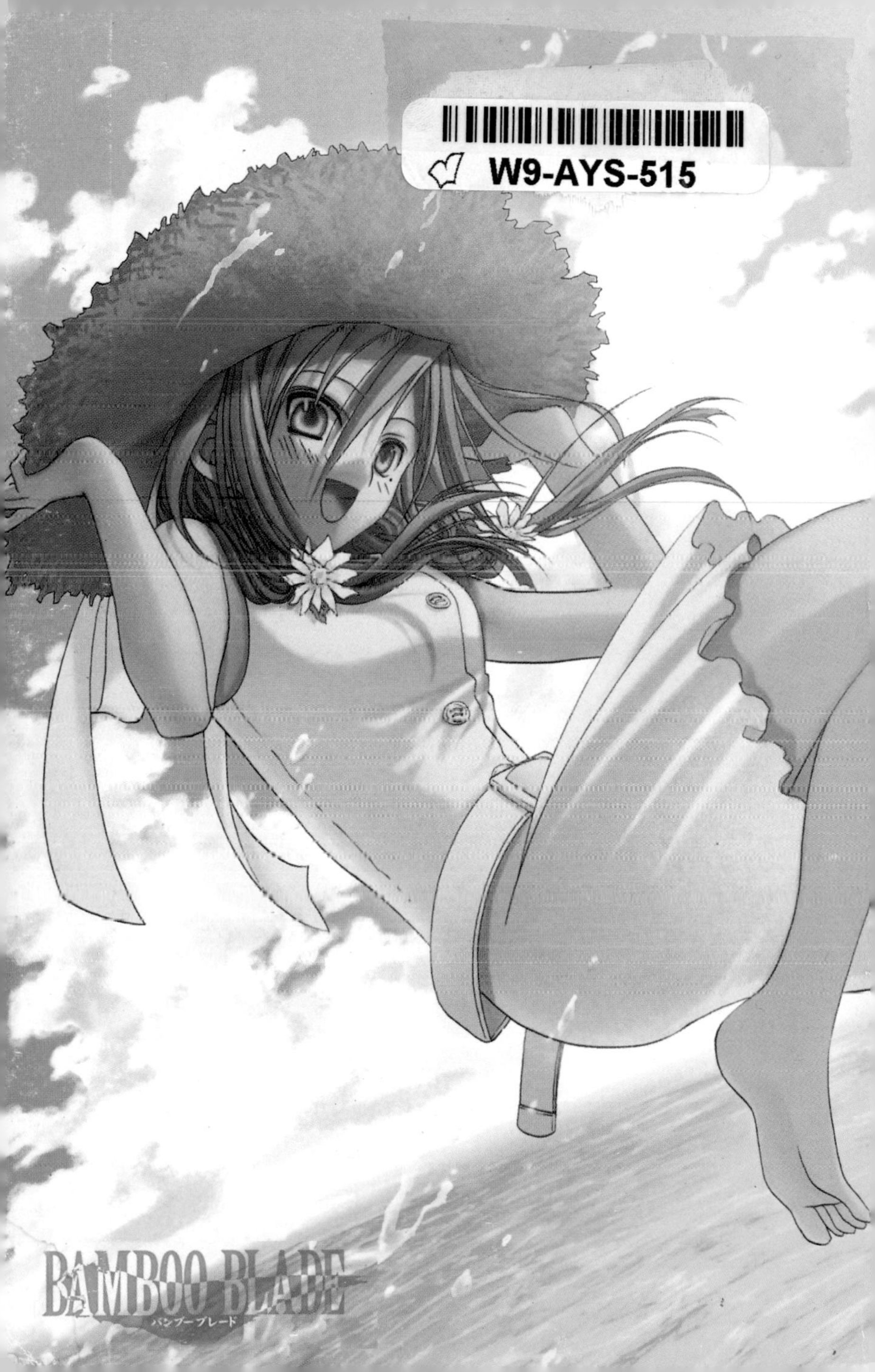
BAMBOO BLADE
バンブーブレード

BAMBOO BLADE 5
CONTENTS

Story: Masahiro Totsuka / Art: Aguri Igarashi

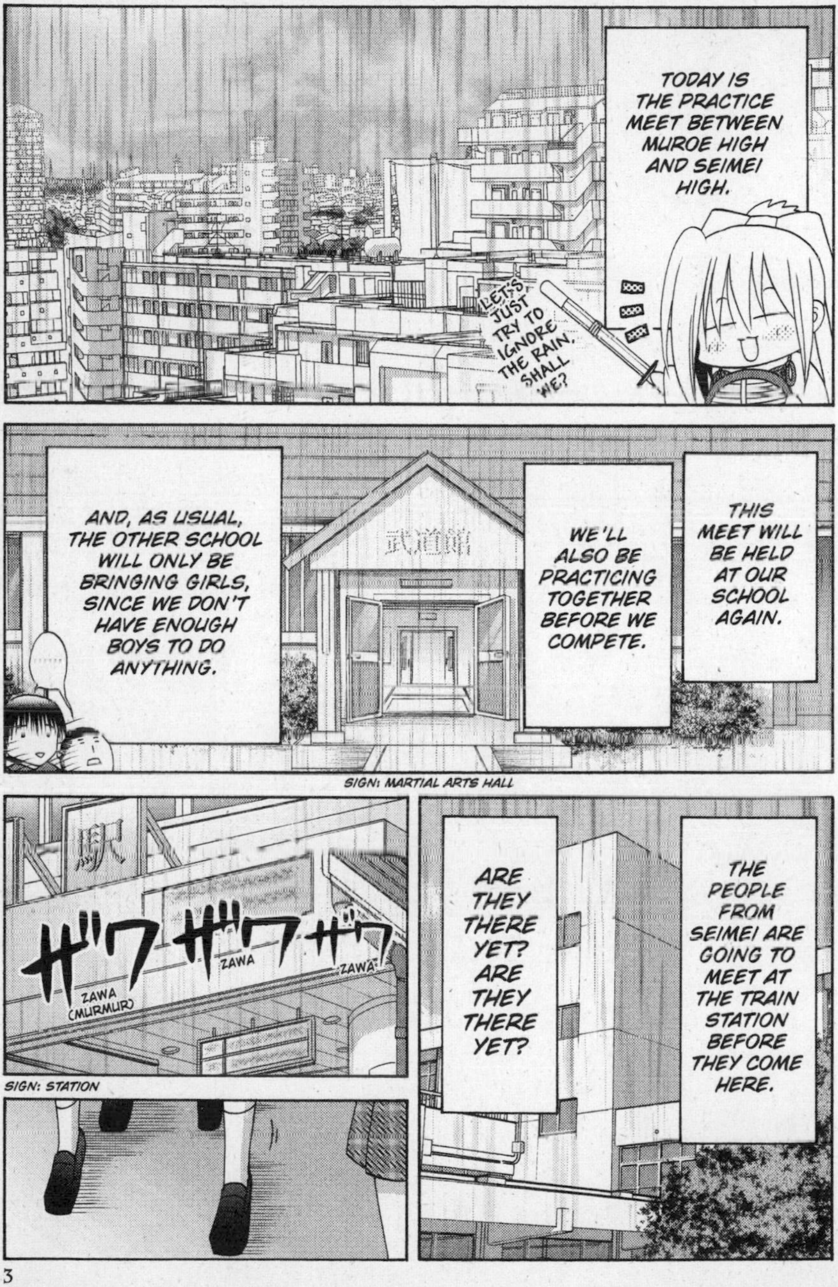
TODAY IS THE PRACTICE MEET BETWEEN MUROE HIGH AND SEIMEI HIGH.
LET'S JUST TRY TO IGNORE THE RAIN, SHALL WE?
THIS MEET WILL BE HELD AT OUR SCHOOL AGAIN.
WE'LL ALSO BE PRACTICING TOGETHER BEFORE WE COMPETE.
武道館
AND, AS USUAL, THE OTHER SCHOOL WILL ONLY BE BRINGING GIRLS, SINCE WE DON'T HAVE ENOUGH BOYS TO DO ANYTHING.
SIGN: MARTIAL ARTS HALL
THE PEOPLE FROM SEIMEI ARE GOING TO MEET AT THE TRAIN STATION BEFORE THEY COME HERE.
ARE THEY THERE YET? ARE THEY THERE YET?
駅
ザワザワザワ
ZAWA (MURMUR)
ZAWA
ZAWA
SIGN: STATION

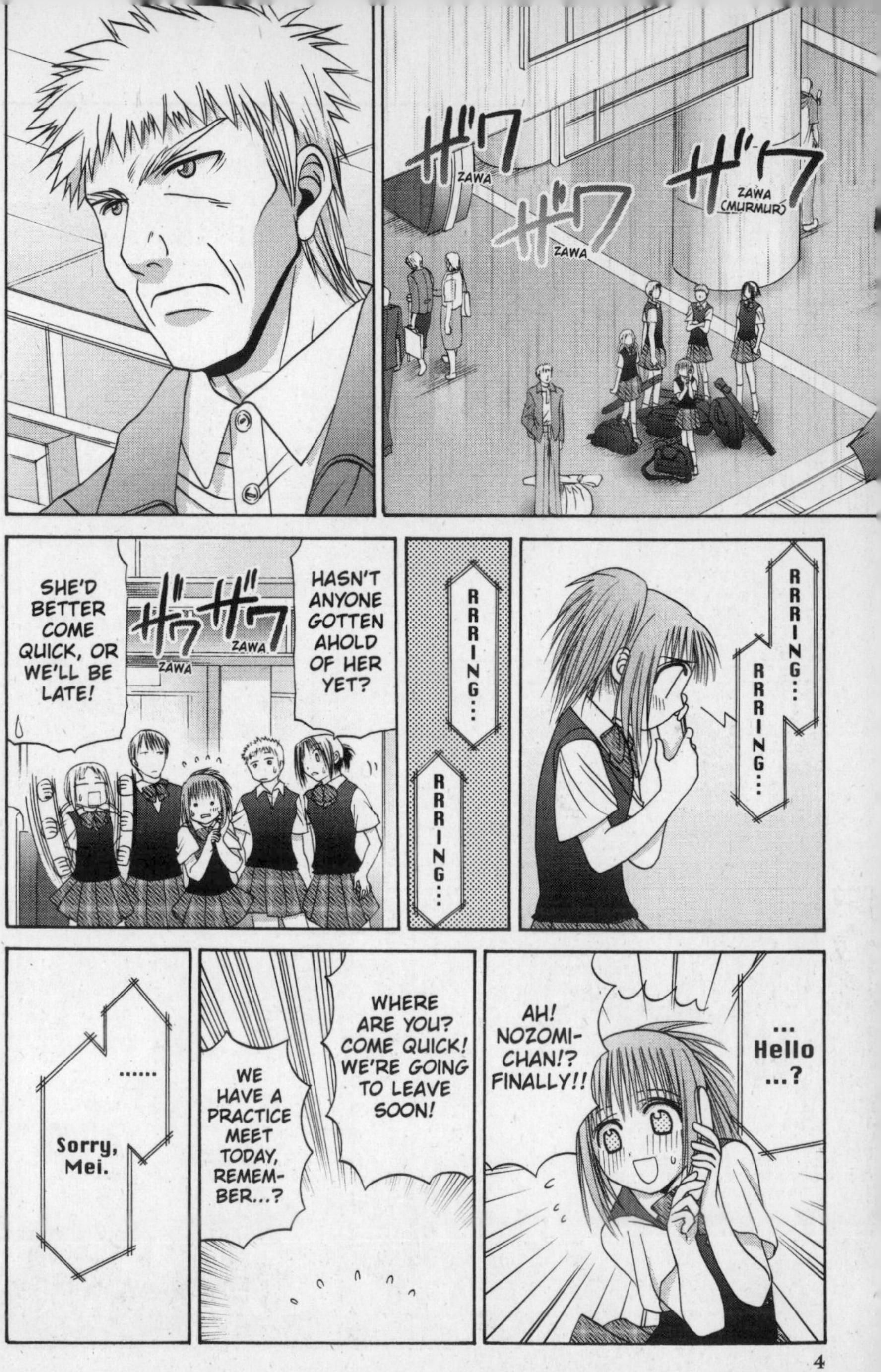
ザワ
ZAWA
ザワ
ZAWA
ザワ
ZAWA (MURMUR)
RRRING...
RRRING...
RRRING...
RRRING...
HASN'T ANYONE GOTTEN AHOLD OF HER YET?
ザワ ザワ
ZAWA ZAWA
SHE'D BETTER COME QUICK, OR WE'LL BE LATE!
... Hello ...?
AH! NOZOMI-CHAN!? FINALLY!!
WHERE ARE YOU? COME QUICK! WE'RE GOING TO LEAVE SOON!
WE HAVE A PRACTICE MEET TODAY, REMEMBER...?
......
Sorry, Mei.

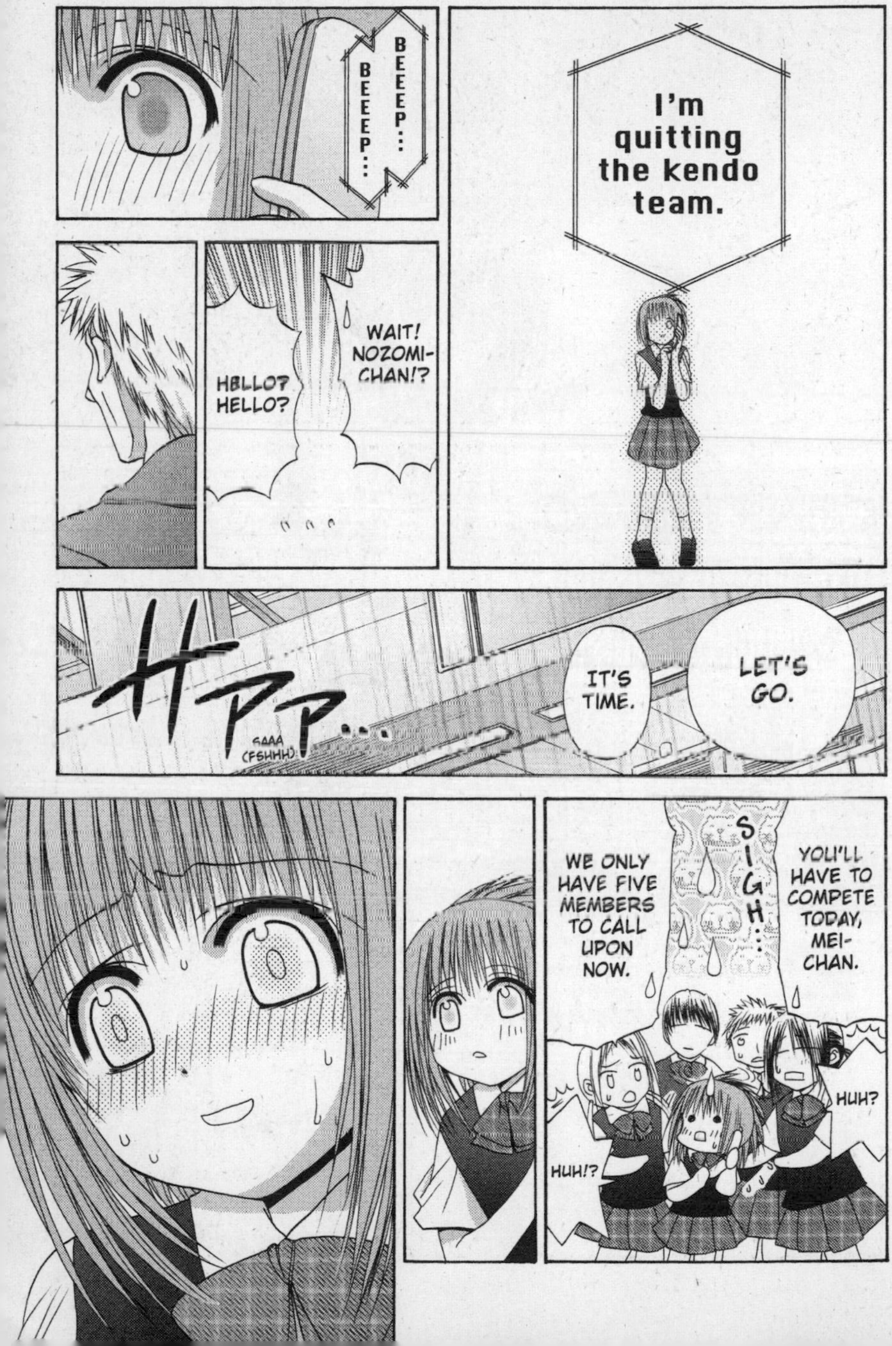
I'm quitting the kendo team.
BEEEP... BEEEP...
WAIT! NOZOMI-CHAN!?
HELLO? HELLO?
...
LET'S GO.
IT'S TIME.
HPP...
SAAA (FSHHH)
YOU'LL HAVE TO COMPETE TODAY, MEI-CHAN.
SIGH...
WE ONLY HAVE FIVE MEMBERS TO CALL UPON NOW.
HUH?
HUH!?

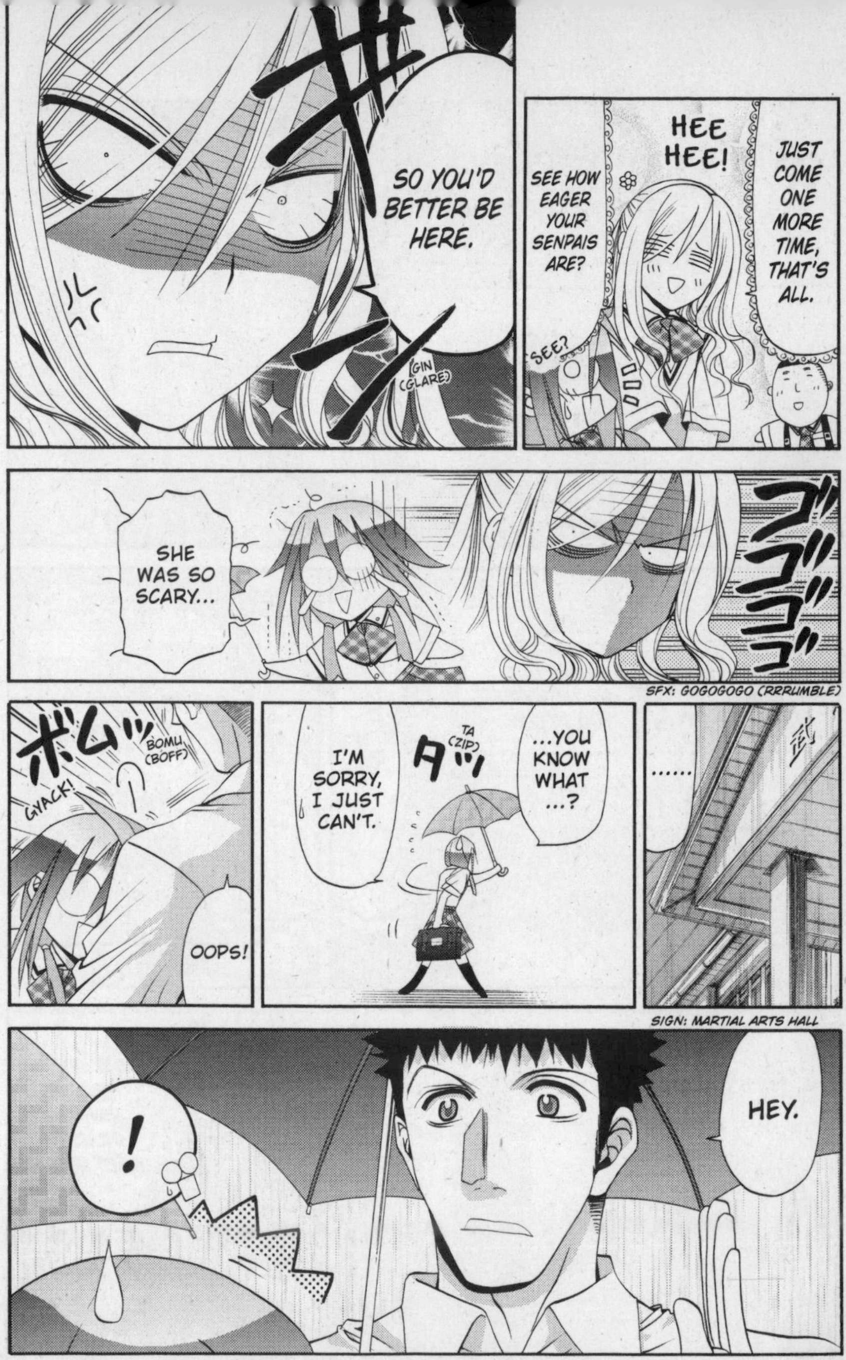
JUST COME ONE MORE TIME, THAT'S ALL.
HEE HEE!
SEE HOW EAGER YOUR SENPAIS ARE?
SEE?
SO YOU'D BETTER BE HERE.
GIN (GLARE)
SHE WAS SO SCARY...
SFX: GOGOGOGO (RRRUMBLE)
......
...YOU KNOW WHAT...?
TA (ZIP)
I'M SORRY, I JUST CAN'T.
BOMU (BOFF)
GYACK!
OOPS!
SIGN: MARTIAL ARTS HALL
HEY.
!

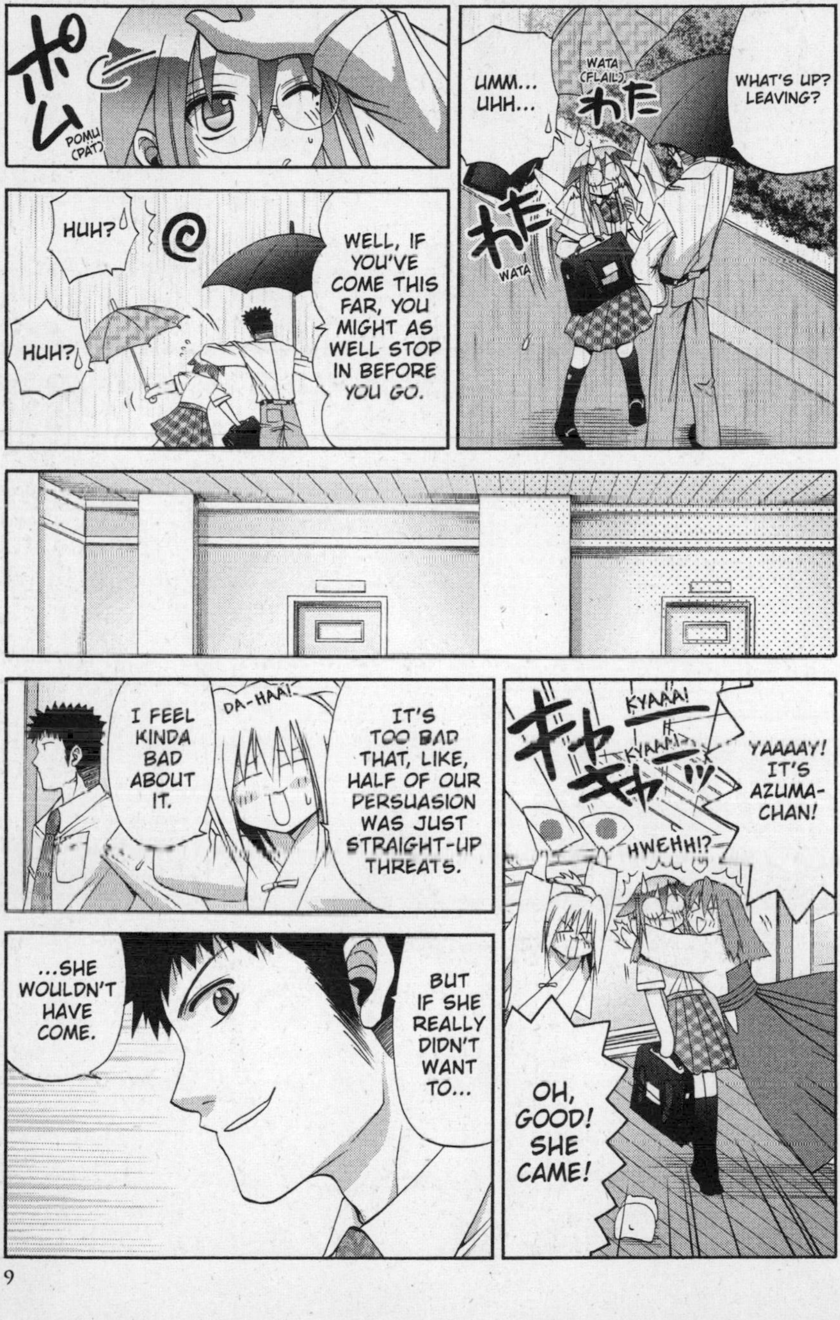
WHAT'S UP? LEAVING?
WATA (FLAIL)
わた
UMM... UHH...
わた
WATA
ポム
POMU (PAT)
WELL, IF YOU'VE COME THIS FAR, YOU MIGHT AS WELL STOP IN BEFORE YOU GO.
HUH?
HUH?
KYAAA!
キャーキャーッ
KYAAA!
YAAAAY! IT'S AZUMA-CHAN!
HWEHH!?
OH, GOOD! SHE CAME!
IT'S TOO BAD THAT, LIKE, HALF OF OUR PERSUASION WAS JUST STRAIGHT-UP THREATS.
DA-HAA!
I FEEL KINDA BAD ABOUT IT.
BUT IF SHE REALLY DIDN'T WANT TO...
...SHE WOULDN'T HAVE COME.

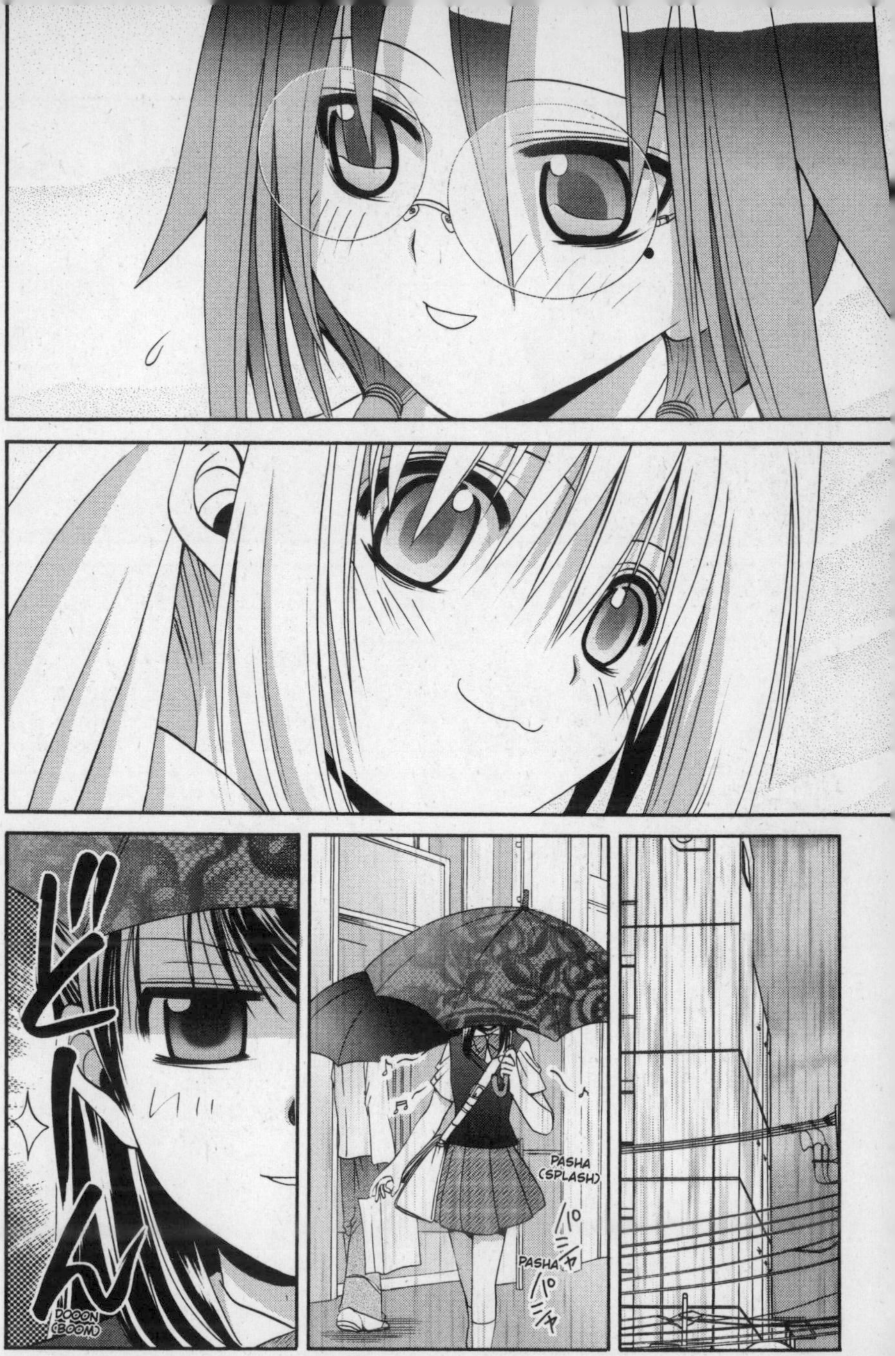
PASHA (SPLASH)
PASHA
DOOON (BOOM)

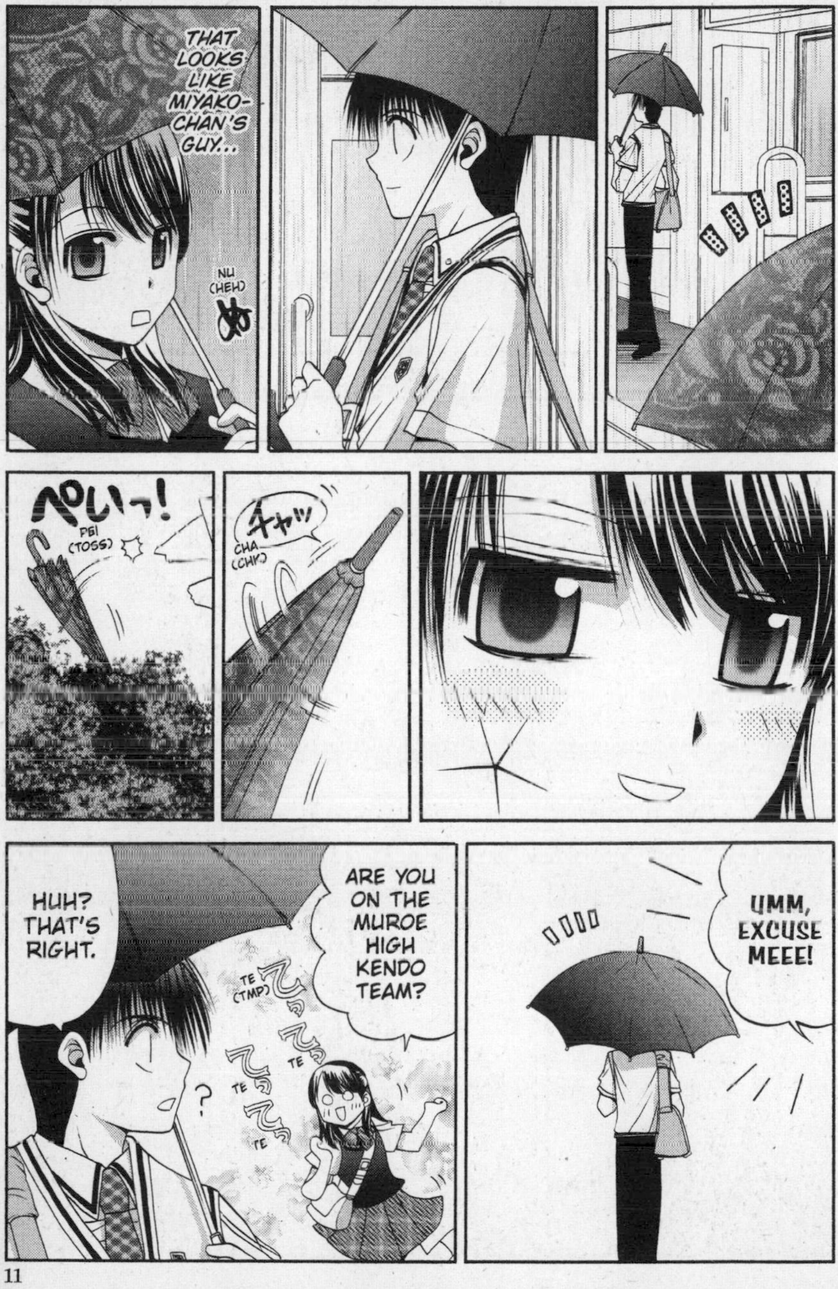
THAT LOOKS LIKE MIYAKO-CHAN'S GUY...
め
NU (HEH)
チャッ
CHA (CHK)
ぺいっ!
PEI (TOSS)
UMM, EXCUSE MEEE!
ARE YOU ON THE MUROE HIGH KENDO TEAM?
TE (TMP)
TE
TE
TE
HUH? THAT'S RIGHT.
?

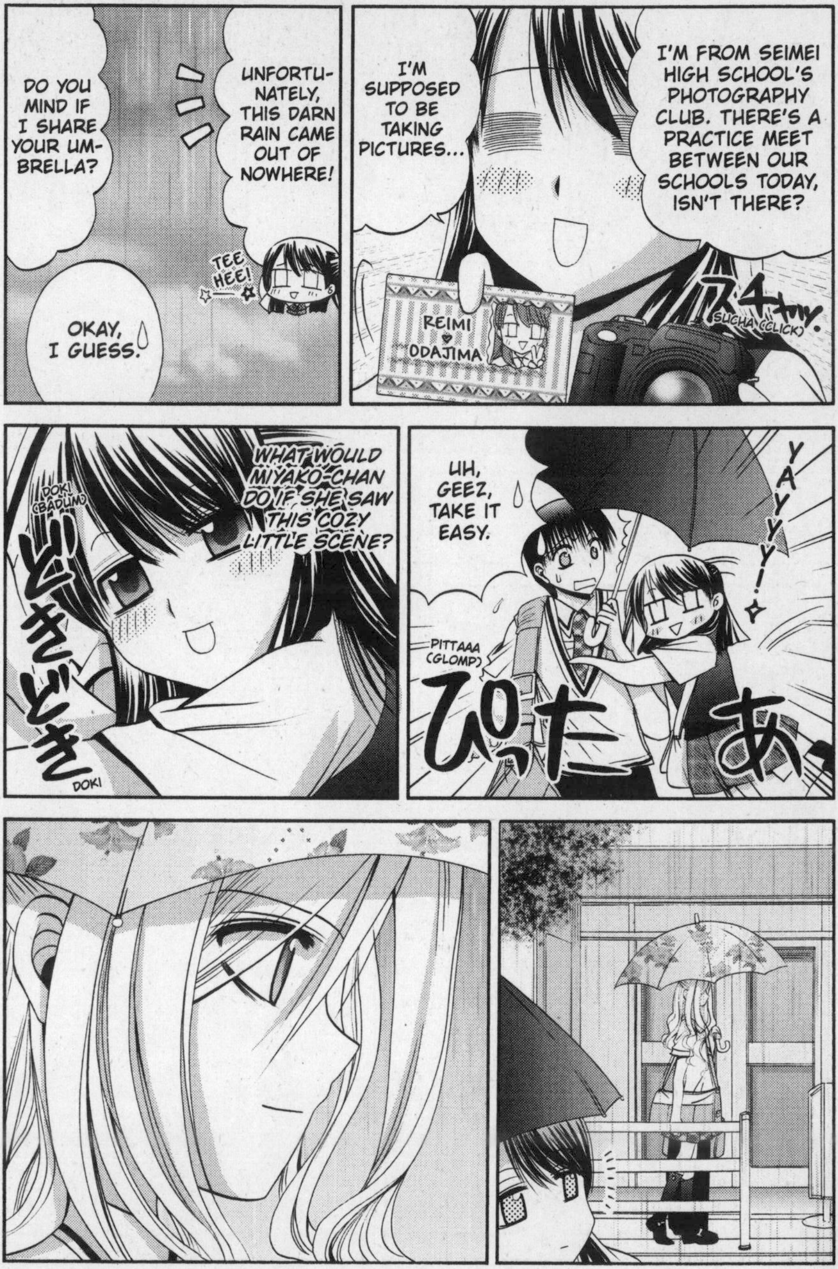
I'M FROM SEIMEI HIGH SCHOOL'S PHOTOGRAPHY CLUB. THERE'S A PRACTICE MEET BETWEEN OUR SCHOOLS TODAY, ISN'T THERE?
I'M SUPPOSED TO BE TAKING PICTURES...
REIMI ♥ ODAJIMA
SUCHA (CLICK)
UNFORTU-NATELY, THIS DARN RAIN CAME OUT OF NOWHERE!
DO YOU MIND IF I SHARE YOUR UM-BRELLA?
TEE HEE!
OKAY, I GUESS.
UH, GEEZ, TAKE IT EASY.
YAYYY!
PITTAAA (GLOMP)
ぴったあっ
WHAT WOULD MIYAKO-CHAN DO IF SHE SAW THIS COZY LITTLE SCENE?
DOKI (BADUM)
どきどき
DOKI

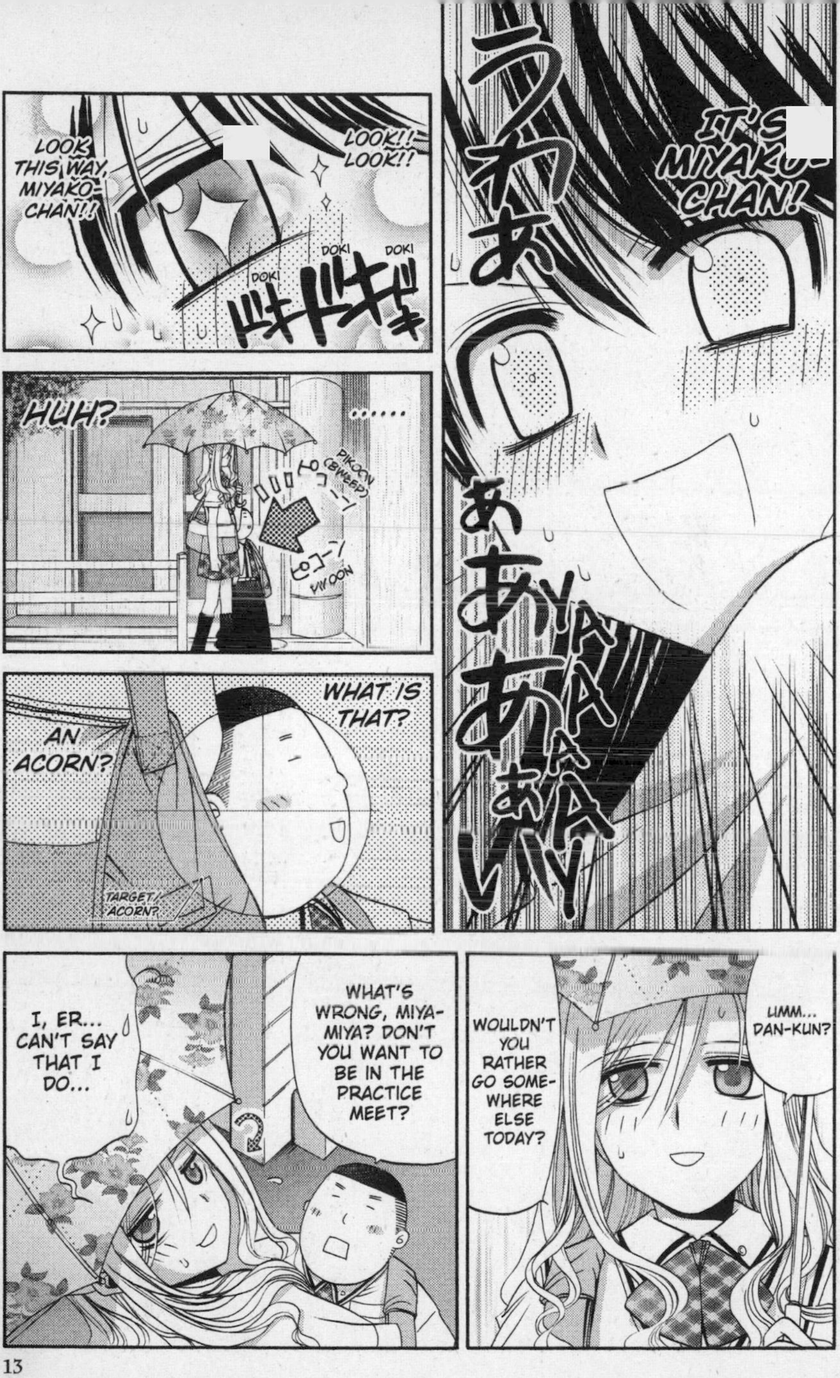
うわあ
IT'S MIYAKO-CHAN!
ああああい
YAAAAY
LOOK!! LOOK!!
LOOK THIS WAY, MIYAKO-CHAN!!
DOKI
DOKI
DOKI
......
ピコーン
PIKOON (BWEEP)
ピコーン
VWOON
HUH?
WHAT IS THAT?
AN ACORN?
TARGET: ACORN?
UMM... DAN-KUN?
WOULDN'T YOU RATHER GO SOMEWHERE ELSE TODAY?
WHAT'S WRONG, MIYA-MIYA? DON'T YOU WANT TO BE IN THE PRACTICE MEET?
I, ER... CAN'T SAY THAT I DO...

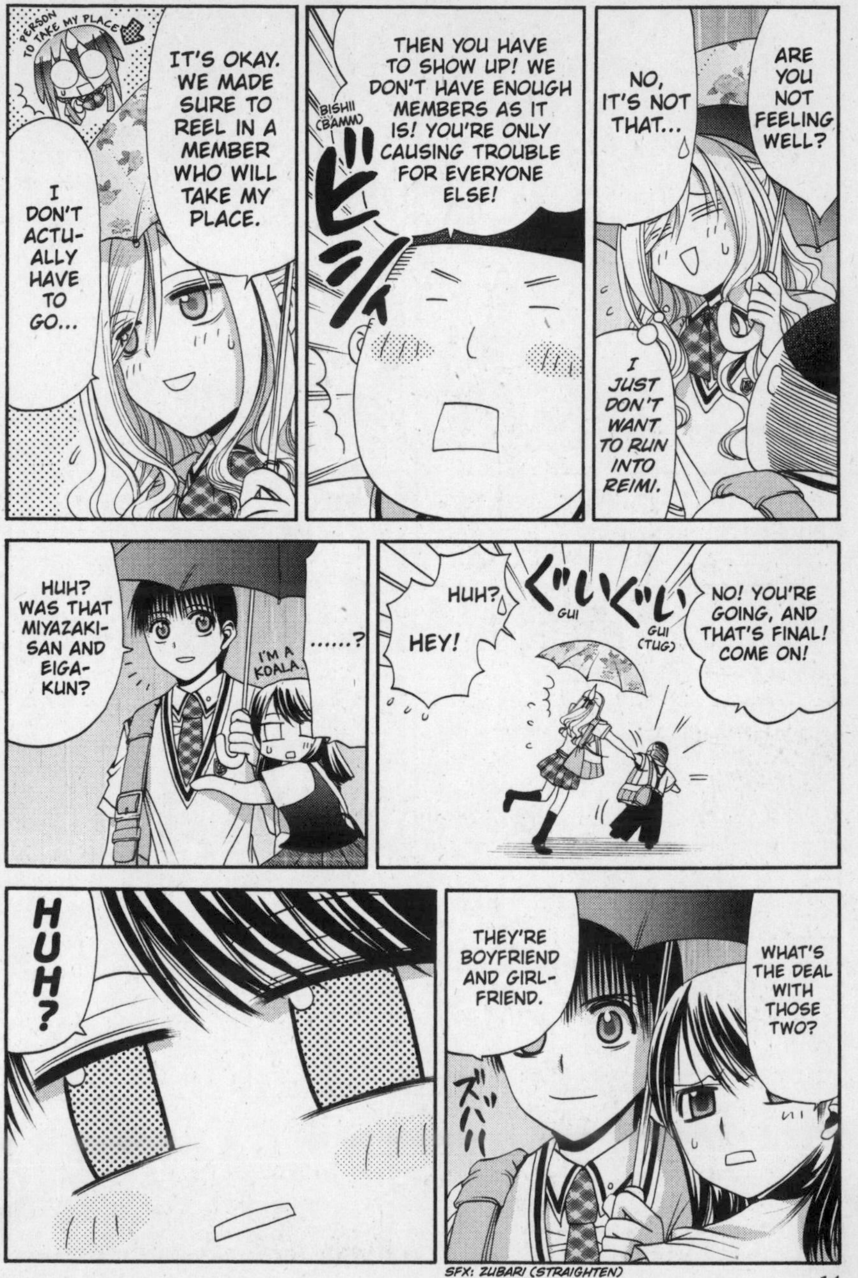
ARE YOU NOT FEELING WELL?
NO, IT'S NOT THAT...
I JUST DON'T WANT TO RUN INTO REIMI.
THEN YOU HAVE TO SHOW UP! WE DON'T HAVE ENOUGH MEMBERS AS IT IS! YOU'RE ONLY CAUSING TROUBLE FOR EVERYONE ELSE!
BISHII (BAMM)
IT'S OKAY. WE MADE SURE TO REEL IN A MEMBER WHO WILL TAKE MY PLACE.
PERSON TO TAKE MY PLACE
I DON'T ACTU-ALLY HAVE TO GO...
NO! YOU'RE GOING, AND THAT'S FINAL! COME ON!
GUI GUI (TUG)
HUH?
HEY!
HUH? WAS THAT MIYAZAKI-SAN AND EIGA-KUN?
I'M A KOALA.
......?
WHAT'S THE DEAL WITH THOSE TWO?
THEY'RE BOYFRIEND AND GIRL-FRIEND.
HUH?

SFX: ZUBARI (STRAIGHTEN)

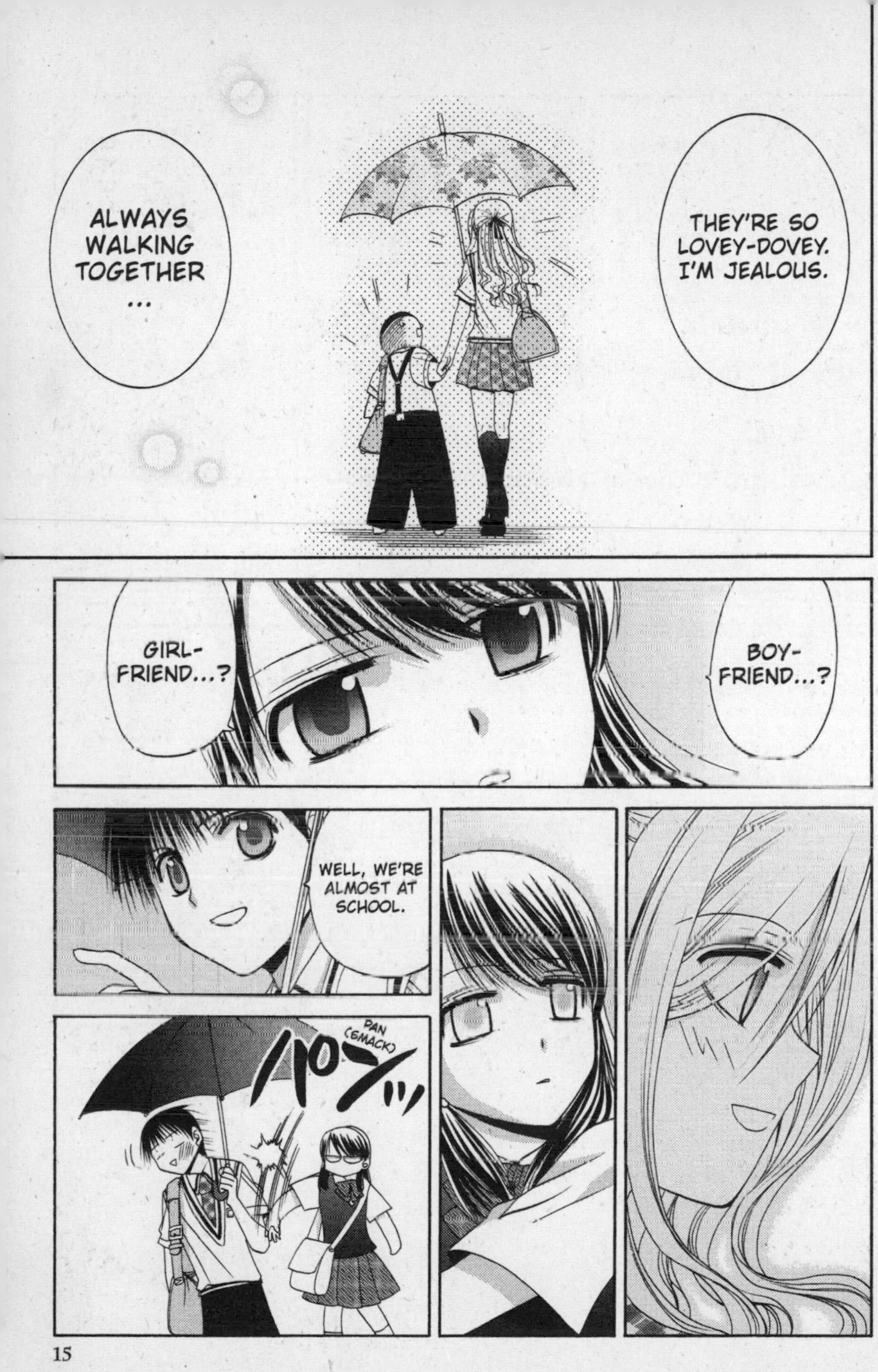
THEY'RE SO LOVEY-DOVEY. I'M JEALOUS.
ALWAYS WALKING TOGETHER ...
BOY-FRIEND...?
GIRL-FRIEND...?
WELL, WE'RE ALMOST AT SCHOOL.
PAN (SMACK)

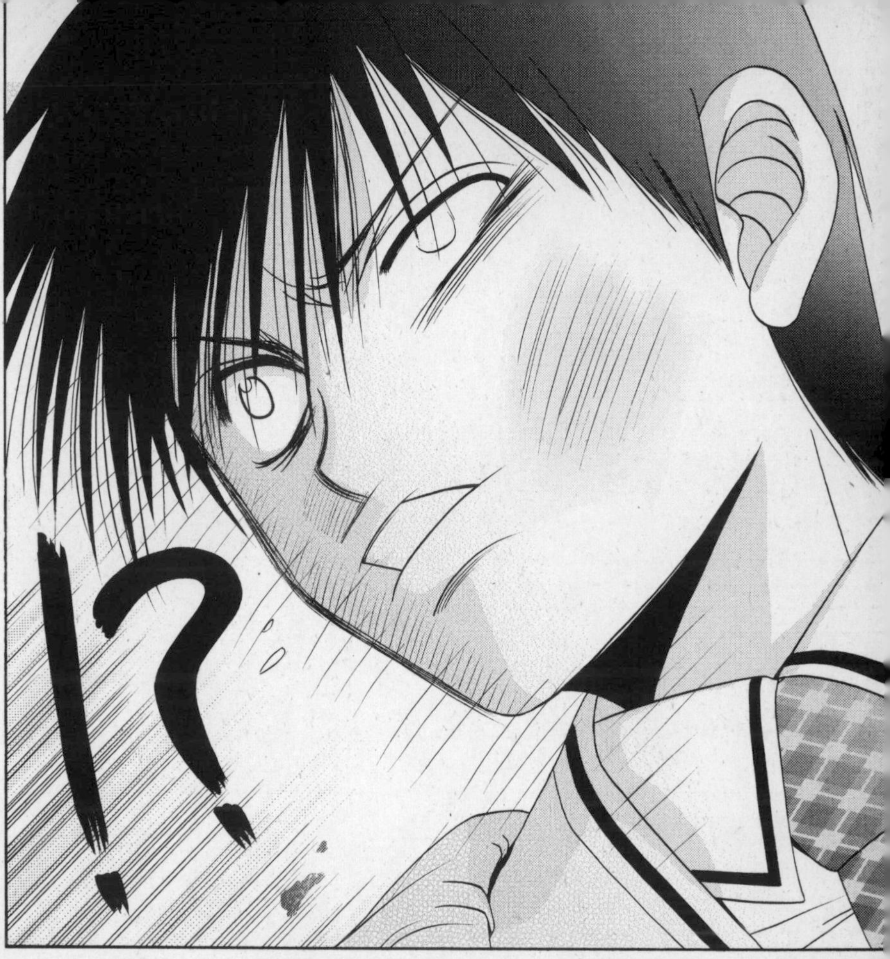
!?

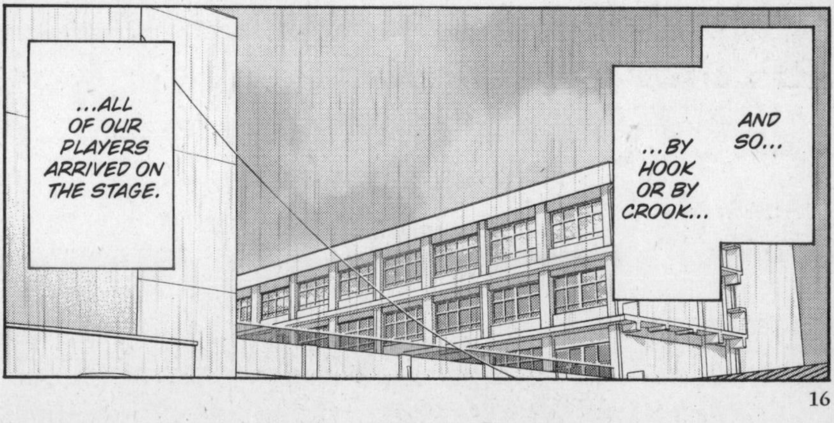
AND SO...
...BY HOOK OR BY CROOK...
...ALL OF OUR PLAYERS ARRIVED ON THE STAGE.

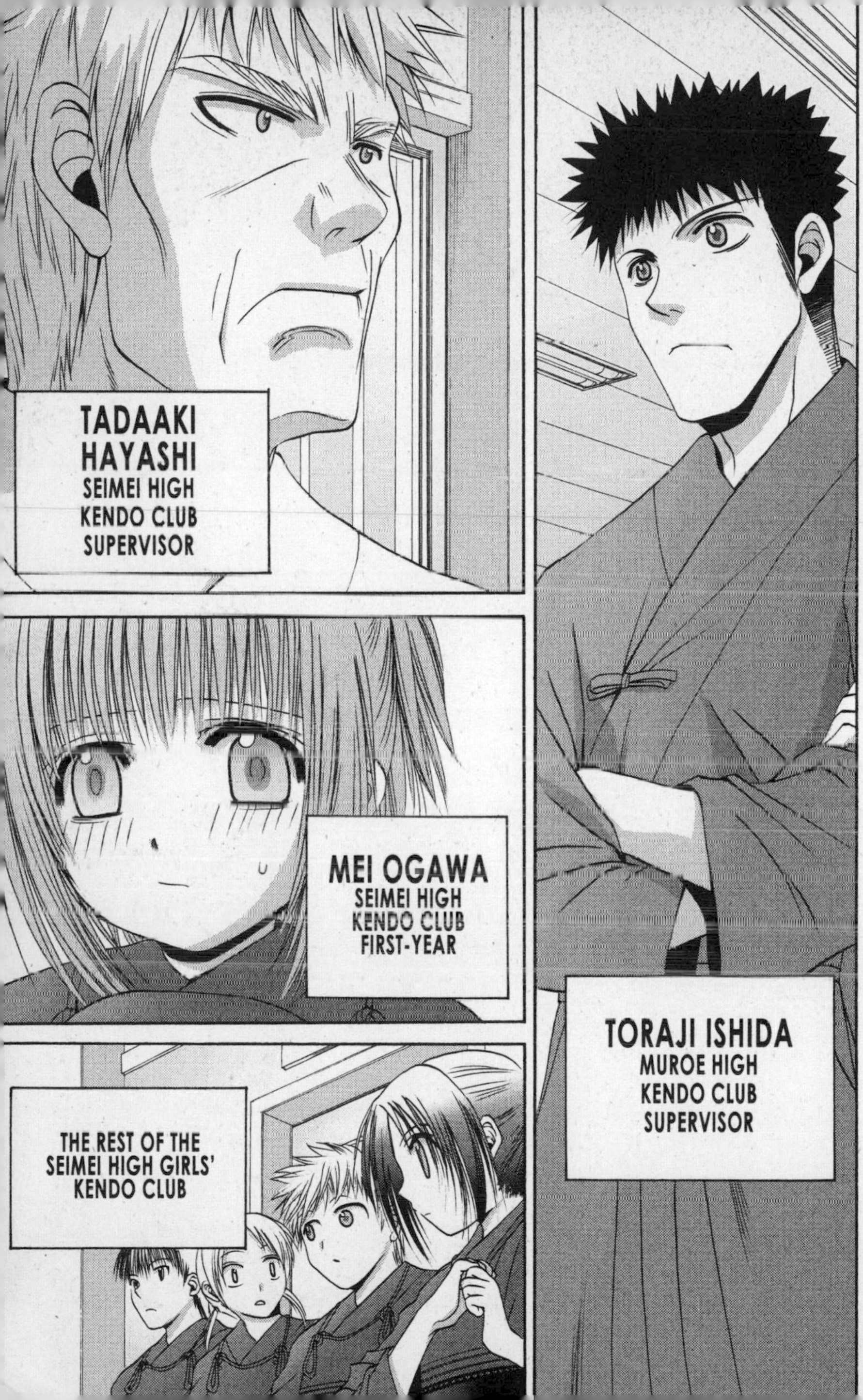
TORAJI ISHIDA
MUROE HIGH
KENDO CLUB
SUPERVISOR
TADAAKI
HAYASHI
SEIMEI HIGH
KENDO CLUB
SUPERVISOR
MEI OGAWA
SEIMEI HIGH
KENDO CLUB
FIRST-YEAR
THE REST OF THE
SEIMEI HIGH GIRLS'
KENDO CLUB

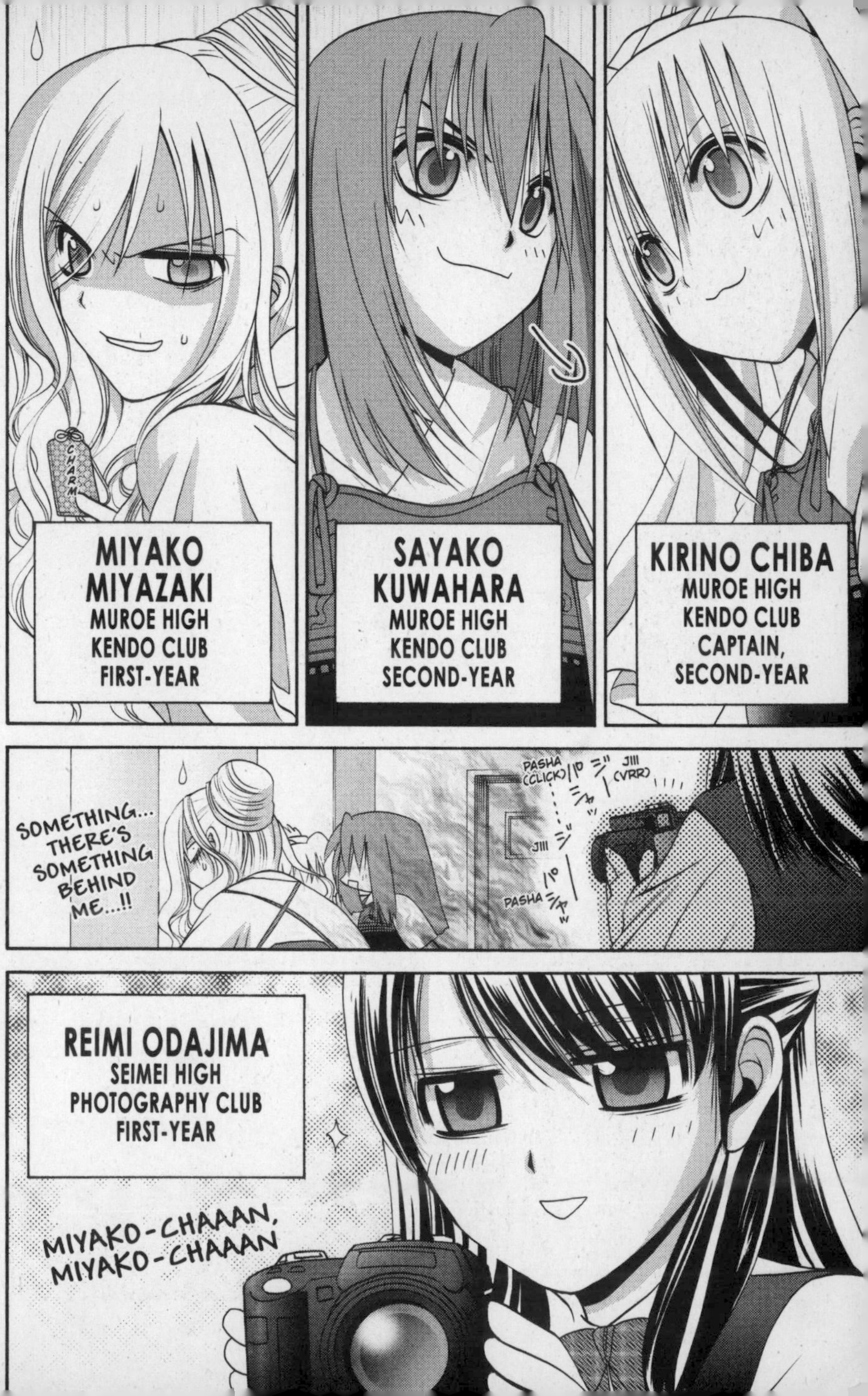
KIRINO CHIBA
MUROE HIGH
KENDO CLUB
CAPTAIN,
SECOND-YEAR
SAYAKO
KUWAHARA
MUROE HIGH
KENDO CLUB
SECOND-YEAR
CHARM
MIYAKO
MIYAZAKI
MUROE HIGH
KENDO CLUB
FIRST-YEAR
JIII
(VRR)
PASHA
(CLICK)
JIII
PASHA
SOMETHING... THERE'S SOMETHING BEHIND ME...!!
REIMI ODAJIMA
SEIMEI HIGH
PHOTOGRAPHY CLUB
FIRST-YEAR
MIYAKO-CHAAAN, MIYAKO-CHAAAN

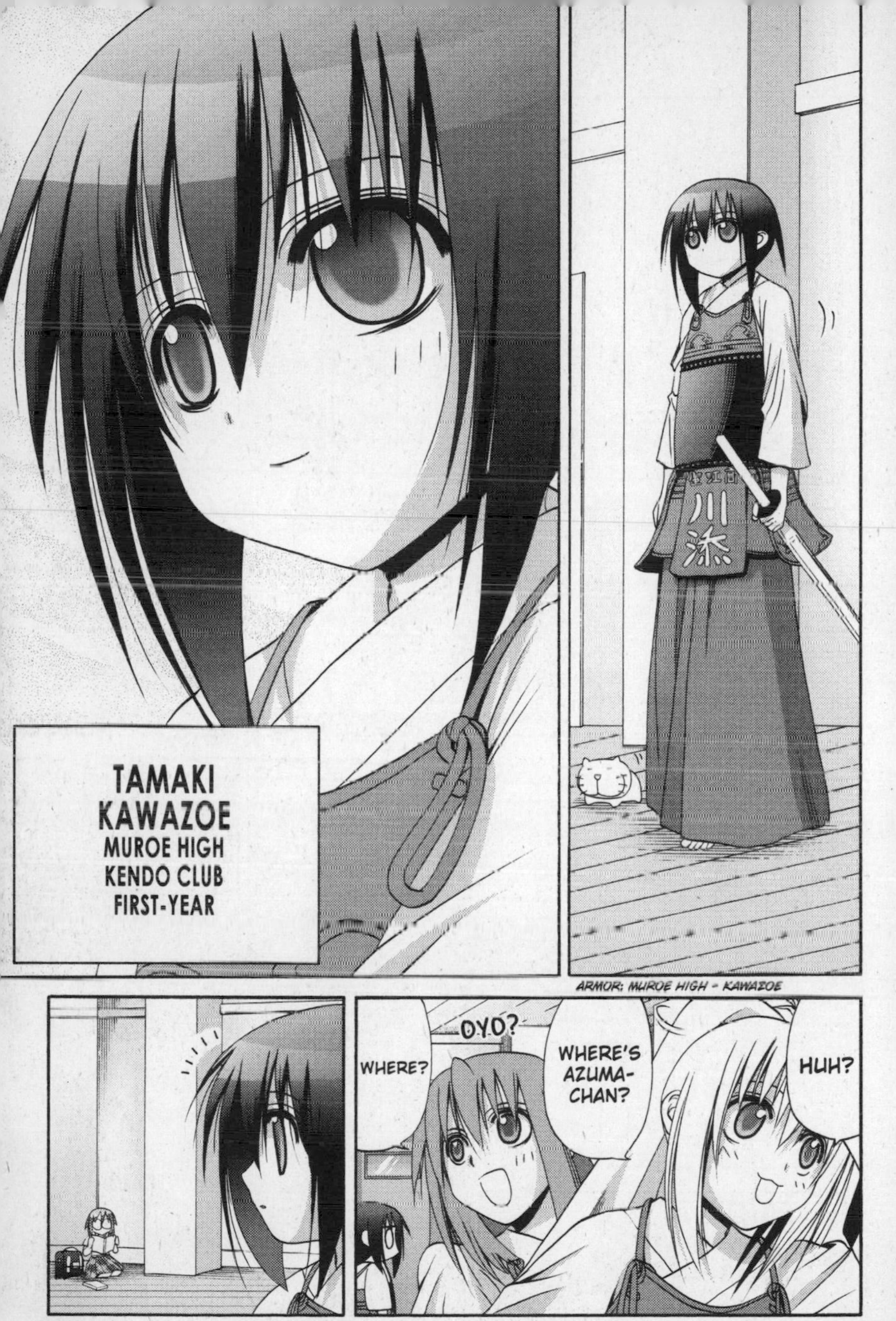
ARMOR: MUROE HIGH - KAWAZOE
TAMAKI KAWAZOE
MUROE HIGH
KENDO CLUB
FIRST-YEAR
HUH?
WHERE'S AZUMA-CHAN?
OYO?
WHERE?

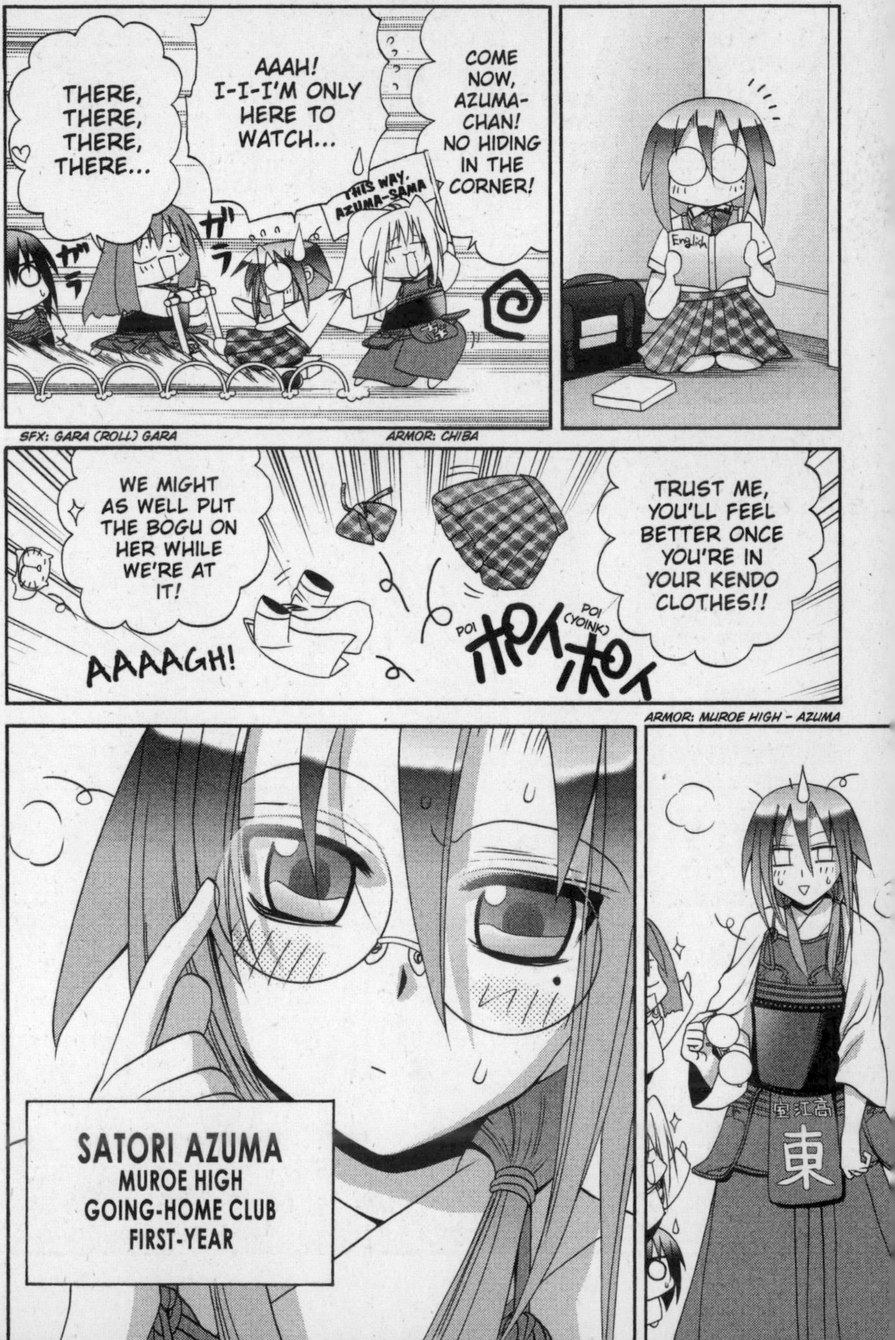
COME NOW, AZUMA-CHAN! NO HIDING IN THE CORNER!
THIS WAY, AZUMA-SAMA
AAAH! I-I-I'M ONLY HERE TO WATCH...
THERE, THERE, THERE, THERE...
SFX: GARA (ROLL) GARA
ARMOR: CHIBA
English
TRUST ME, YOU'LL FEEL BETTER ONCE YOU'RE IN YOUR KENDO CLOTHES!!
POI (YOINK) POI
WE MIGHT AS WELL PUT THE BOGU ON HER WHILE WE'RE AT IT!
AAAAGH!
ARMOR: MUROE HIGH - AZUMA
室江高
東
SATORI AZUMA
MUROE HIGH
GOING-HOME CLUB
FIRST-YEAR

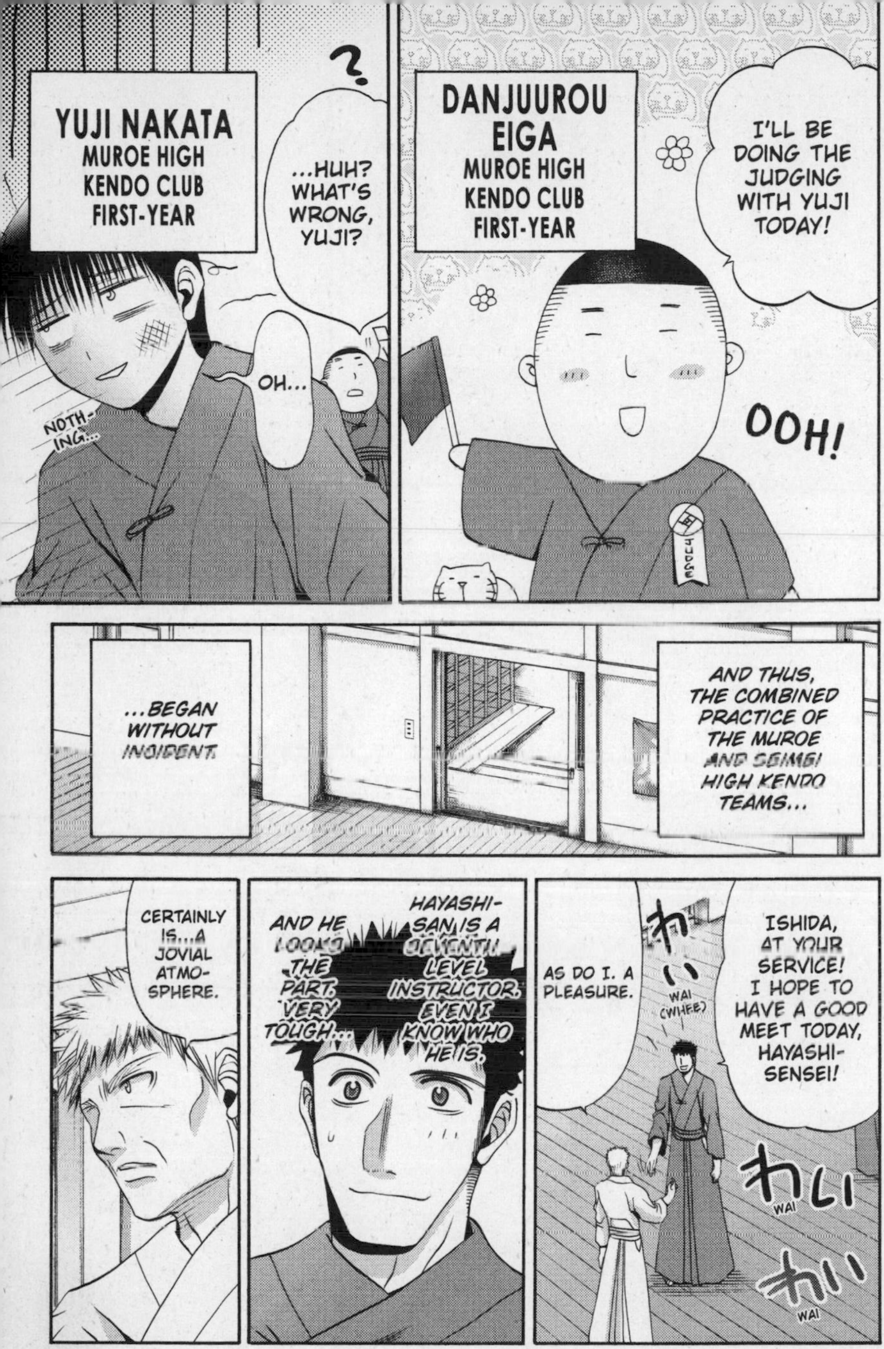
DANJUUROU EIGA
MUROE HIGH KENDO CLUB FIRST-YEAR
I'LL BE DOING THE JUDGING WITH YUJI TODAY!
OOH!
JUDGE
YUJI NAKATA
MUROE HIGH KENDO CLUB FIRST-YEAR
...HUH? WHAT'S WRONG, YUJI?
OH...
NOTHING...
AND THUS, THE COMBINED PRACTICE OF THE MUROE AND SEIMEI HIGH KENDO TEAMS...
...BEGAN WITHOUT INCIDENT.
ISHIDA, AT YOUR SERVICE! I HOPE TO HAVE A GOOD MEET TODAY, HAYASHI-SENSEI!
わい
WAI (WHEE)
AS DO I. A PLEASURE.
わい
WAI
わい
WAI
HAYASHI-SAN IS A SEVENTH-LEVEL INSTRUCTOR. EVEN I KNOW WHO HE IS.
AND HE LOOKS THE PART. VERY TOUGH...
CERTAINLY IS... A JOVIAL ATMOSPHERE.

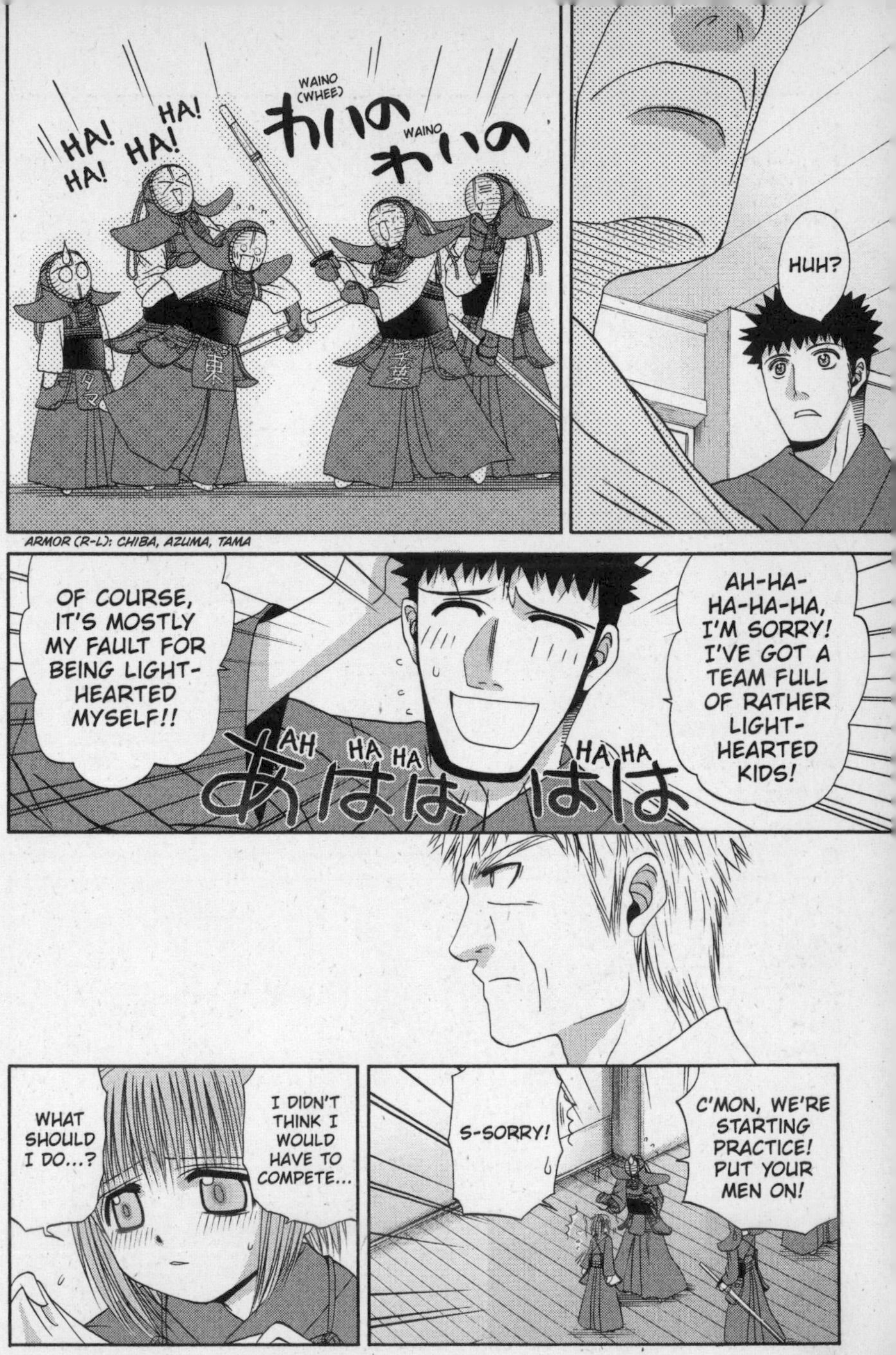
HUH?
WAINO (WHEE)
わいの
WAINO
わいの
HA!
HA!
HA!
HA!
AH-HA-HA-HA-HA, I'M SORRY! I'VE GOT A TEAM FULL OF RATHER LIGHT-HEARTED KIDS!
AH HA HA HA HA
あはははは
OF COURSE, IT'S MOSTLY MY FAULT FOR BEING LIGHT-HEARTED MYSELF!!
C'MON, WE'RE STARTING PRACTICE! PUT YOUR MEN ON!
S-SORRY!
I DIDN'T THINK I WOULD HAVE TO COMPETE...
WHAT SHOULD I DO...?
ARMOR (R-L): CHIBA, AZUMA, TAMA

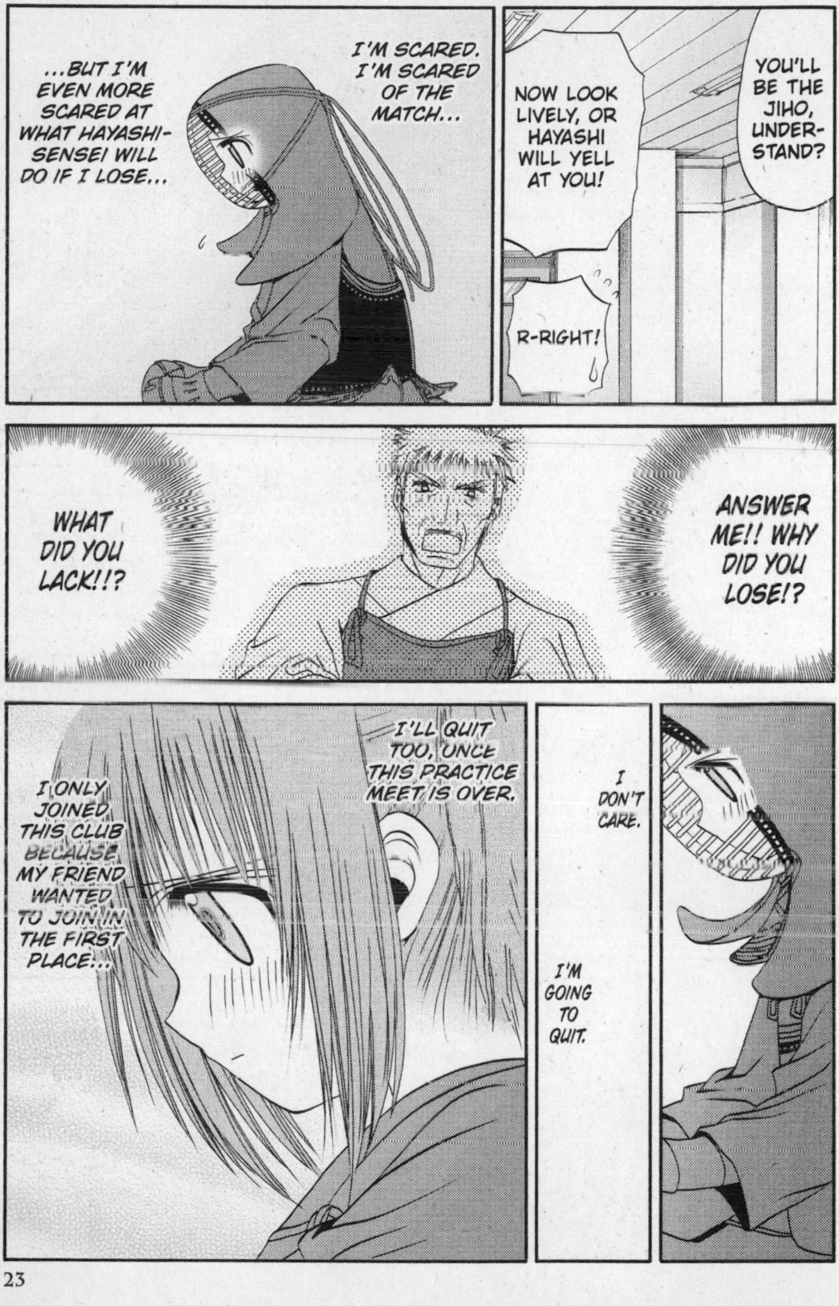
YOU'LL BE THE JIHO, UNDERSTAND?
NOW LOOK LIVELY, OR HAYASHI WILL YELL AT YOU!
R-RIGHT!
I'M SCARED. I'M SCARED OF THE MATCH...
...BUT I'M EVEN MORE SCARED AT WHAT HAYASHI-SENSEI WILL DO IF I LOSE...
ANSWER ME!! WHY DID YOU LOSE!?
WHAT DID YOU LACK!!?
I DON'T CARE.
I'M GOING TO QUIT.
I'LL QUIT TOO, ONCE THIS PRACTICE MEET IS OVER.
I ONLY JOINED THIS CLUB BECAUSE MY FRIEND WANTED TO JOIN IN THE FIRST PLACE...

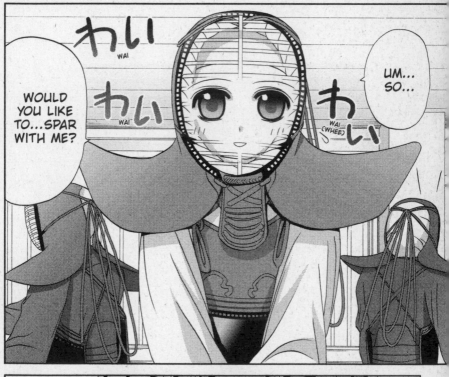

わい
WAI

わい
WAI

わい
WAI
(WHEE)

WOULD YOU LIKE TO...SPAR WITH ME?

UM... SO...

どきどき
DOKI
(BADUM)
DOKI

NICE TO MEET YOU.

BAMBOO BLADE

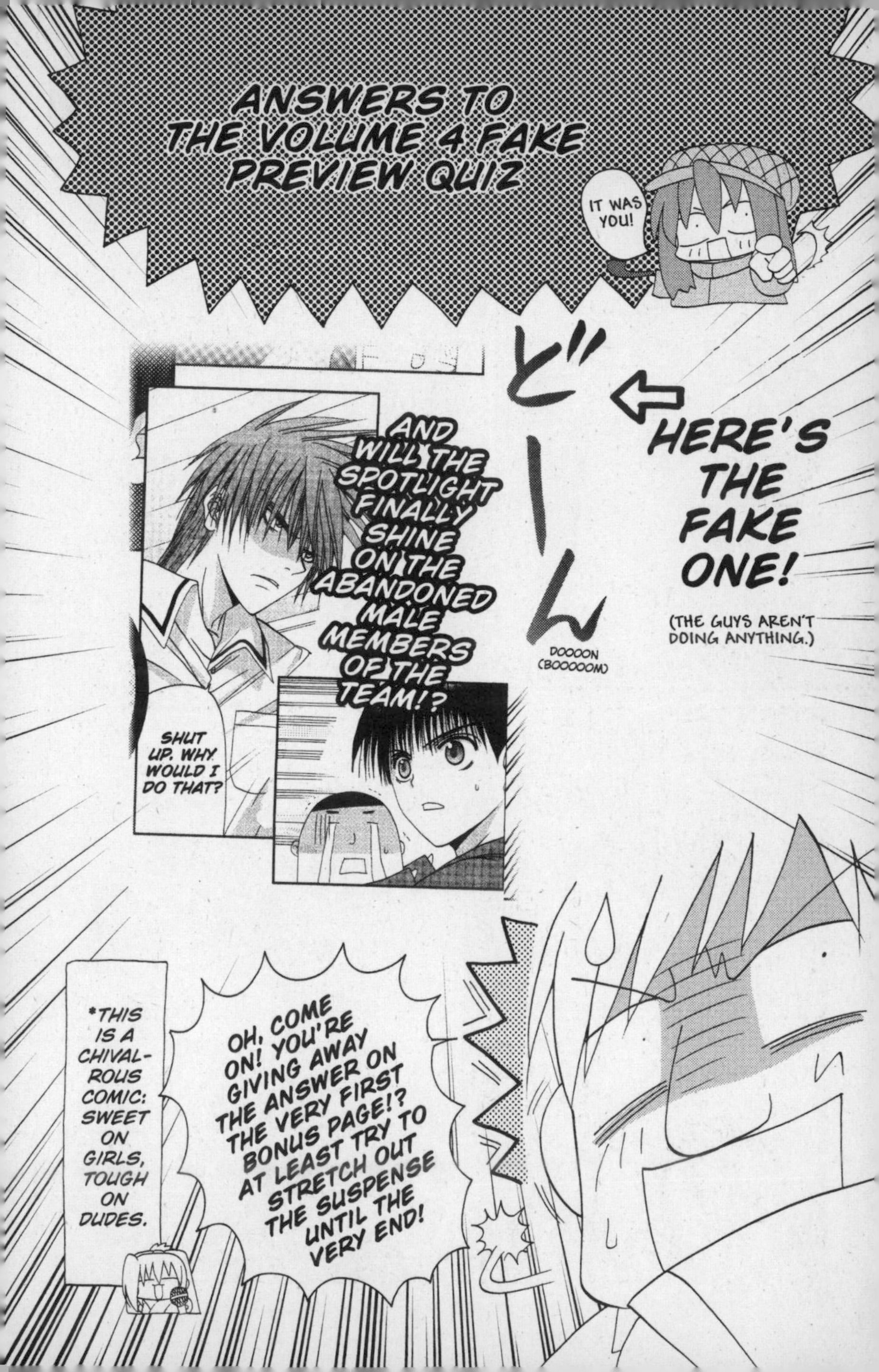
ANSWERS TO THE VOLUME 4 FAKE PREVIEW QUIZ
IT WAS YOU!
HERE'S THE FAKE ONE!
(THE GUYS AREN'T DOING ANYTHING.)
どーん
DOOOON (BOOOOOM)
AND WILL THE SPOTLIGHT FINALLY SHINE ON THE ABANDONED MALE MEMBERS OF THE TEAM!?
SHUT UP. WHY WOULD I DO THAT?
OH, COME ON! YOU'RE GIVING AWAY THE ANSWER ON THE VERY FIRST BONUS PAGE!? AT LEAST TRY TO STRETCH OUT THE SUSPENSE UNTIL THE VERY END!
*THIS IS A CHIVAL-ROUS COMIC: SWEET ON GIRLS, TOUGH ON DUDES.

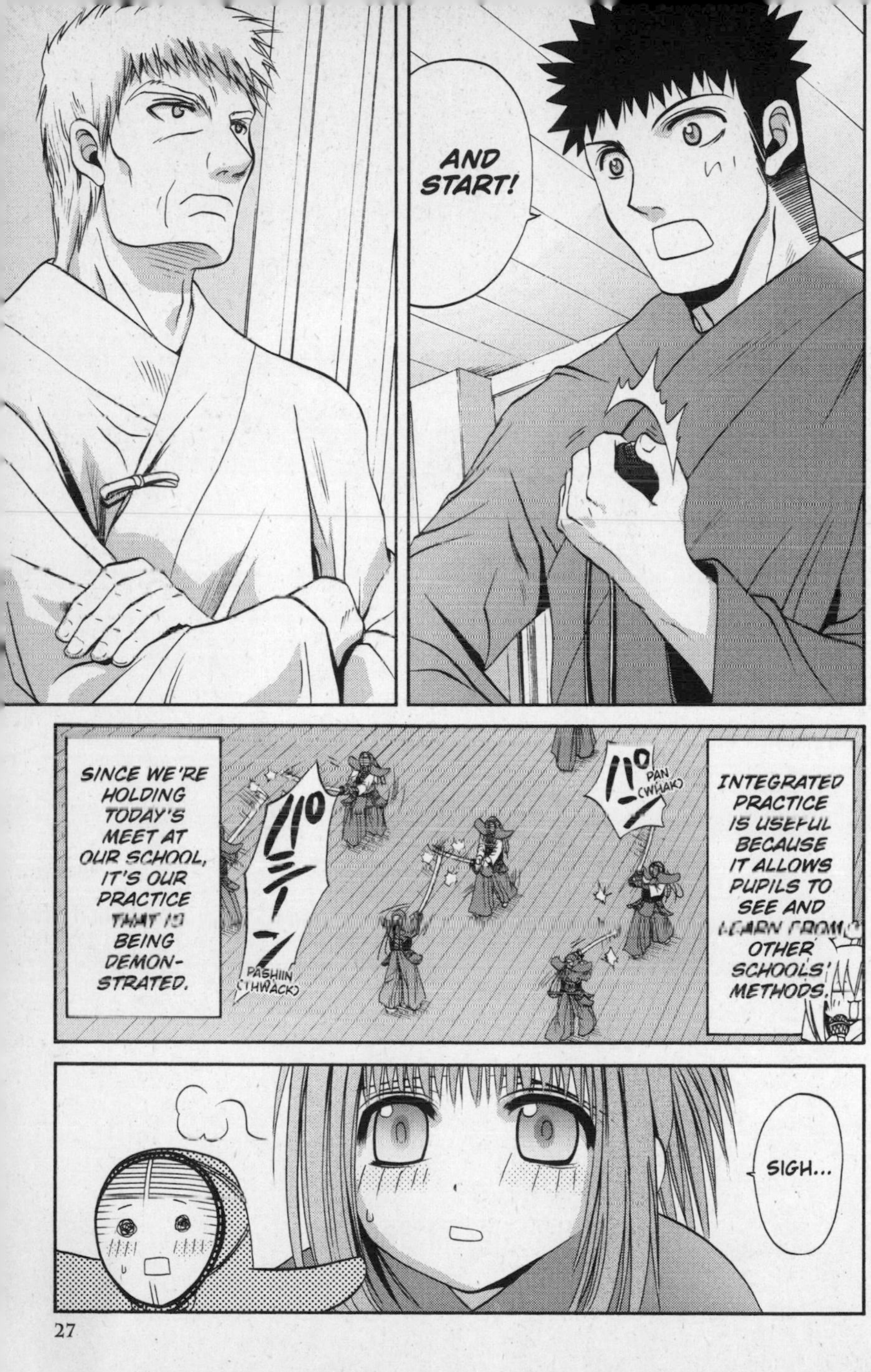
AND START!
INTEGRATED PRACTICE IS USEFUL BECAUSE IT ALLOWS PUPILS TO SEE AND LEARN FROM OTHER SCHOOLS' METHODS.
PAN (WHAK)
SINCE WE'RE HOLDING TODAY'S MEET AT OUR SCHOOL, IT'S OUR PRACTICE THAT IS BEING DEMON-STRATED.
PASHIIN (THWACK)
SIGH...

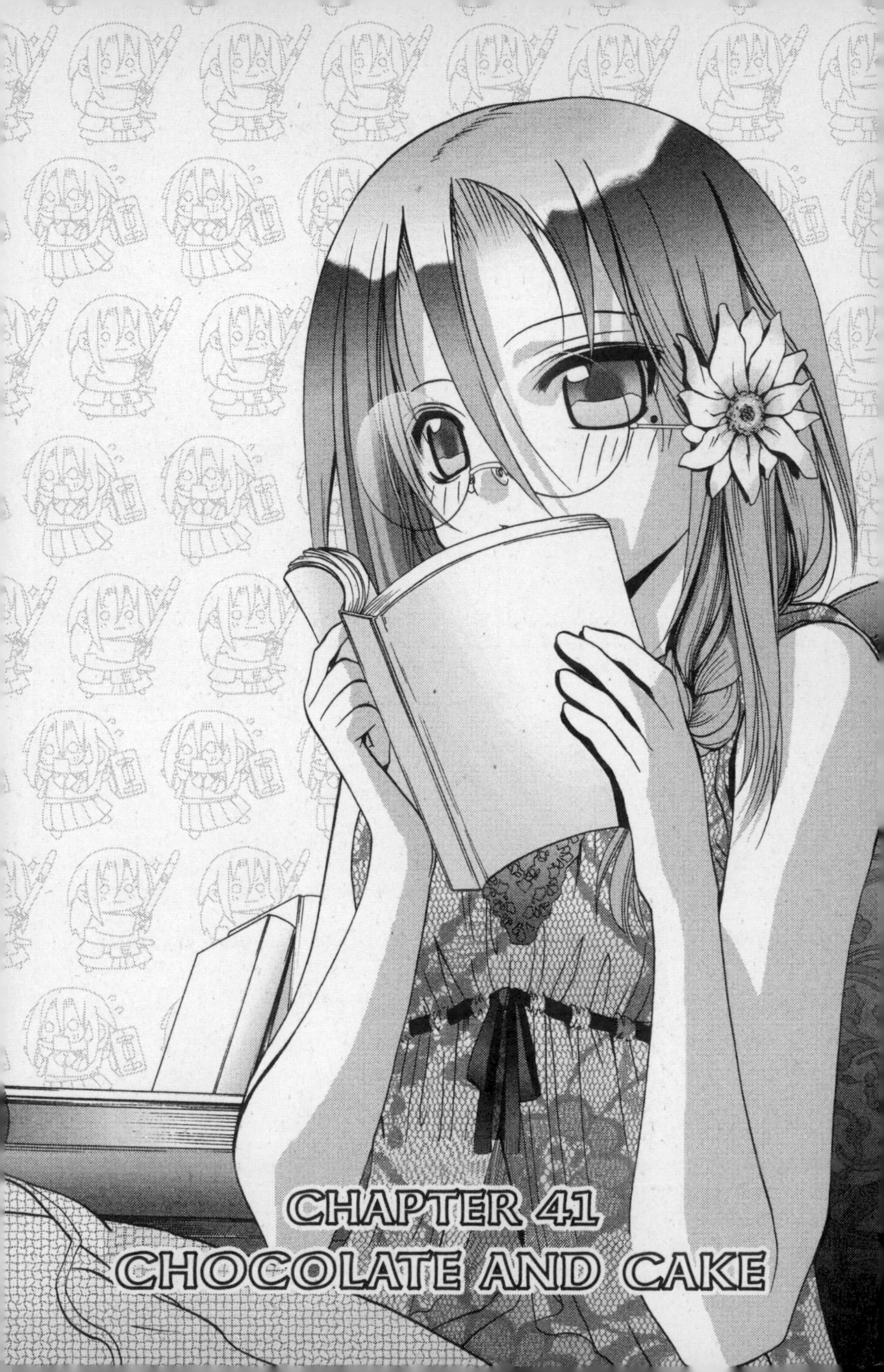
CHAPTER 41
CHOCOLATE AND CAKE

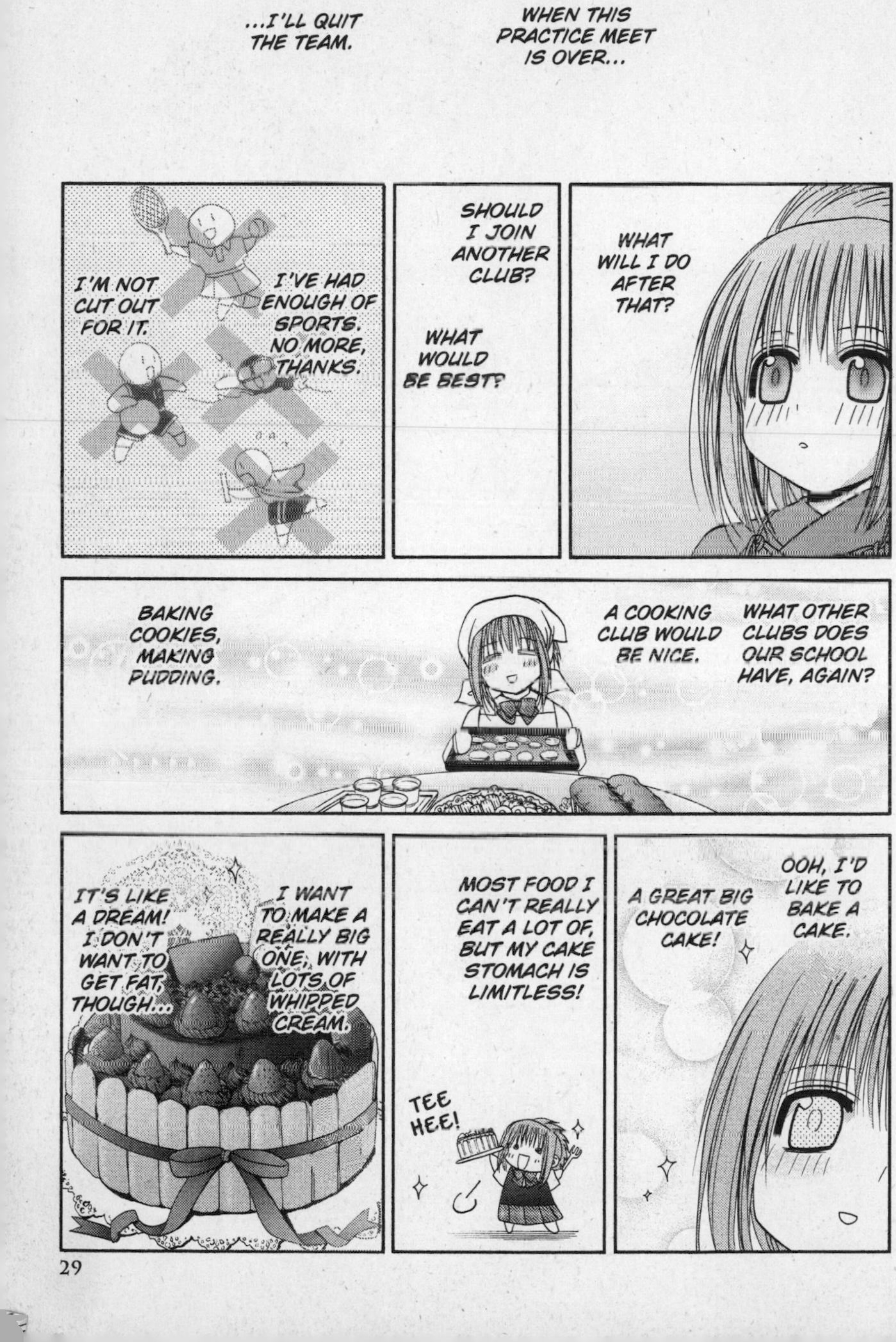
WHEN THIS PRACTICE MEET IS OVER...
...I'LL QUIT THE TEAM.
WHAT WILL I DO AFTER THAT?
SHOULD I JOIN ANOTHER CLUB?
WHAT WOULD BE BEST?
I'VE HAD ENOUGH OF SPORTS. NO MORE, THANKS.
I'M NOT CUT OUT FOR IT.
WHAT OTHER CLUBS DOES OUR SCHOOL HAVE, AGAIN?
A COOKING CLUB WOULD BE NICE.
BAKING COOKIES, MAKING PUDDING.
OOH, I'D LIKE TO BAKE A CAKE.
A GREAT BIG CHOCOLATE CAKE!
MOST FOOD I CAN'T REALLY EAT A LOT OF, BUT MY CAKE STOMACH IS LIMITLESS!
TEE HEE!
I WANT TO MAKE A REALLY BIG ONE, WITH LOTS OF WHIPPED CREAM.
IT'S LIKE A DREAM! I DON'T WANT TO GET FAT, THOUGH...

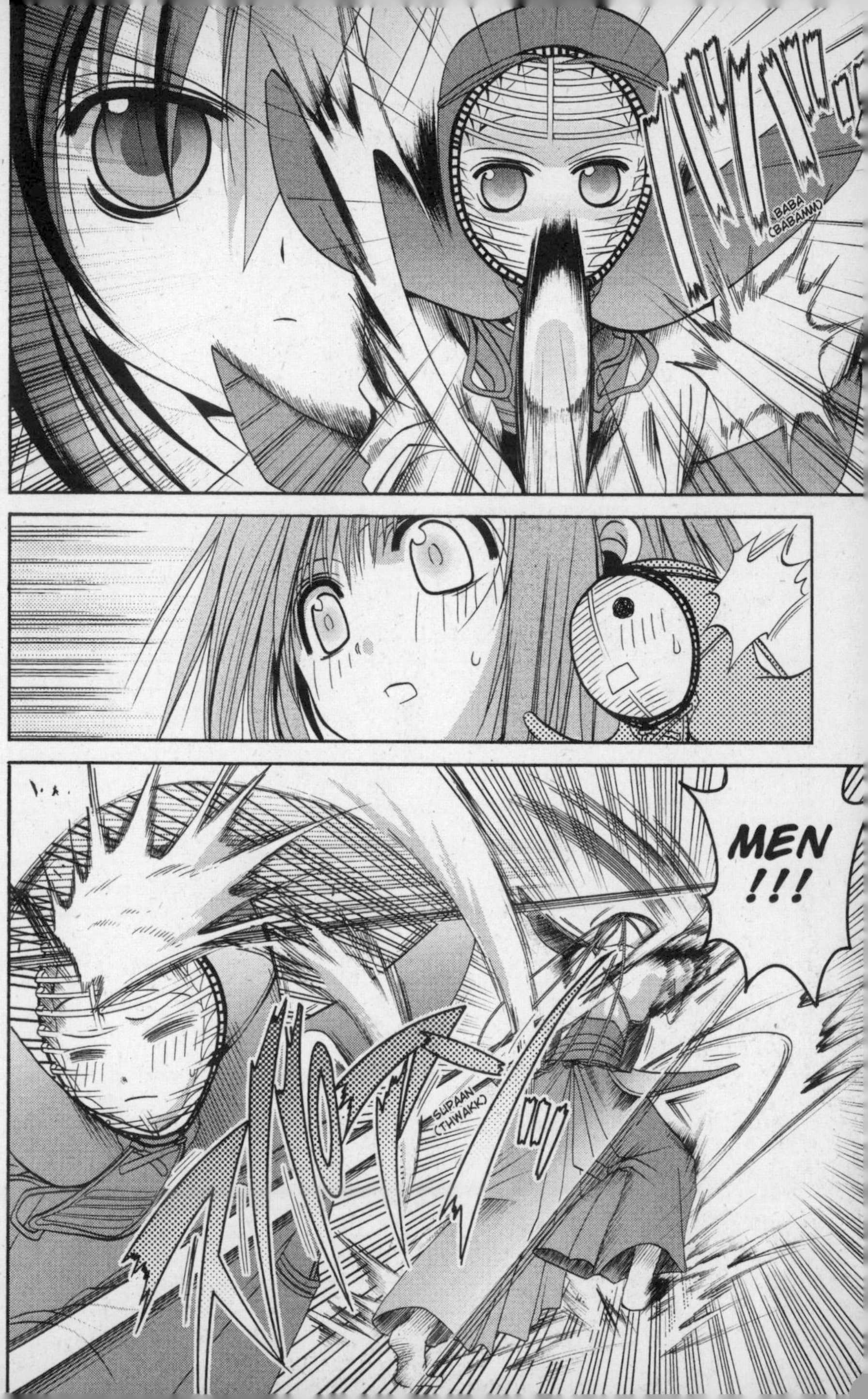
BABA
(BABAMM)
MEN
!!!
SUPAAN
(THWAKK)

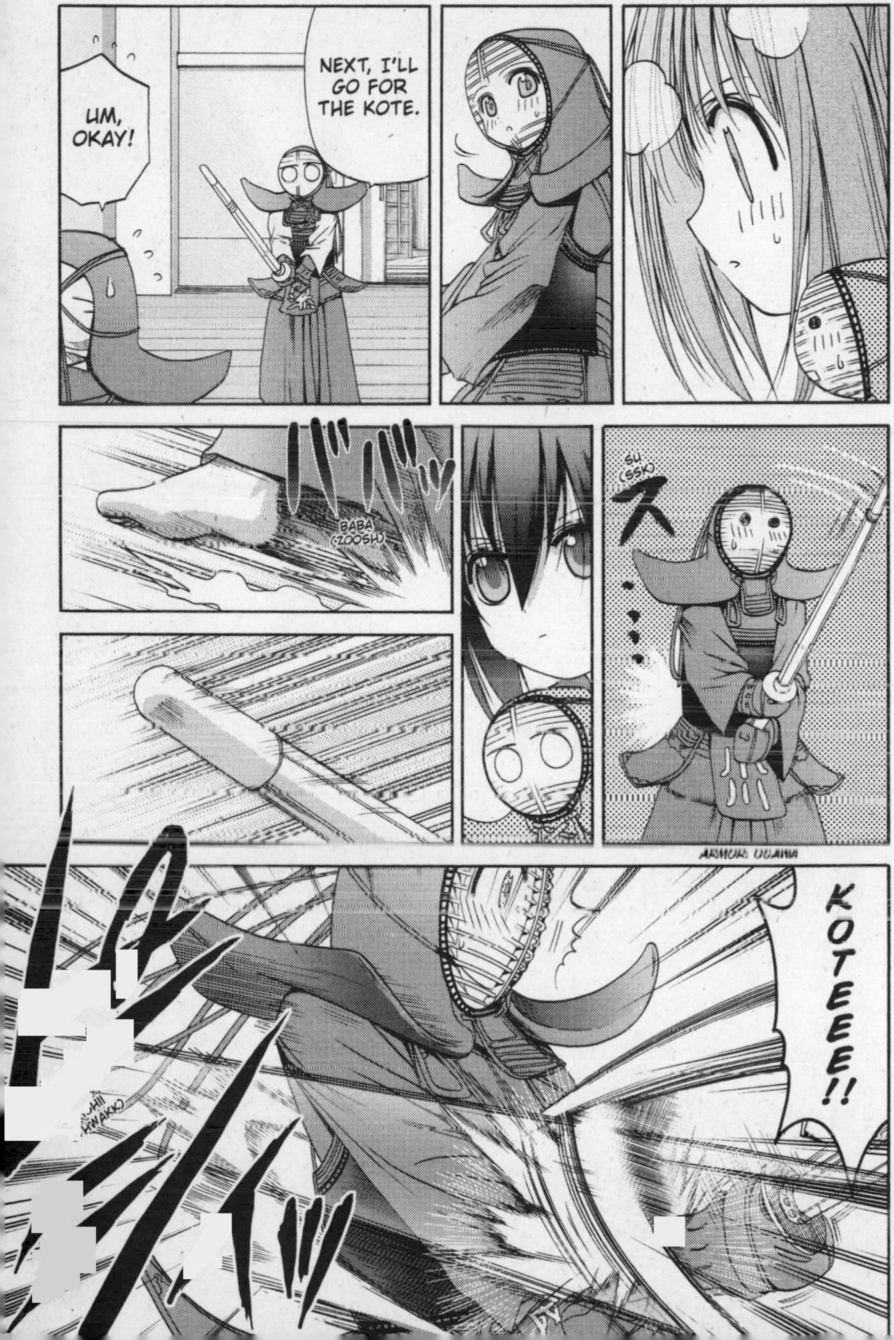
NEXT, I'LL GO FOR THE KOTE.
UM, OKAY!
SU (SSK)
BABA (ZOOSH)
KOTEEE!!

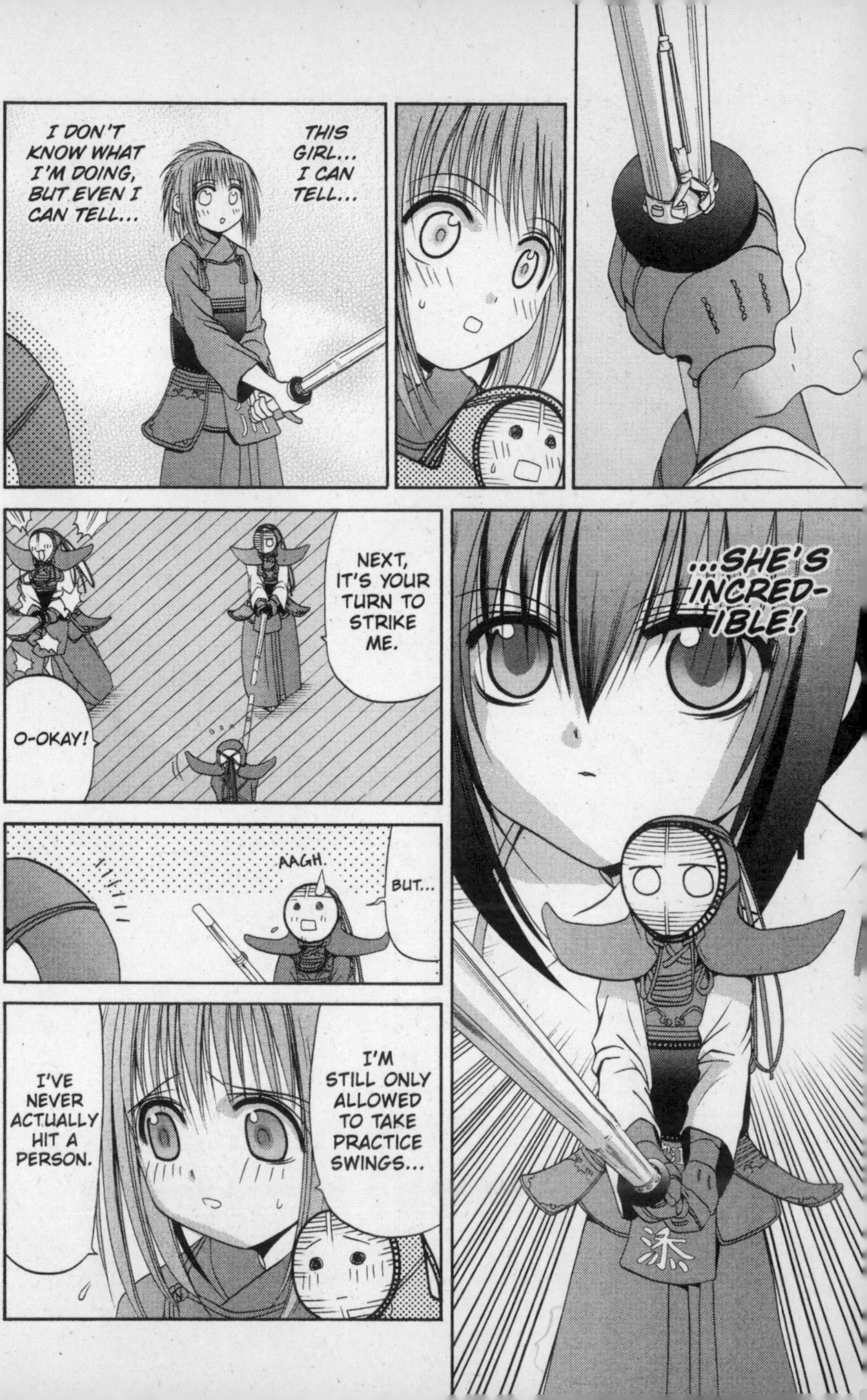
THIS GIRL... I CAN TELL...
I DON'T KNOW WHAT I'M DOING, BUT EVEN I CAN TELL...
...SHE'S INCRED-IBLE!
NEXT, IT'S YOUR TURN TO STRIKE ME.
O-OKAY!
BUT...
AAGH.
I'M STILL ONLY ALLOWED TO TAKE PRACTICE SWINGS...
I'VE NEVER ACTUALLY HIT A PERSON.

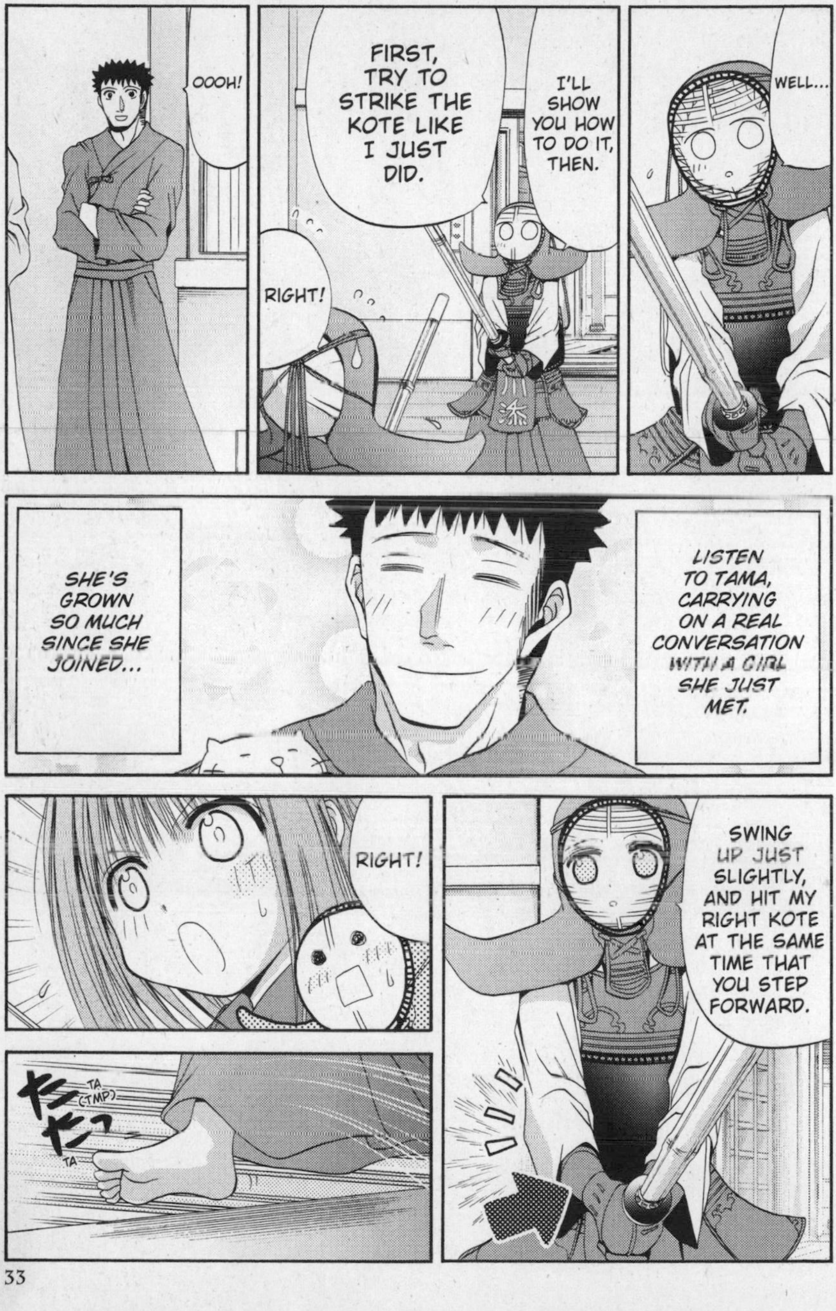
WELL...
I'LL SHOW YOU HOW TO DO IT, THEN.
FIRST, TRY TO STRIKE THE KOTE LIKE I JUST DID.
RIGHT!
OOOH!
LISTEN TO TAMA, CARRYING ON A REAL CONVERSATION WITH A GIRL SHE JUST MET.
SHE'S GROWN SO MUCH SINCE SHE JOINED...
SWING UP JUST SLIGHTLY, AND HIT MY RIGHT KOTE AT THE SAME TIME THAT YOU STEP FORWARD.
RIGHT!
TA (TMP) TA

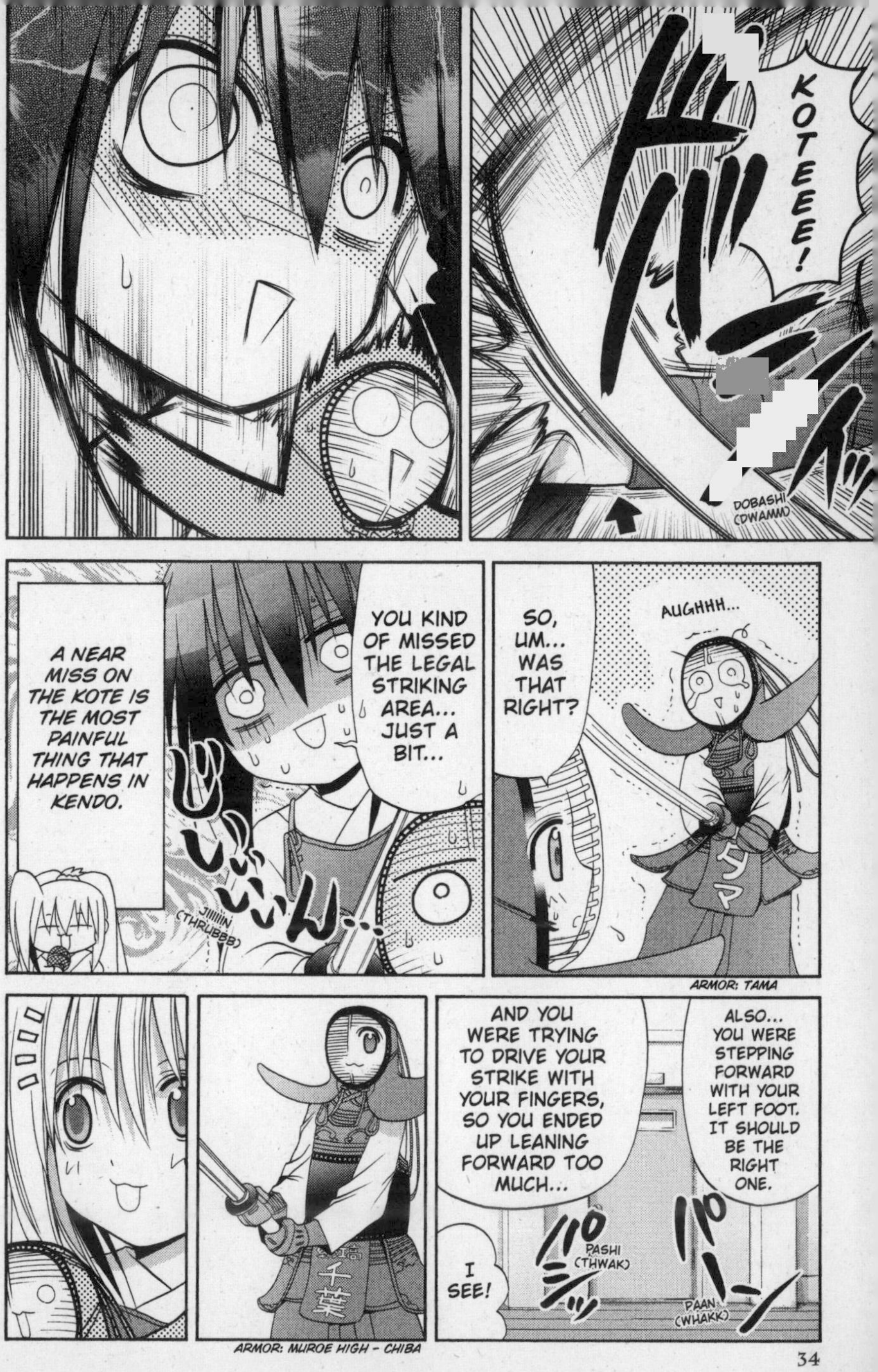
KOTEEE!
DOBASHI (DWAMM)
AUGHHH...
SO, UM... WAS THAT RIGHT?
ARMOR: TAMA
YOU KIND OF MISSED THE LEGAL STRIKING AREA... JUST A BIT...
A NEAR MISS ON THE KOTE IS THE MOST PAINFUL THING THAT HAPPENS IN KENDO.
JIIIIIN (THRUBBB)
ALSO... YOU WERE STEPPING FORWARD WITH YOUR LEFT FOOT. IT SHOULD BE THE RIGHT ONE.
AND YOU WERE TRYING TO DRIVE YOUR STRIKE WITH YOUR FINGERS, SO YOU ENDED UP LEANING FORWARD TOO MUCH...
PAAN (WHAKK)
PASHI (THWAK)
I SEE!
ARMOR: MUROE HIGH - CHIBA

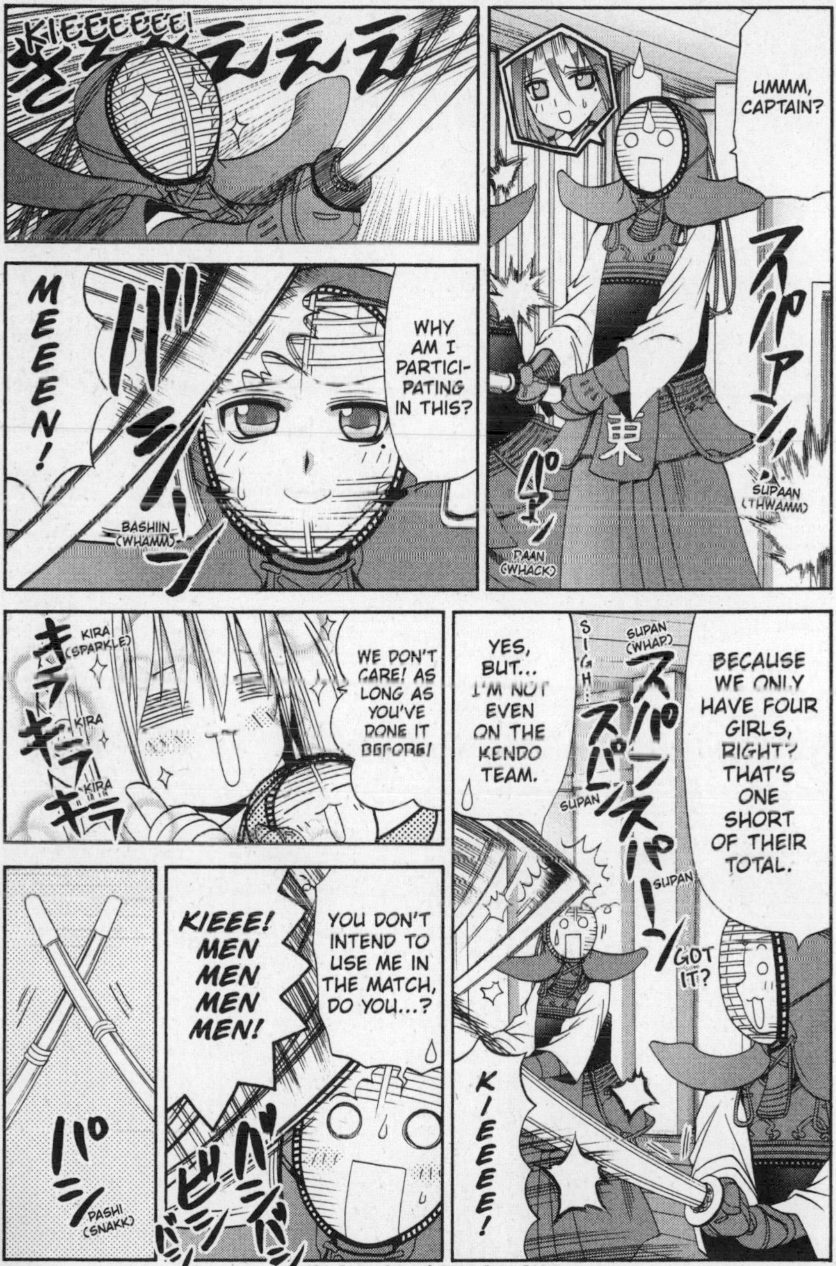
UMMM, CAPTAIN?
SUPAAN (THWAMM)
PAAN (WHACK)
KIEEEEEEE!
WHY AM I PARTICI-PATING IN THIS?
MEEEEN!
BASHIIN (WHAMM)
BECAUSE WE ONLY HAVE FOUR GIRLS, RIGHT? THAT'S ONE SHORT OF THEIR TOTAL.
SUPAN (WHAP)
SIGH...
YES, BUT... I'M NOT EVEN ON THE KENDO TEAM.
SUPAN
SUPAN
GOT IT?
KIEEEEE!
WE DON'T CARE! AS LONG AS YOU'VE DONE IT BEFORE!
KIRA (SPARKLE)
KIRA
KIRA
YOU DON'T INTEND TO USE ME IN THE MATCH, DO YOU...?
KIEEE! MEN MEN MEN MEN!
PASHI (SNAKK)

SFX: BASHI (WHAM) BASHI BISHI BASHI

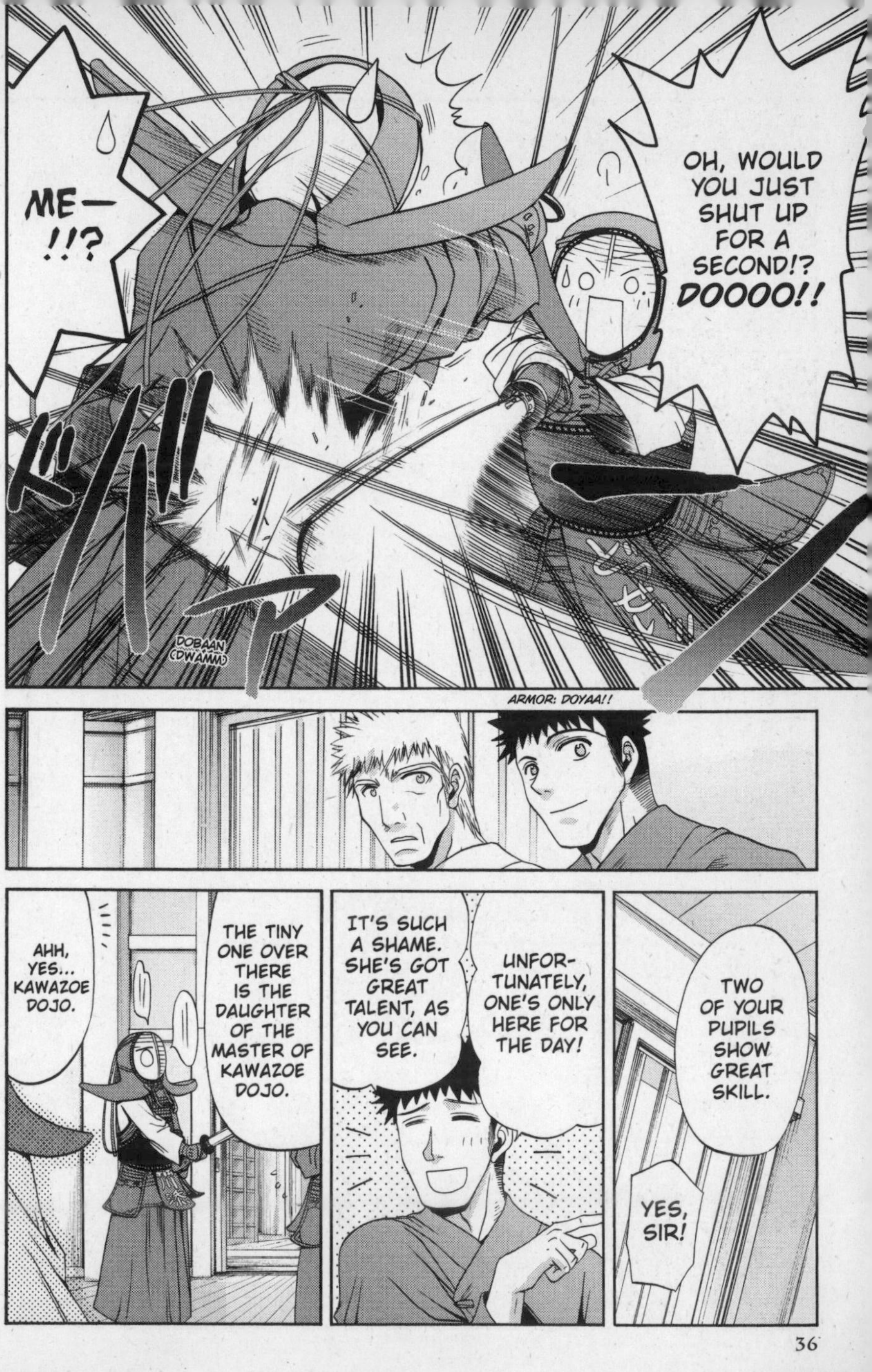
OH, WOULD YOU JUST SHUT UP FOR A SECOND!? DOOOO!!
ME— !!?
DOBAAN (DWAMM)
ARMOR: DOYAA!!
TWO OF YOUR PUPILS SHOW GREAT SKILL.
YES, SIR!
UNFORTUNATELY, ONE'S ONLY HERE FOR THE DAY!
IT'S SUCH A SHAME. SHE'S GOT GREAT TALENT, AS YOU CAN SEE.
THE TINY ONE OVER THERE IS THE DAUGHTER OF THE MASTER OF KAWAZOE DOJO.
AHH, YES... KAWAZOE DOJO.

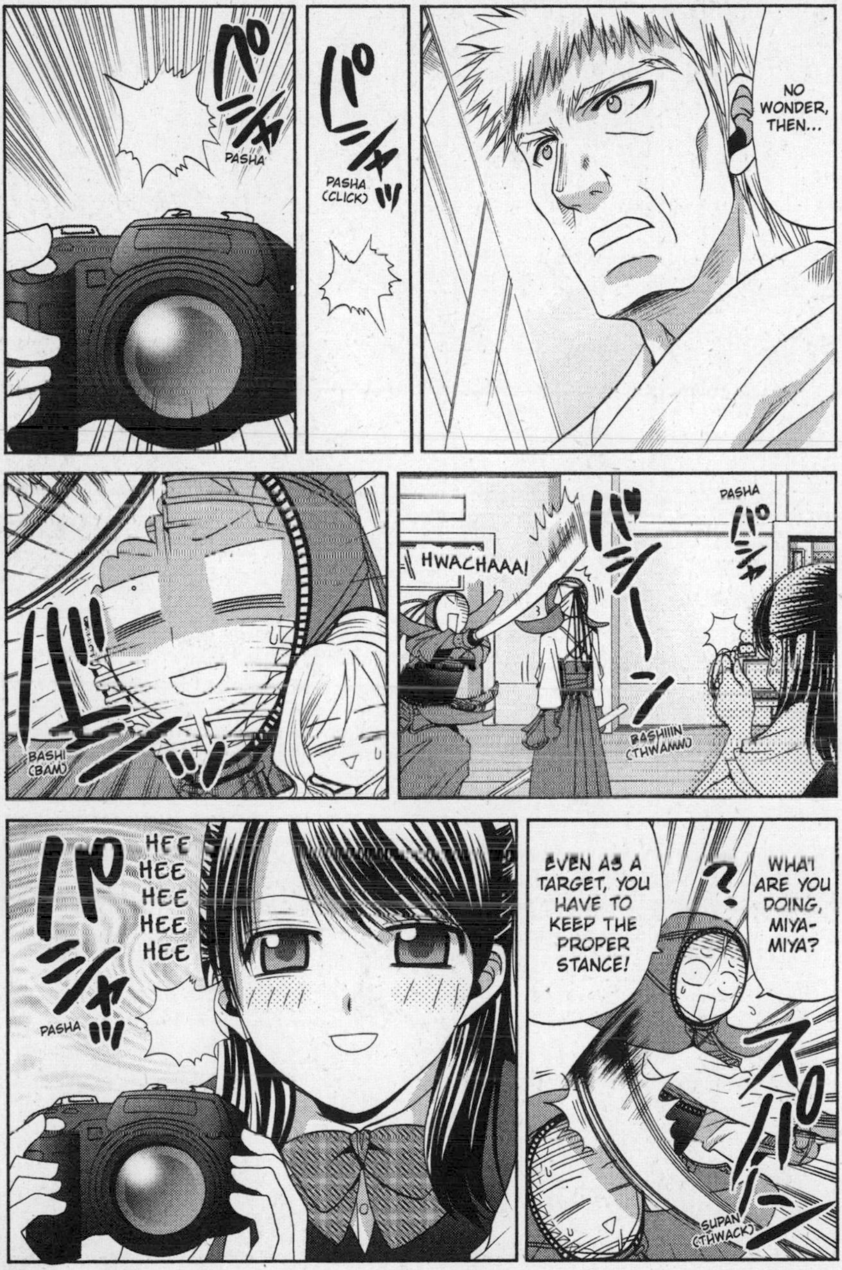
NO WONDER, THEN...
PASHA (CLICK)
PASHA
PASHA
HWACHAAA!
BASHIIIN (THWAMM)
BASHI (BAM)
WHAT ARE YOU DOING, MIYA-MIYA?
EVEN AS A TARGET, YOU HAVE TO KEEP THE PROPER STANCE!
SUPAN (THWACK)
HEE HEE HEE HEE HEE
PASHA

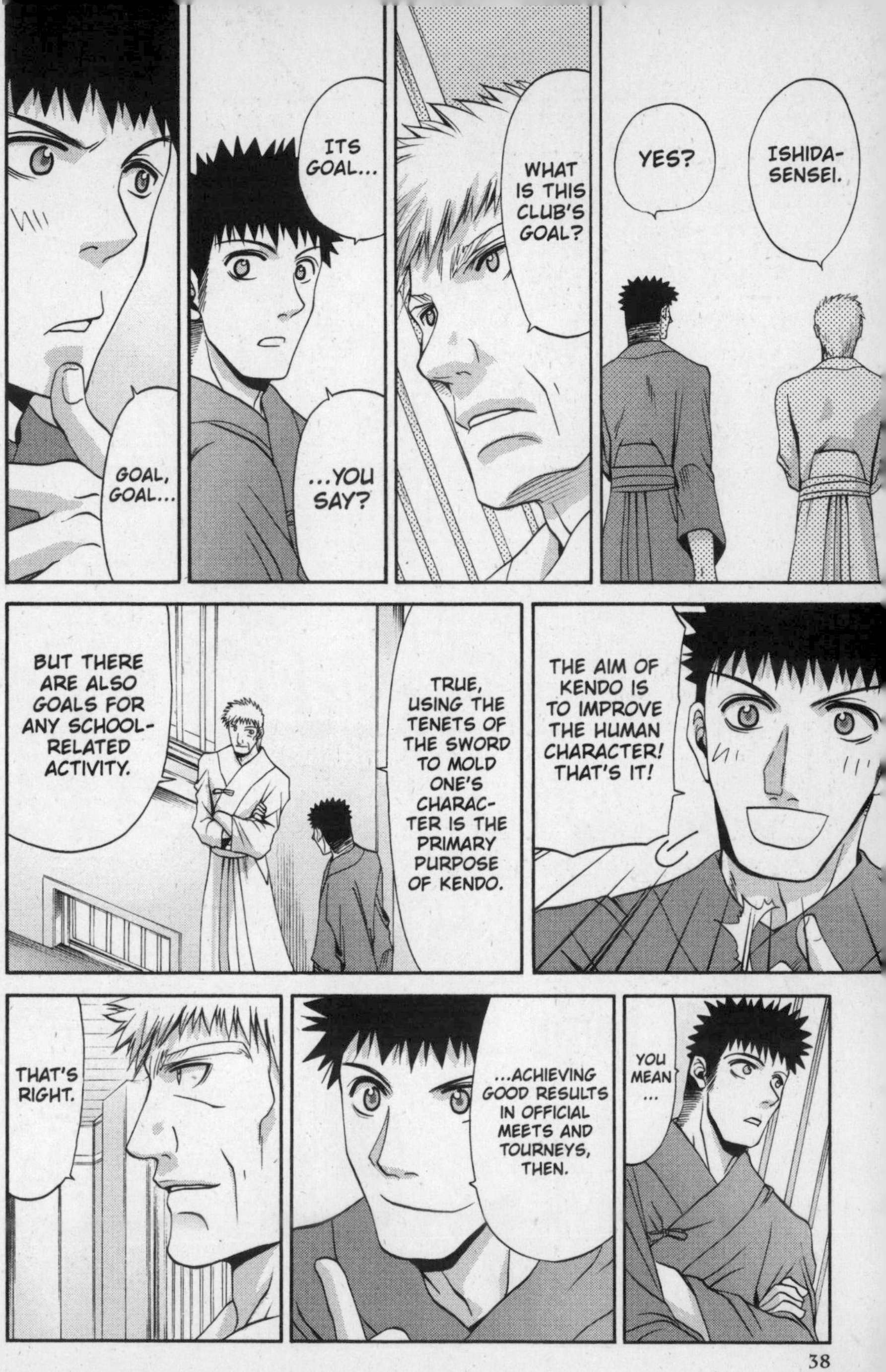
ISHIDA-SENSEI.
YES?
WHAT IS THIS CLUB'S GOAL?
ITS GOAL...
...YOU SAY?
GOAL, GOAL...
THE AIM OF KENDO IS TO IMPROVE THE HUMAN CHARACTER! THAT'S IT!
TRUE, USING THE TENETS OF THE SWORD TO MOLD ONE'S CHARACTER IS THE PRIMARY PURPOSE OF KENDO.
BUT THERE ARE ALSO GOALS FOR ANY SCHOOL-RELATED ACTIVITY.
YOU MEAN ...
...ACHIEVING GOOD RESULTS IN OFFICIAL MEETS AND TOURNEYS, THEN.
THAT'S RIGHT.

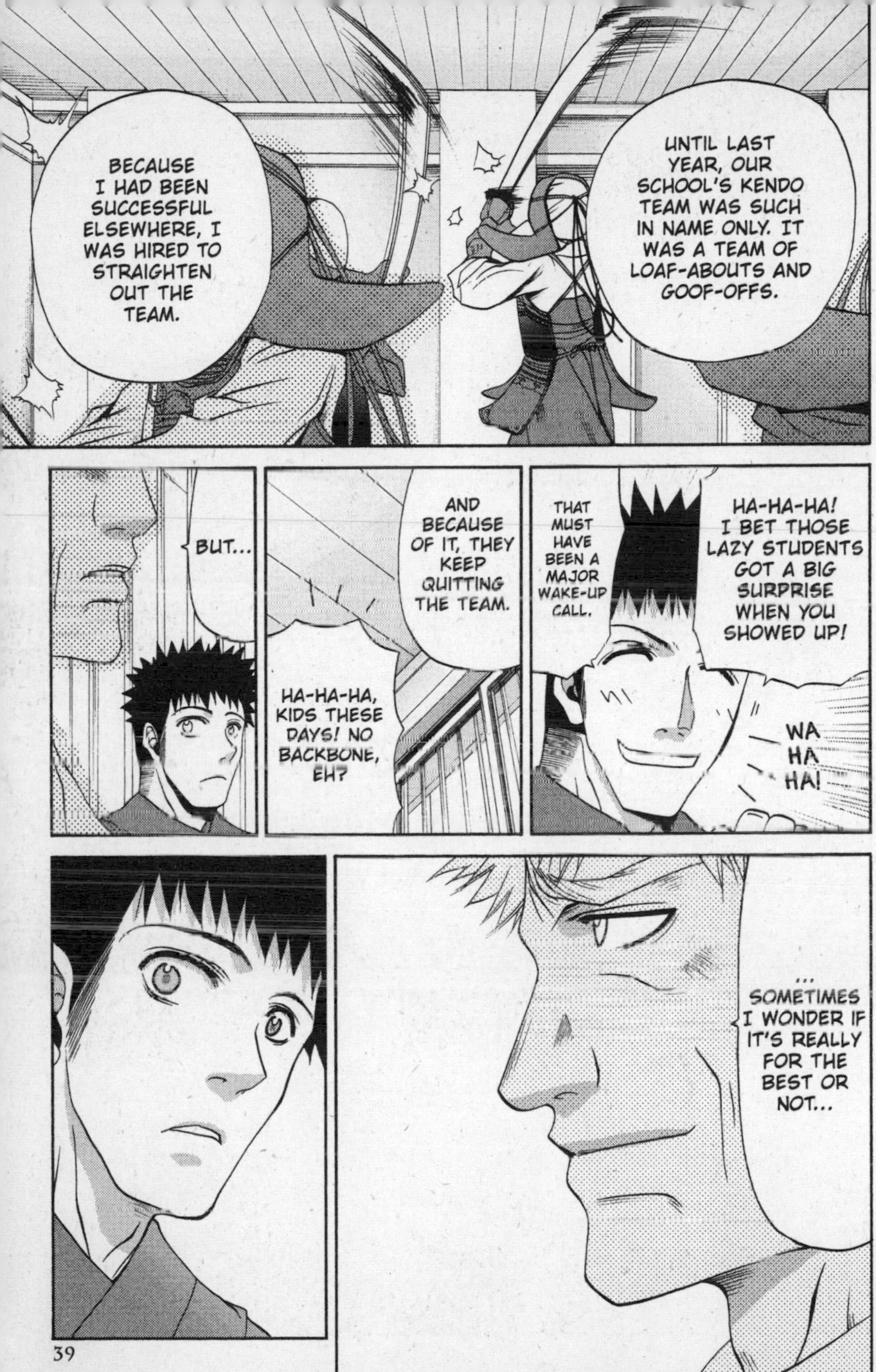

UNTIL LAST YEAR, OUR SCHOOL'S KENDO TEAM WAS SUCH IN NAME ONLY. IT WAS A TEAM OF LOAF-ABOUTS AND GOOF-OFFS.
BECAUSE I HAD BEEN SUCCESSFUL ELSEWHERE, I WAS HIRED TO STRAIGHTEN OUT THE TEAM.
HA-HA-HA! I BET THOSE LAZY STUDENTS GOT A BIG SURPRISE WHEN YOU SHOWED UP!
THAT MUST HAVE BEEN A MAJOR WAKE-UP CALL.
WA HA HA!
AND BECAUSE OF IT, THEY KEEP QUITTING THE TEAM.
HA-HA-HA, KIDS THESE DAYS! NO BACKBONE, EH?
BUT...
... SOMETIMES I WONDER IF IT'S REALLY FOR THE BEST OR NOT...

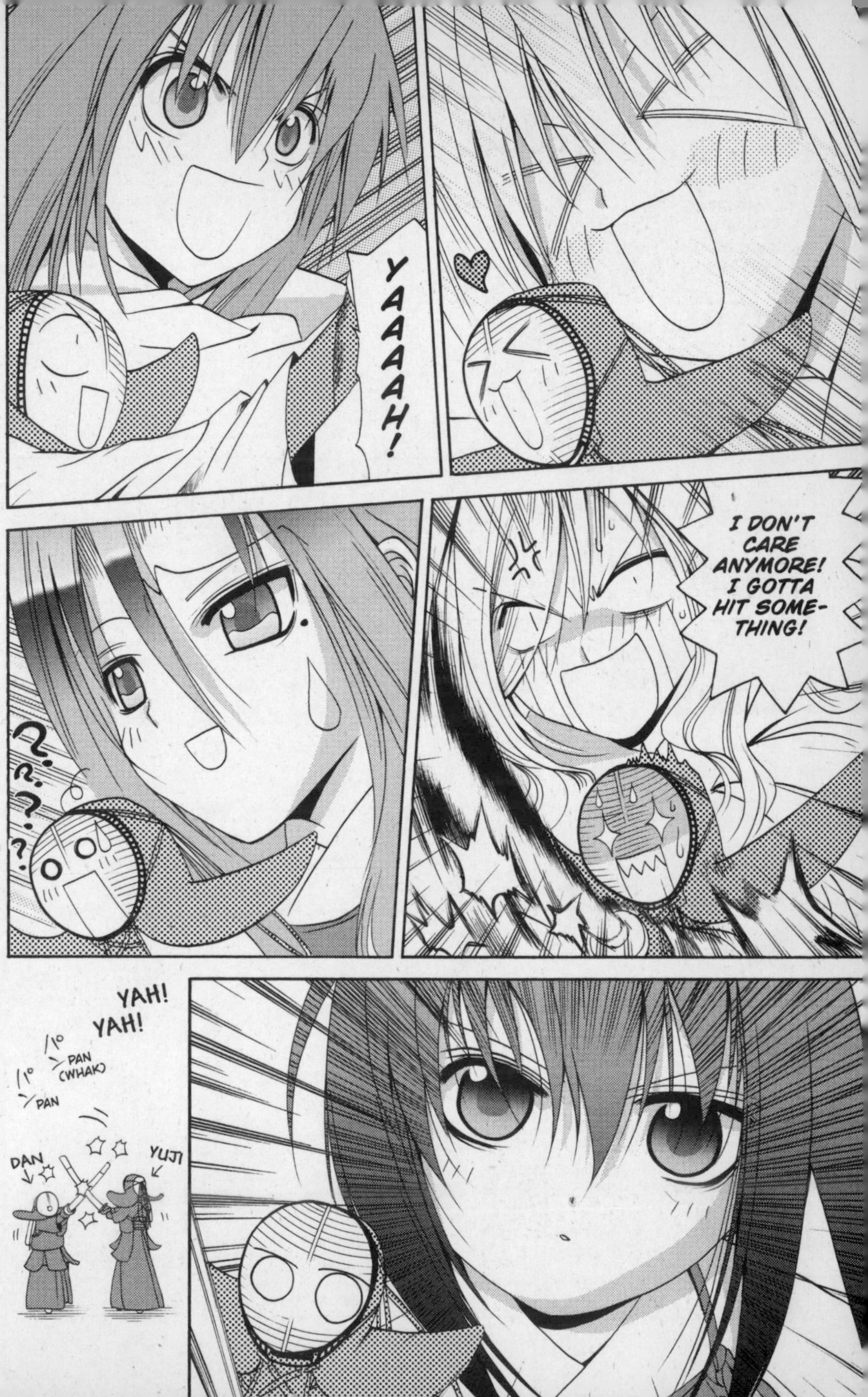
YAAAAAH!
I DON'T CARE ANYMORE! I GOTTA HIT SOME-THING!
YAH! YAH!
パ PAN (WHAK)
パ PAN
DAN
YUJI

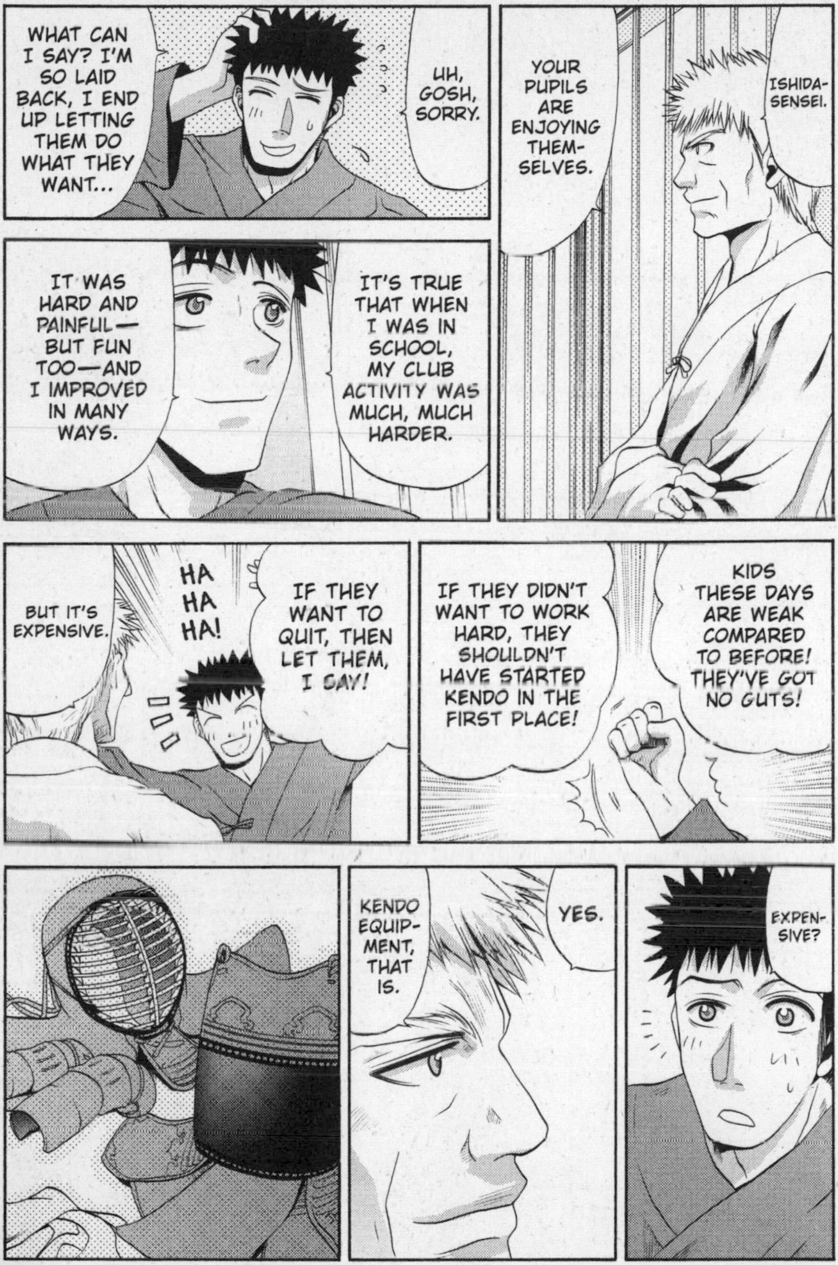
ISHIDA-SENSEI.
YOUR PUPILS ARE ENJOYING THEM-SELVES.
UH, GOSH, SORRY.
WHAT CAN I SAY? I'M SO LAID BACK, I END UP LETTING THEM DO WHAT THEY WANT...
IT'S TRUE THAT WHEN I WAS IN SCHOOL, MY CLUB ACTIVITY WAS MUCH, MUCH HARDER.
IT WAS HARD AND PAINFUL—BUT FUN TOO—AND I IMPROVED IN MANY WAYS.
KIDS THESE DAYS ARE WEAK COMPARED TO BEFORE! THEY'VE GOT NO GUTS!
IF THEY DIDN'T WANT TO WORK HARD, THEY SHOULDN'T HAVE STARTED KENDO IN THE FIRST PLACE!
IF THEY WANT TO QUIT, THEN LET THEM, I SAY!
HA HA HA!
BUT IT'S EXPENSIVE.
EXPEN-SIVE?
YES.
KENDO EQUIP-MENT, THAT IS.

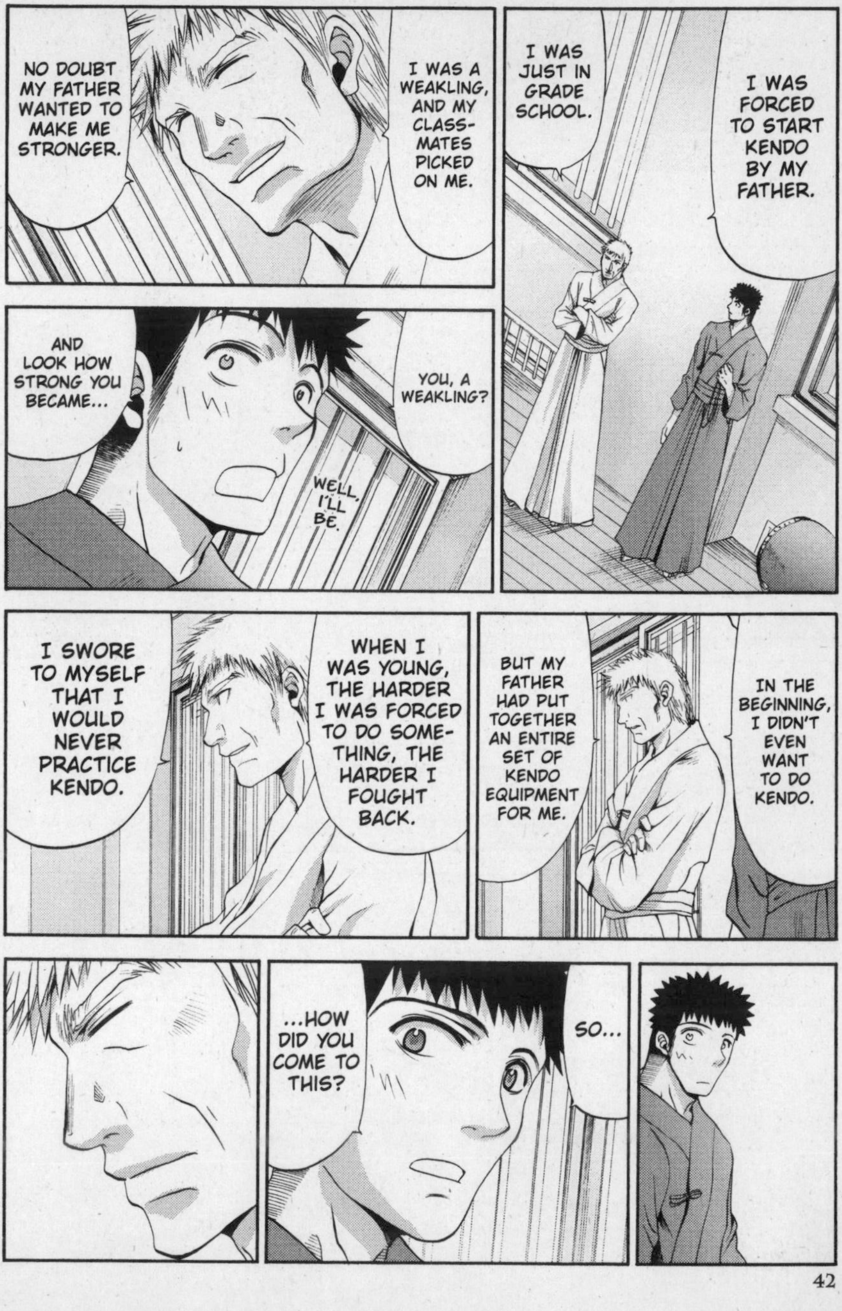
I WAS FORCED TO START KENDO BY MY FATHER.
I WAS JUST IN GRADE SCHOOL.
I WAS A WEAKLING, AND MY CLASS-MATES PICKED ON ME.
NO DOUBT MY FATHER WANTED TO MAKE ME STRONGER.
YOU, A WEAKLING?
WELL, I'LL BE.
AND LOOK HOW STRONG YOU BECAME...
IN THE BEGINNING, I DIDN'T EVEN WANT TO DO KENDO.
BUT MY FATHER HAD PUT TOGETHER AN ENTIRE SET OF KENDO EQUIPMENT FOR ME.
WHEN I WAS YOUNG, THE HARDER I WAS FORCED TO DO SOME-THING, THE HARDER I FOUGHT BACK.
I SWORE TO MYSELF THAT I WOULD NEVER PRACTICE KENDO.
SO...
...HOW DID YOU COME TO THIS?

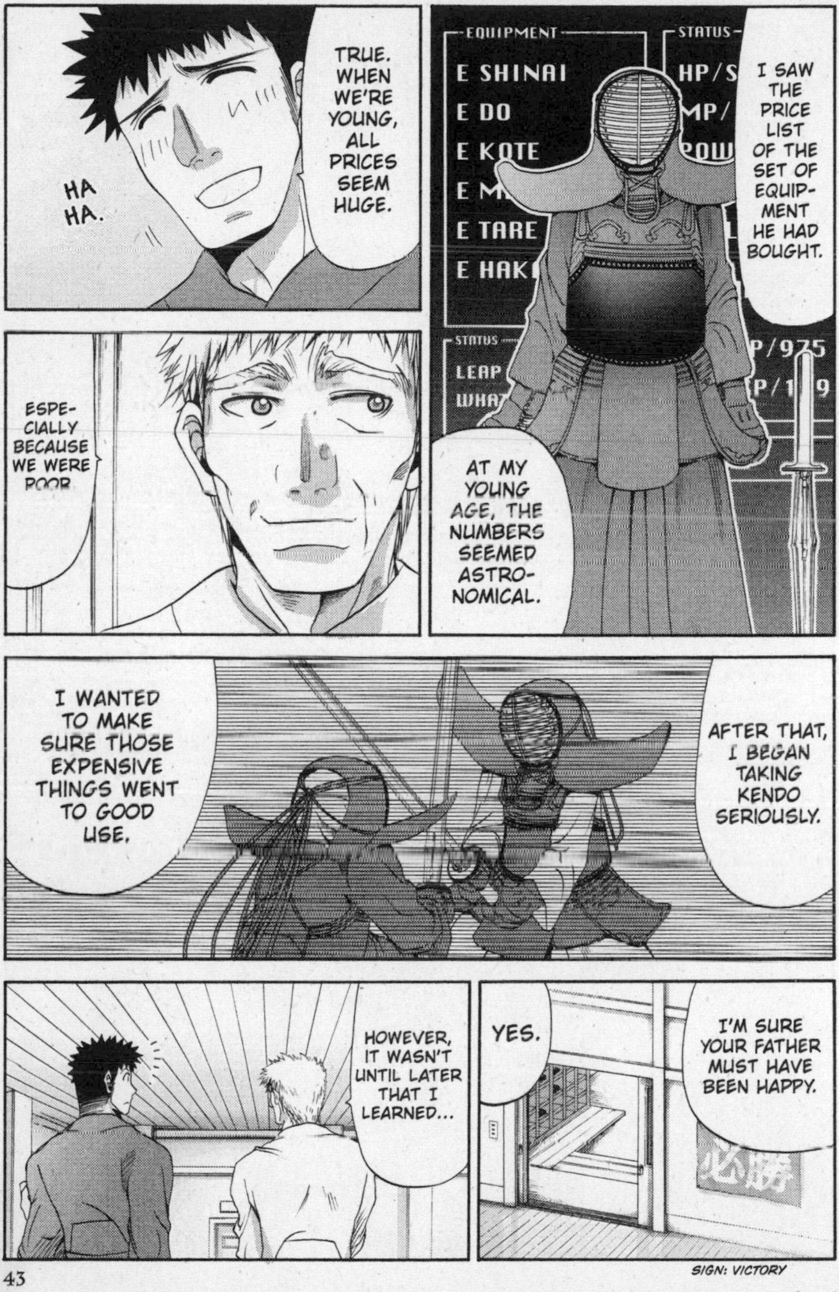
EQUIPMENT
E SHINAI
E DO
E KOTE
E TARE
STATUS
STATUS
LEAP
P/975
I SAW THE PRICE LIST OF THE SET OF EQUIP-MENT HE HAD BOUGHT.
AT MY YOUNG AGE, THE NUMBERS SEEMED ASTRO-NOMICAL.
TRUE. WHEN WE'RE YOUNG, ALL PRICES SEEM HUGE.
HA HA.
ESPE-CIALLY BECAUSE WE WERE POOR.
AFTER THAT, I BEGAN TAKING KENDO SERIOUSLY.
I WANTED TO MAKE SURE THOSE EXPENSIVE THINGS WENT TO GOOD USE.
I'M SURE YOUR FATHER MUST HAVE BEEN HAPPY.
YES.
必勝
HOWEVER, IT WASN'T UNTIL LATER THAT I LEARNED...

SIGN: VICTORY

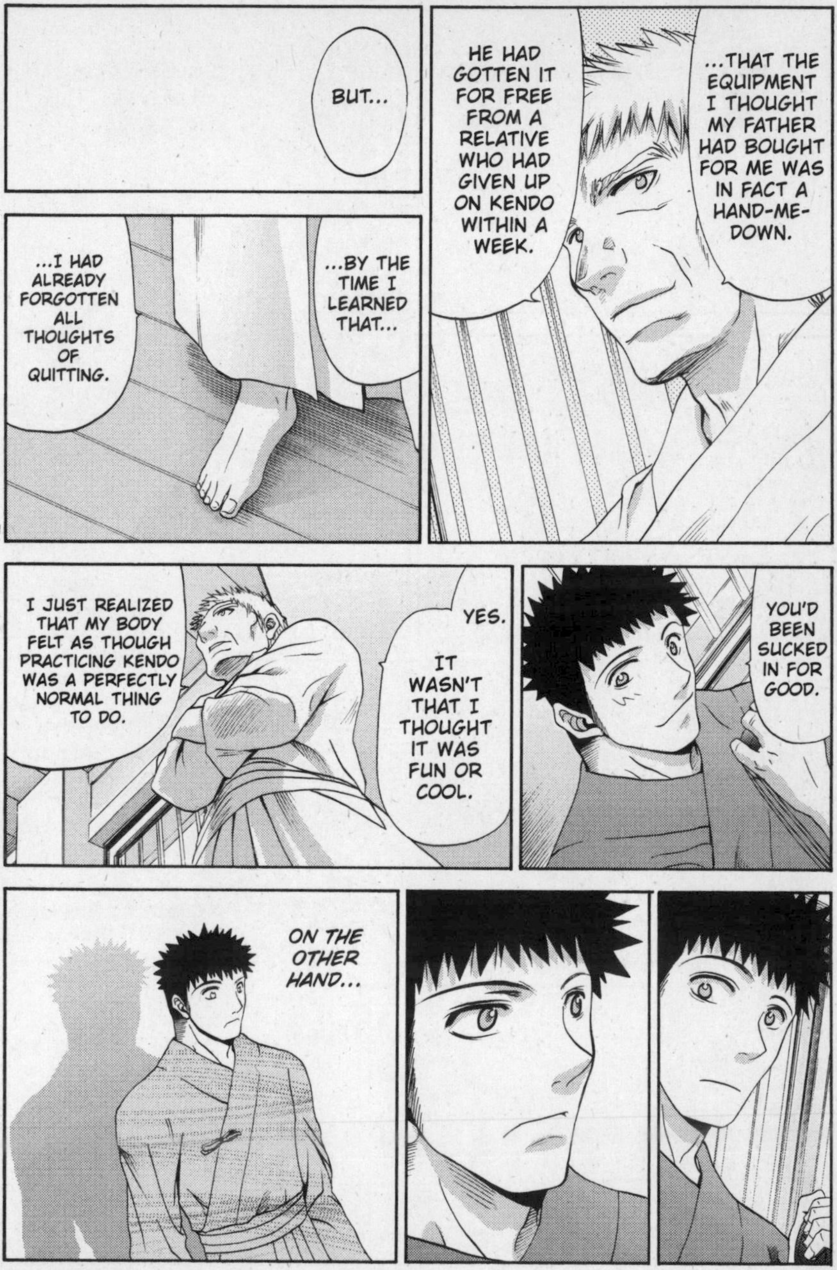
...THAT THE EQUIPMENT I THOUGHT MY FATHER HAD BOUGHT FOR ME WAS IN FACT A HAND-ME-DOWN.
HE HAD GOTTEN IT FOR FREE FROM A RELATIVE WHO HAD GIVEN UP ON KENDO WITHIN A WEEK.
BUT...
...BY THE TIME I LEARNED THAT...
...I HAD ALREADY FORGOTTEN ALL THOUGHTS OF QUITTING.
YOU'D BEEN SUCKED IN FOR GOOD.
YES.
IT WASN'T THAT I THOUGHT IT WAS FUN OR COOL.
I JUST REALIZED THAT MY BODY FELT AS THOUGH PRACTICING KENDO WAS A PERFECTLY NORMAL THING TO DO.
ON THE OTHER HAND...

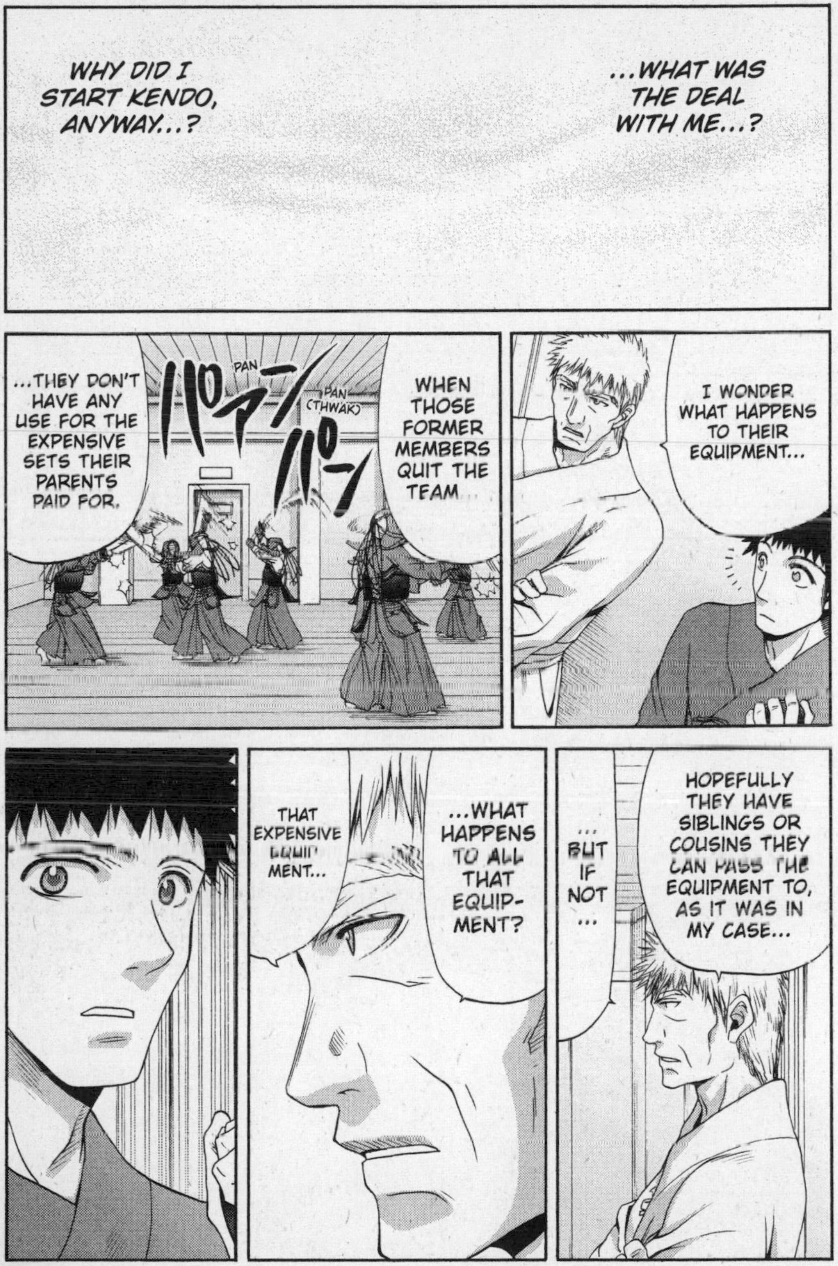
...WHAT WAS THE DEAL WITH ME...?
WHY DID I START KENDO, ANYWAY...?
I WONDER WHAT HAPPENS TO THEIR EQUIPMENT...
WHEN THOSE FORMER MEMBERS QUIT THE TEAM...
パァーン
PAN
パーン
PAN (THWAK)
...THEY DON'T HAVE ANY USE FOR THE EXPENSIVE SETS THEIR PARENTS PAID FOR.
HOPEFULLY THEY HAVE SIBLINGS OR COUSINS THEY CAN PASS THE EQUIPMENT TO, AS IT WAS IN MY CASE...
...BUT IF NOT...
...WHAT HAPPENS TO ALL THAT EQUIPMENT?
THAT EXPENSIVE EQUIPMENT...

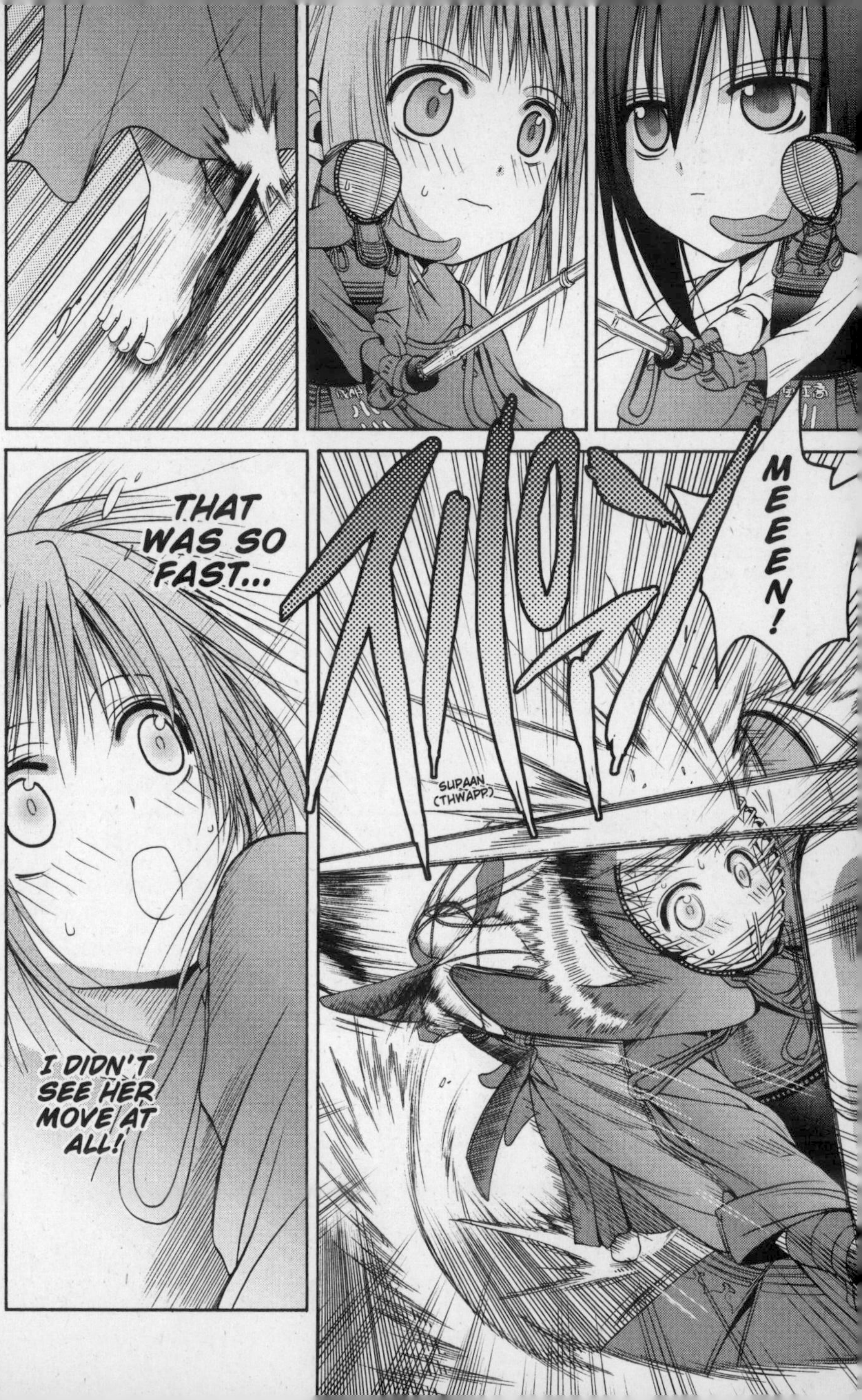
MEEEN!
SUPAAN (THWAPP)
THAT WAS SO FAST...
I DIDN'T SEE HER MOVE AT ALL!

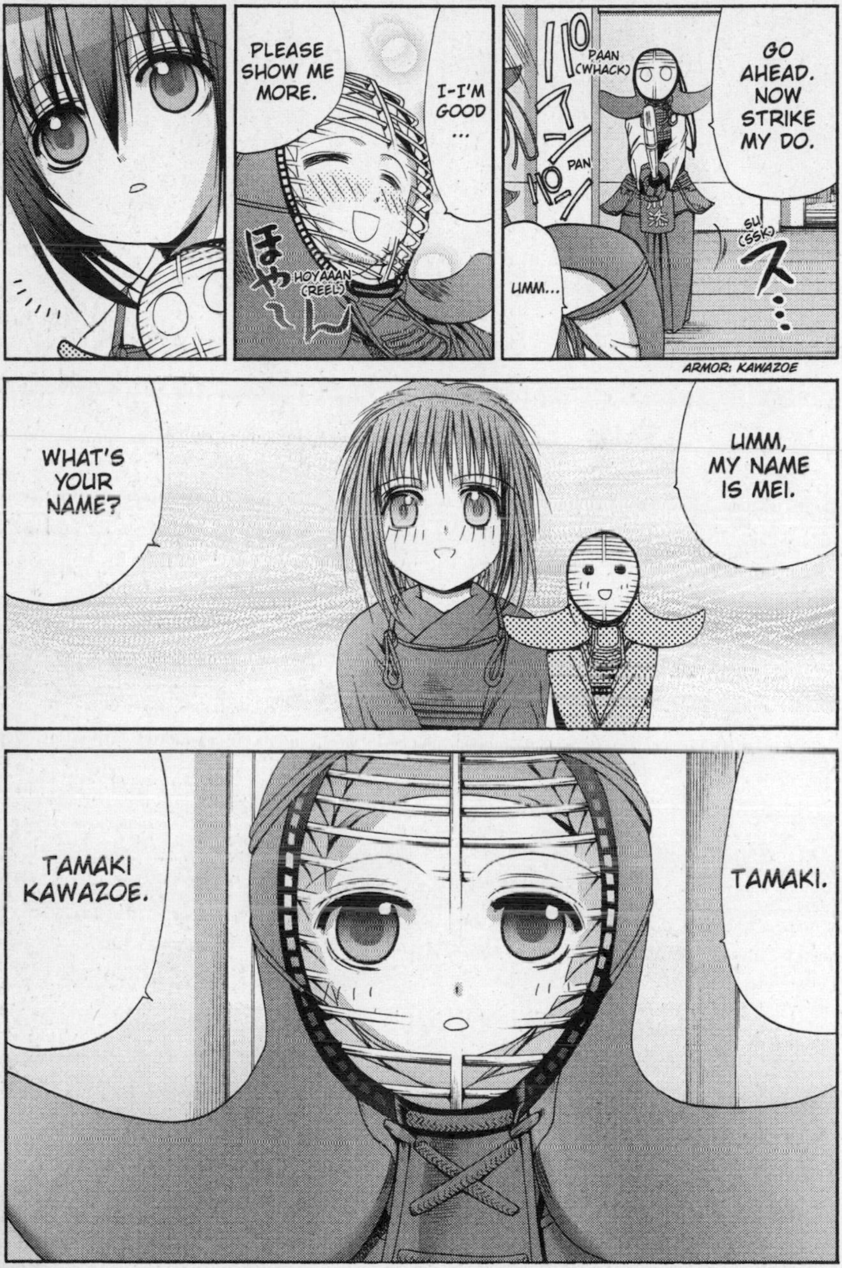
GO AHEAD. NOW STRIKE MY DO.
PAAN (WHACK)
PAN
SU (SSK)
UMM...
I-I'M GOOD ...
PLEASE SHOW ME MORE.
HOYAAAN (REEL)
ARMOR: KAWAZOE
UMM, MY NAME IS MEI.
WHAT'S YOUR NAME?
TAMAKI.
TAMAKI KAWAZOE.

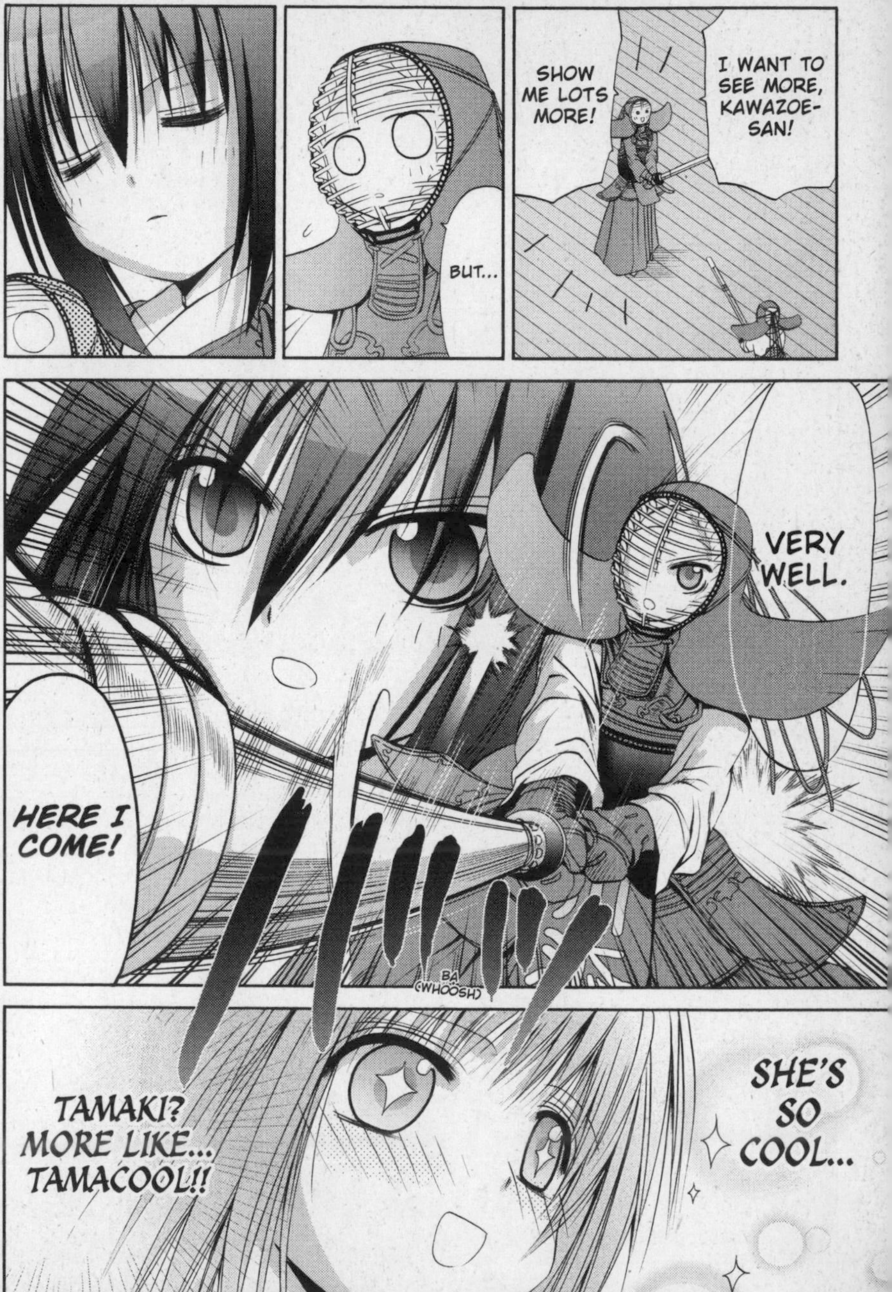
I WANT TO SEE MORE, KAWAZOE-SAN!
SHOW ME LOTS MORE!
BUT...
VERY WELL.
HERE I COME!
BA (WHOOSH)
SHE'S SO COOL...
TAMAKI? MORE LIKE... TAMACOOL!!

BAMBOO BLADE

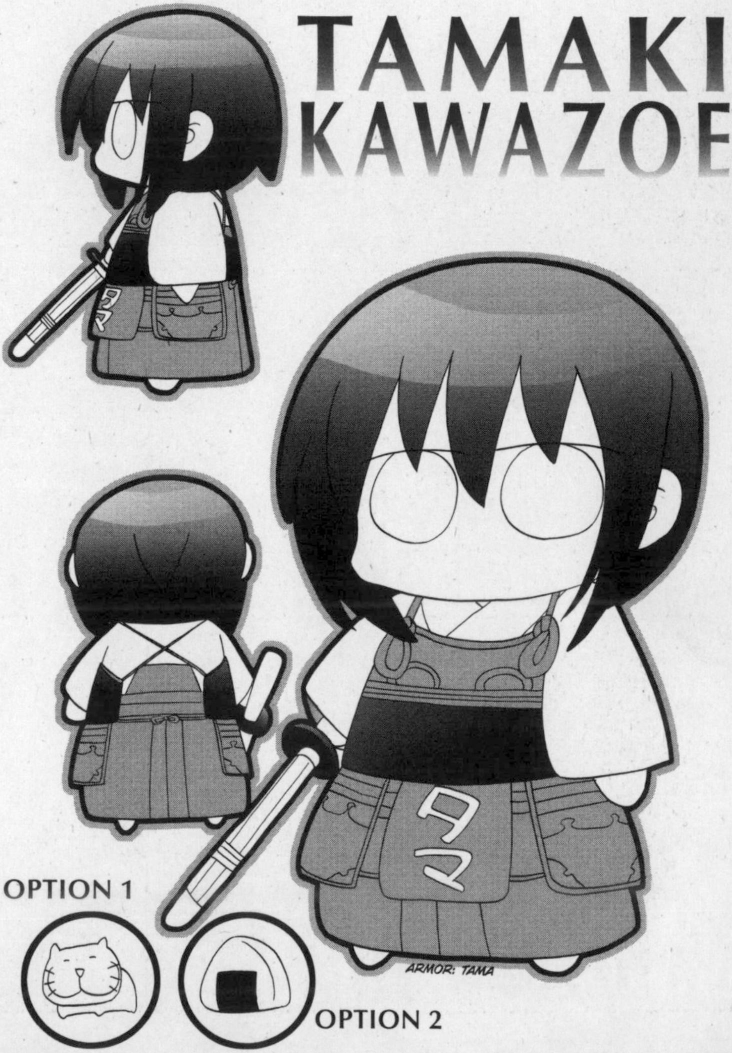
TAMAKI
KAWAZOE
タマ
OPTION 1
OPTION 2
ARMOR: TAMA

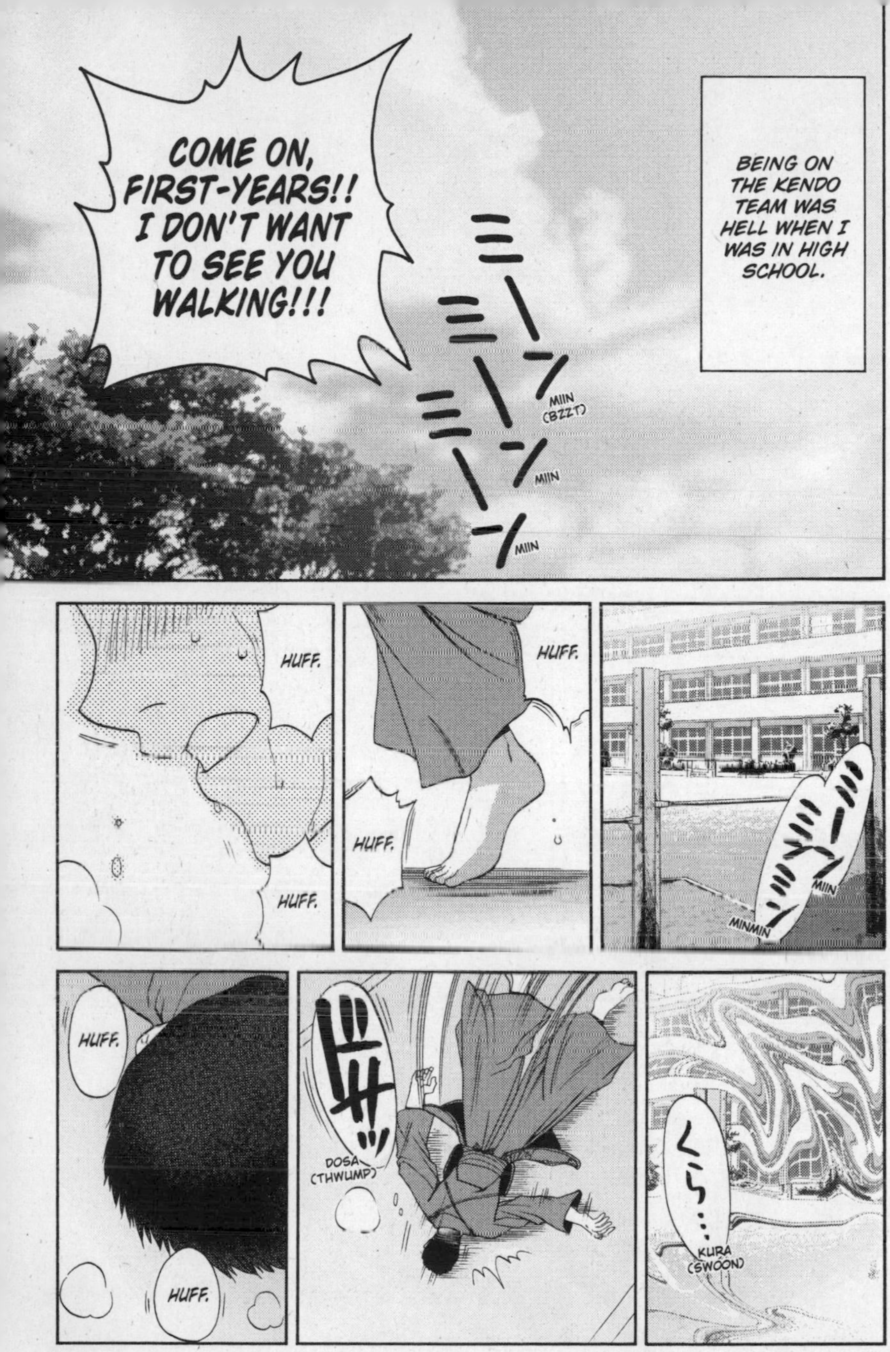
BEING ON THE KENDO TEAM WAS HELL WHEN I WAS IN HIGH SCHOOL.
COME ON, FIRST-YEARS!! I DON'T WANT TO SEE YOU WALKING!!!
MIIN (BZZT)
MIIN
MIIN
MIIN
MINMIN
HUFF.
HUFF.
HUFF.
HUFF.
くら…
KURA (SWOON)
DOSA (THWUMP)
HUFF.
HUFF.

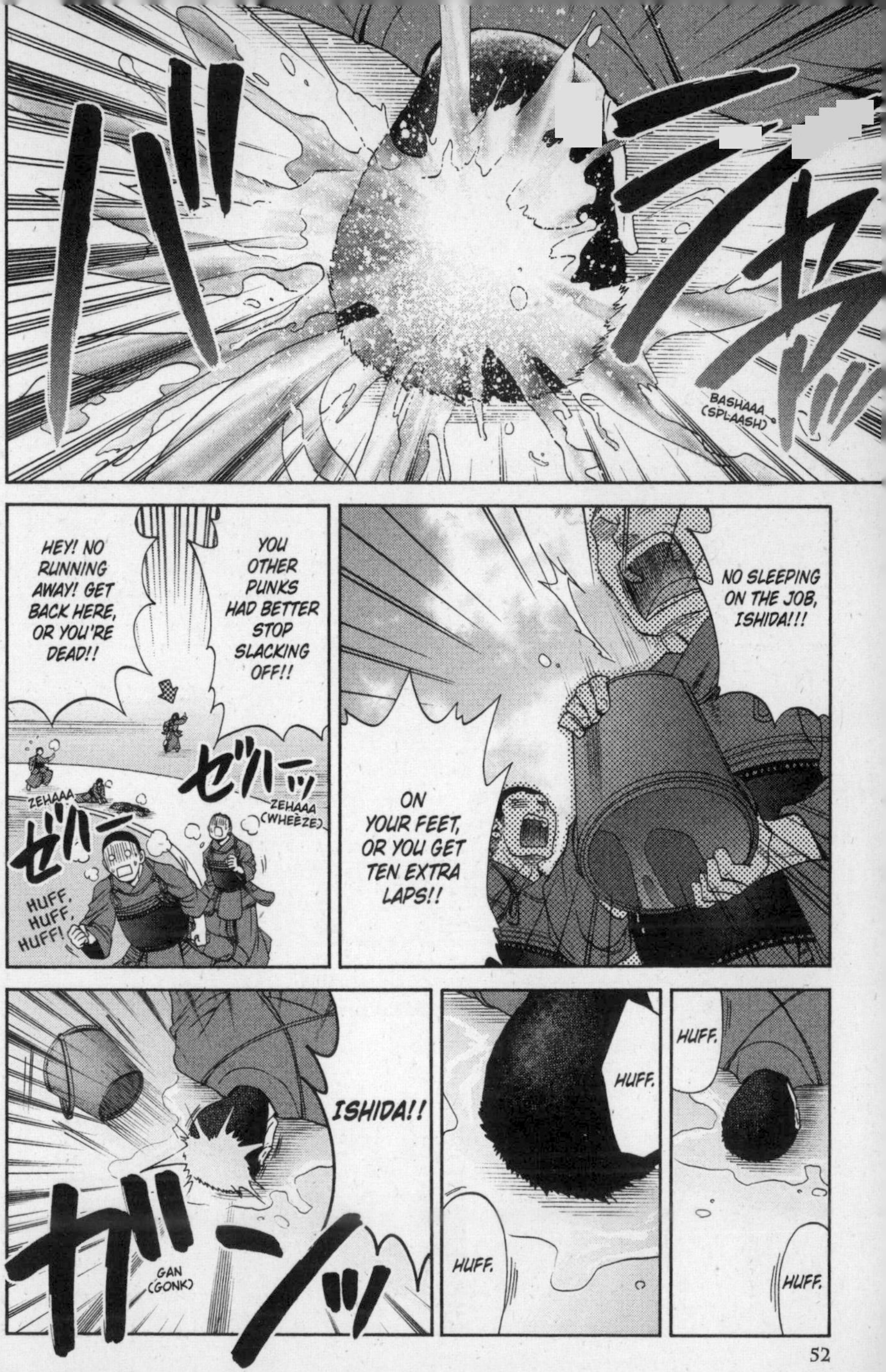
BASHAAA (SPLAASH)
NO SLEEPING ON THE JOB, ISHIDA!!!
ON YOUR FEET, OR YOU GET TEN EXTRA LAPS!!
YOU OTHER PUNKS HAD BETTER STOP SLACKING OFF!!
HEY! NO RUNNING AWAY! GET BACK HERE, OR YOU'RE DEAD!!
ZEHAAA (WHEEZE)
ZEHAAA
HUFF, HUFF, HUFF!
HUFF.
HUFF.
HUFF.
HUFF.
ISHIDA!!
GAN (GONK)

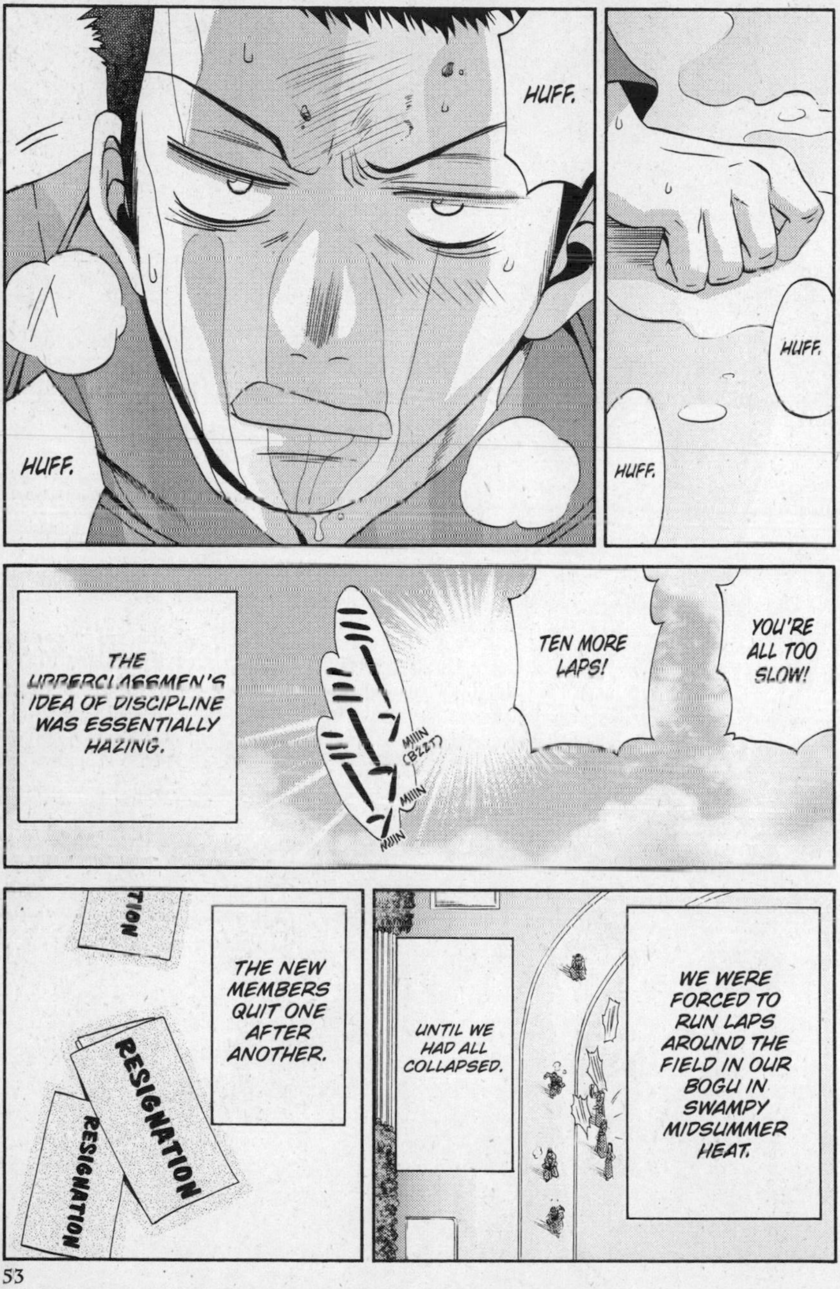
HUFF.
HUFF.
HUFF.
HUFF.
YOU'RE ALL TOO SLOW!
TEN MORE LAPS!
MIIIN (BZZT)
MIIIN
MIIIN
THE UPPERCLASSMEN'S IDEA OF DISCIPLINE WAS ESSENTIALLY HAZING.
WE WERE FORCED TO RUN LAPS AROUND THE FIELD IN OUR BOGU IN SWAMPY MIDSUMMER HEAT.
UNTIL WE HAD ALL COLLAPSED.
THE NEW MEMBERS QUIT ONE AFTER ANOTHER.
RESIGNATION
RESIGNATION

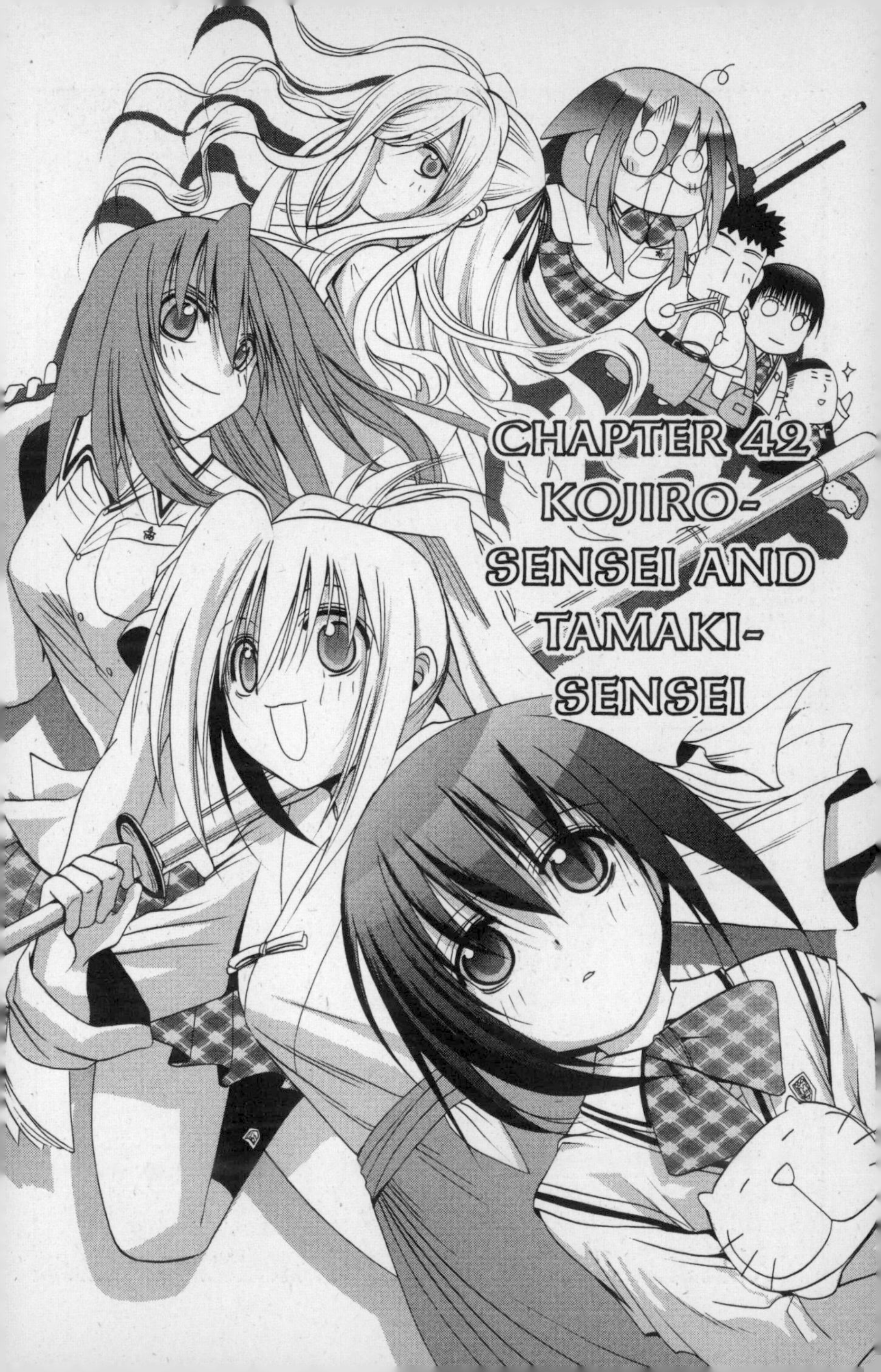
CHAPTER 42
KOJIRO-SENSEI AND TAMAKI-SENSEI

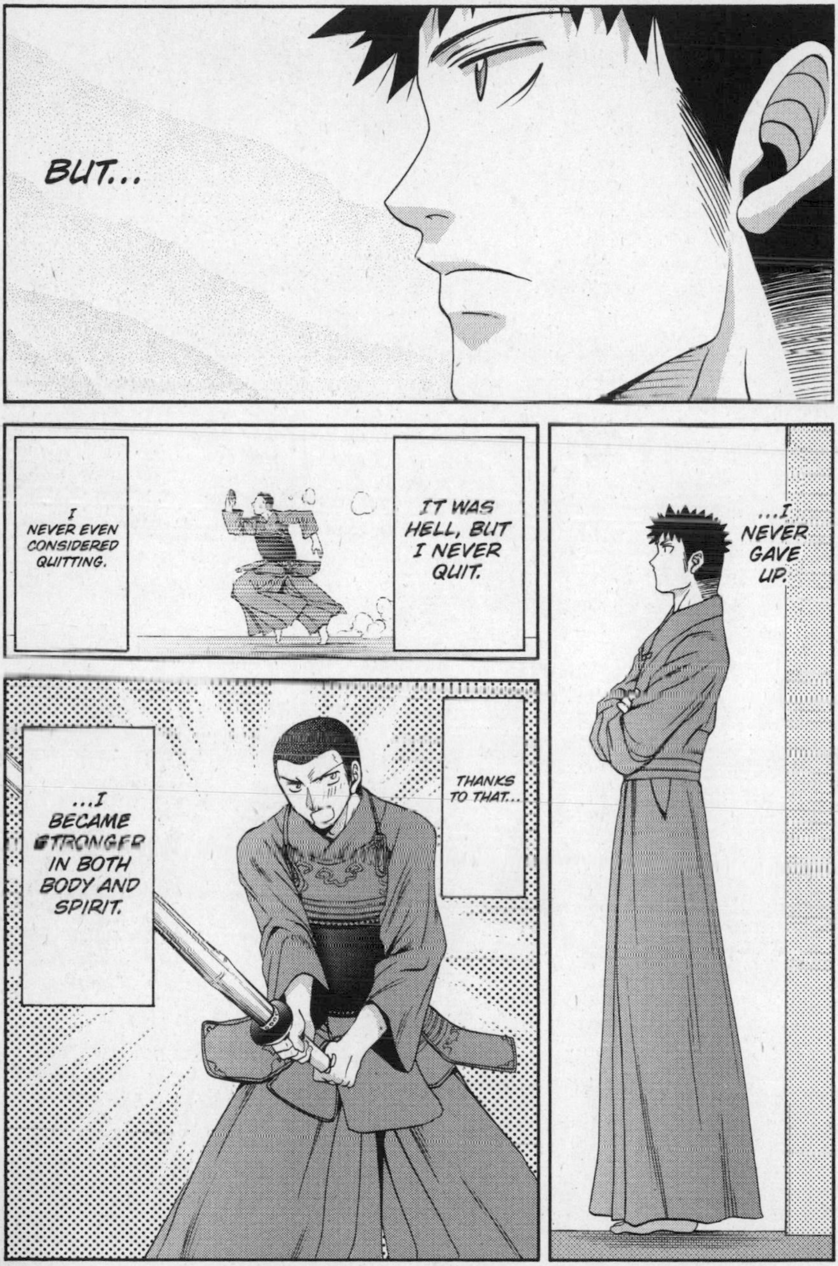
BUT...
...I NEVER GAVE UP.
IT WAS HELL, BUT I NEVER QUIT.
I NEVER EVEN CONSIDERED QUITTING.
THANKS TO THAT...
...I BECAME STRONGER IN BOTH BODY AND SPIRIT.

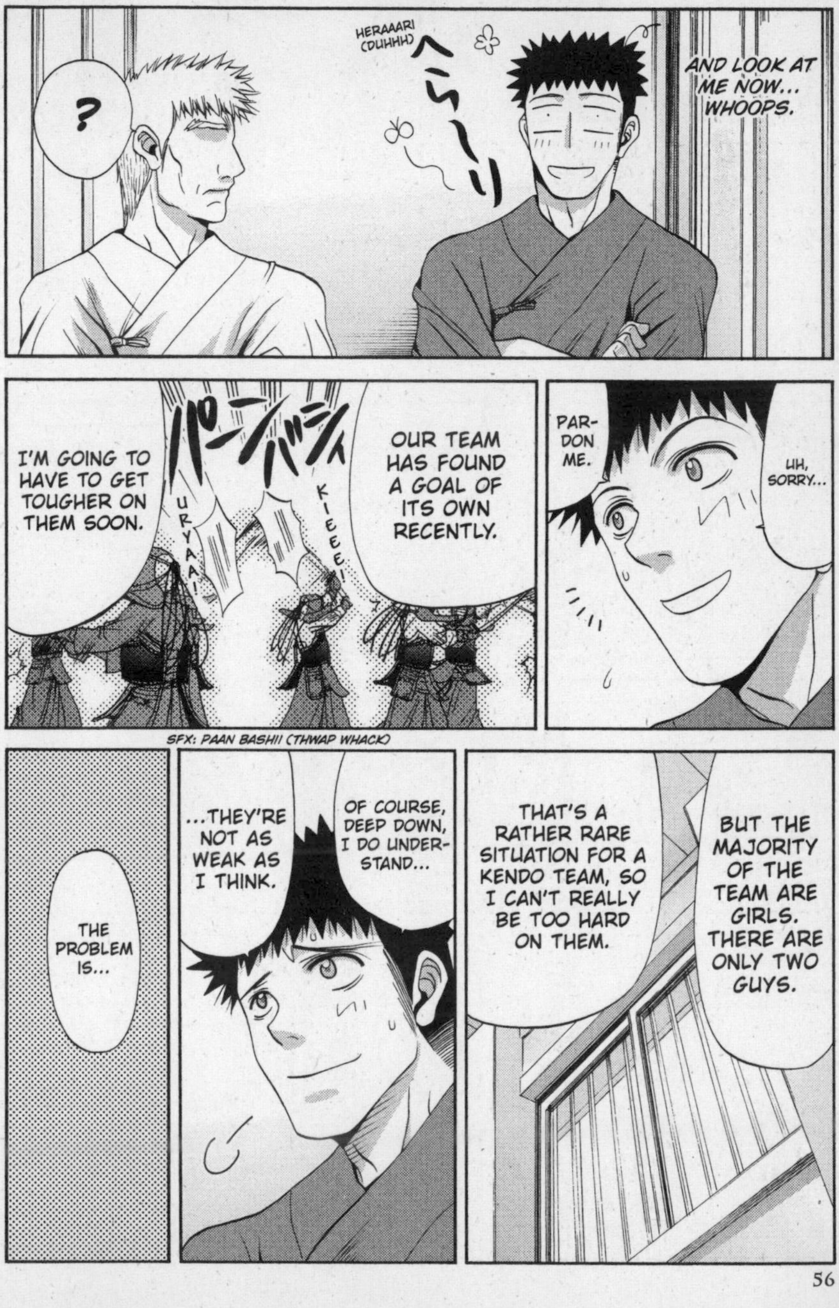
AND LOOK AT ME NOW... WHOOPS.
HERAAARI (DUHHH)
?
PAR-DON ME.
UH, SORRY...
OUR TEAM HAS FOUND A GOAL OF ITS OWN RECENTLY.
KIEEEE!
URYAA!
I'M GOING TO HAVE TO GET TOUGHER ON THEM SOON.
SFX: PAAN BASHII (THWAP WHACK)
BUT THE MAJORITY OF THE TEAM ARE GIRLS. THERE ARE ONLY TWO GUYS.
THAT'S A RATHER RARE SITUATION FOR A KENDO TEAM, SO I CAN'T REALLY BE TOO HARD ON THEM.
OF COURSE, DEEP DOWN, I DO UNDER-STAND...
...THEY'RE NOT AS WEAK AS I THINK.
THE PROBLEM IS...

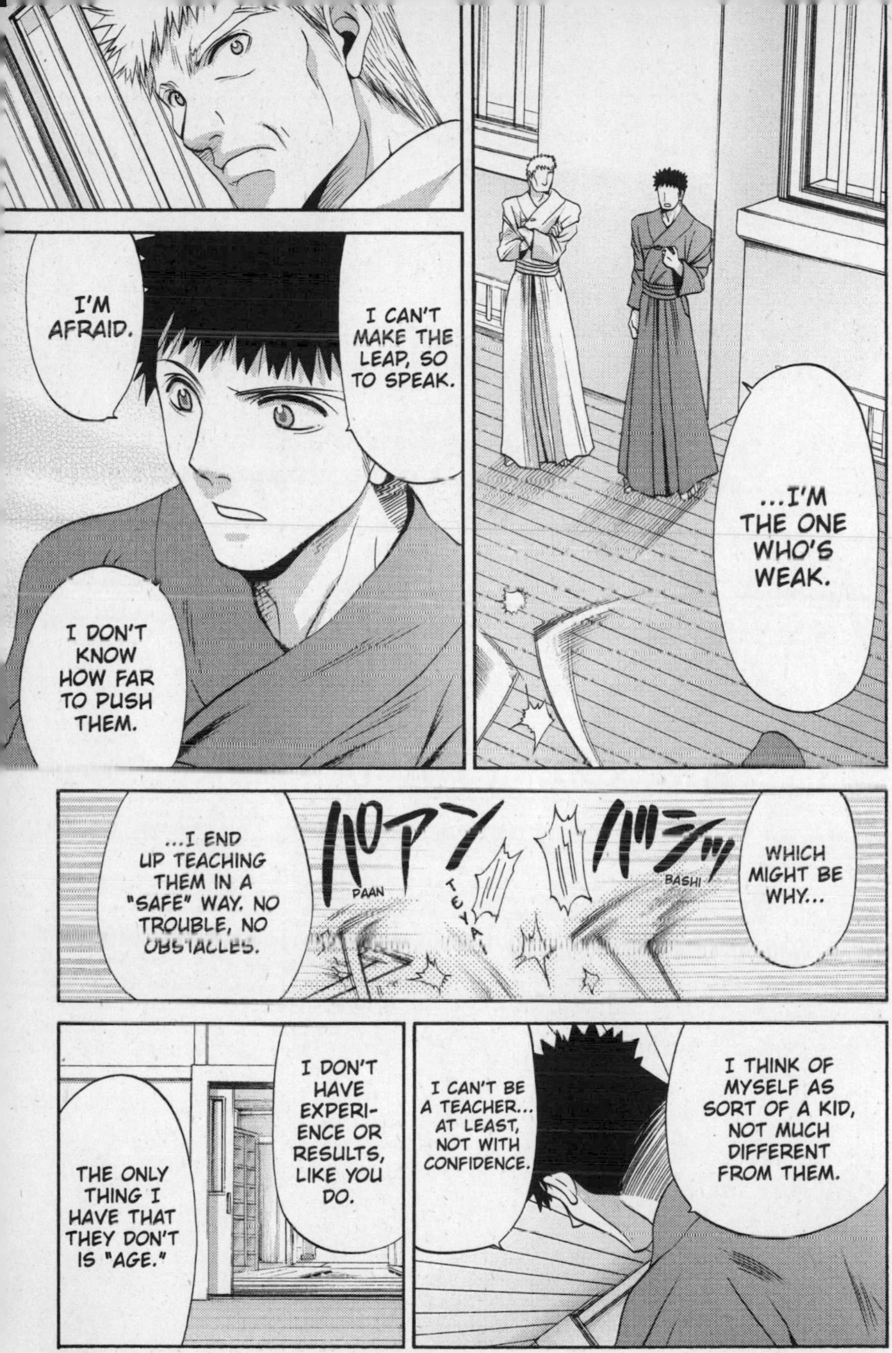
...I'M THE ONE WHO'S WEAK.
I CAN'T MAKE THE LEAP, SO TO SPEAK.
I'M AFRAID.
I DON'T KNOW HOW FAR TO PUSH THEM.
WHICH MIGHT BE WHY...
バシッ
BASHI
TEYA!
パアン
PAAN
...I END UP TEACHING THEM IN A "SAFE" WAY. NO TROUBLE, NO OBSTACLES.
I THINK OF MYSELF AS SORT OF A KID, NOT MUCH DIFFERENT FROM THEM.
I CAN'T BE A TEACHER... AT LEAST, NOT WITH CONFIDENCE.
I DON'T HAVE EXPERIENCE OR RESULTS, LIKE YOU DO.
THE ONLY THING I HAVE THAT THEY DON'T IS "AGE."

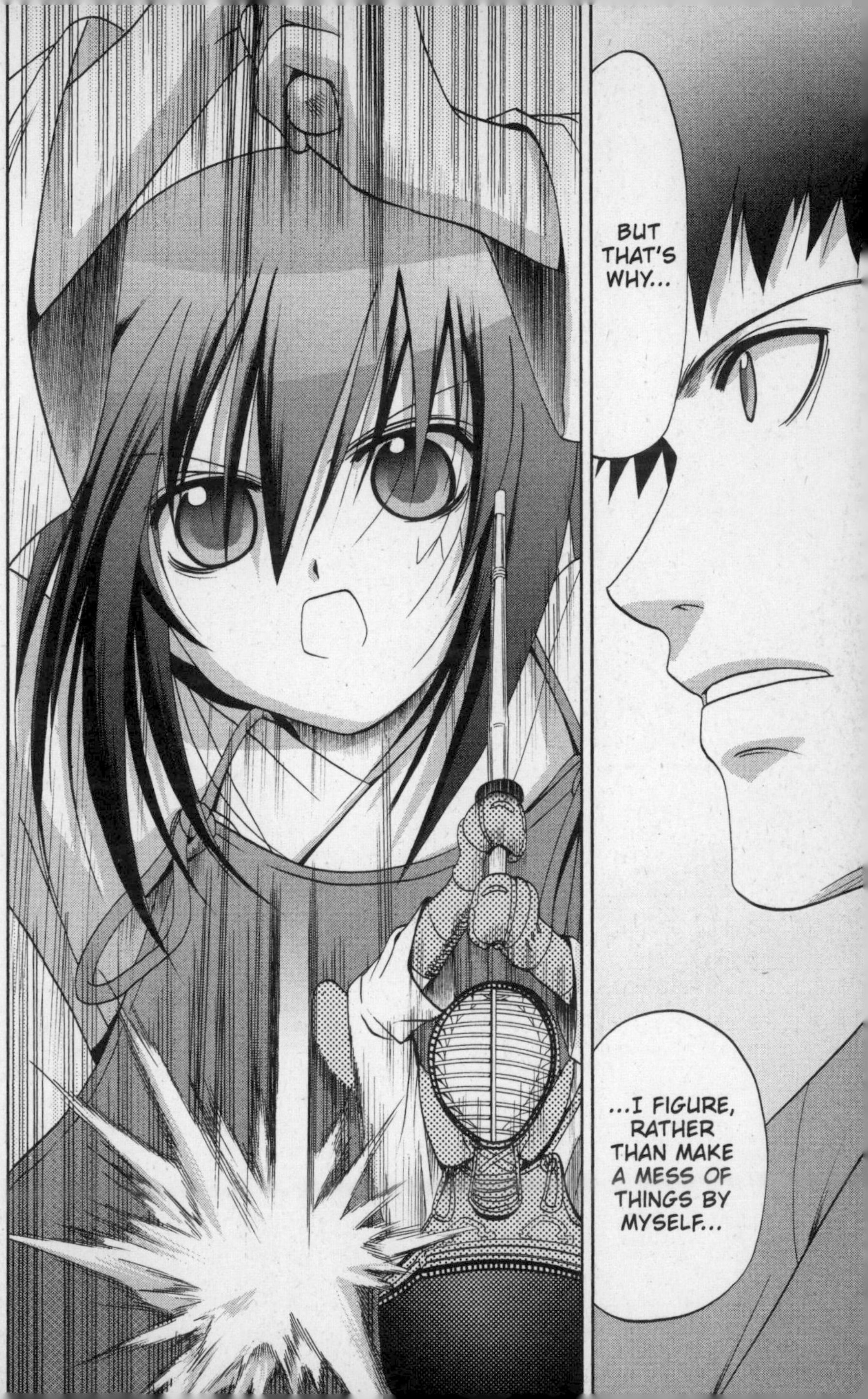
BUT THAT'S WHY...
...I FIGURE, RATHER THAN MAKE A MESS OF THINGS BY MYSELF...

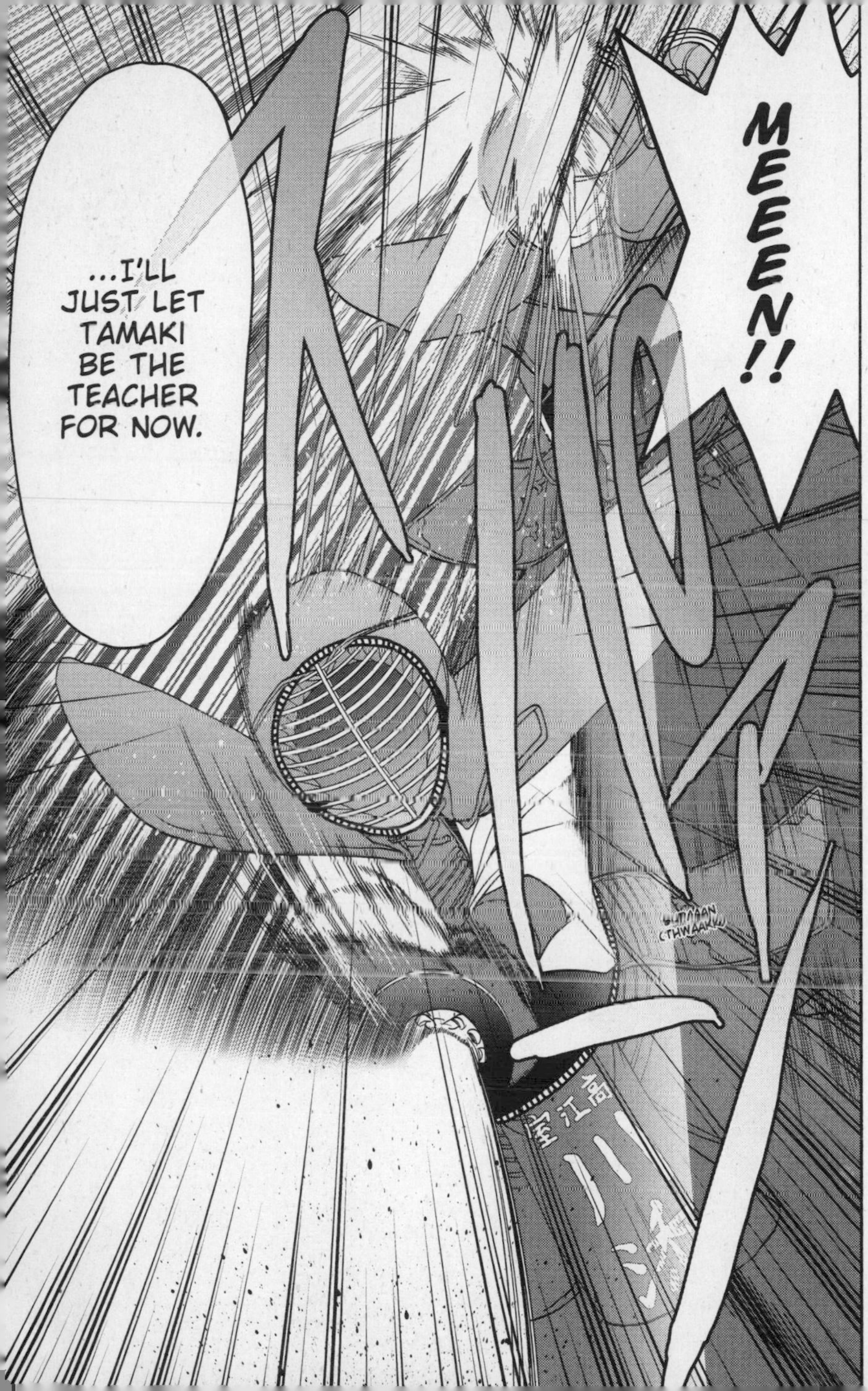
MEEEEN!!
(THWAAK!)
室江高
...I'LL JUST LET TAMAKI BE THE TEACHER FOR NOW.

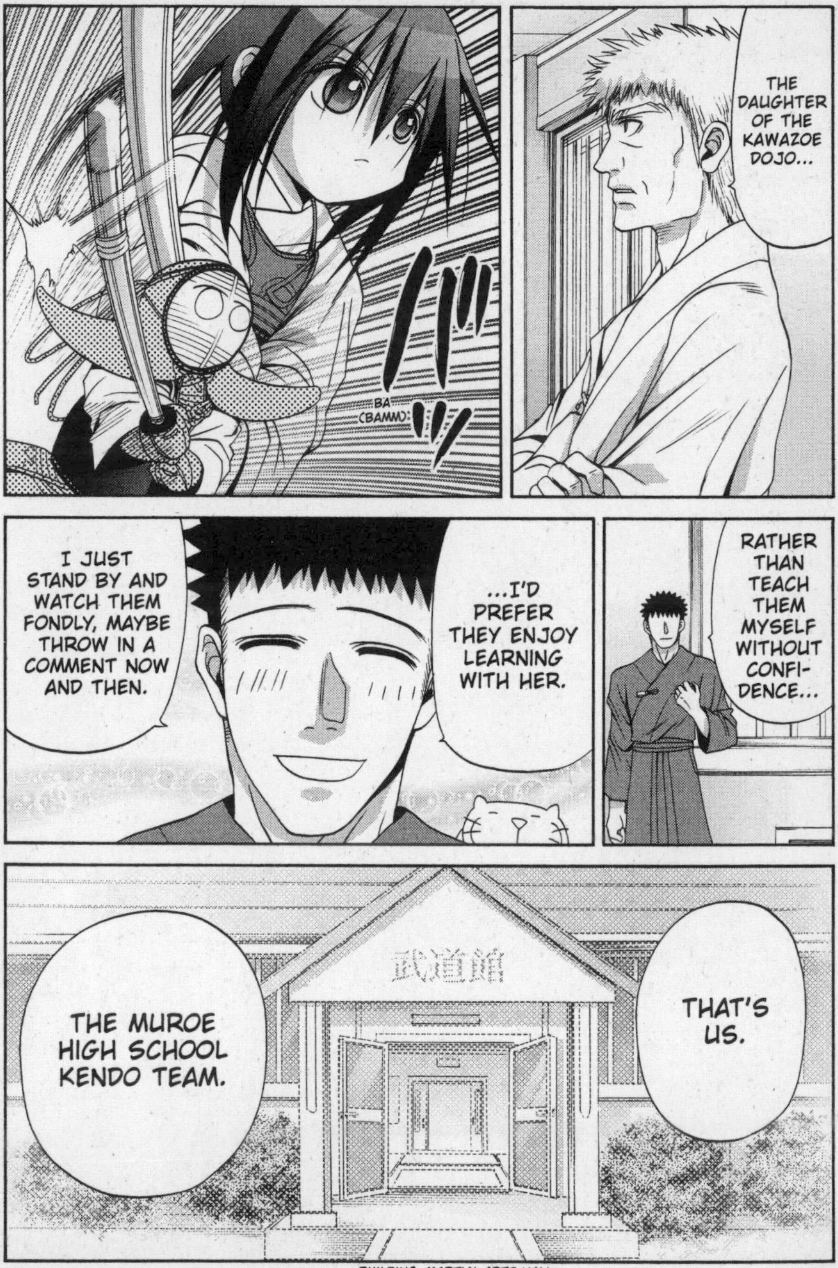
THE DAUGHTER OF THE KAWAZOE DOJO...
BA (BAMM)
RATHER THAN TEACH THEM MYSELF WITHOUT CONFIDENCE...
...I'D PREFER THEY ENJOY LEARNING WITH HER.
I JUST STAND BY AND WATCH THEM FONDLY, MAYBE THROW IN A COMMENT NOW AND THEN.
THAT'S US.
武道館
THE MUROE HIGH SCHOOL KENDO TEAM.
BUILDING: MARTIAL ARTS HALL

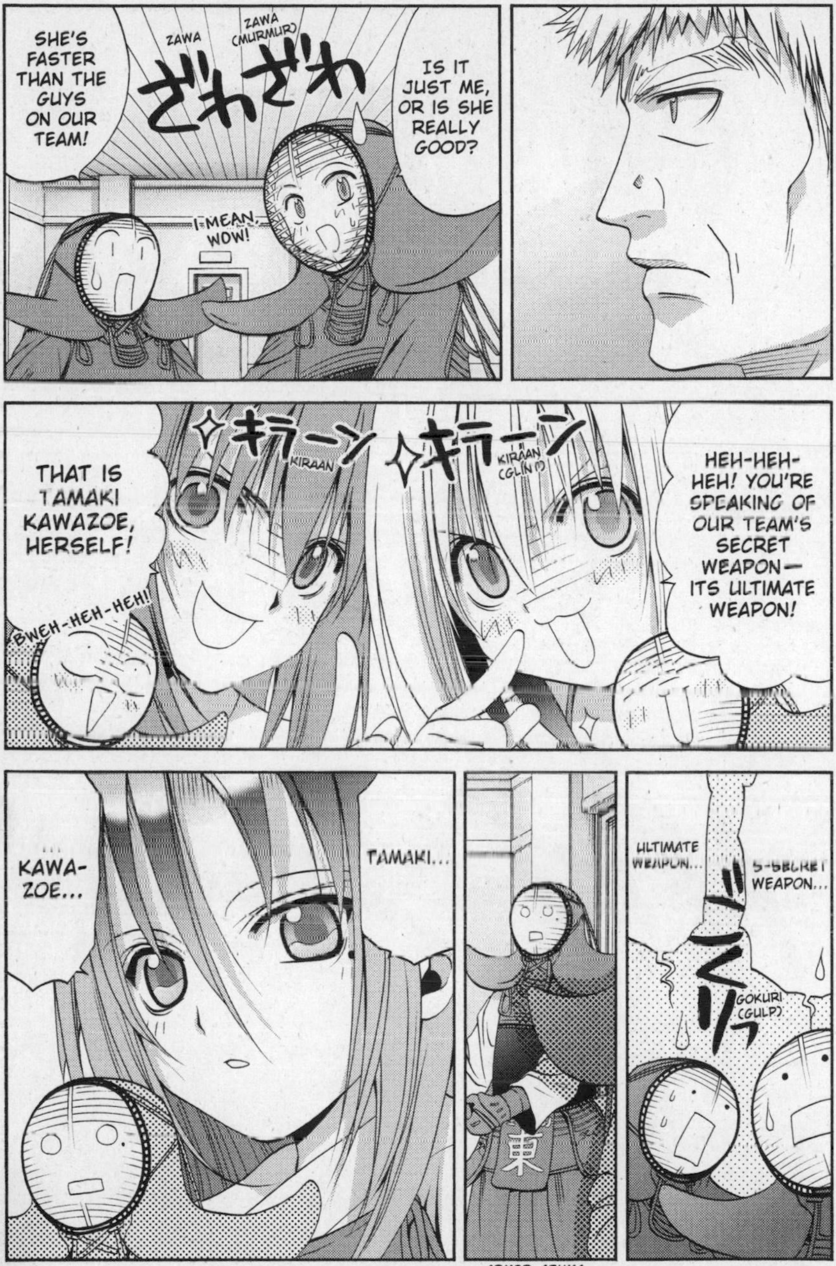
IS IT JUST ME, OR IS SHE REALLY GOOD?
ZAWA (MURMUR)
ざわざわ
ZAWA
SHE'S FASTER THAN THE GUYS ON OUR TEAM!
I MEAN, WOW!
HEH-HEH-HEH! YOU'RE SPEAKING OF OUR TEAM'S SECRET WEAPON—ITS ULTIMATE WEAPON!
キラーン
KIRAAN (GLINT)
キラーン
KIRAAN
THAT IS TAMAKI KAWAZOE, HERSELF!
BWEH-HEH-HEH!
S-SECRET WEAPON...
ULTIMATE WEAPON...
GOKURI (GULP)
TAMAKI...
... KAWAZOE...

ARMOR: AZUMA

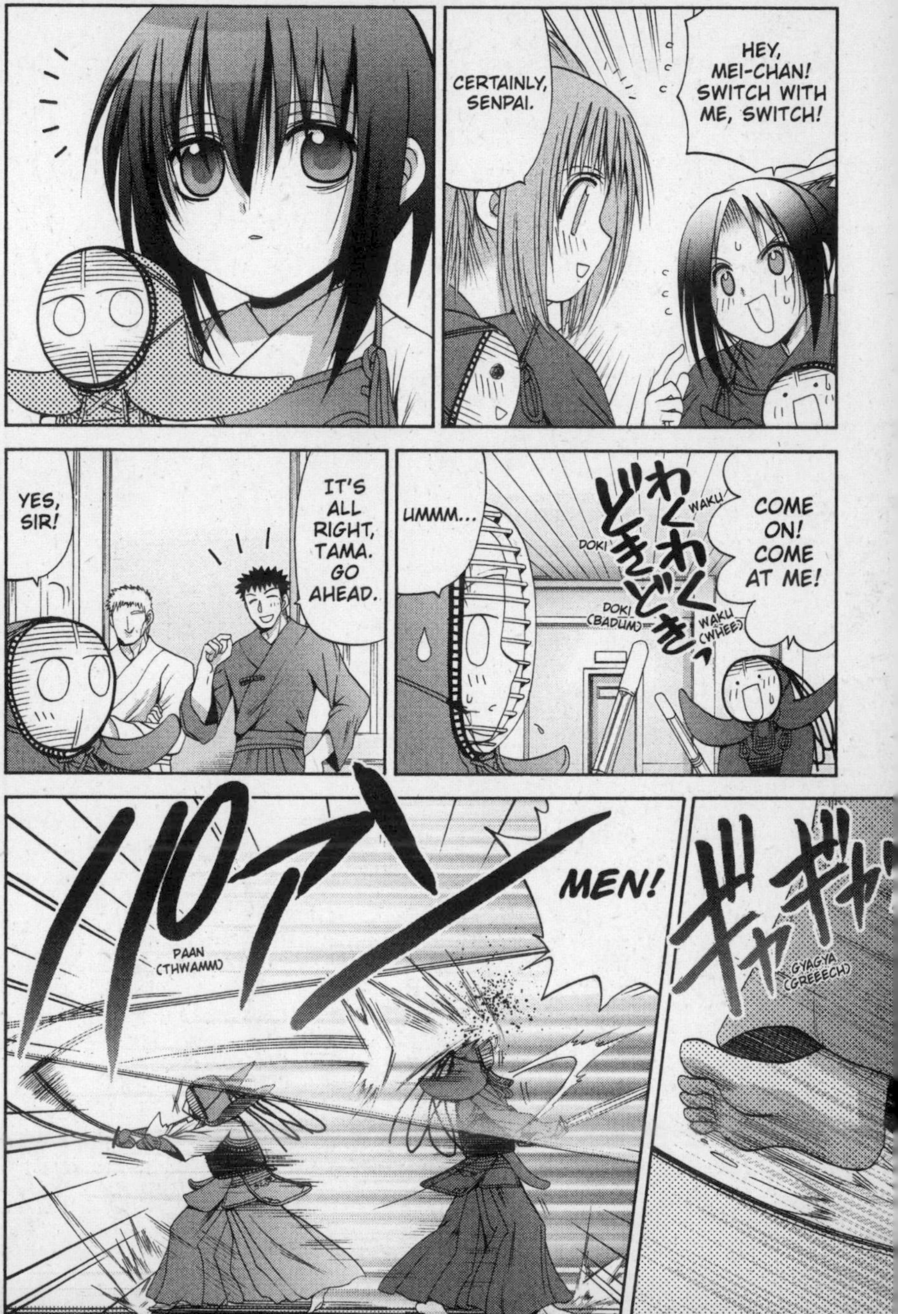
HEY, MEI-CHAN! SWITCH WITH ME, SWITCH!
CERTAINLY, SENPAI.
COME ON! COME AT ME!
わくわくどきどき
WAKU
DOKI
DOKI (BADUMP)
WAKU (WHEE)
UMMM...
IT'S ALL RIGHT, TAMA. GO AHEAD.
YES, SIR!
GYAGYA (GREEECH)
MEN!
PAAN (THWAMM)

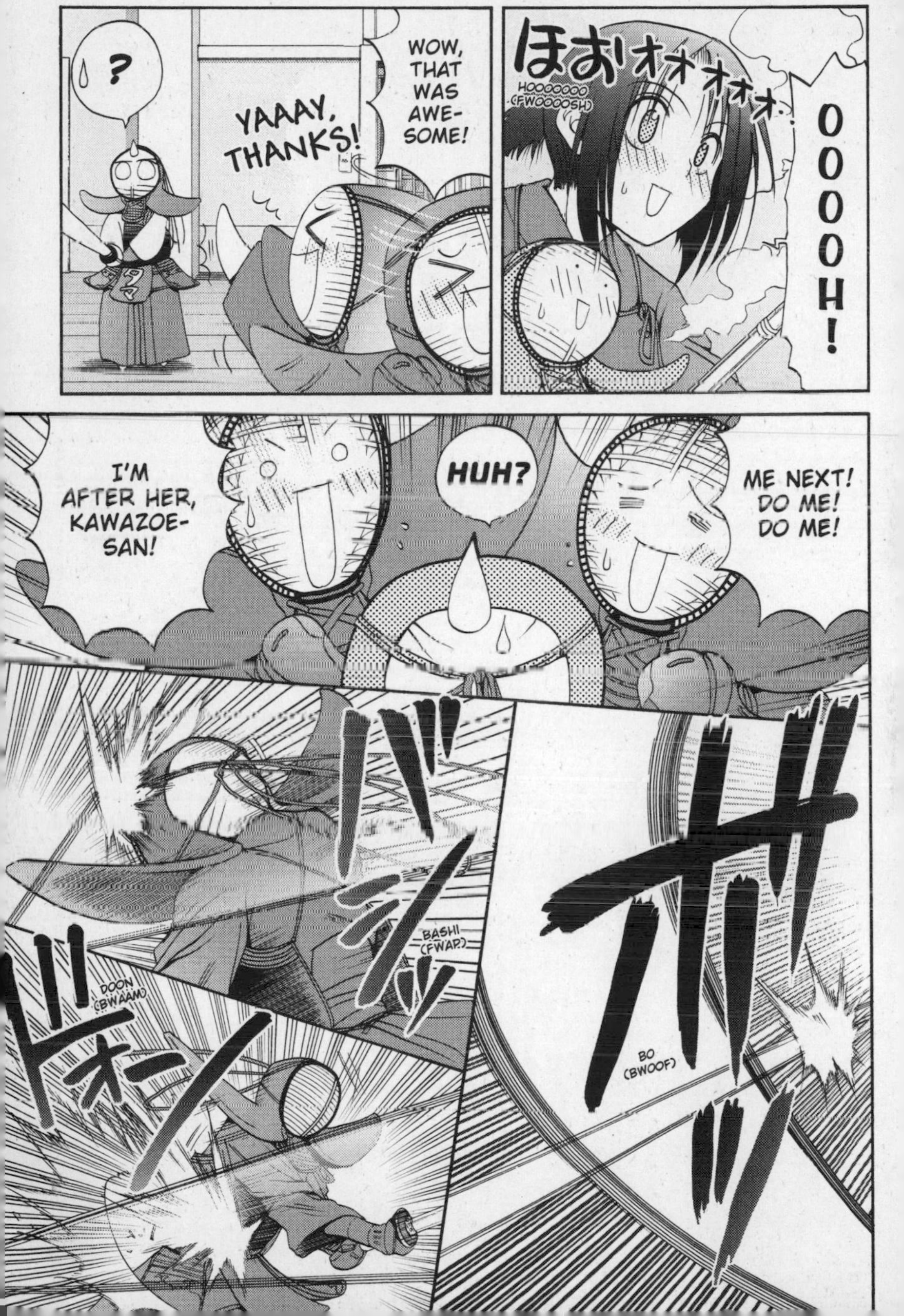
ほおオオオオオ
HOOOOOOO (FWOOOOSH)
OOOOOH!
WOW, THAT WAS AWE-SOME!
YAAAY, THANKS!
?
ME NEXT! DO ME! DO ME!
HUH?
I'M AFTER HER, KAWAZOE-SAN!
BO (BWOOF)
BASHI (FWAP)
DOON (BWAAM)

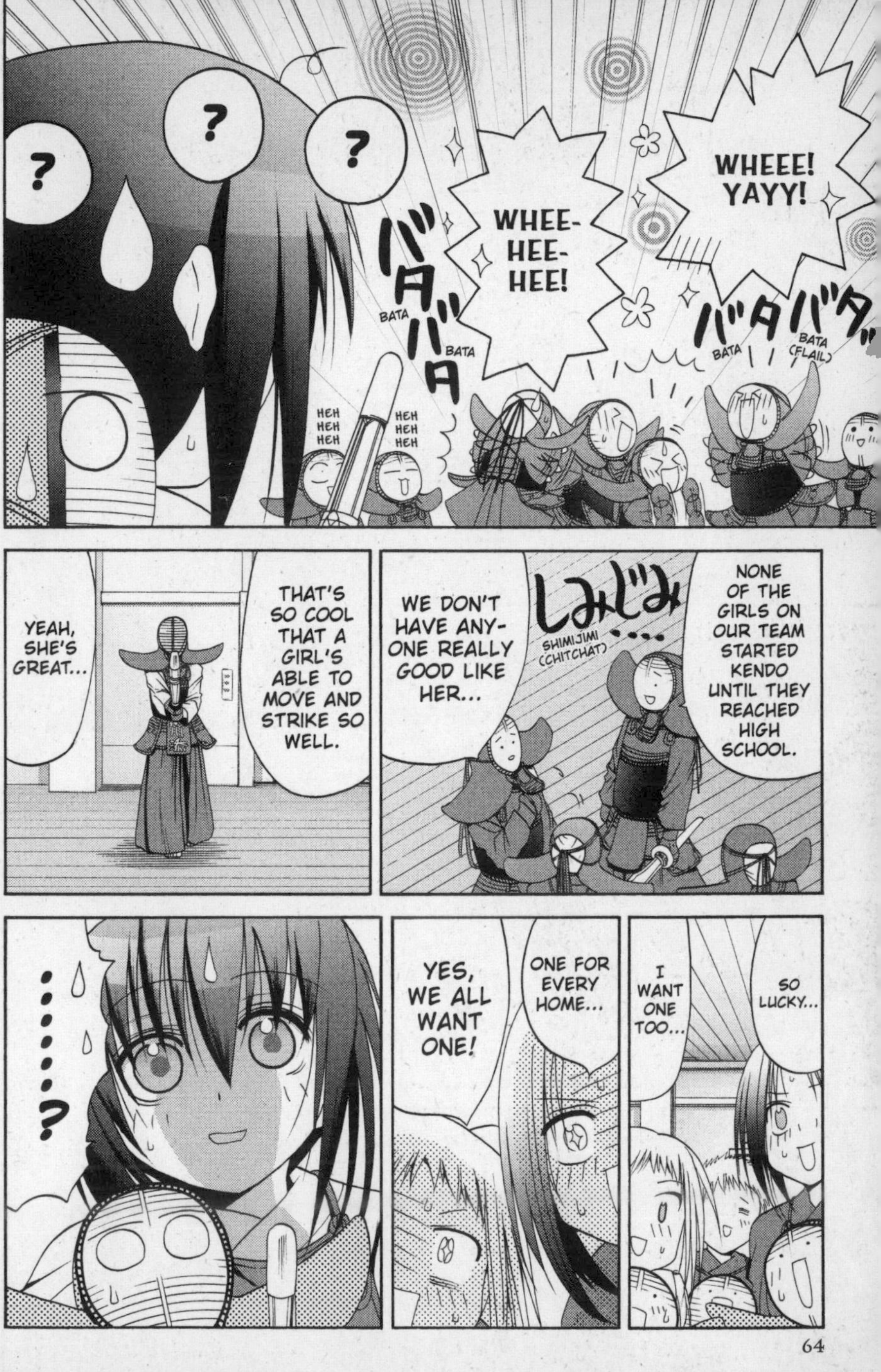
WHEEE! YAYY!
バタバタ
BATA
BATA (FLAIL)
WHEE-HEE-HEE!
バタバタ
BATA
BATA
HEH HEH HEH
HEH HEH HEH
?
?
?
NONE OF THE GIRLS ON OUR TEAM STARTED KENDO UNTIL THEY REACHED HIGH SCHOOL.
しみじみ
SHIMIJIMI (CHITCHAT)
WE DON'T HAVE ANY-ONE REALLY GOOD LIKE HER...
THAT'S SO COOL THAT A GIRL'S ABLE TO MOVE AND STRIKE SO WELL.
YEAH, SHE'S GREAT...
SO LUCKY...
I WANT ONE TOO...
ONE FOR EVERY HOME...
YES, WE ALL WANT ONE!
......?

GU
(GRIP)

SHE'S SO SHARP...

I WAS BETTER...

IT'S BEEN SO LONG... BUT NOW I REMEMBER.

I'M SORRY, MA'AM, WE CAN'T DO THAT.

DO YOU MIND IF I GET ONE OF THESE TO GO?

ARMOR: AZUMA

LIKE THIS!!

MORE!!

MORE LIKE THIS!!

BA (WHAM)

DOSHU (DSHH)

LIKE THIS!!

GYA (GYAP)

THE BOGU ARE SO HEAVY ON ME, I MOVE LIKE A ROBOT.

IT'S SO NEAT TO SEE SOMEONE MOVE LIKE TAMA-SAN...

GIKU (JERK)

SHAKU (SHUDDER)

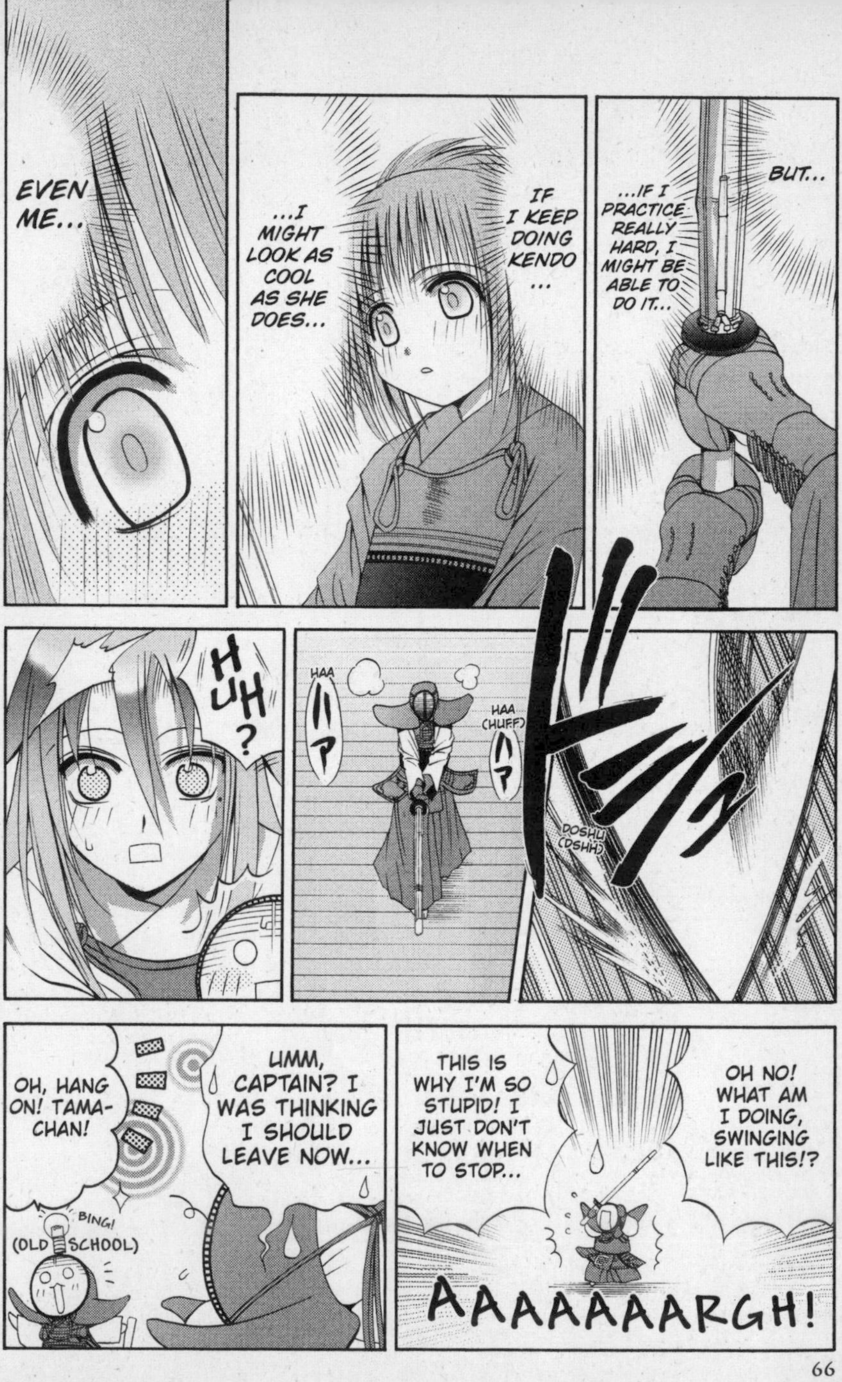
BUT...
...IF I PRACTICE REALLY HARD, I MIGHT BE ABLE TO DO IT...
IF I KEEP DOING KENDO ...
...I MIGHT LOOK AS COOL AS SHE DOES...
EVEN ME...
ドシュ
DOSHU (DSHH)
ハァ
HAA (HUFF)
ハァ
HAA
HUH?
OH NO! WHAT AM I DOING, SWINGING LIKE THIS!?
THIS IS WHY I'M SO STUPID! I JUST DON'T KNOW WHEN TO STOP...
AAAAAAARGH!
UMM, CAPTAIN? I WAS THINKING I SHOULD LEAVE NOW...
OH, HANG ON! TAMA-CHAN!
BING!
(OLD SCHOOL)

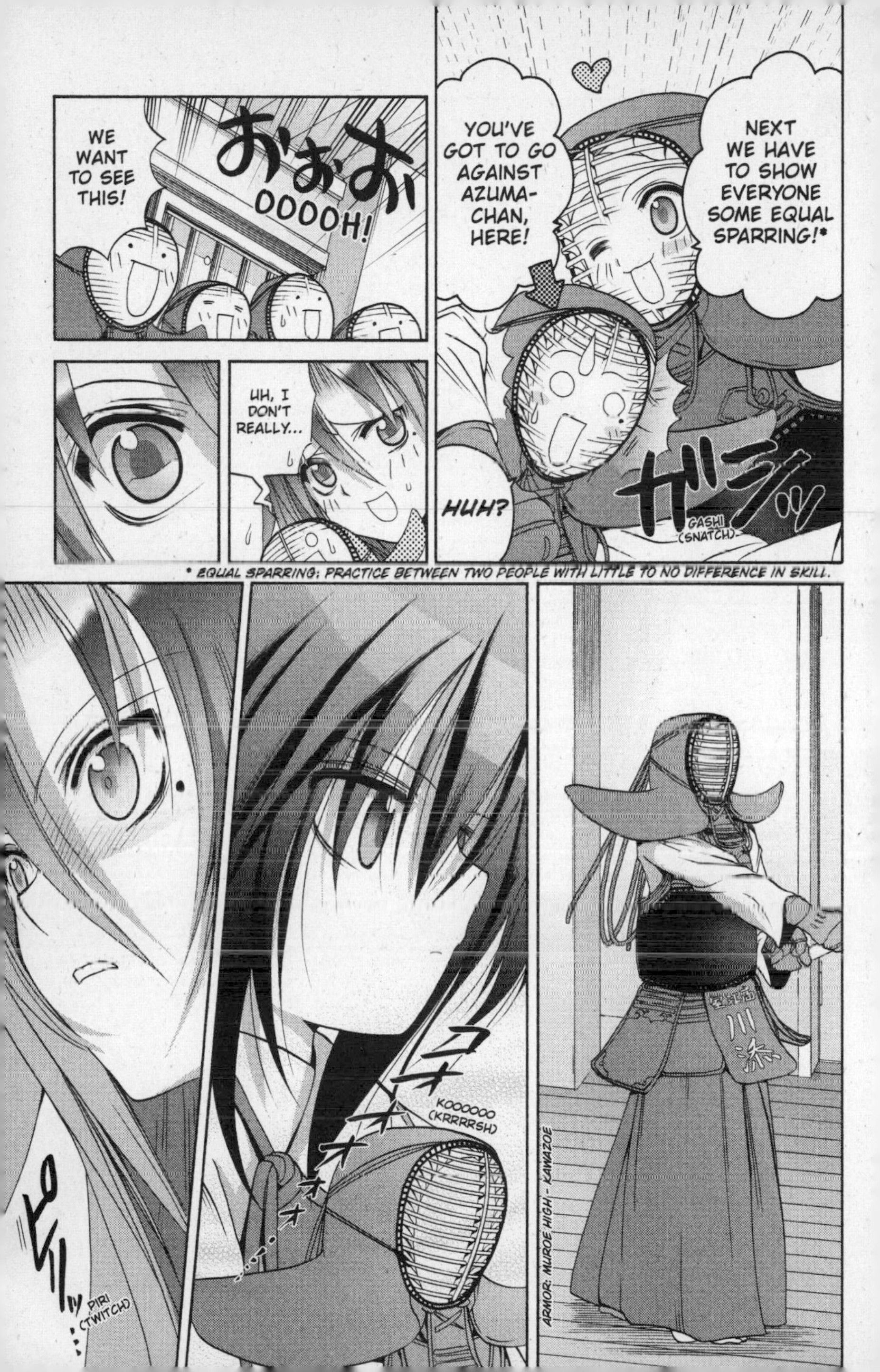
NEXT WE HAVE TO SHOW EVERYONE SOME EQUAL SPARRING!*
YOU'VE GOT TO GO AGAINST AZUMA-CHAN, HERE!
GASHI (SNATCH)
HUH?
WE WANT TO SEE THIS!
OOOOH!
UH, I DON'T REALLY...
* EQUAL SPARRING: PRACTICE BETWEEN TWO PEOPLE WITH LITTLE TO NO DIFFERENCE IN SKILL.
ARMOR: MUROE HIGH - KAWAZOE
KOOOOOO (KRRRRSH)
PIRI (TWITCH)

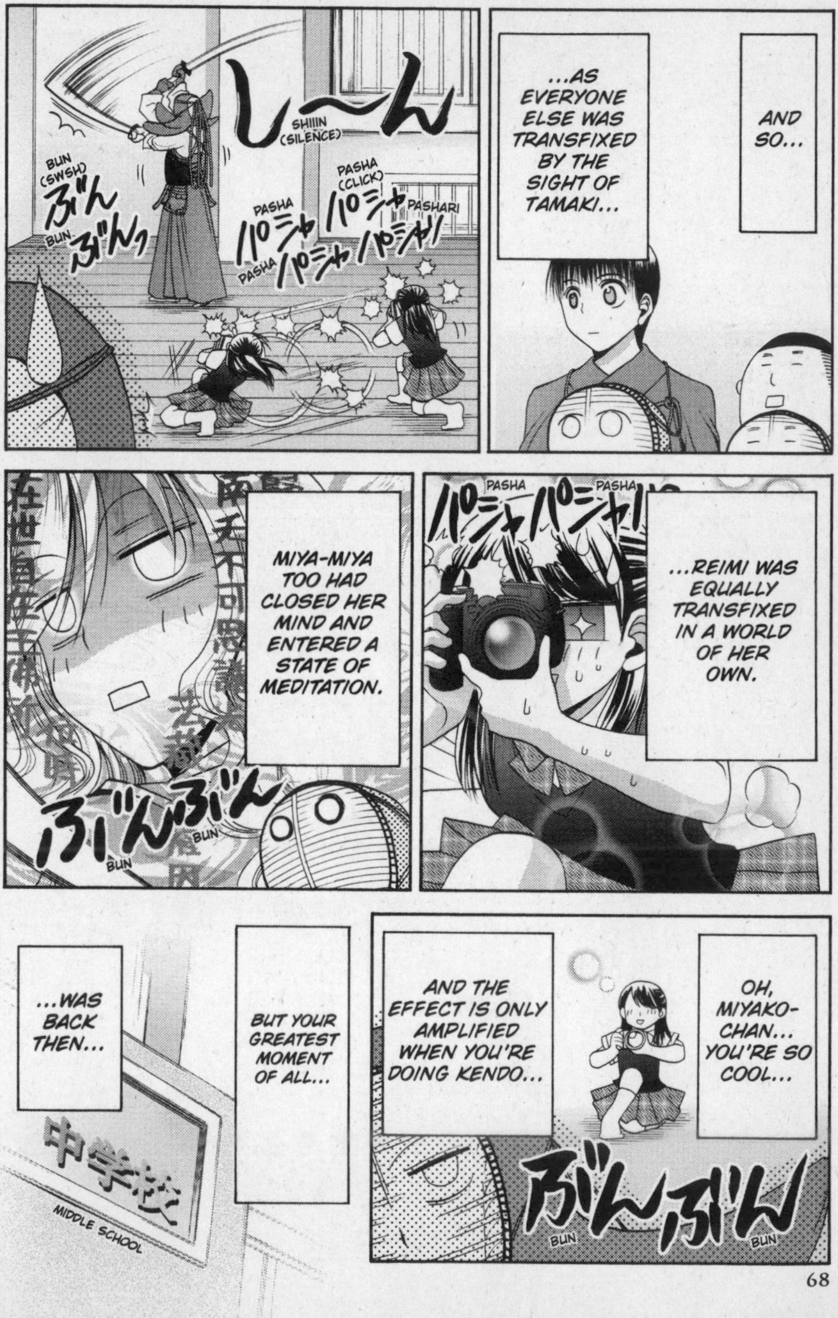
AND SO...
...AS EVERYONE ELSE WAS TRANSFIXED BY THE SIGHT OF TAMAKI...
しーん
SHIIIN (SILENCE)
PASHA (CLICK)
パシャ
PASHARI
PASHA
パシャ
PASHA
パシャ パシャリ
BUN (SWSH)
ぶん
BUN
ぶんっ
PASHA PASHA
パシャパシャ
...REIMI WAS EQUALLY TRANSFIXED IN A WORLD OF HER OWN.
MIYA-MIYA TOO HAD CLOSED HER MIND AND ENTERED A STATE OF MEDITATION.
ぶんぶん
BUN BUN
OH, MIYAKO-CHAN... YOU'RE SO COOL...
AND THE EFFECT IS ONLY AMPLIFIED WHEN YOU'RE DOING KENDO...
ぶんぶん
BUN BUN
BUT YOUR GREATEST MOMENT OF ALL...
...WAS BACK THEN...
中学校
MIDDLE SCHOOL

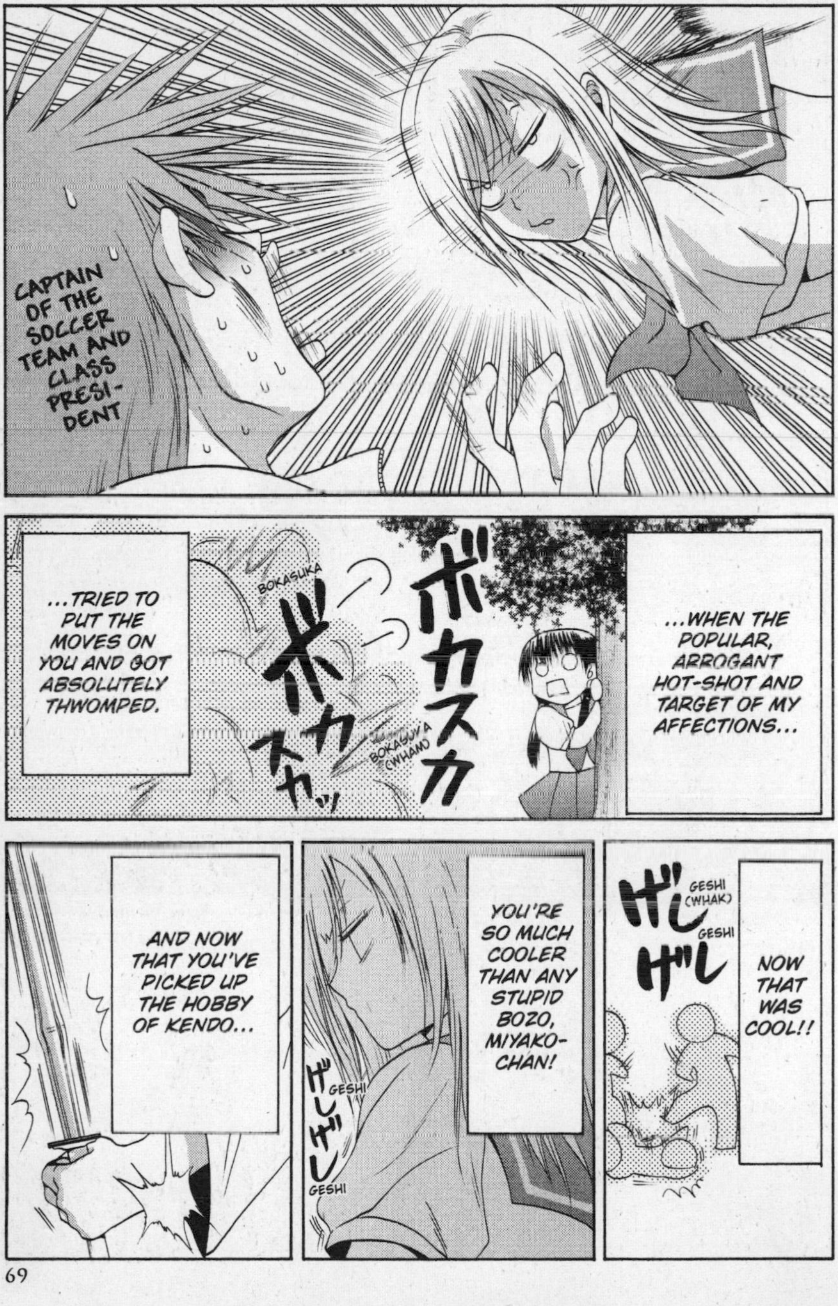
CAPTAIN OF THE SOCCER TEAM AND CLASS PRESIDENT
...WHEN THE POPULAR, ARROGANT HOT-SHOT AND TARGET OF MY AFFECTIONS...
ボカスカ
BOKASUKA
ボカスカッ
BOKASUKA (WHAM)
...TRIED TO PUT THE MOVES ON YOU AND GOT ABSOLUTELY THWOMPED.
NOW THAT WAS COOL!!
げしげし
GESHI (WHAK)
GESHI
YOU'RE SO MUCH COOLER THAN ANY STUPID BOZO, MIYAKO-CHAN!
げしげし
GESHI
GESHI
AND NOW THAT YOU'VE PICKED UP THE HOBBY OF KENDO...

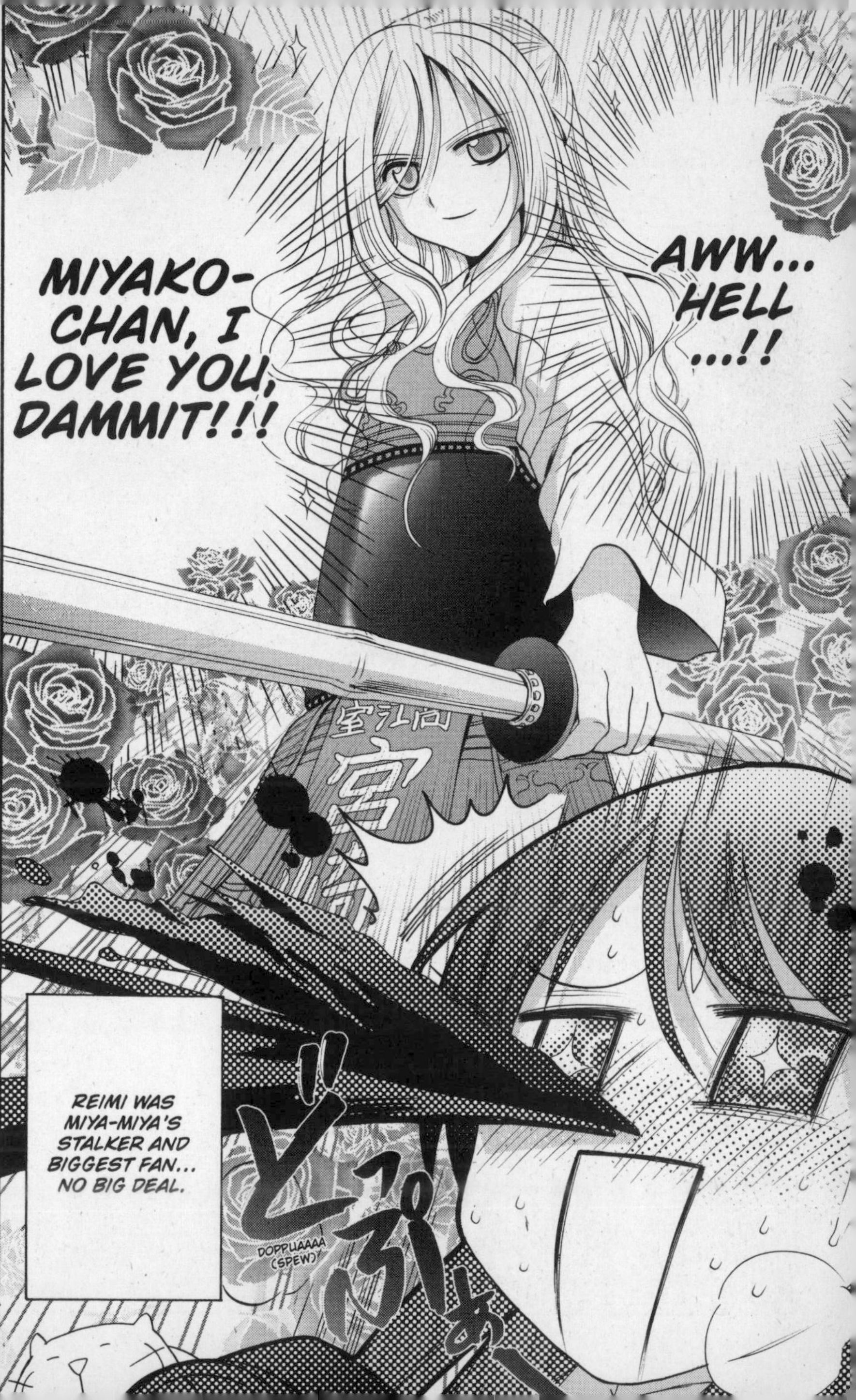
AWW... HELL ...!!
MIYAKO-CHAN, I LOVE YOU, DAMMIT!!!
REIMI WAS MIYA-MIYA'S STALKER AND BIGGEST FAN... NO BIG DEAL.
DOPPUAAAA (SPEW)

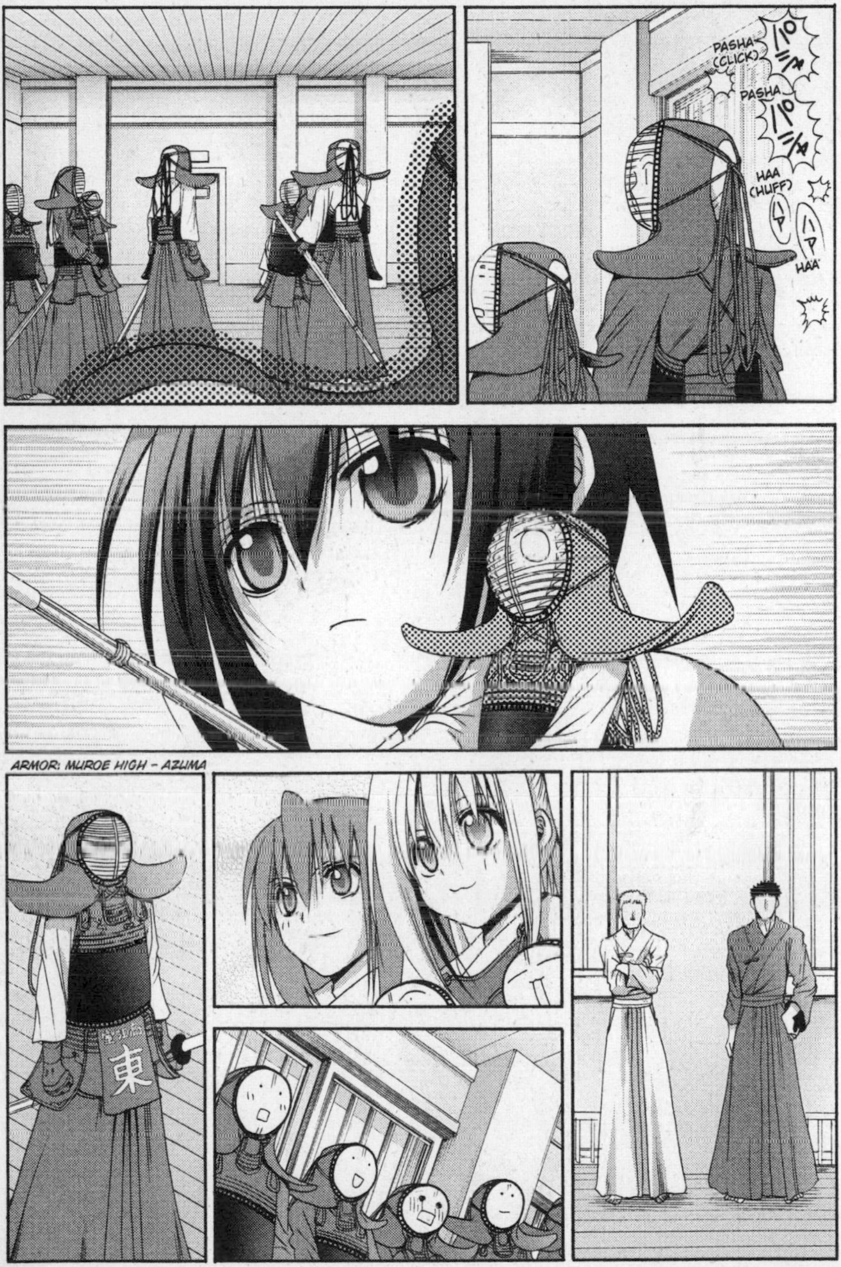
PASHA (CLICK)
PASHA
HAA (HUFF)
HAA
ARMOR: MUROE HIGH - AZUMA
東

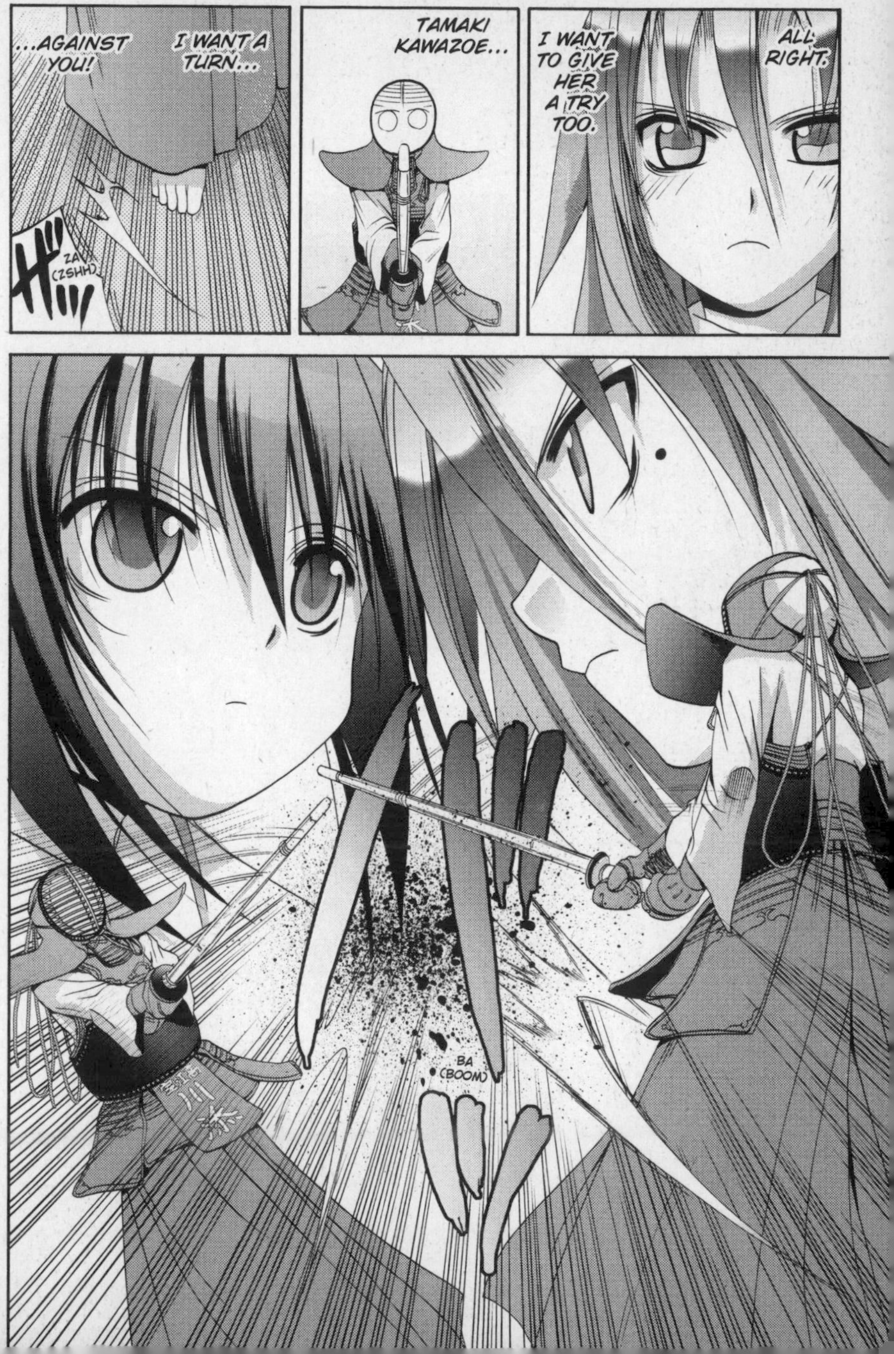
ALL RIGHT.
I WANT TO GIVE HER A TRY TOO.
TAMAKI KAWAZOE...
I WANT A TURN...
...AGAINST YOU!
ZA (ZSHH)
BA (BOOM)

BAMBOO BLADE

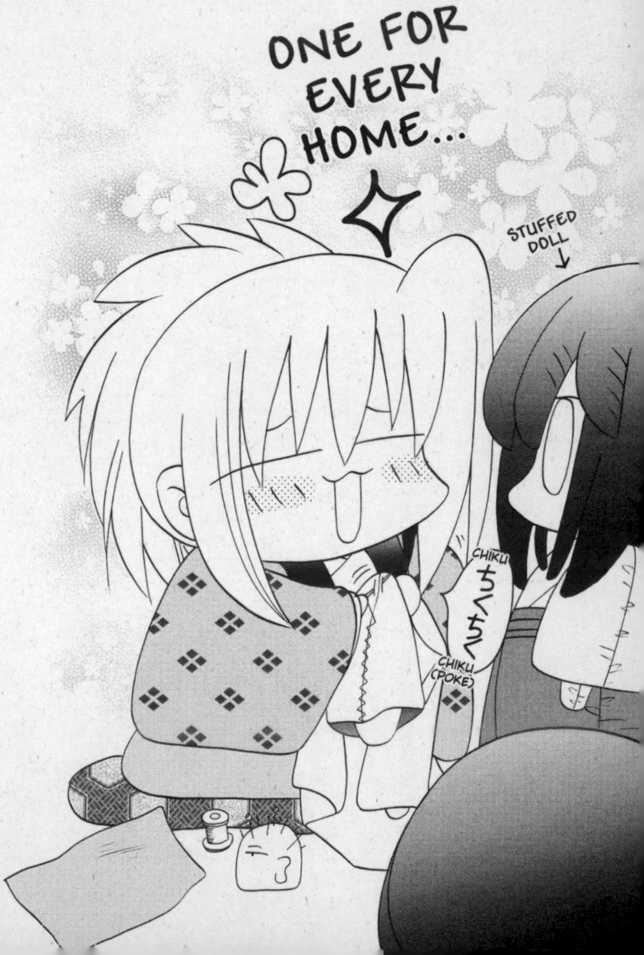
ONE FOR EVERY HOME...
STUFFED DOLL
CHIKU
ちくちく
CHIKU (POKE)

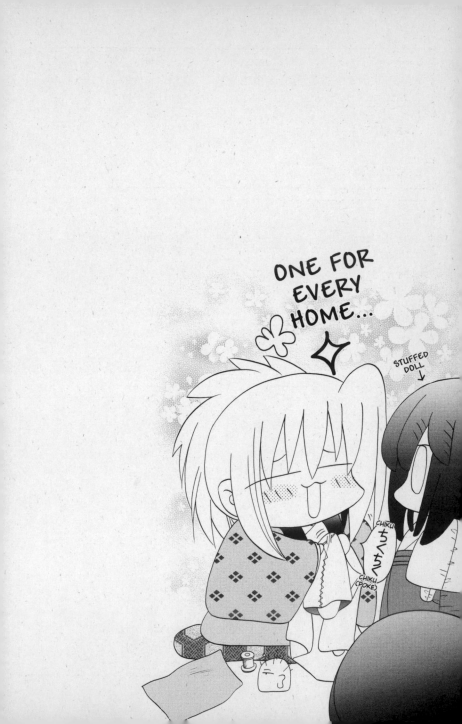

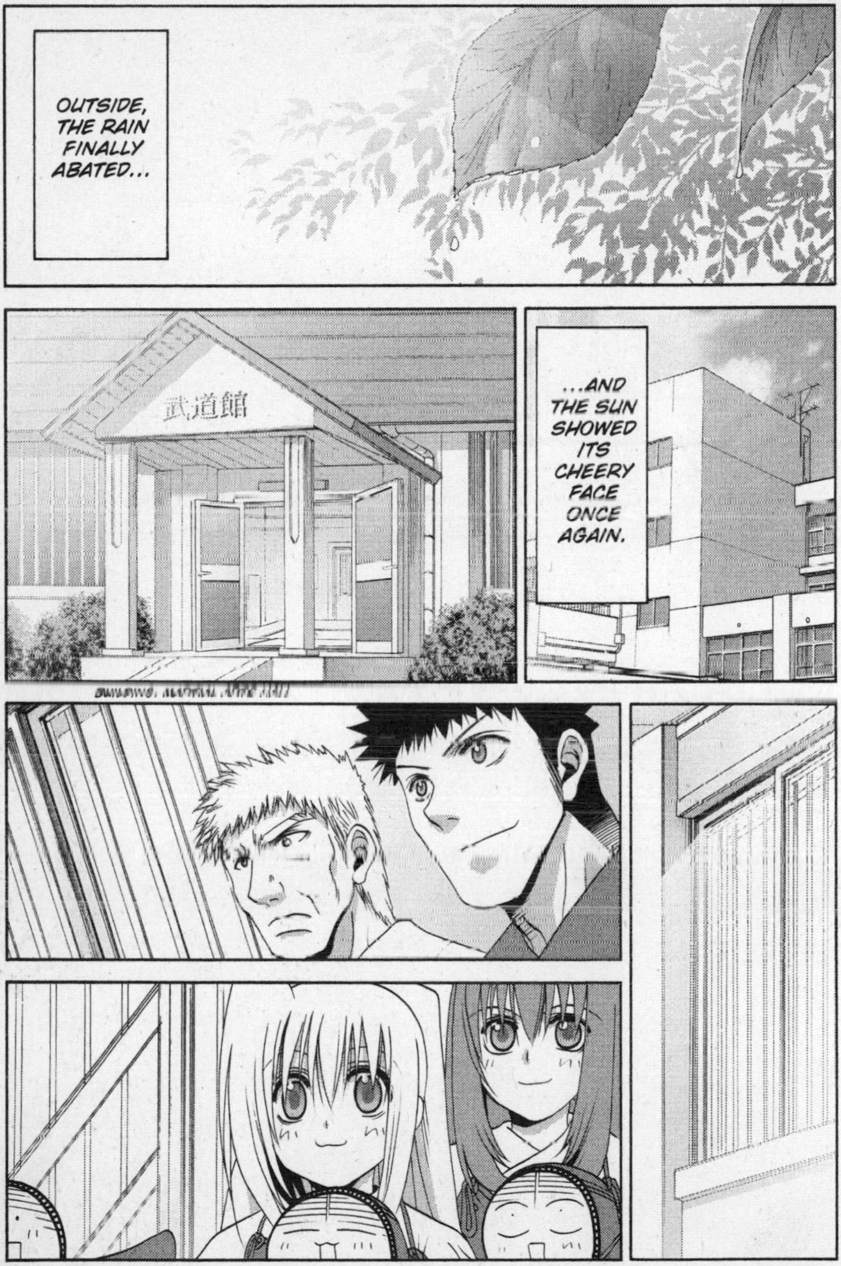
OUTSIDE, THE RAIN FINALLY ABATED...
...AND THE SUN SHOWED ITS CHEERY FACE ONCE AGAIN.
武道館

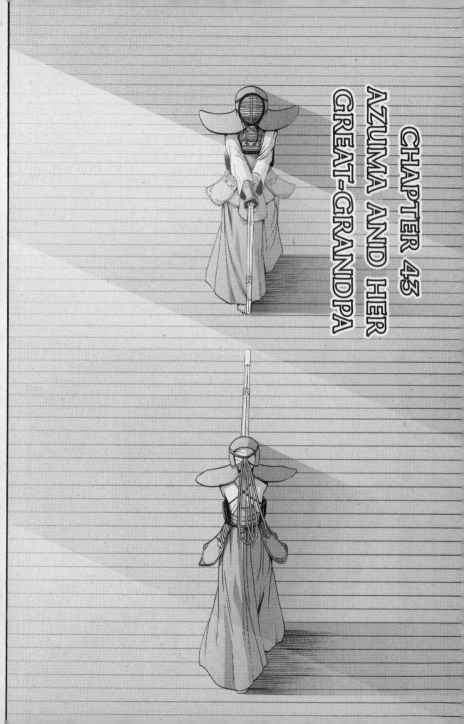

CHAPTER 43
AZUMA AND HER
GREAT-GRANDPA

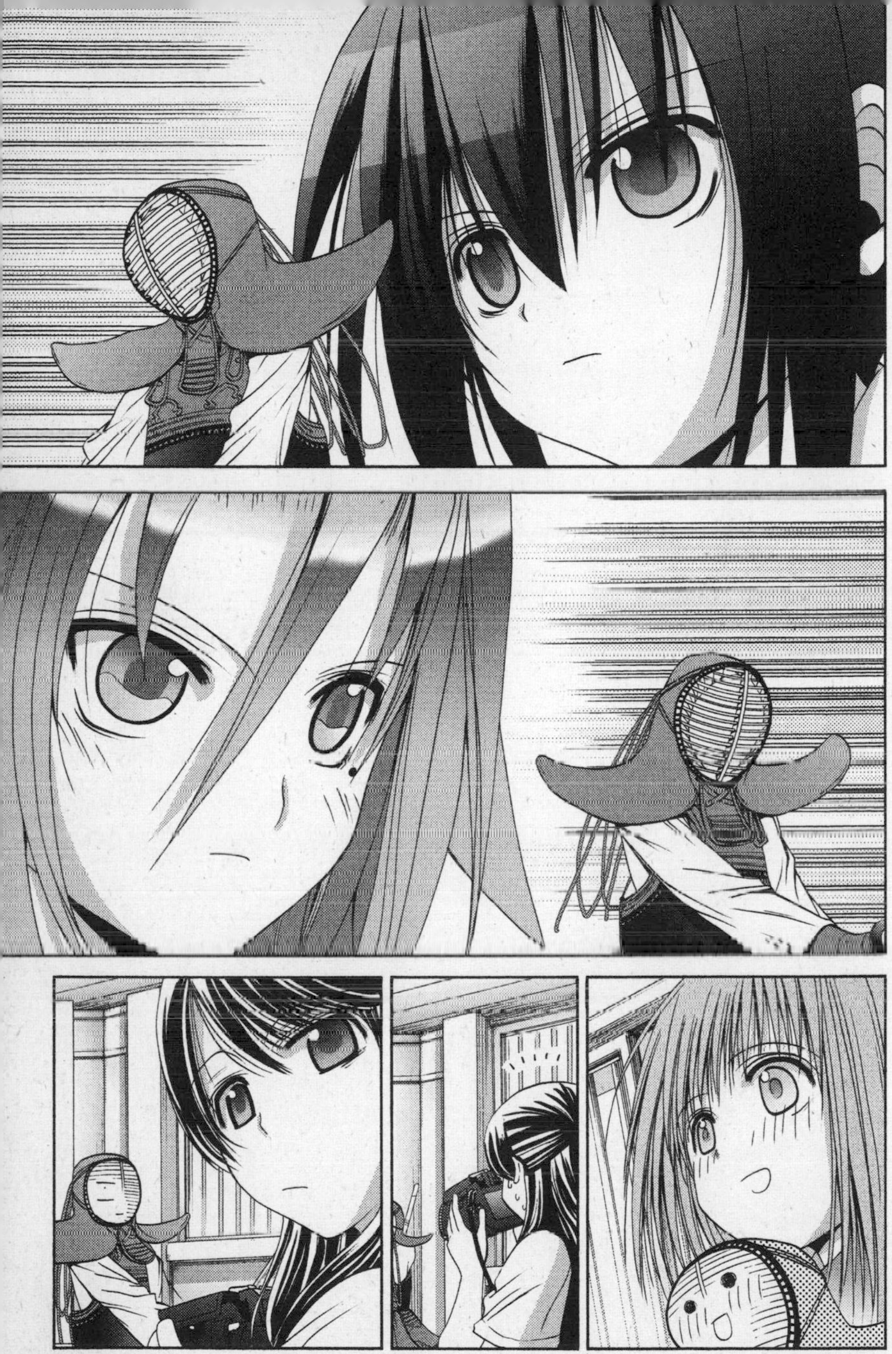

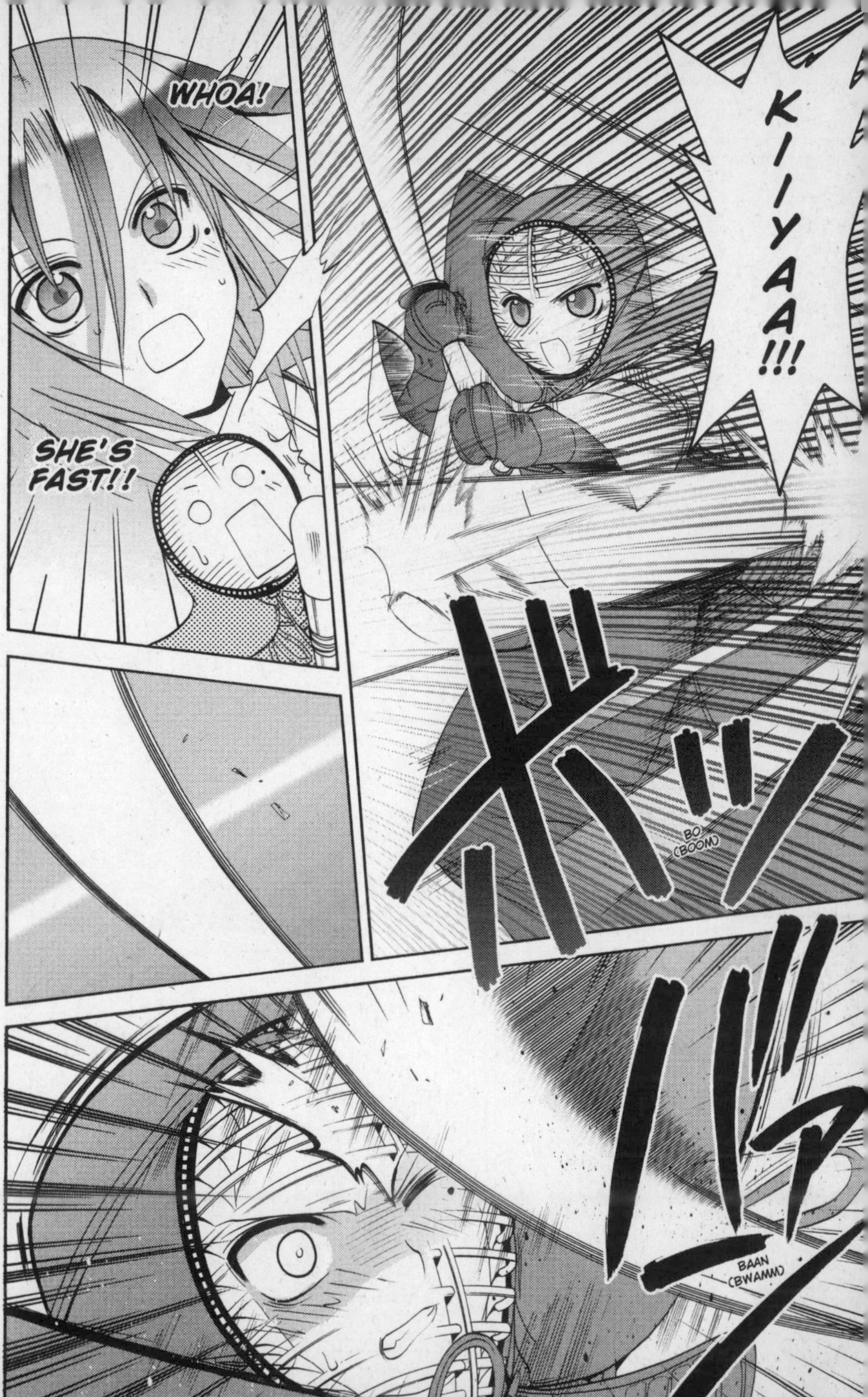
KIIYAA!!!
BO (BOOM)
WHOA!
SHE'S FAST!!
BAAN (BWAMM)

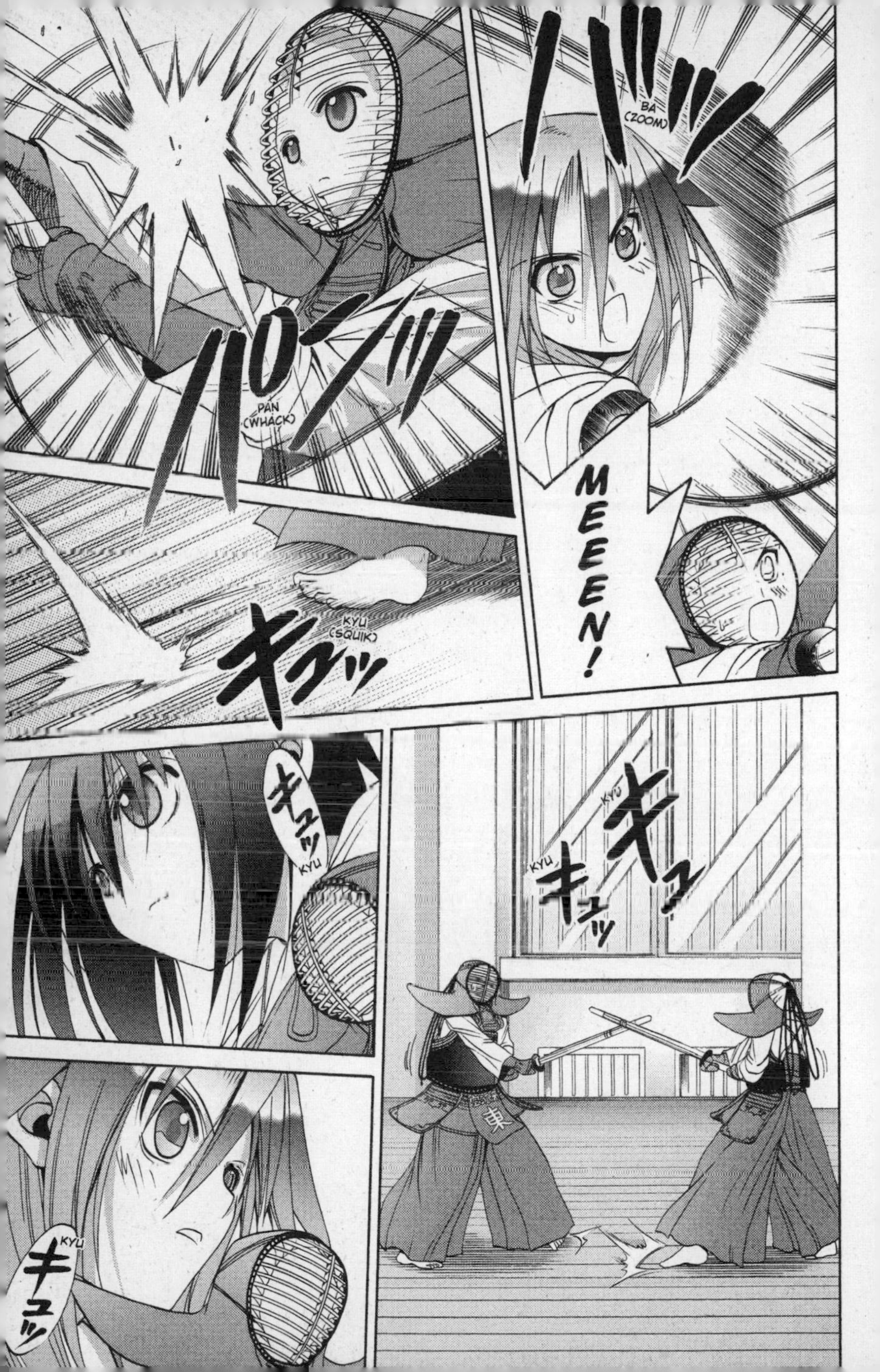

BA (ZOOM)
MEEEN!
PAN (WHACK)
KYU (SQUIK)
KYU
KYU
KYU
KYU

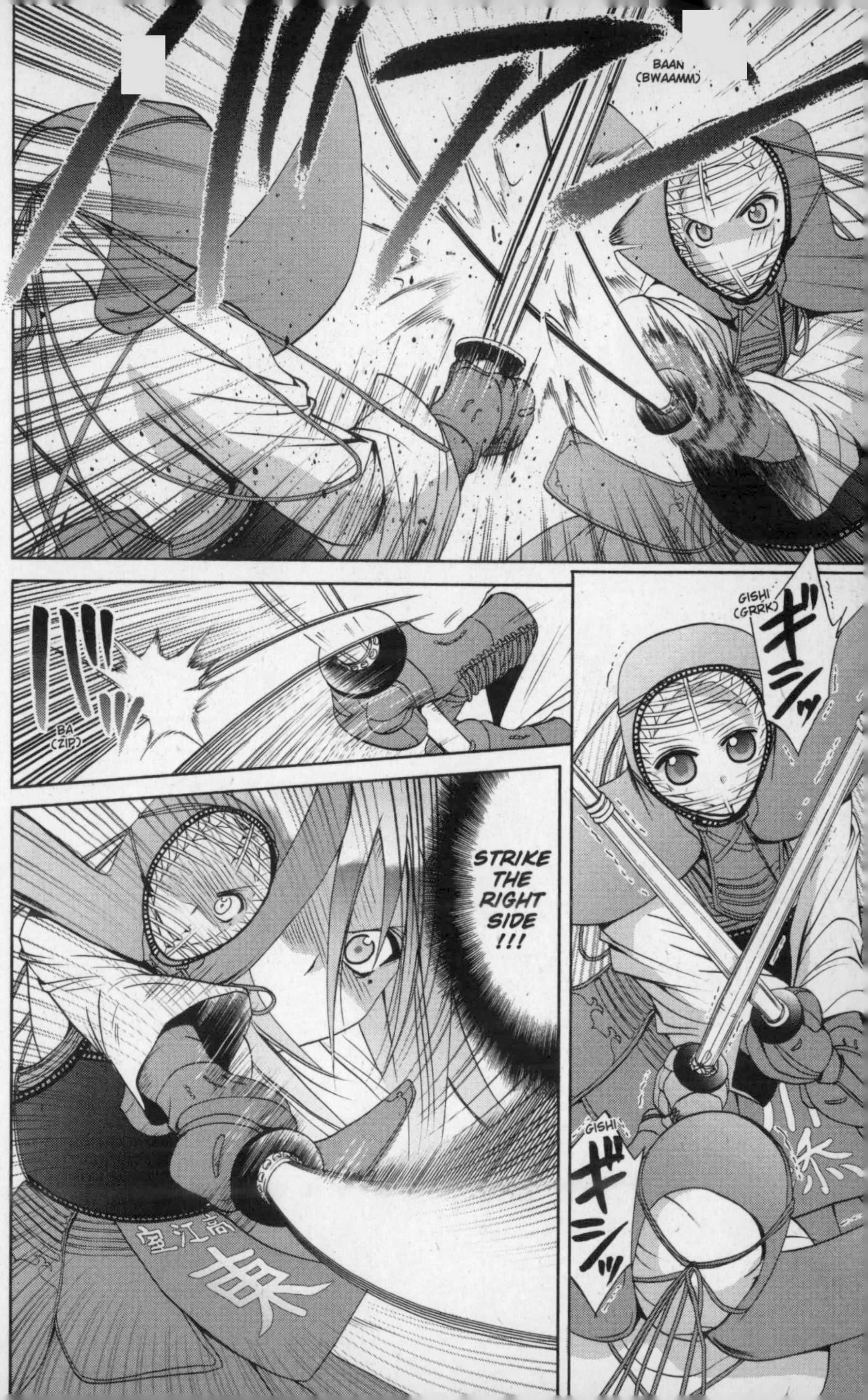
BAAN (BWAAMM)
GISHI (GRRK)
ギシッ
GISHI
ギシッ
BA (ZIP)
STRIKE THE RIGHT SIDE!!!

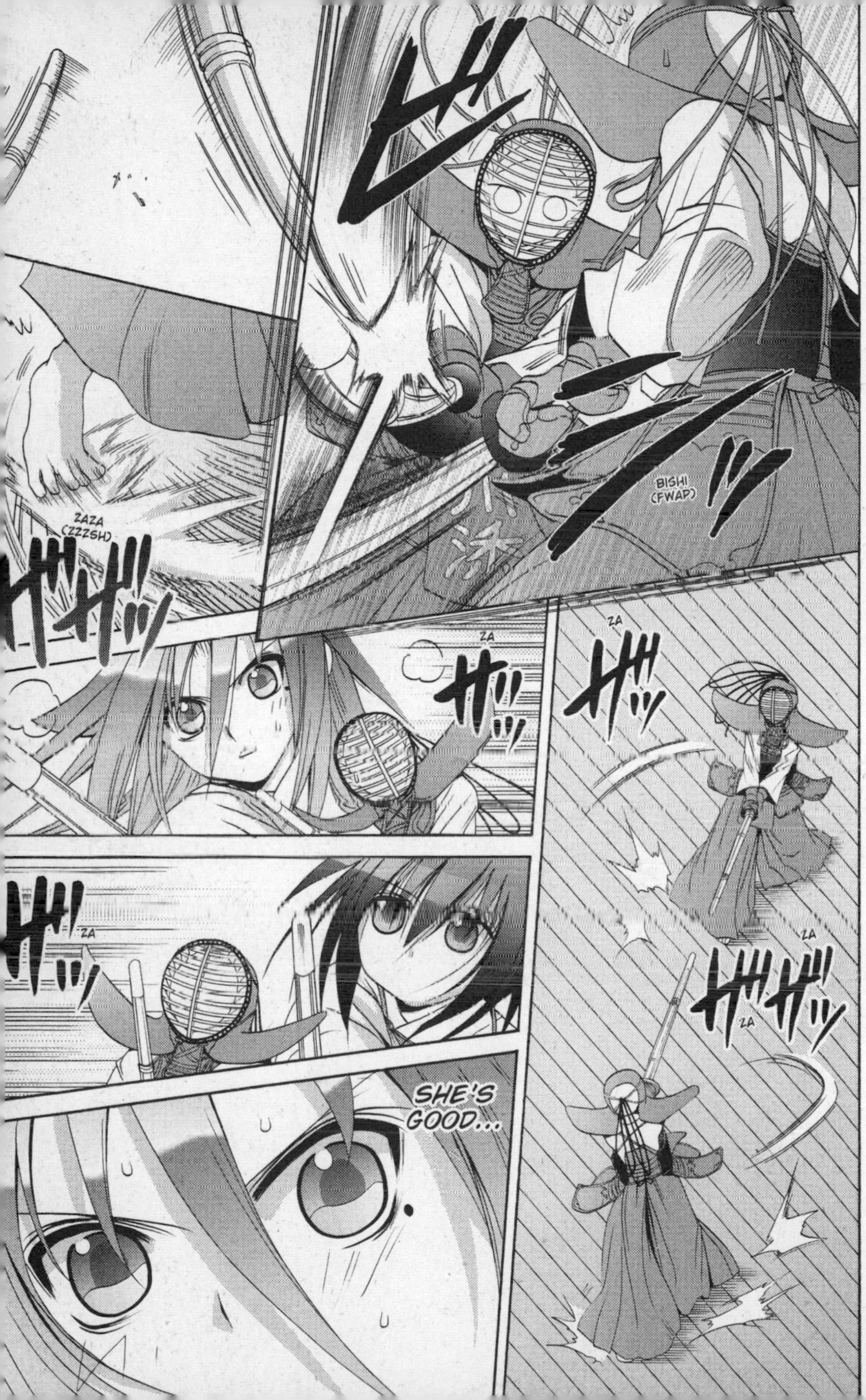
BISHI (FWAP)
ZAZA (ZZZSH)
ZA
ZA
ZA
ZA
ZA
SHE'S GOOD...

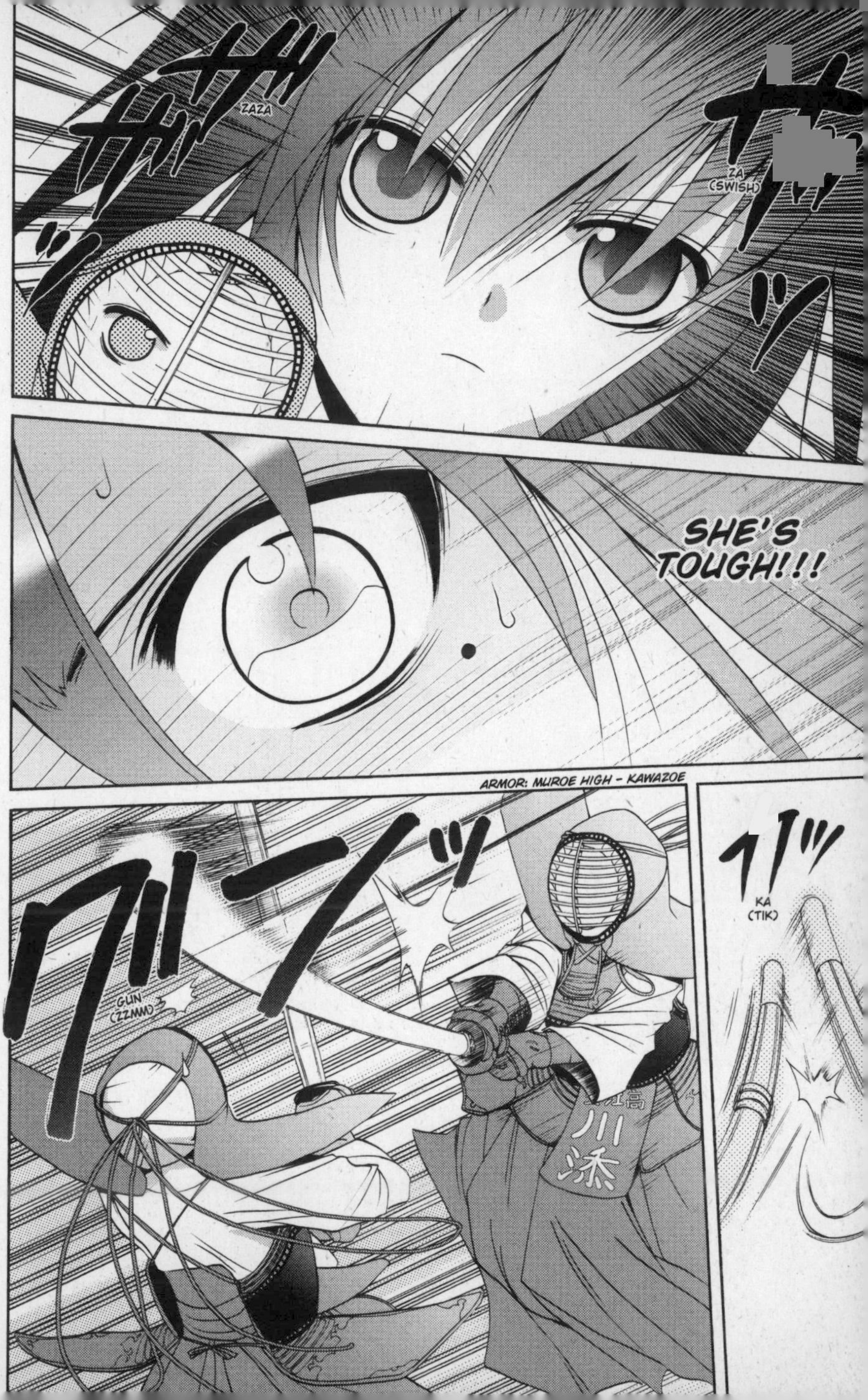
ZA
(SWISH)
ZAZA
SHE'S TOUGH!!!
ARMOR: MUROE HIGH - KAWAZOE
KA
(TIK)
GUN
(ZZMM)
川添

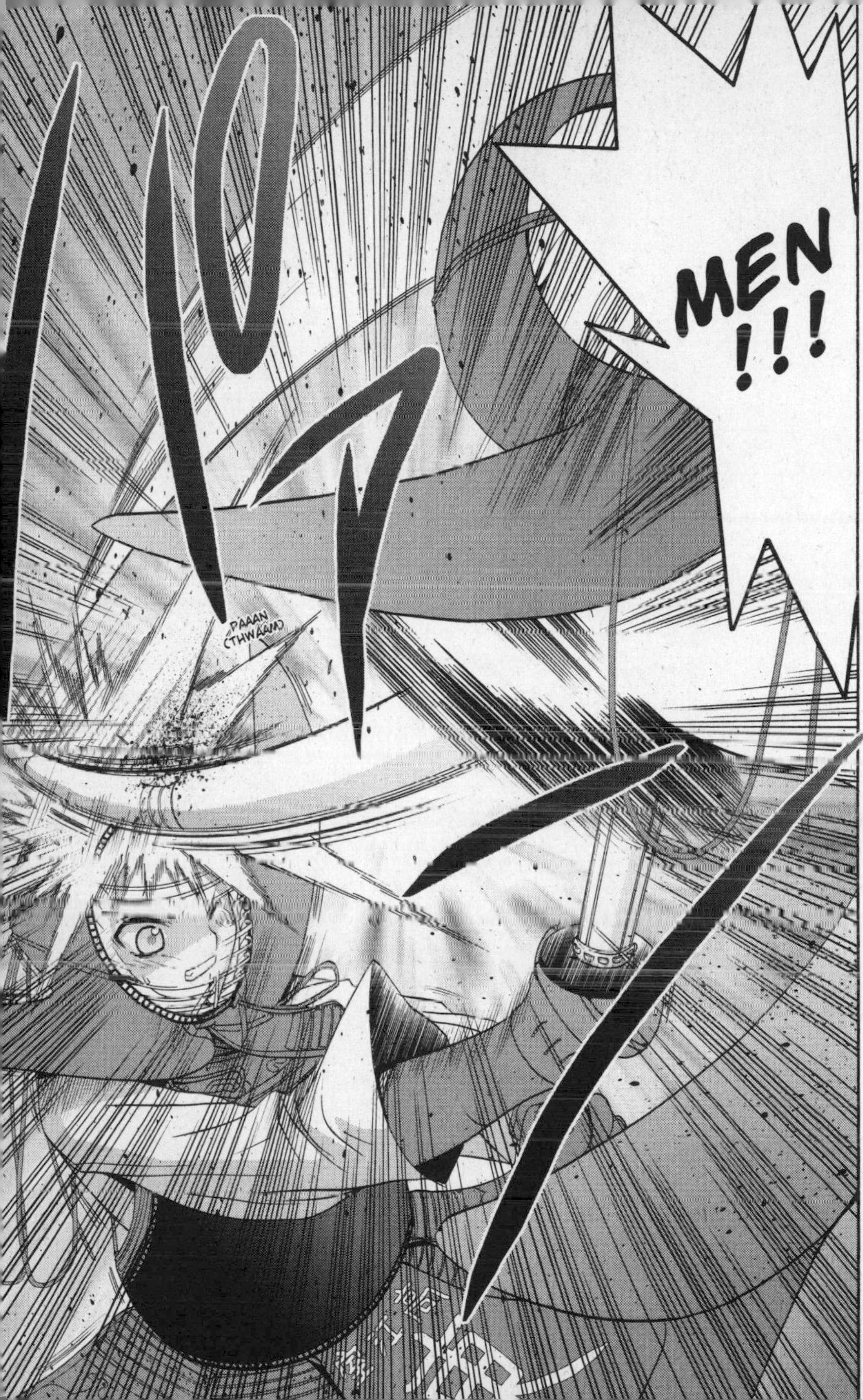
MEN !!!
PAAAN (THWAAM)

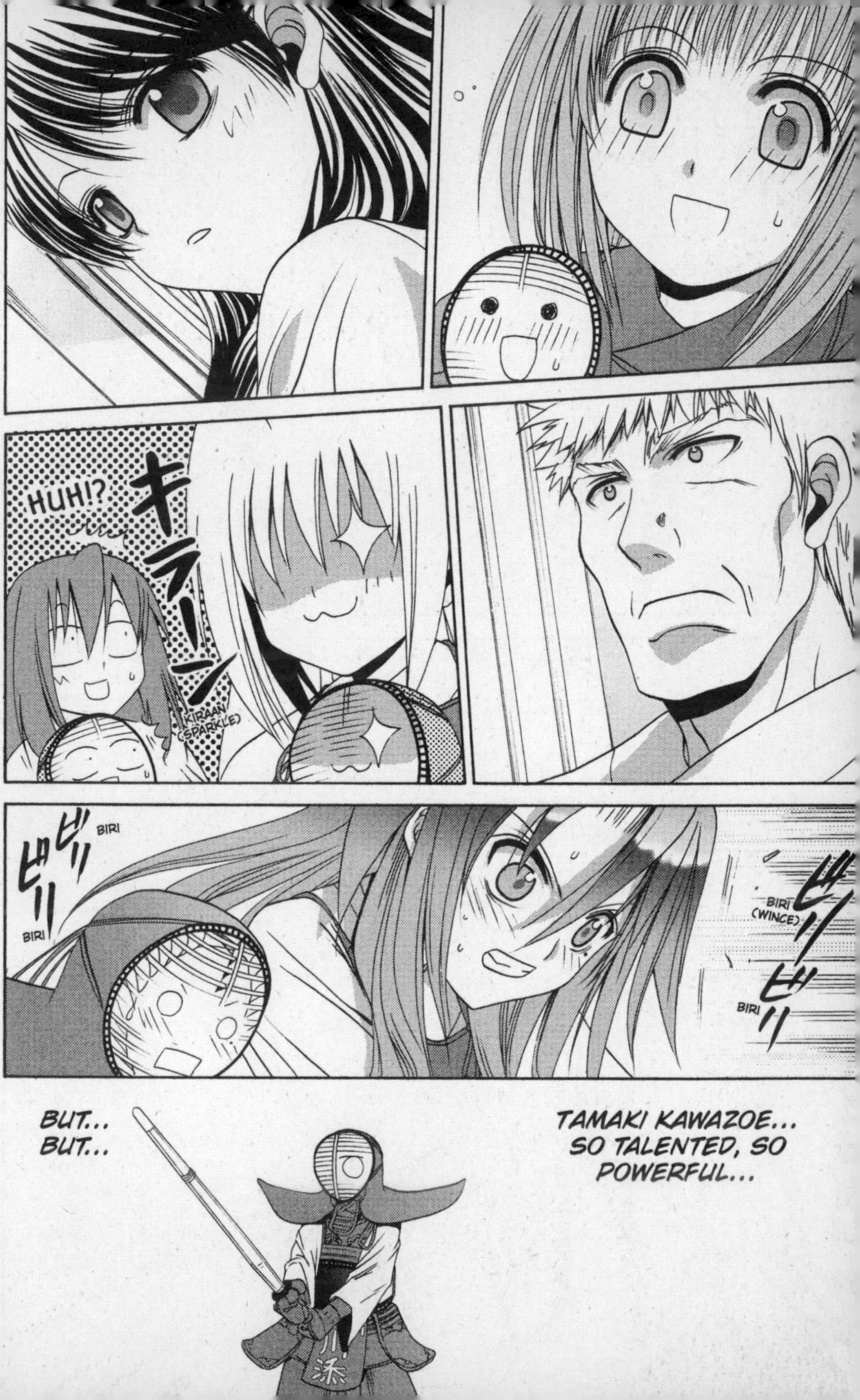
キラーン
KIRAAN (SPARKLE)
HUH!?
ビリビリ
BIRI (WINCE)
BIRI
ビリビリ
BIRI
BIRI
TAMAKI KAWAZOE... SO TALENTED, SO POWERFUL...
BUT... BUT...

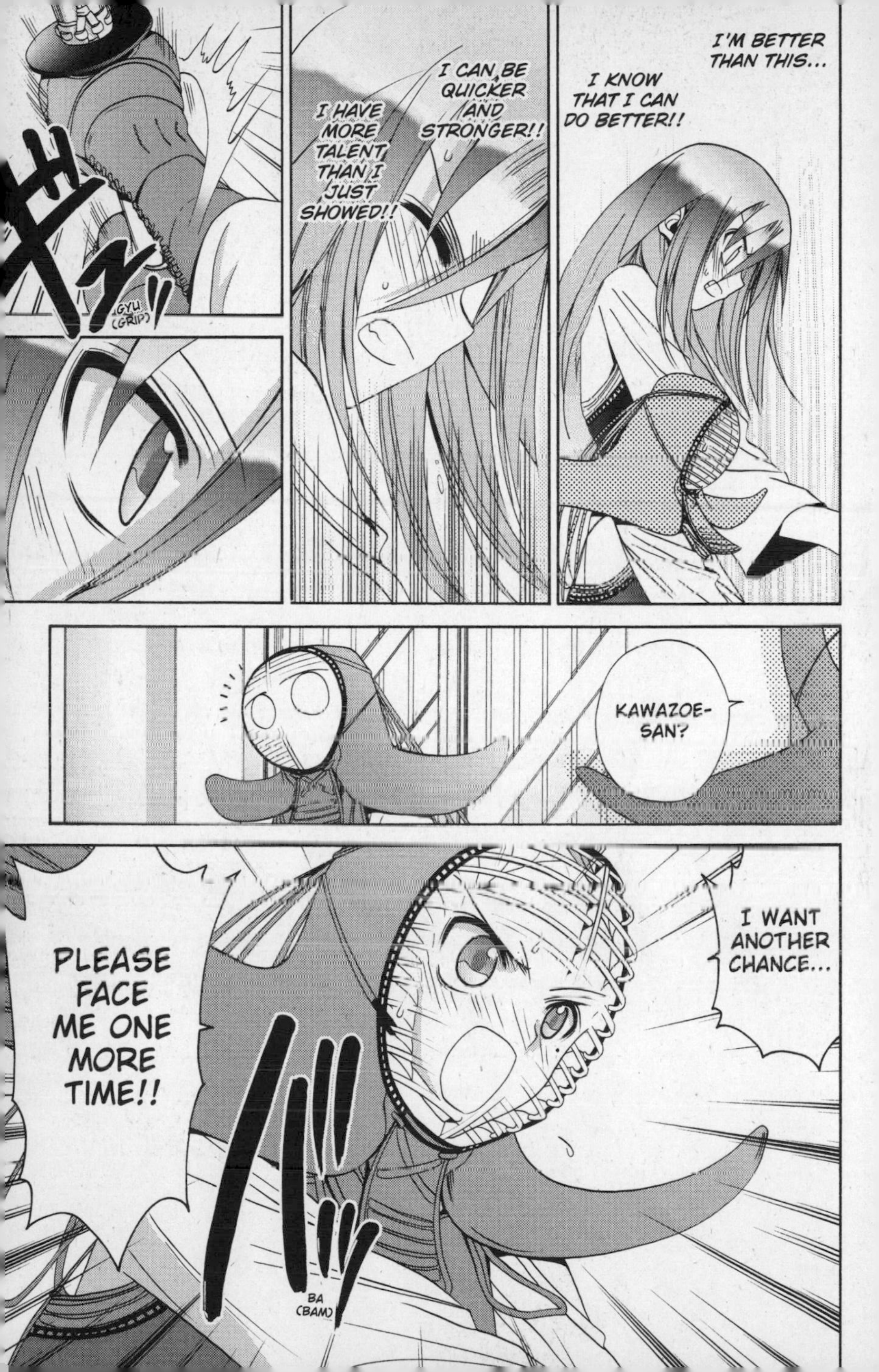
I'M BETTER THAN THIS...
I KNOW THAT I CAN DO BETTER!!
I CAN BE QUICKER AND STRONGER!!
I HAVE MORE TALENT THAN I JUST SHOWED!!
GYU (GRIP)
KAWAZOE-SAN?
I WANT ANOTHER CHANCE...
PLEASE FACE ME ONE MORE TIME!!
BA (BAM)

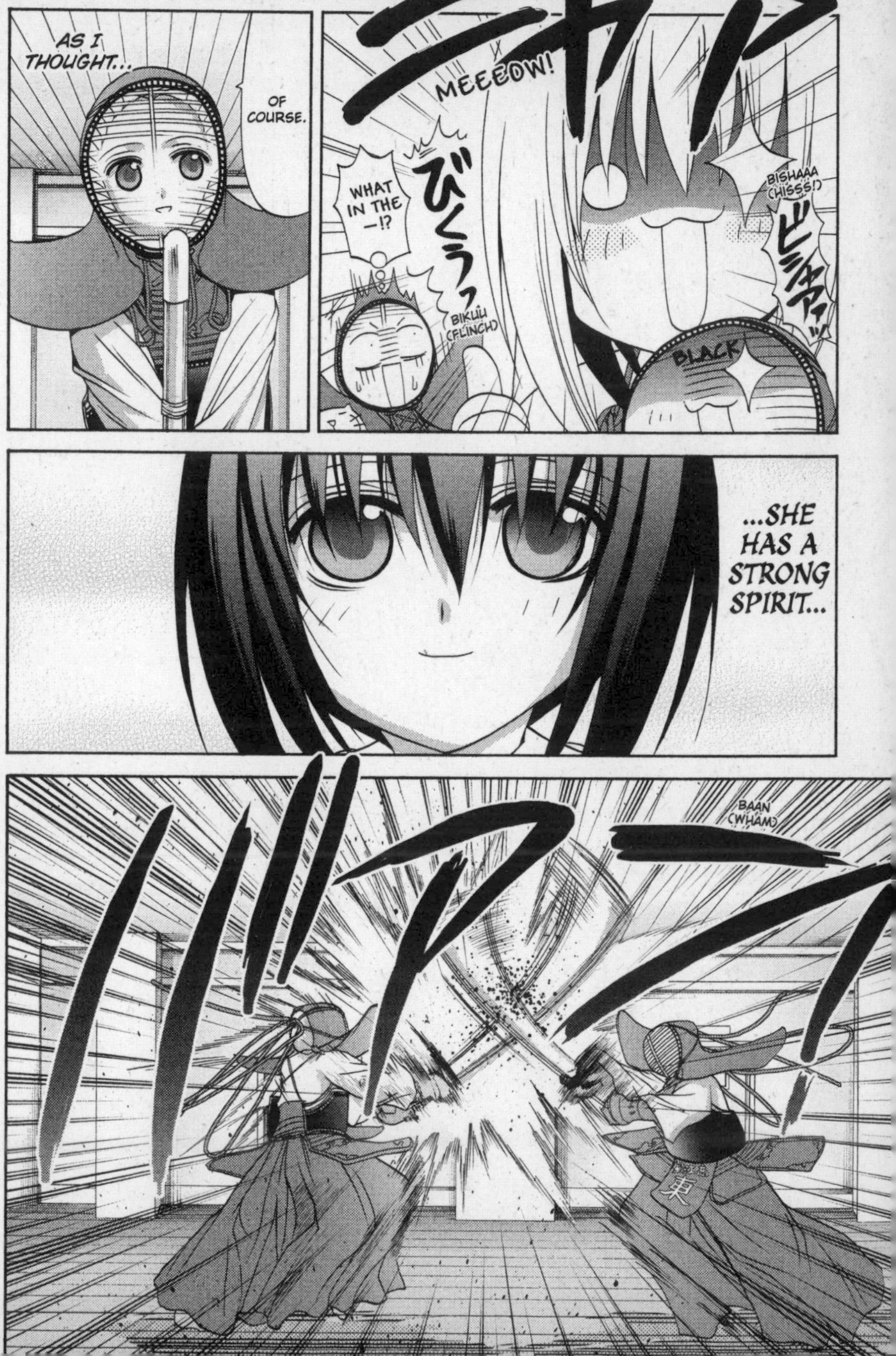
ニャア
MEEEOW!
BISHAAA (HISSS!)
ビシャァッ
WHAT IN THE—!?
びくぅっ
BIKÛÛ (FLINCH)
BLACK
AS I THOUGHT...
OF COURSE.
...SHE HAS A STRONG SPIRIT...
BAAN (WHAM)
バァーン

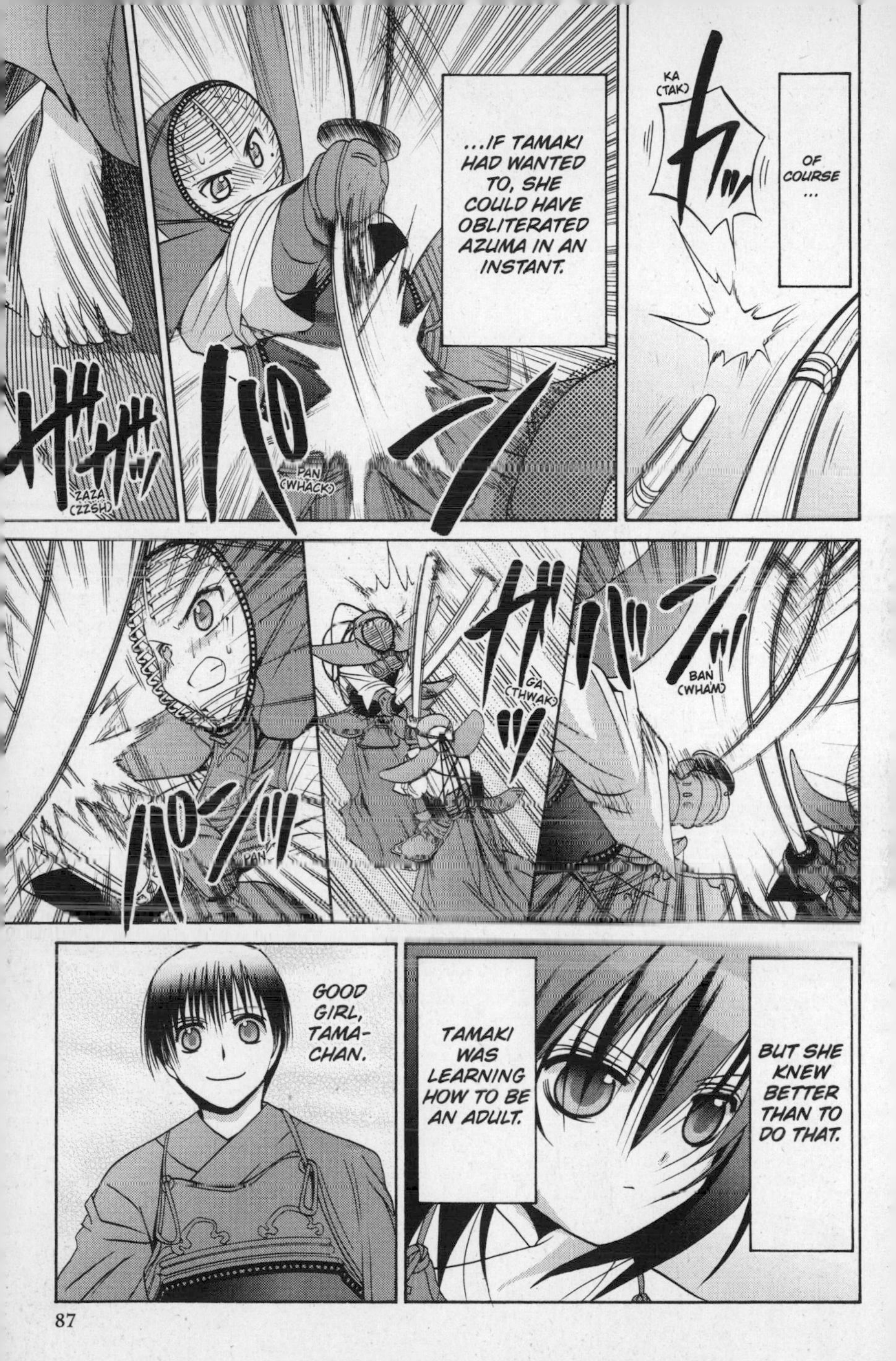
KA (TAK)
OF COURSE...
...IF TAMAKI HAD WANTED TO, SHE COULD HAVE OBLITERATED AZUMA IN AN INSTANT.
PAN (WHACK)
ZAZA (ZZSH)
BAN (WHAM)
GA (THWAK)
PAN
BUT SHE KNEW BETTER THAN TO DO THAT.
TAMAKI WAS LEARNING HOW TO BE AN ADULT.
GOOD GIRL, TAMA-CHAN.

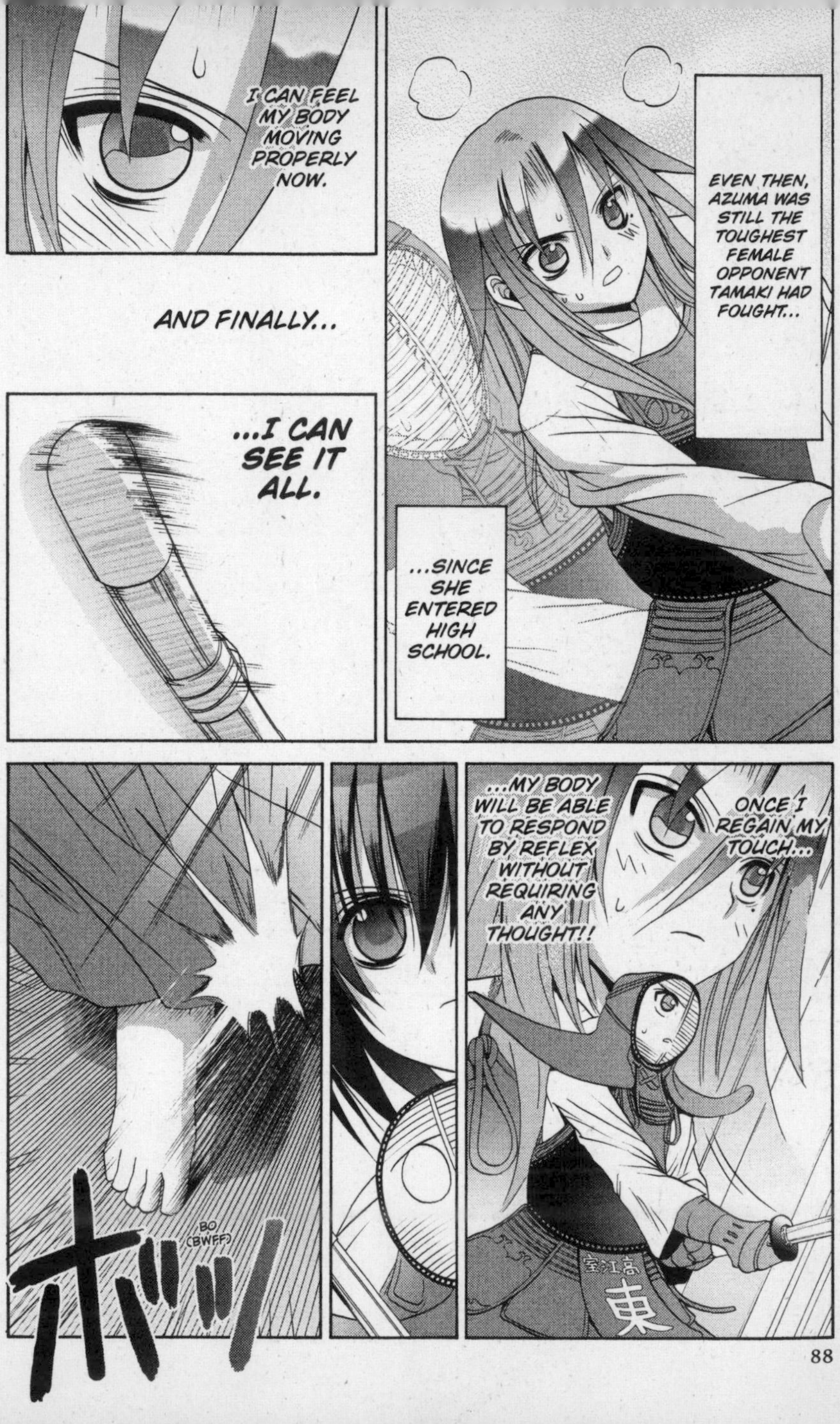
EVEN THEN, AZUMA WAS STILL THE TOUGHEST FEMALE OPPONENT TAMAKI HAD FOUGHT...
...SINCE SHE ENTERED HIGH SCHOOL.
I CAN FEEL MY BODY MOVING PROPERLY NOW.
AND FINALLY...
...I CAN SEE IT ALL.
ONCE I REGAIN MY TOUCH...
...MY BODY WILL BE ABLE TO RESPOND BY REFLEX WITHOUT REQUIRING ANY THOUGHT!!
ボッ
BO (BWFF)

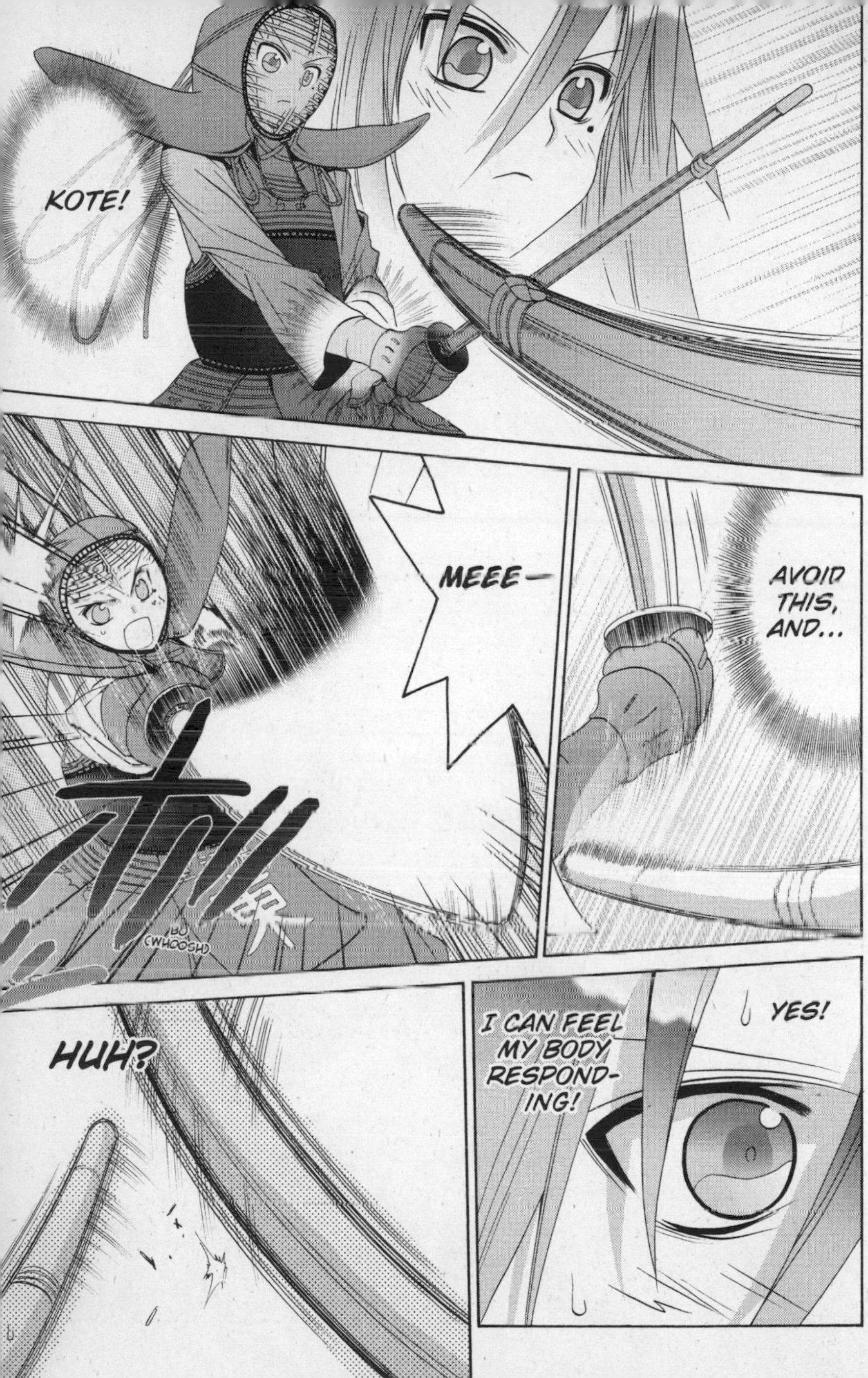
KOTE!
AVOID THIS, AND...
MEEE—
BU
(WHOOSH)
YES!
I CAN FEEL MY BODY RESPOND-ING!
HUH?

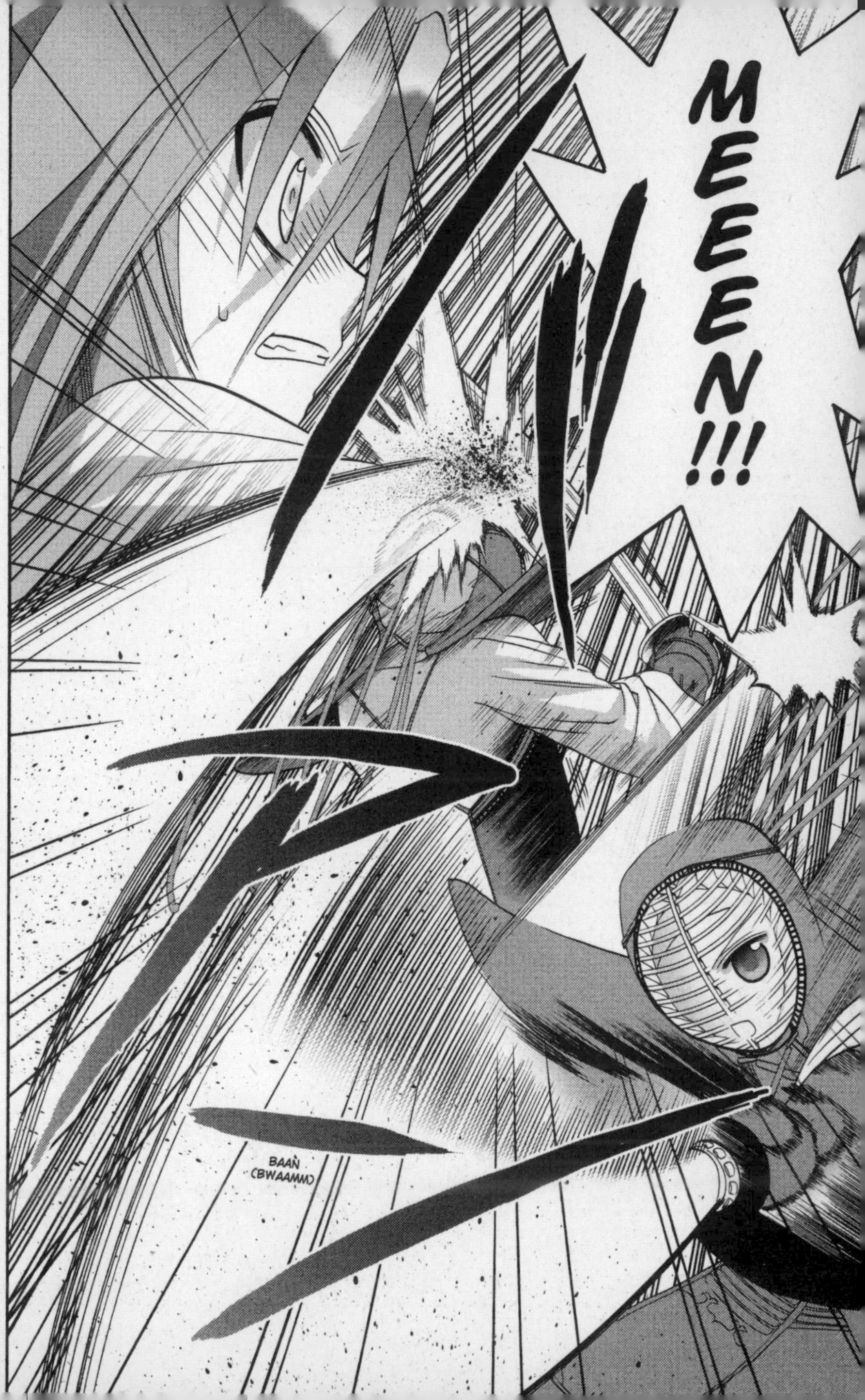
MEEEEN!!!
BAAN
(BWAAMM)

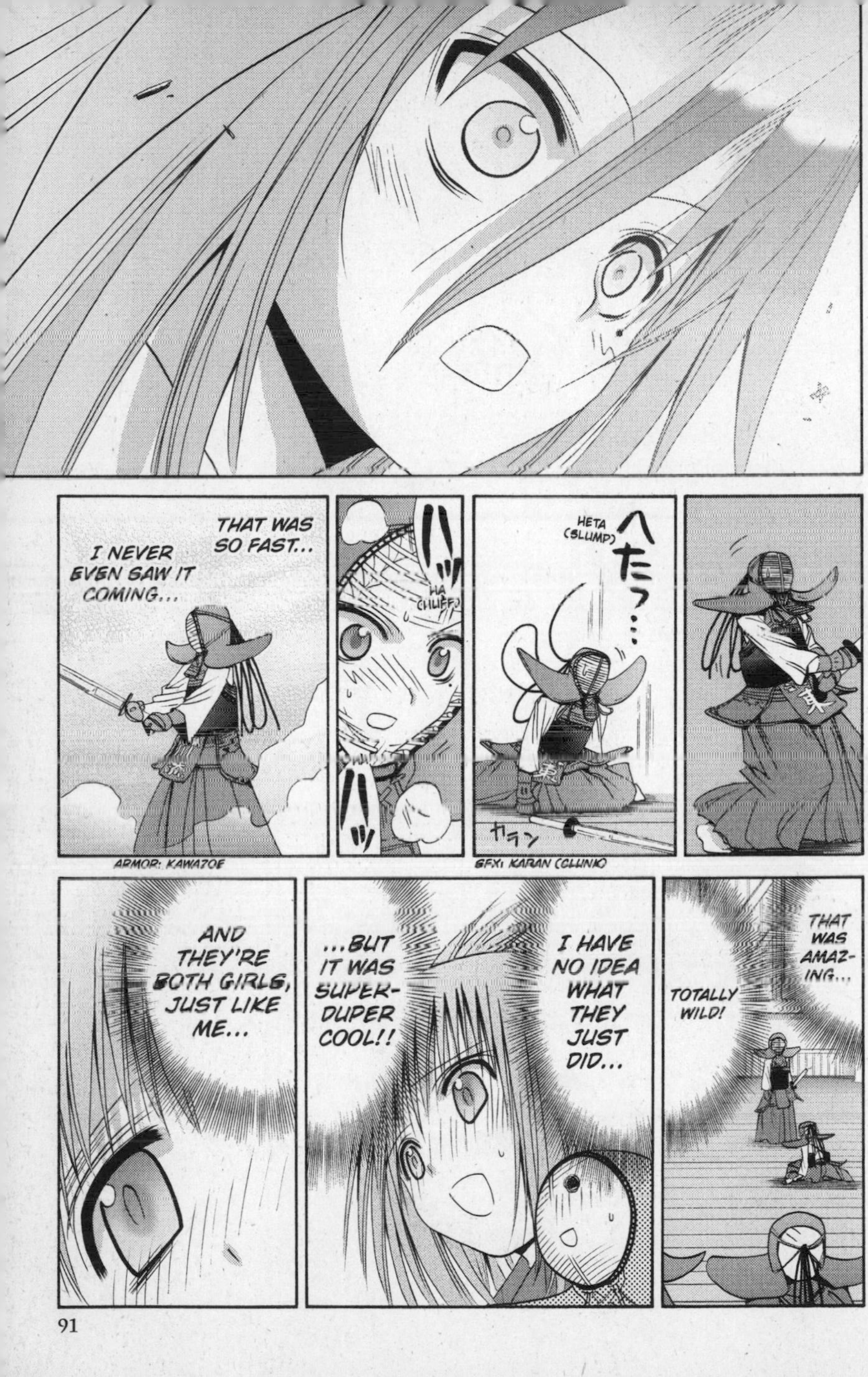

HETA (SLUMP)
へたっ…
カラン
SFX: KARAN (CLUNK)
ハッ
HA (HUFF)
ハッ
THAT WAS SO FAST...
I NEVER EVEN SAW IT COMING...
ARMOR: KAWAZOE
THAT WAS AMAZING...
TOTALLY WILD!
I HAVE NO IDEA WHAT THEY JUST DID...
...BUT IT WAS SUPER-DUPER COOL!!
AND THEY'RE BOTH GIRLS, JUST LIKE ME...

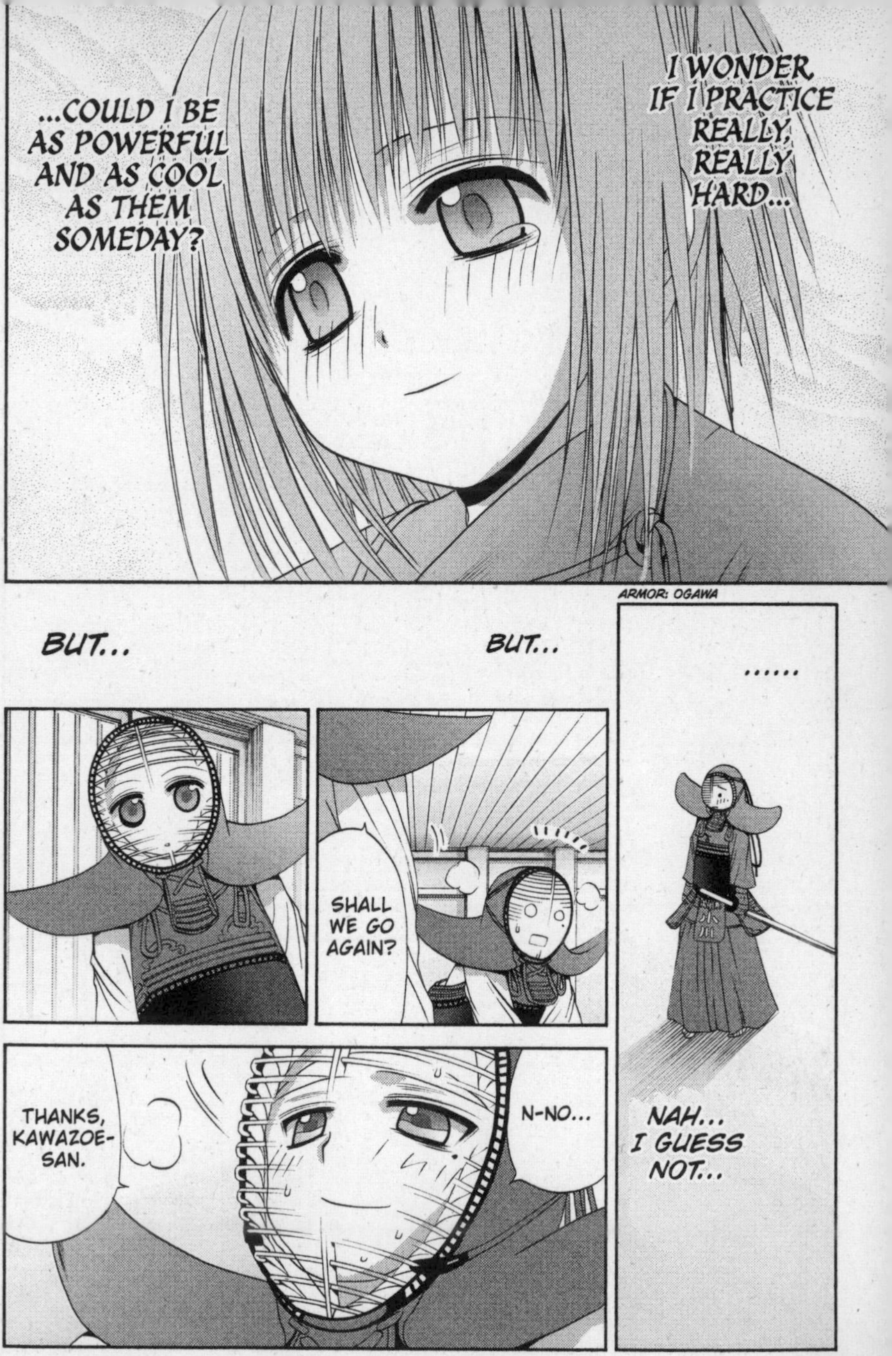
I WONDER IF I PRACTICE REALLY, REALLY HARD...
...COULD I BE AS POWERFUL AND AS COOL AS THEM SOMEDAY?
BUT...
BUT...
ARMOR: OGAWA
......
NAH... I GUESS NOT...
SHALL WE GO AGAIN?
N-NO...
THANKS, KAWAZOE-SAN.

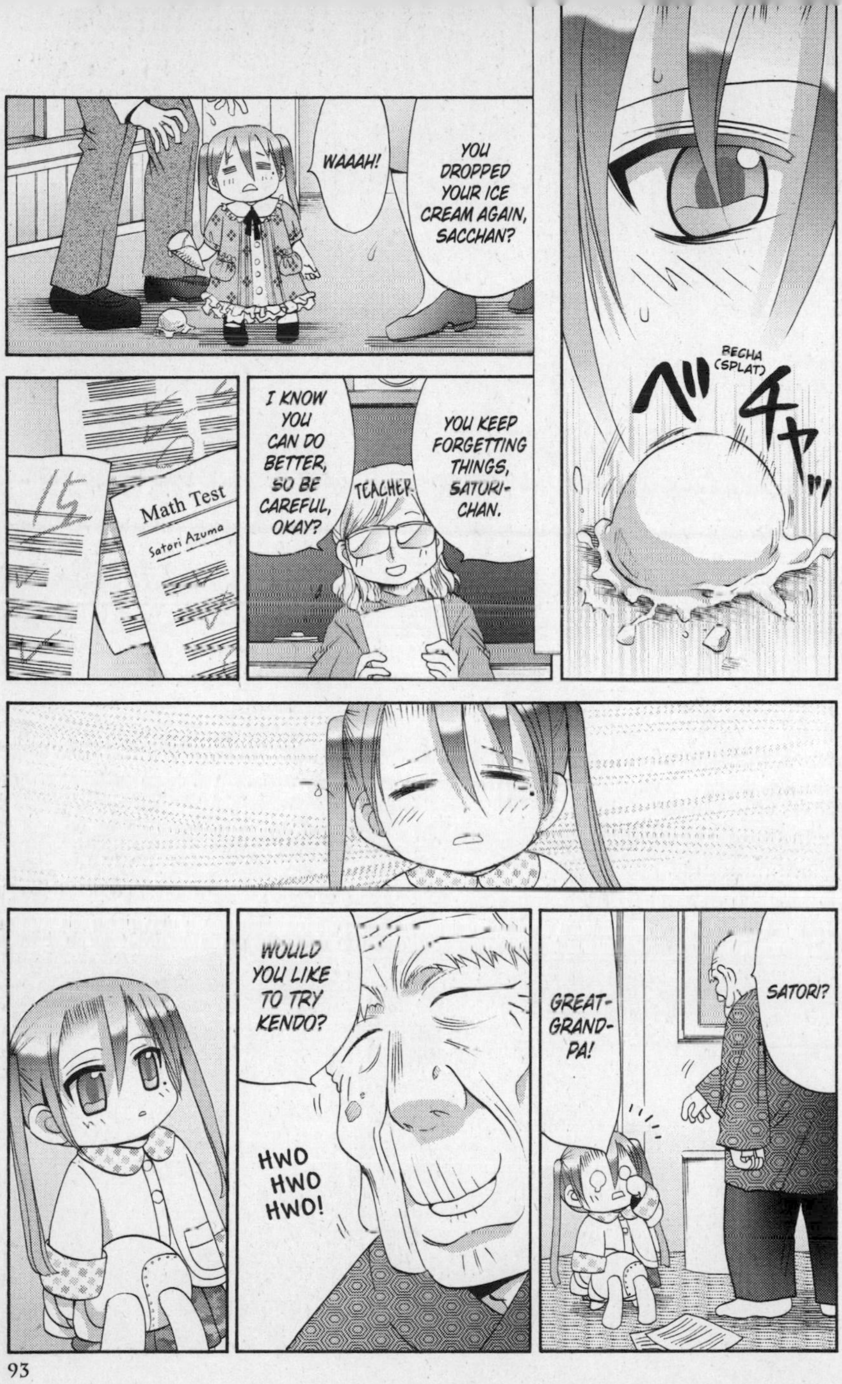
BECHA (SPLAT)
ベチャッ
YOU DROPPED YOUR ICE CREAM AGAIN, SACCHAN?
WAAAH!
YOU KEEP FORGETTING THINGS, SATORI-CHAN.
I KNOW YOU CAN DO BETTER, SO BE CAREFUL, OKAY?
TEACHER
15
Math Test
Satori Azuma
SATORI?
GREAT-GRANDPA!
WOULD YOU LIKE TO TRY KENDO?
HWO HWO HWO!

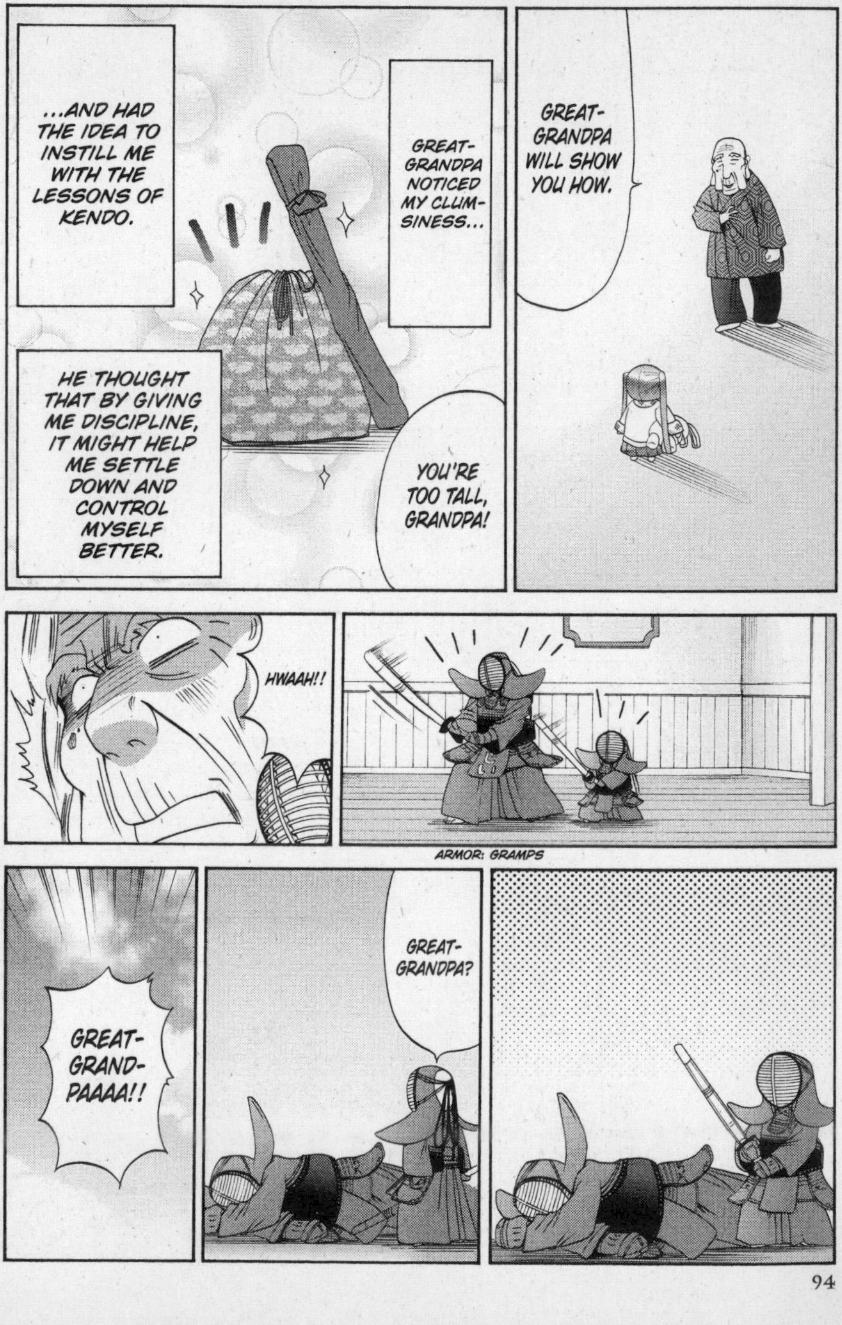
GREAT-GRANDPA WILL SHOW YOU HOW.
GREAT-GRANDPA NOTICED MY CLUMSINESS...
...AND HAD THE IDEA TO INSTILL ME WITH THE LESSONS OF KENDO.
HE THOUGHT THAT BY GIVING ME DISCIPLINE, IT MIGHT HELP ME SETTLE DOWN AND CONTROL MYSELF BETTER.
YOU'RE TOO TALL, GRANDPA!
ARMOR: GRAMPS
HWAAH!!
GREAT-GRANDPA?
GREAT-GRAND-PAAAA!!

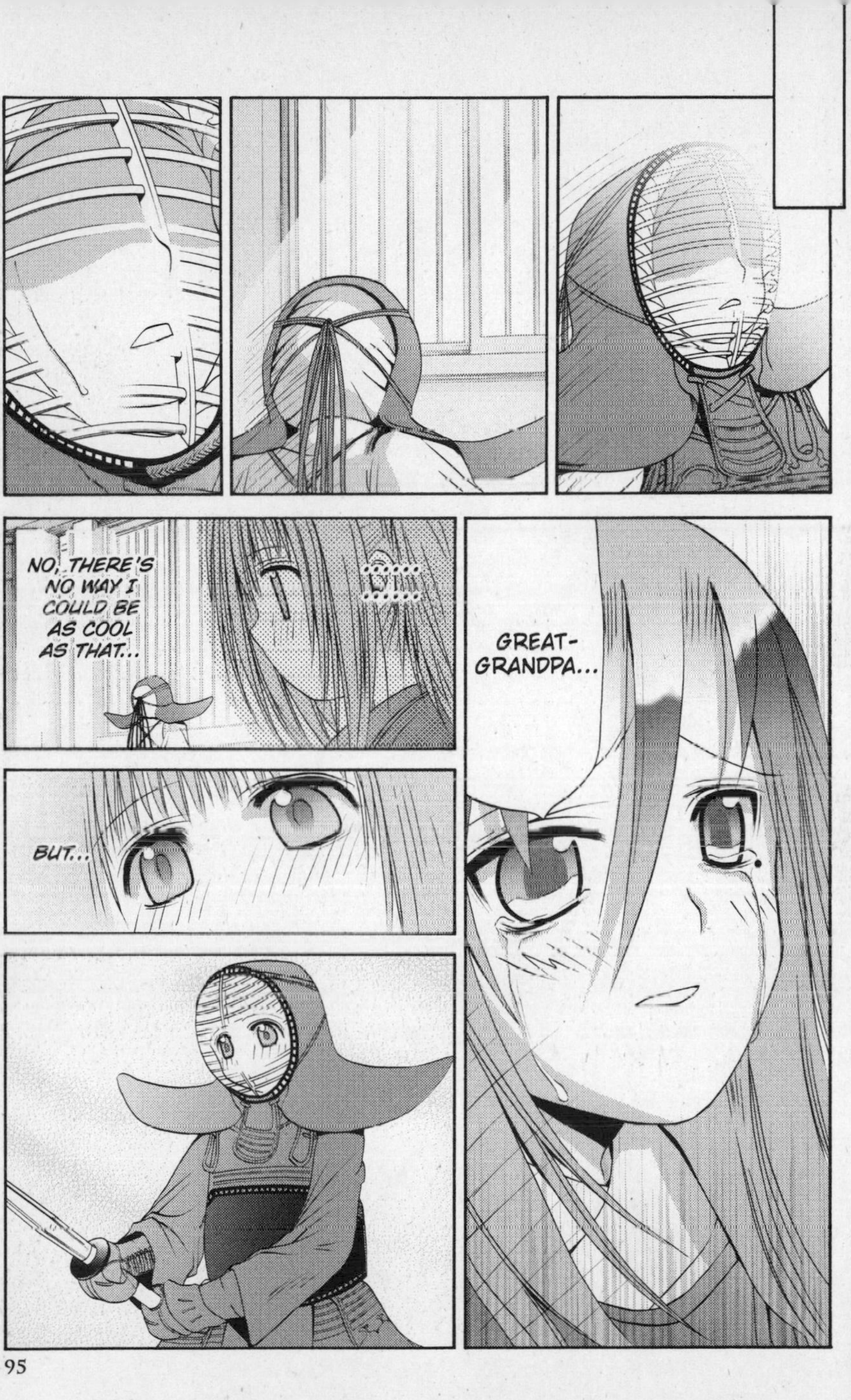
GREAT-GRANDPA...
......
NO, THERE'S NO WAY I COULD BE AS COOL AS THAT...
BUT...

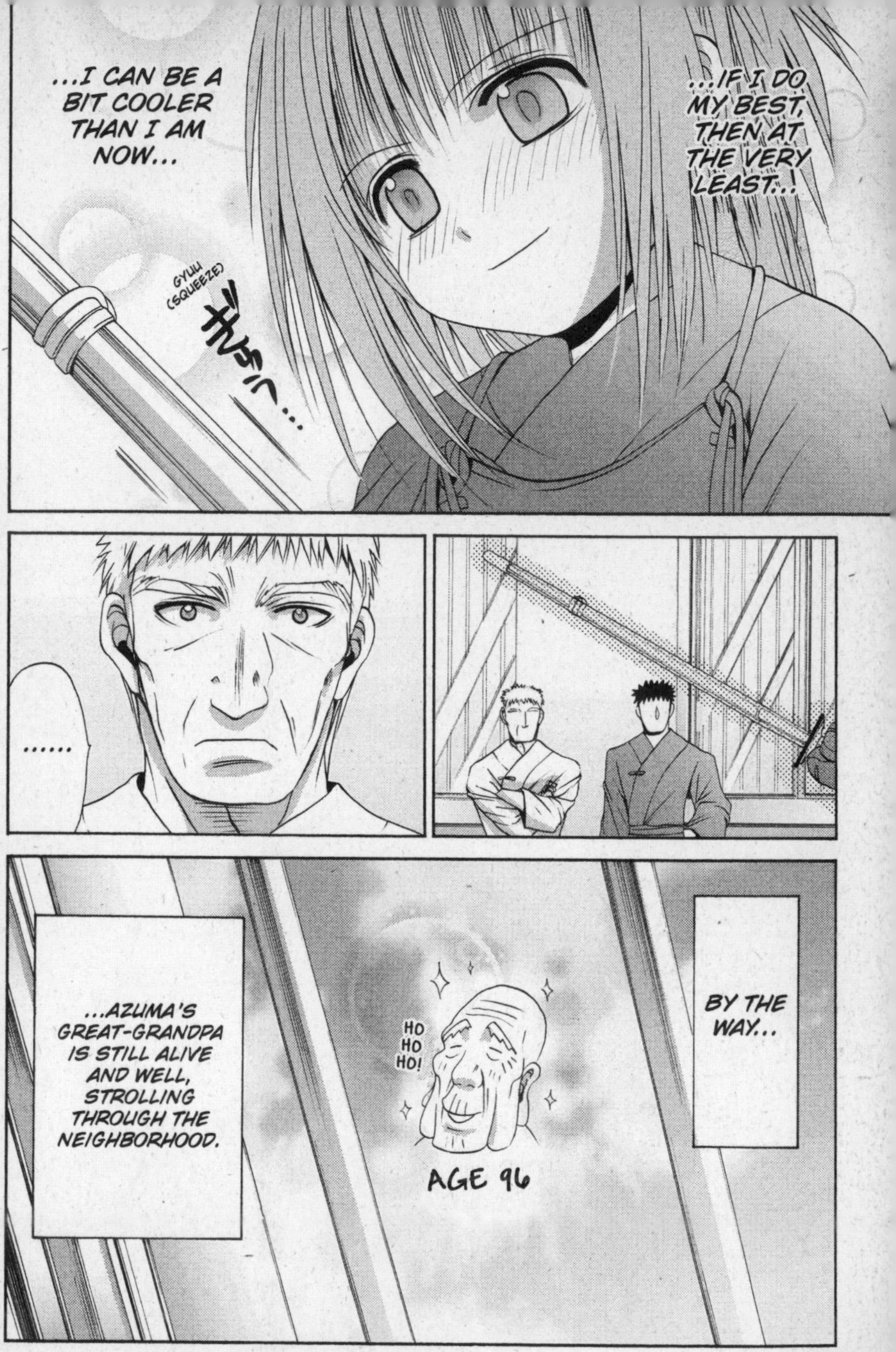
...IF I DO MY BEST, THEN AT THE VERY LEAST...
...I CAN BE A BIT COOLER THAN I AM NOW...
GYUU (SQUEEZE)
......
BY THE WAY...
...AZUMA'S GREAT-GRANDPA IS STILL ALIVE AND WELL, STROLLING THROUGH THE NEIGHBORHOOD.
HO HO HO!
AGE 96

BAMBOO BLADE

KIRINO CHIBA

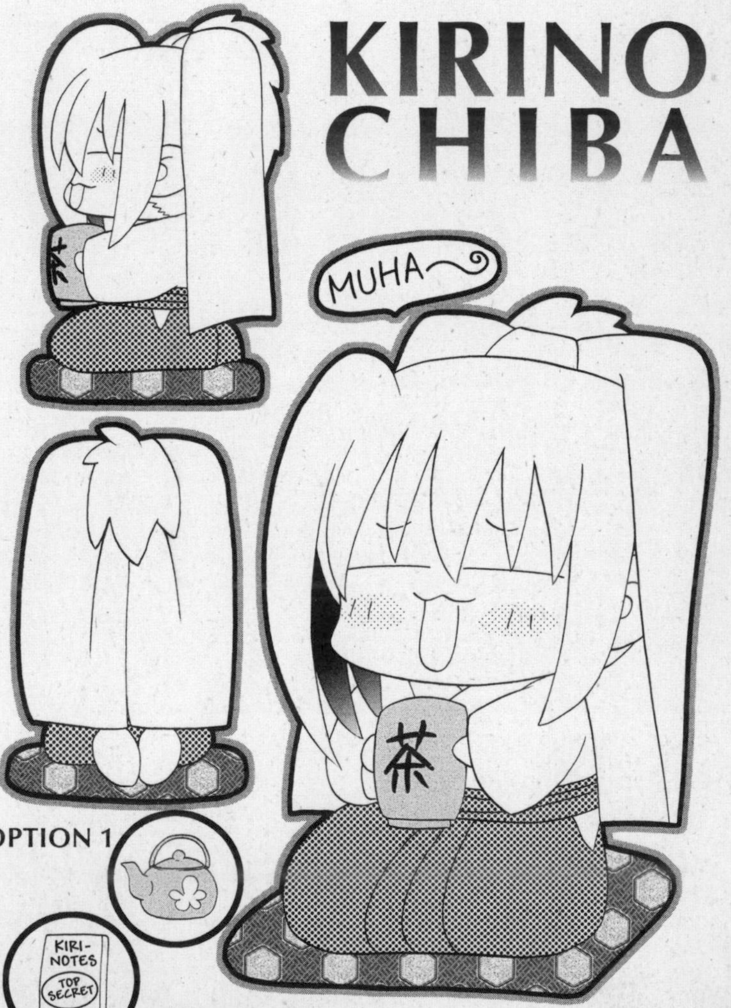
MUHA~
茶
OPTION 1
KIRI-NOTES
TOP SECRET
OPTION 2

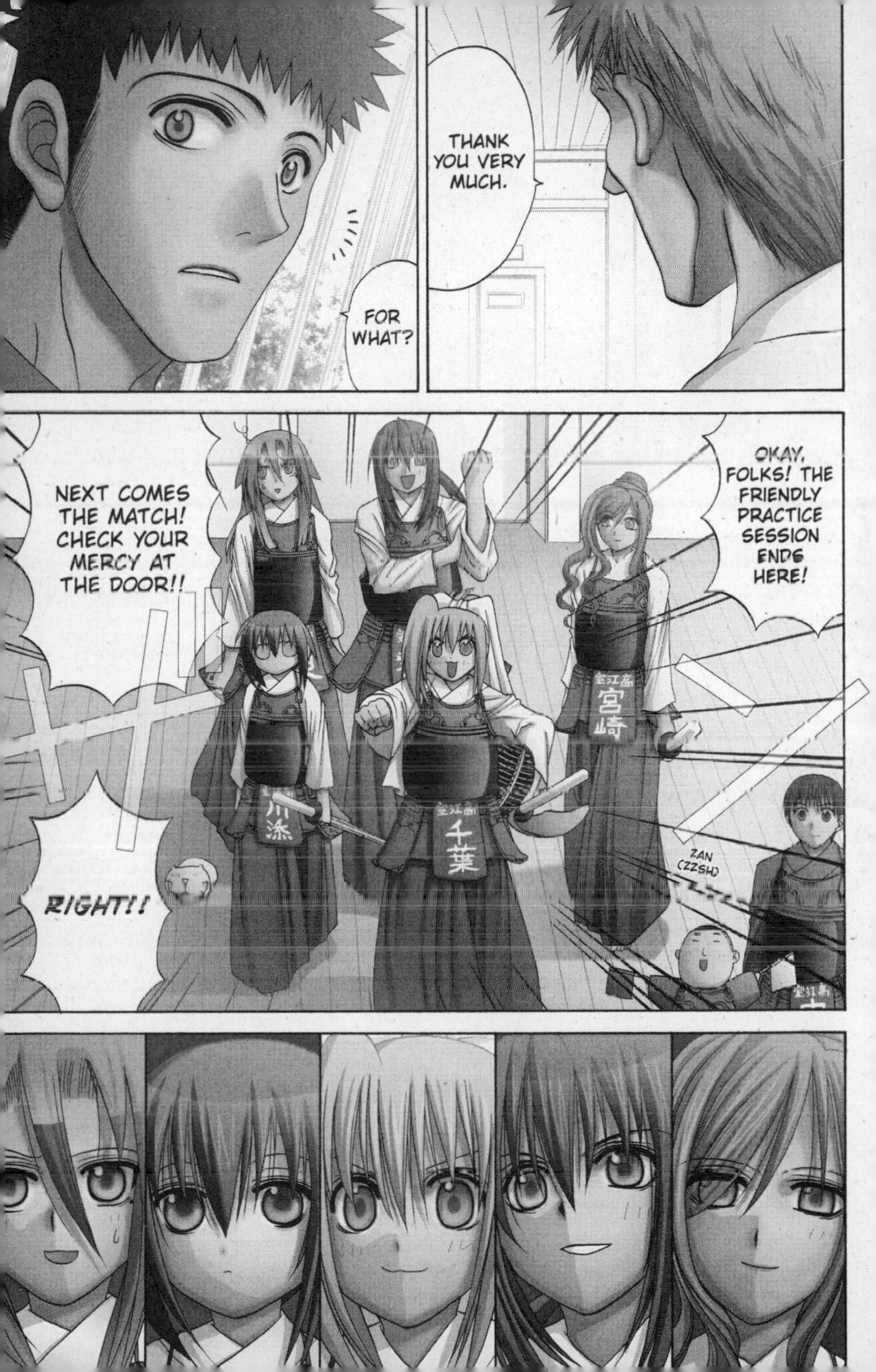
THANK YOU VERY MUCH.
FOR WHAT?
OKAY, FOLKS! THE FRIENDLY PRACTICE SESSION ENDS HERE!
宮崎
ZAN (ZZSH)
千葉
川添
NEXT COMES THE MATCH! CHECK YOUR MERCY AT THE DOOR!!
RIGHT!!

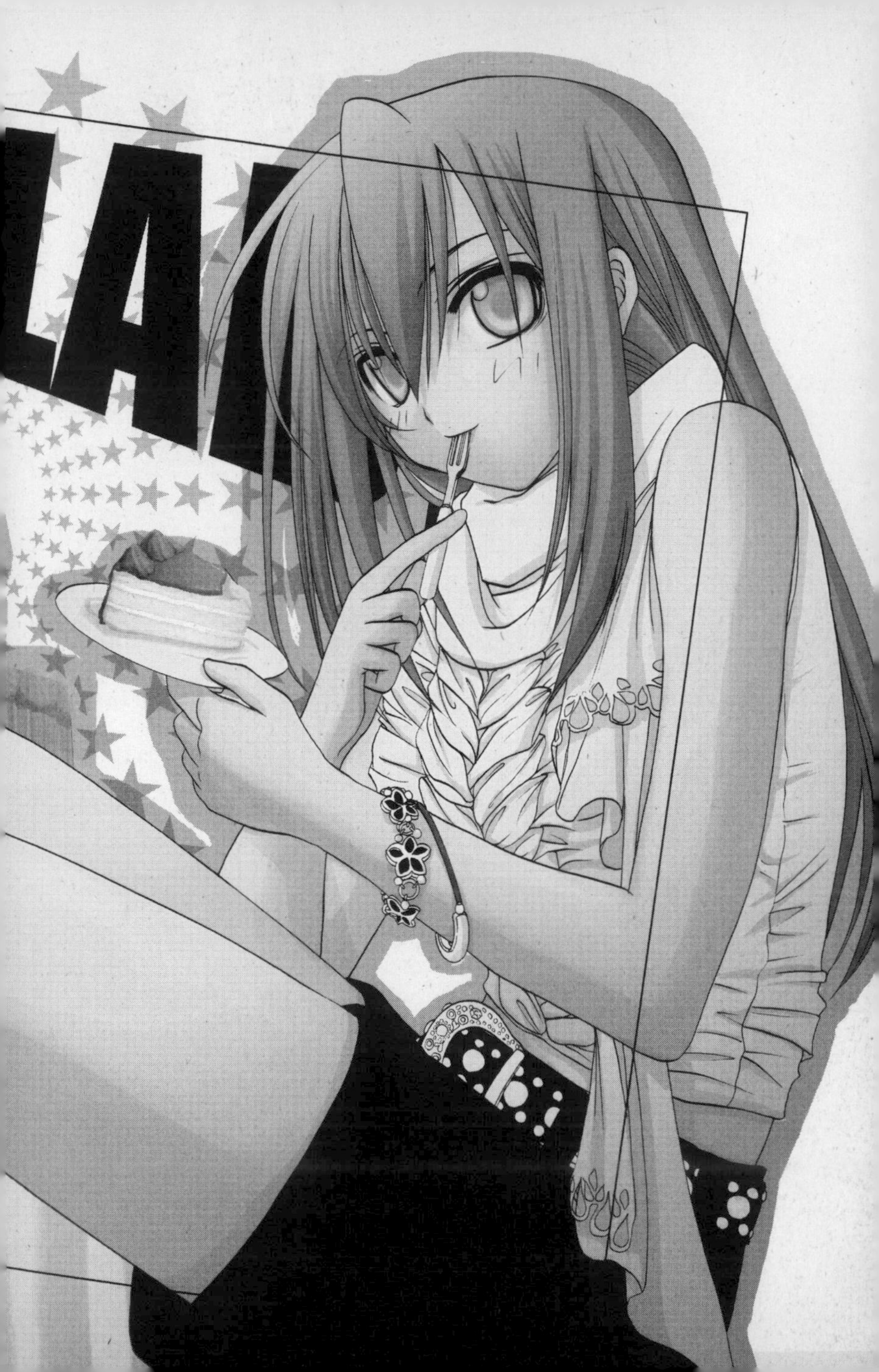
LA

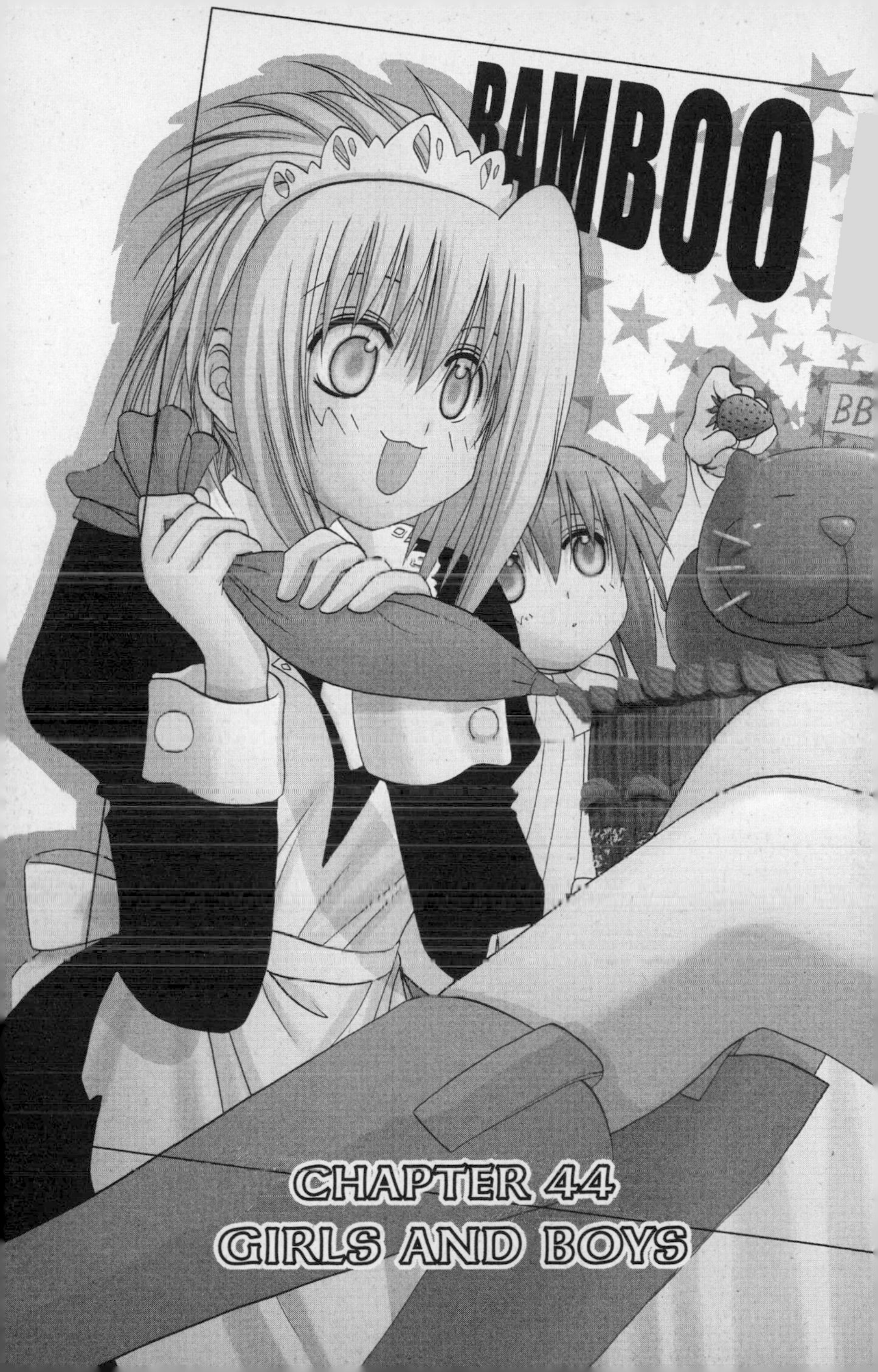
BAMBOO
BB
CHAPTER 44
GIRLS AND BOYS

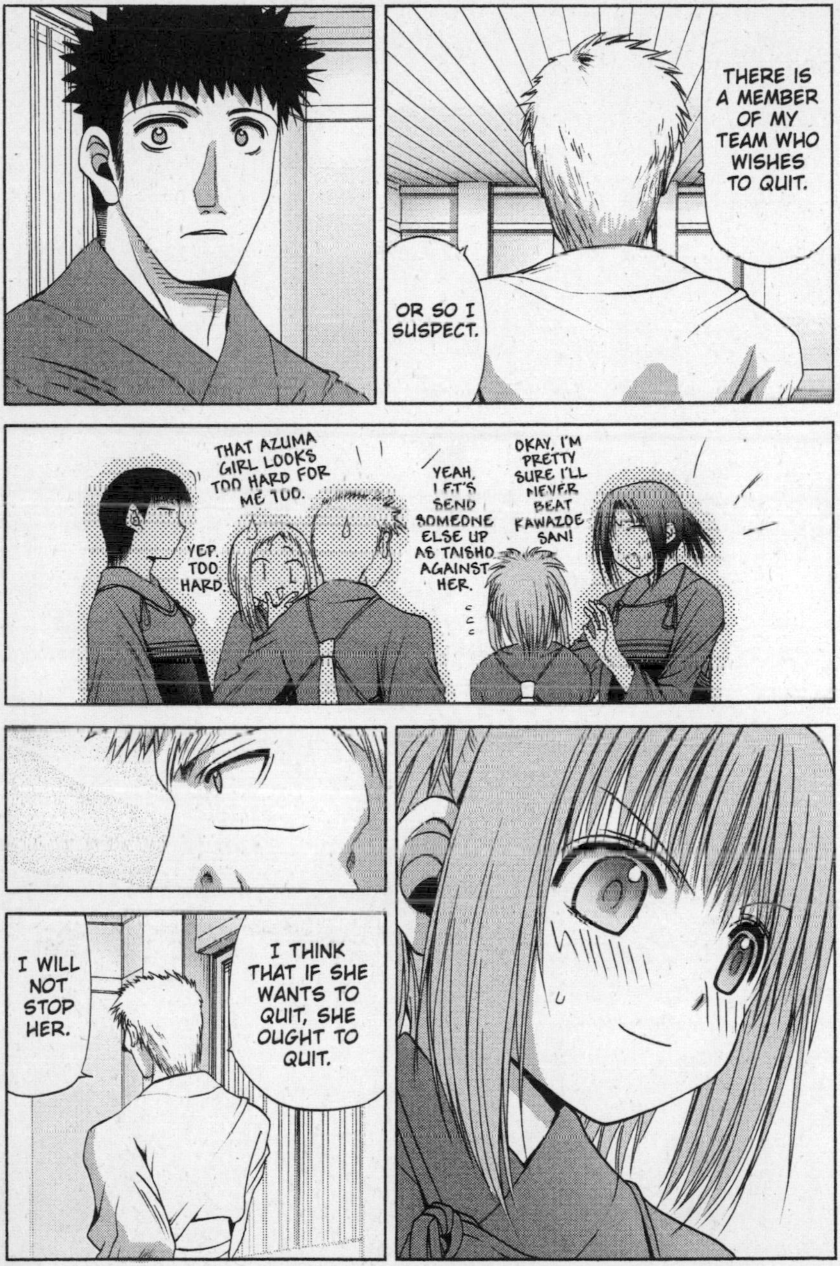
THERE IS A MEMBER OF MY TEAM WHO WISHES TO QUIT.
OR SO I SUSPECT.
OKAY, I'M PRETTY SURE I'LL NEVER BEAT KAWAZOE SAN!
YEAH, LET'S SEND SOMEONE ELSE UP AS TAISHO AGAINST HER.
THAT AZUMA GIRL LOOKS TOO HARD FOR ME TOO.
YEP. TOO HARD.
I THINK THAT IF SHE WANTS TO QUIT, SHE OUGHT TO QUIT.
I WILL NOT STOP HER.

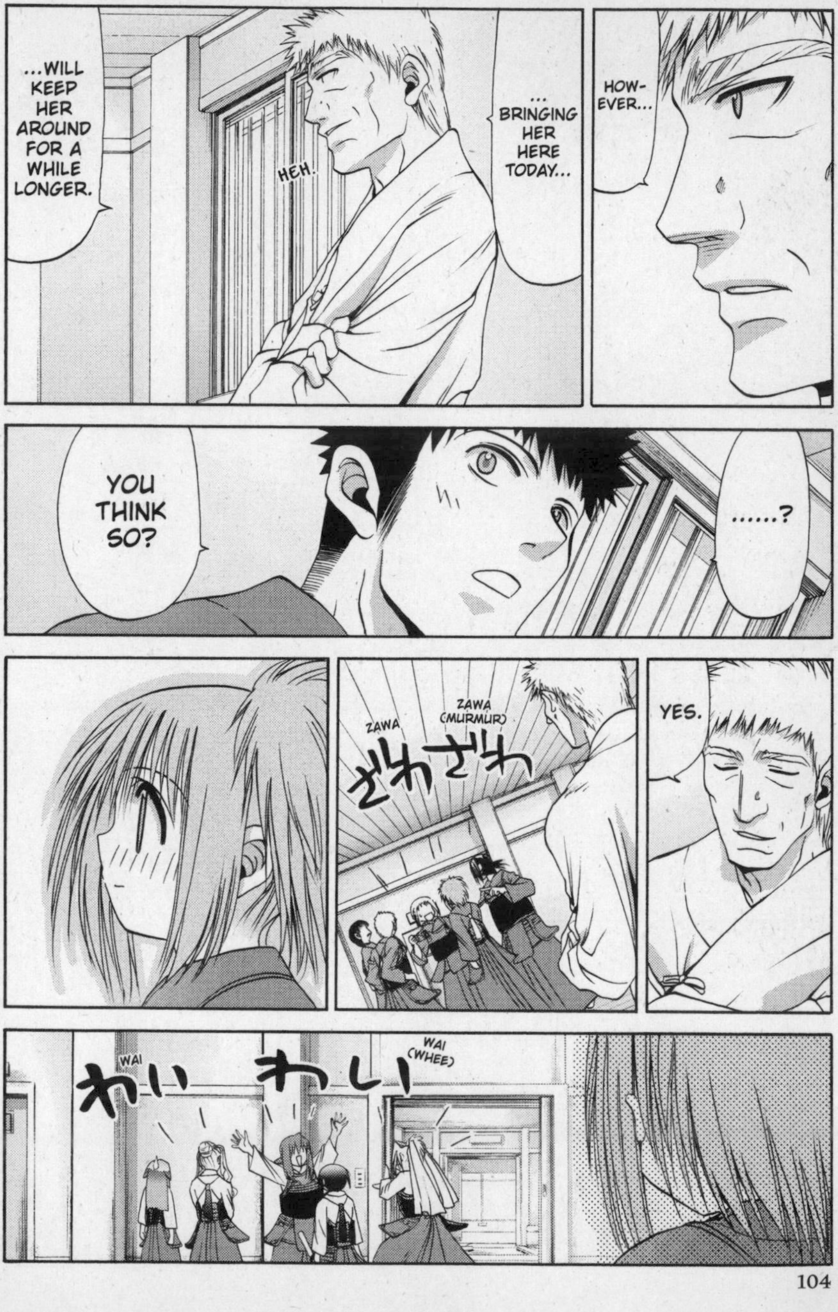
HOW-EVER...
...BRINGING HER HERE TODAY...
HEH!
...WILL KEEP HER AROUND FOR A WHILE LONGER.
......?
YOU THINK SO?
YES.
ZAWA (MURMUR)
ZAWA
ざわざわ
WAI (WHEE)
WAI
わいわい

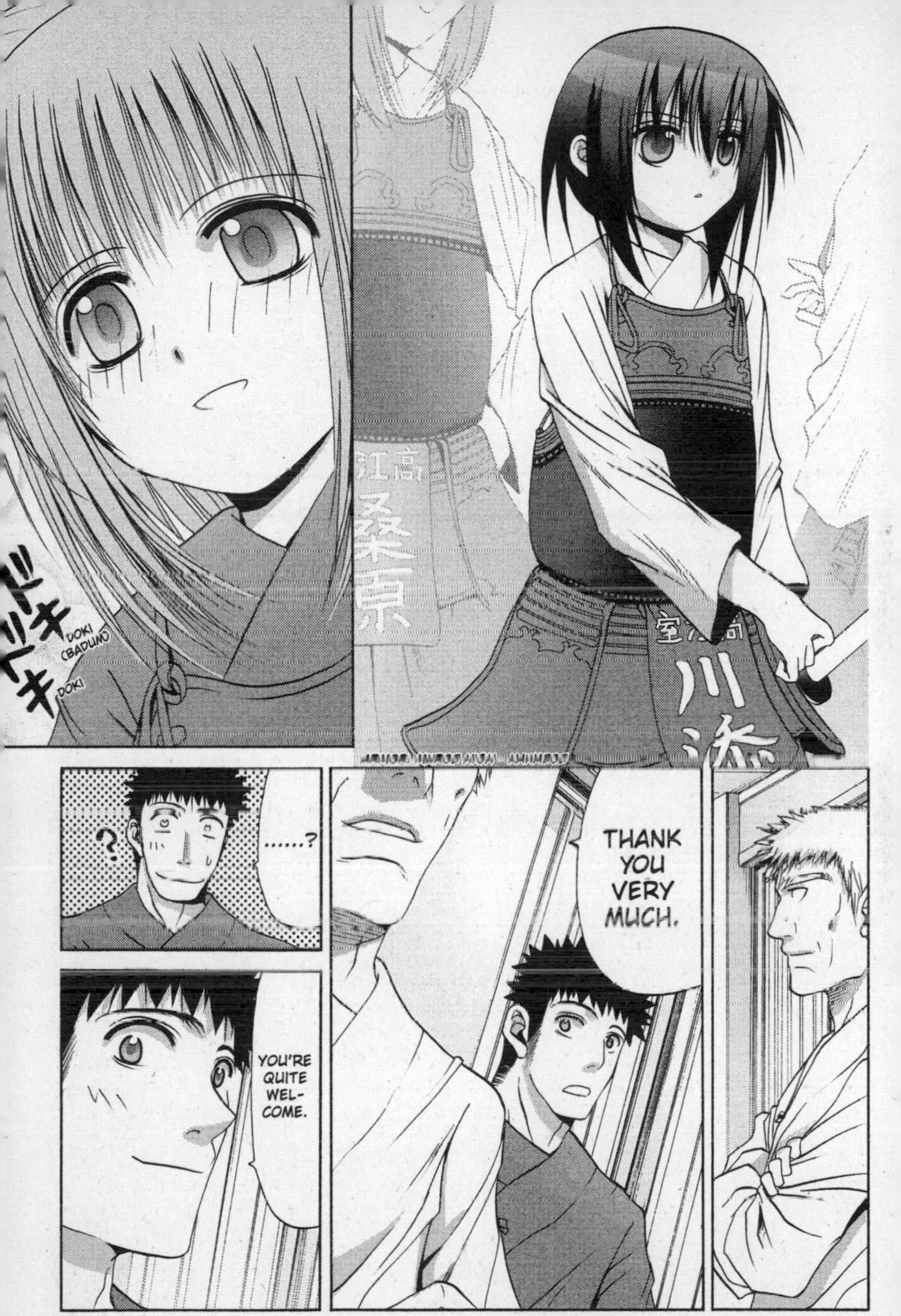
江高
桑原
ドキ
ドキ
DOKI (BADUM)
DOKI
THANK YOU VERY MUCH.
?
......?
YOU'RE QUITE WEL-COME.

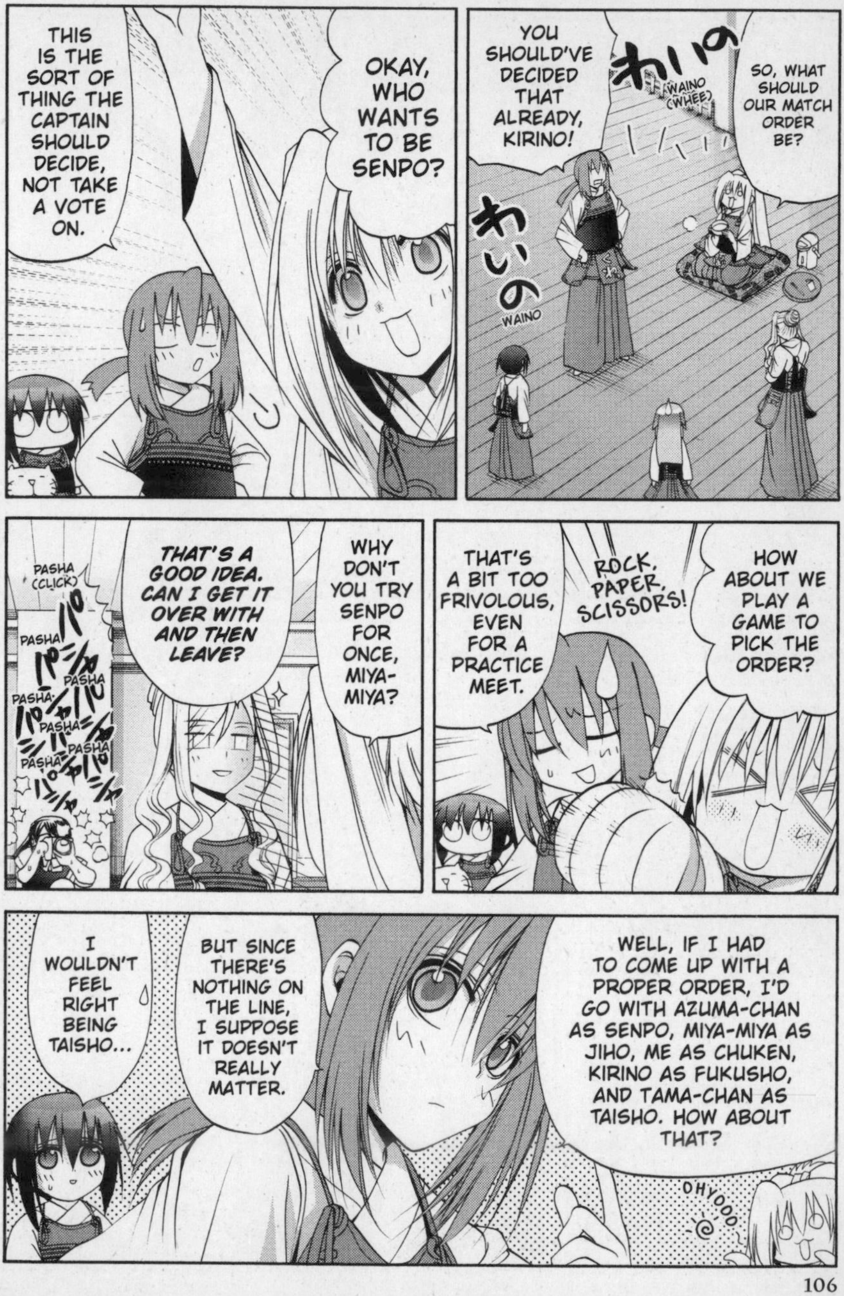
SO, WHAT SHOULD OUR MATCH ORDER BE?
わいの
WAINO (WHEE)
YOU SHOULD'VE DECIDED THAT ALREADY, KIRINO!
わいの
WAINO
OKAY, WHO WANTS TO BE SENPO?
THIS IS THE SORT OF THING THE CAPTAIN SHOULD DECIDE, NOT TAKE A VOTE ON.
HOW ABOUT WE PLAY A GAME TO PICK THE ORDER?
ROCK, PAPER, SCISSORS!
THAT'S A BIT TOO FRIVOLOUS, EVEN FOR A PRACTICE MEET.
WHY DON'T YOU TRY SENPO FOR ONCE, MIYA-MIYA?
THAT'S A GOOD IDEA. CAN I GET IT OVER WITH AND THEN LEAVE?
PASHA (CLICK)
PASHA
PASHA
PASHA
PASHA
PASHA
PASHA
WELL, IF I HAD TO COME UP WITH A PROPER ORDER, I'D GO WITH AZUMA-CHAN AS SENPO, MIYA-MIYA AS JIHO, ME AS CHUKEN, KIRINO AS FUKUSHO, AND TAMA-CHAN AS TAISHO. HOW ABOUT THAT?
OHYOOO
BUT SINCE THERE'S NOTHING ON THE LINE, I SUPPOSE IT DOESN'T REALLY MATTER.
I WOULDN'T FEEL RIGHT BEING TAISHO...

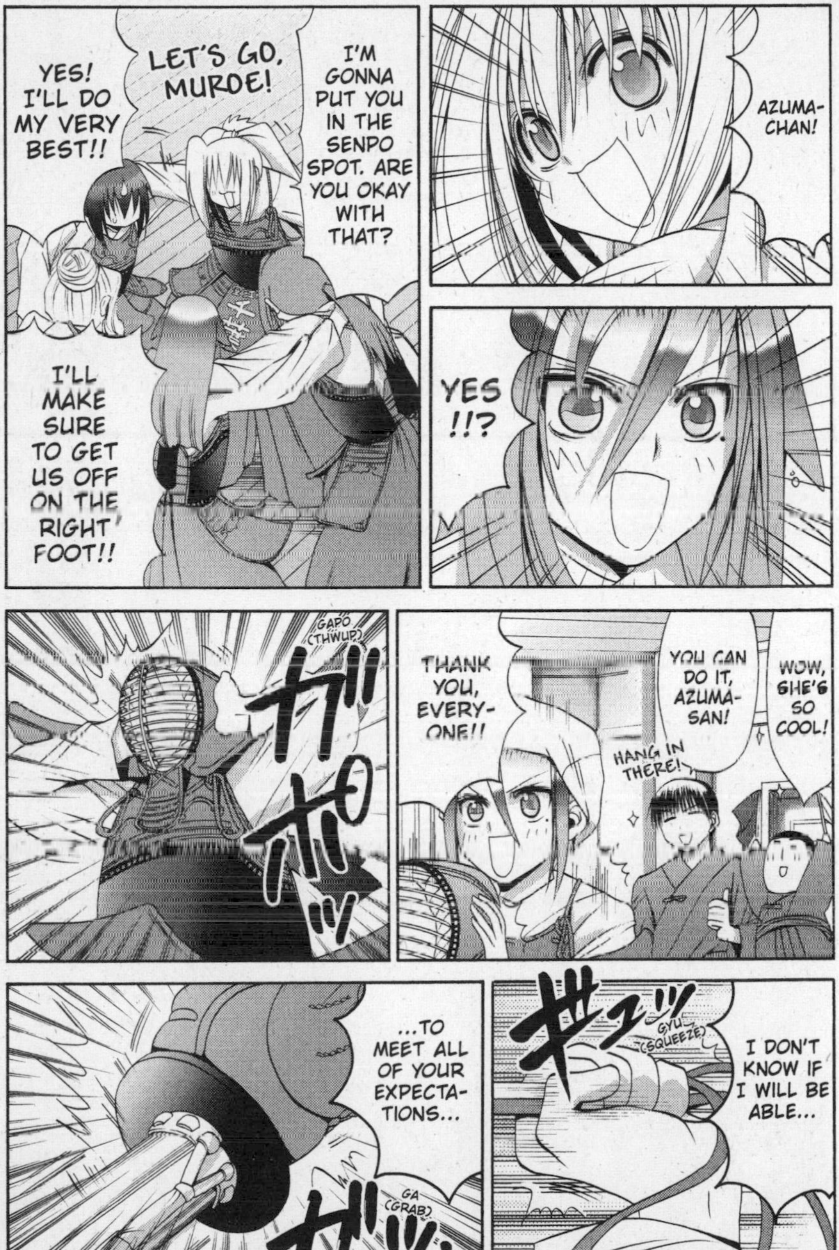
AZUMA-CHAN!
YES!!?
I'M GONNA PUT YOU IN THE SENPO SPOT. ARE YOU OKAY WITH THAT?
LET'S GO, MURDE!
YES! I'LL DO MY VERY BEST!!
I'LL MAKE SURE TO GET US OFF ON THE RIGHT FOOT!!
WOW, SHE'S SO COOL!
YOU CAN DO IT, AZUMA-SAN!
HANG IN THERE!
THANK YOU, EVERYONE!!
GAPO (THWUP)
GYU (SQUEEZE)
I DON'T KNOW IF I WILL BE ABLE...
...TO MEET ALL OF YOUR EXPECTATIONS...
GA (GRAB)

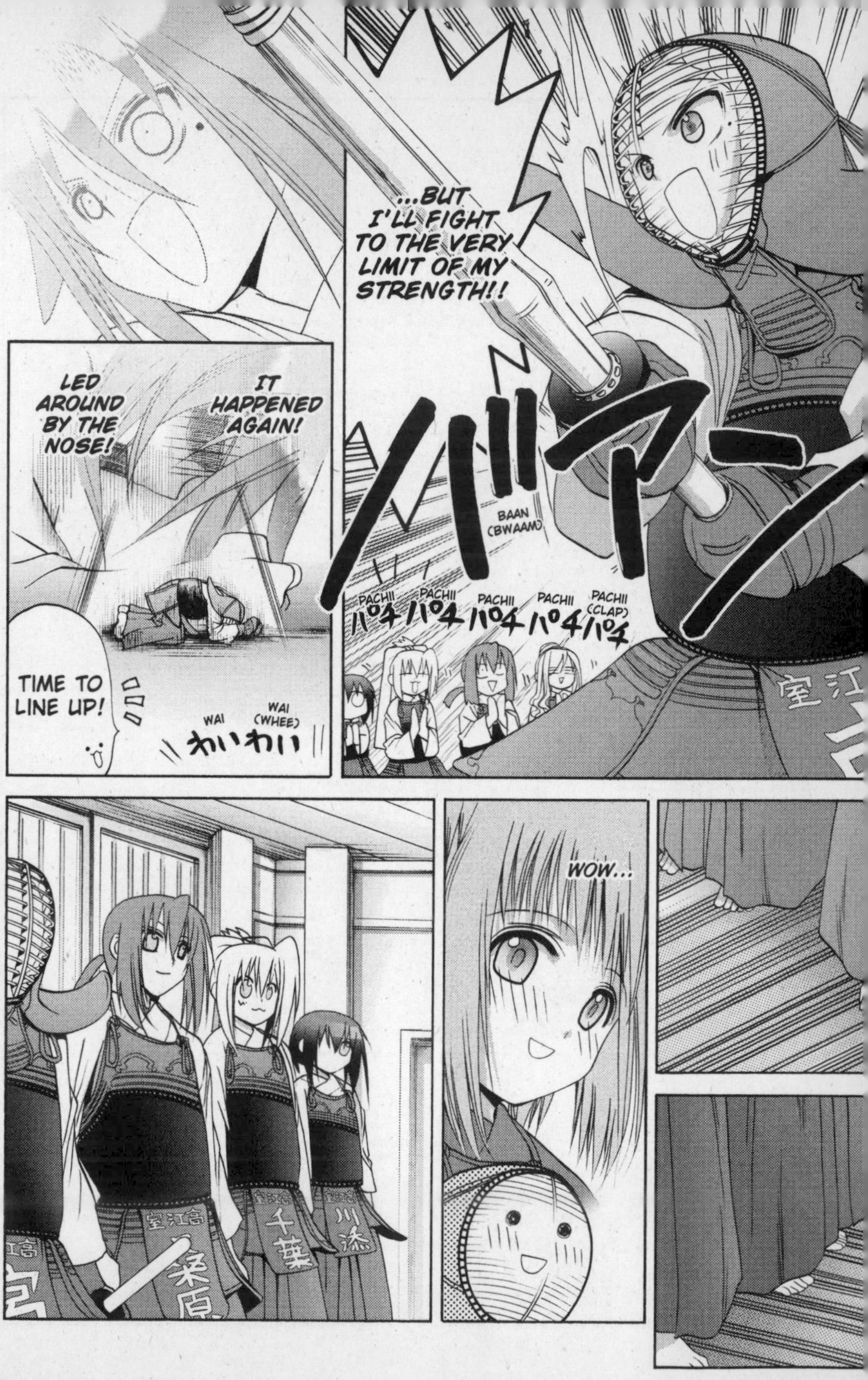
...BUT I'LL FIGHT TO THE VERY LIMIT OF MY STRENGTH!!
BAAN (BWAAM)
PACHII PACHII PACHII PACHII PACHII (CLAP)
パチパチパチパチパチ
IT HAPPENED AGAIN!
LED AROUND BY THE NOSE!
TIME TO LINE UP!
WAI WAI (WHEE)
わいわい
WOW...

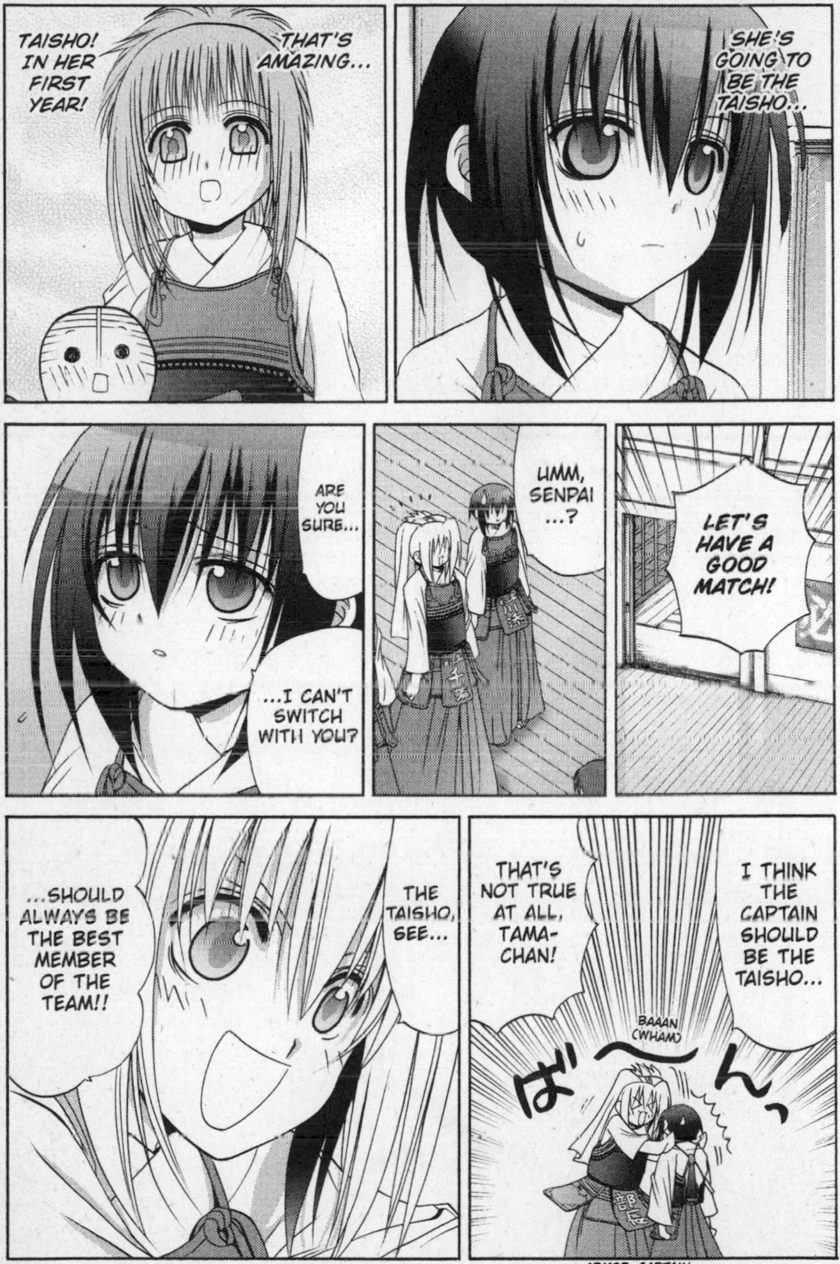
SHE'S GOING TO BE THE TAISHO...
THAT'S AMAZING...
TAISHO! IN HER FIRST YEAR!
LET'S HAVE A GOOD MATCH!
UMM, SENPAI...?
ARE YOU SURE...
...I CAN'T SWITCH WITH YOU?
I THINK THE CAPTAIN SHOULD BE THE TAISHO...
THAT'S NOT TRUE AT ALL, TAMA-CHAN!
BAAAN (WHAM)
ば〜ん
THE TAISHO, SEE...
...SHOULD ALWAYS BE THE BEST MEMBER OF THE TEAM!!

ARMOR: CAPTAIN

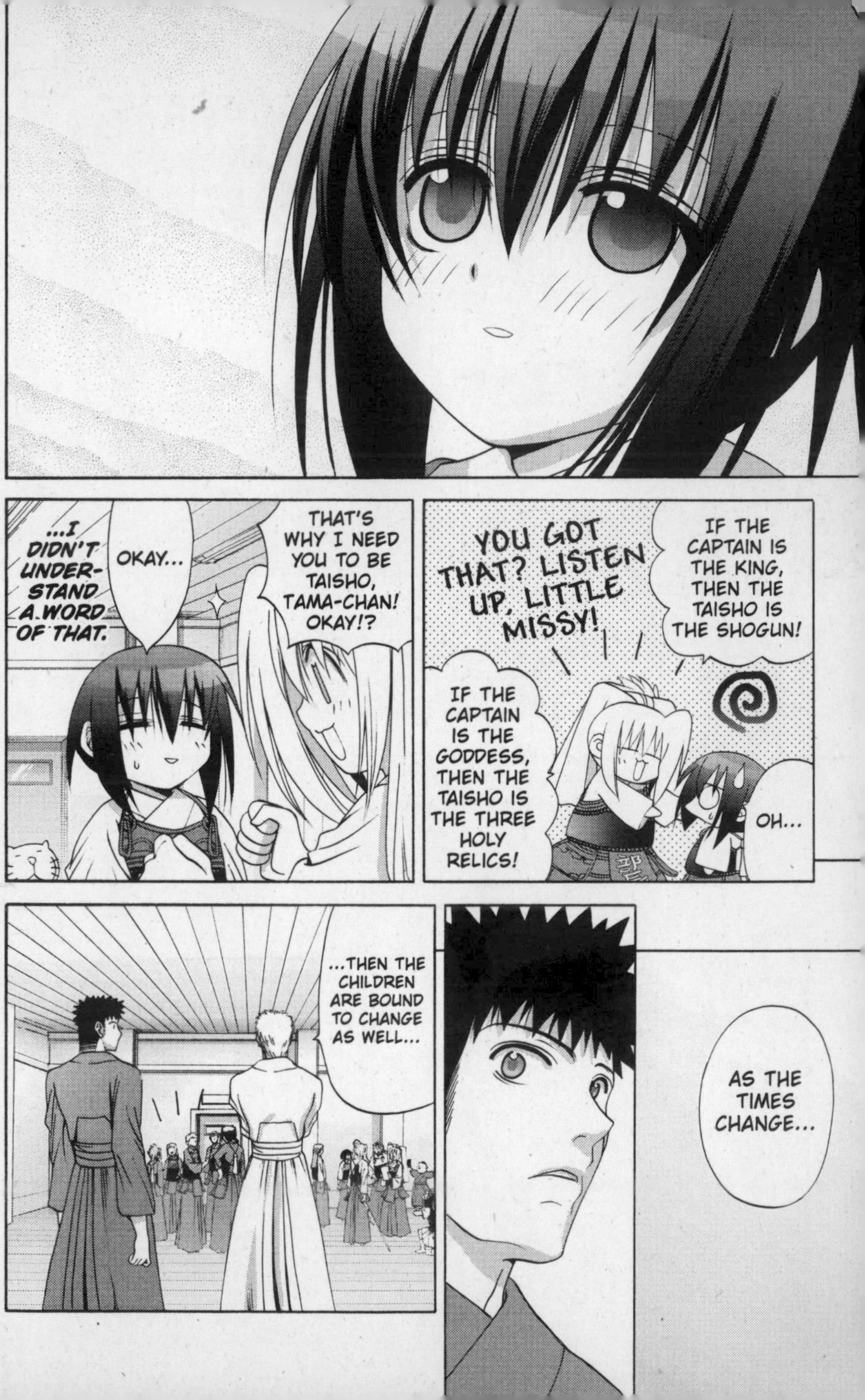
IF THE CAPTAIN IS THE KING, THEN THE TAISHO IS THE SHOGUN!
YOU GOT THAT? LISTEN UP, LITTLE MISSY!
IF THE CAPTAIN IS THE GODDESS, THEN THE TAISHO IS THE THREE HOLY RELICS!
OH...
THAT'S WHY I NEED YOU TO BE TAISHO, TAMA-CHAN! OKAY!?
OKAY...
...I DIDN'T UNDER-STAND A WORD OF THAT.
AS THE TIMES CHANGE...
...THEN THE CHILDREN ARE BOUND TO CHANGE AS WELL...

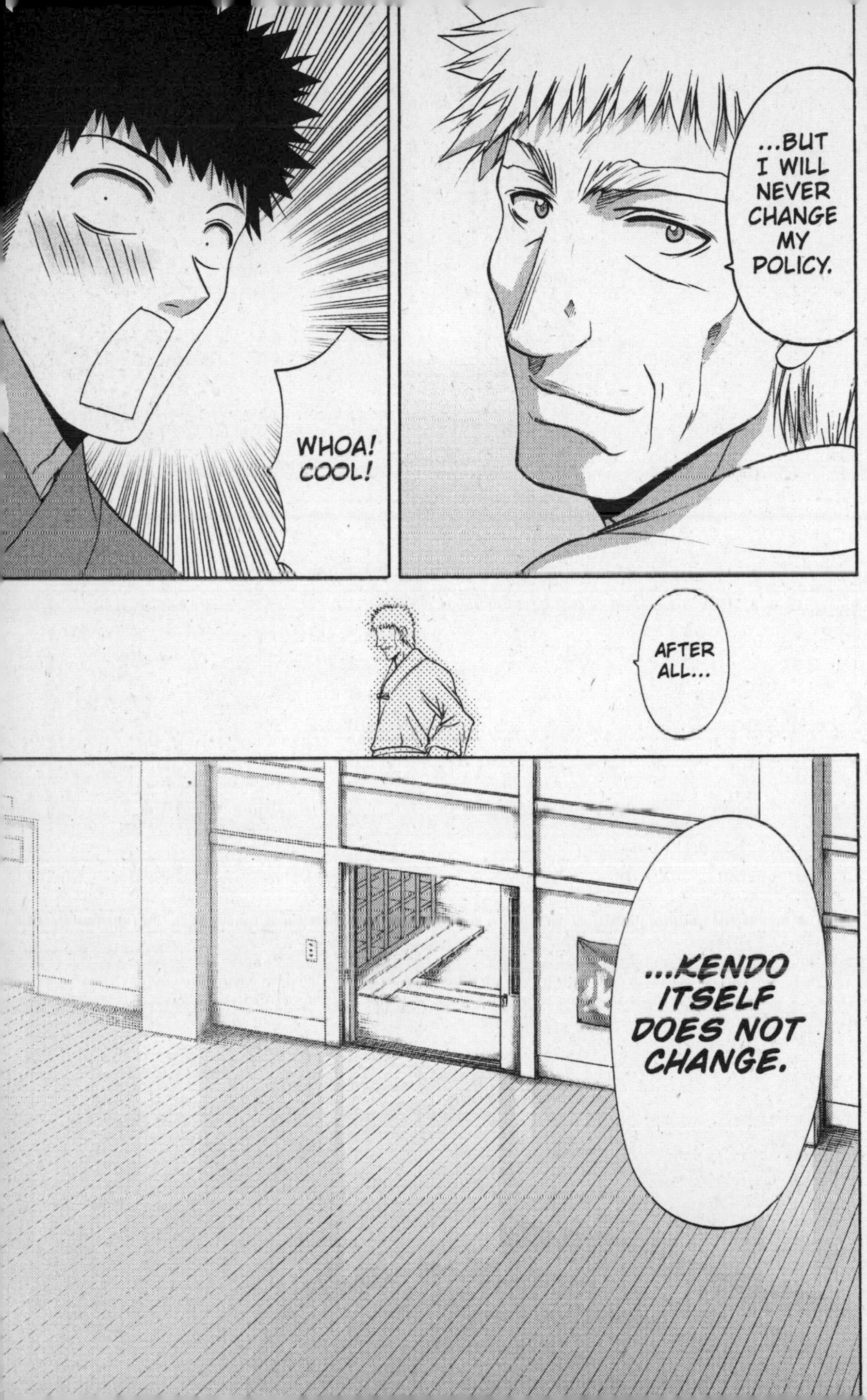
...BUT I WILL NEVER CHANGE MY POLICY.
WHOA! COOL!
AFTER ALL...
...KENDO ITSELF DOES NOT CHANGE.

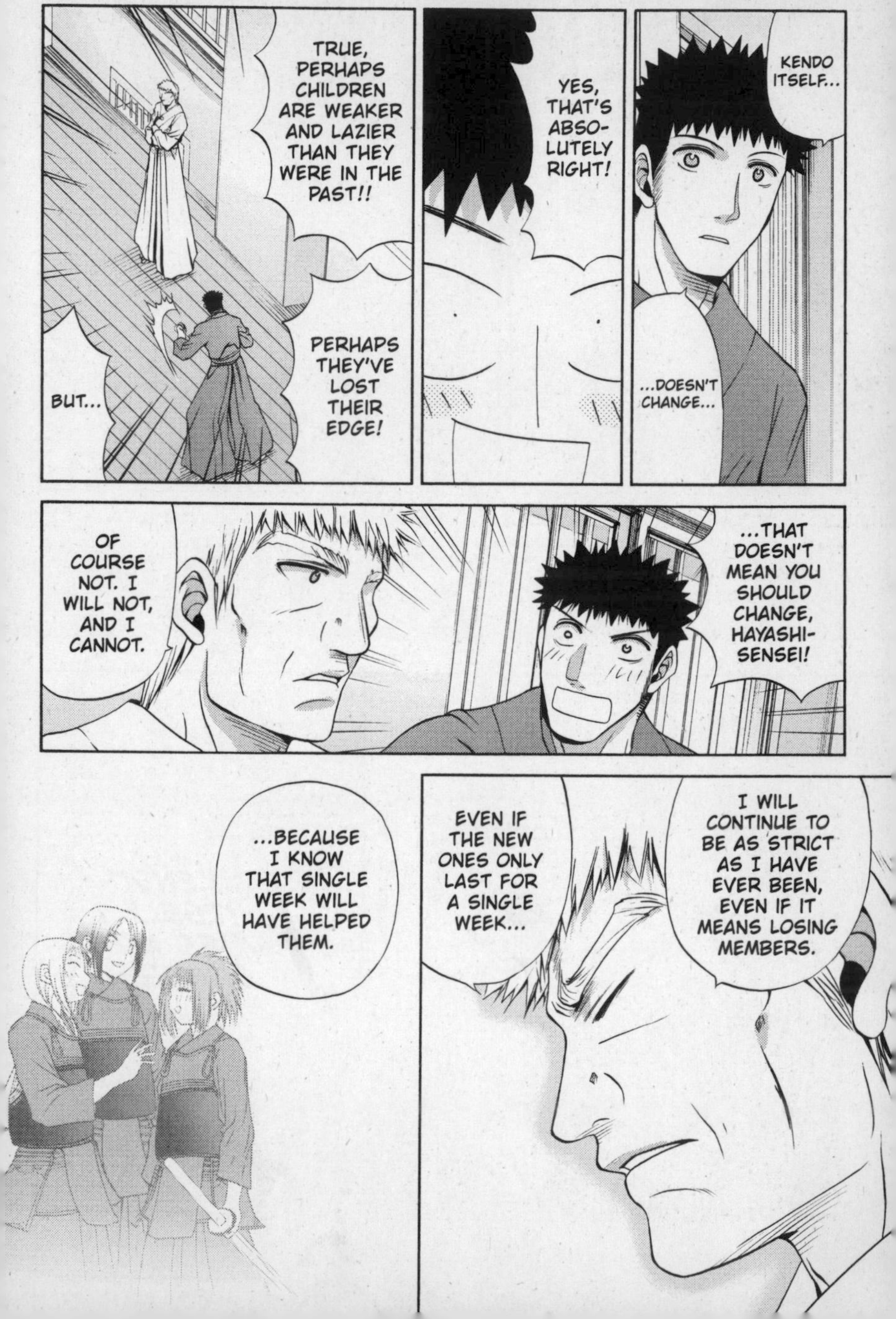
KENDO ITSELF...
...DOESN'T CHANGE...
YES, THAT'S ABSOLUTELY RIGHT!
TRUE, PERHAPS CHILDREN ARE WEAKER AND LAZIER THAN THEY WERE IN THE PAST!!
PERHAPS THEY'VE LOST THEIR EDGE!
BUT...
...THAT DOESN'T MEAN YOU SHOULD CHANGE, HAYASHI-SENSEI!
OF COURSE NOT. I WILL NOT, AND I CANNOT.
I WILL CONTINUE TO BE AS STRICT AS I HAVE EVER BEEN, EVEN IF IT MEANS LOSING MEMBERS.
EVEN IF THE NEW ONES ONLY LAST FOR A SINGLE WEEK...
...BECAUSE I KNOW THAT SINGLE WEEK WILL HAVE HELPED THEM.

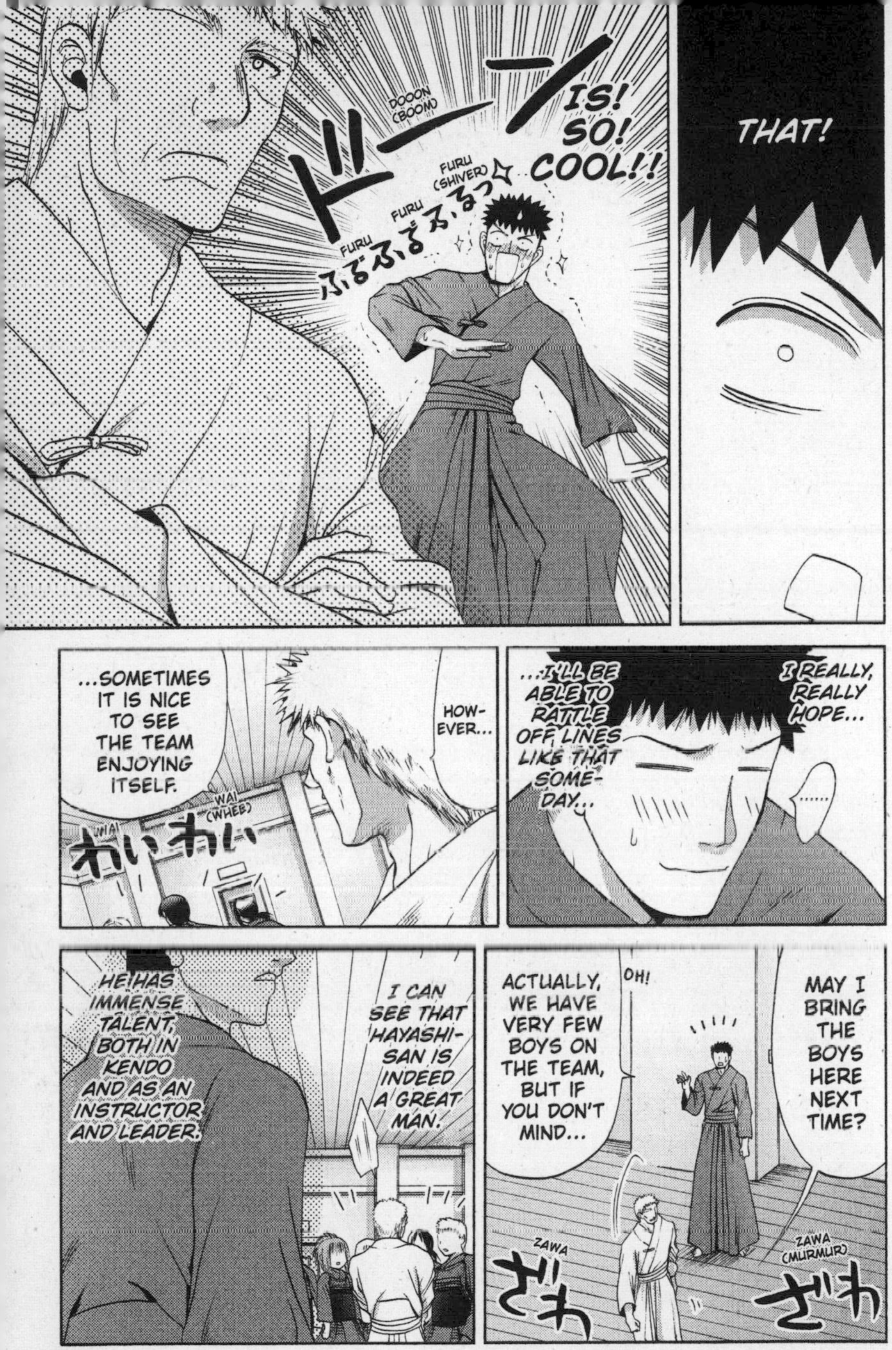

THAT!
IS! SO! COOL!!
DOOON (BOOM)
ドーーン
FURU FURU FURU (SHIVER)
ぶるぶるぶるっ
I REALLY, REALLY HOPE...
...I'LL BE ABLE TO RATTLE OFF LINES LIKE THAT SOME-DAY...
......
HOW-EVER...
...SOMETIMES IT IS NICE TO SEE THE TEAM ENJOYING ITSELF.
WAI WAI (WHEE)
わいわい
MAY I BRING THE BOYS HERE NEXT TIME?
OH!
ACTUALLY, WE HAVE VERY FEW BOYS ON THE TEAM, BUT IF YOU DON'T MIND...
ZAWA (MURMUR)
ざわ
ZAWA
ざわ
I CAN SEE THAT HAYASHI-SAN IS INDEED A GREAT MAN.
HE HAS IMMENSE TALENT, BOTH IN KENDO AND AS AN INSTRUCTOR AND LEADER.

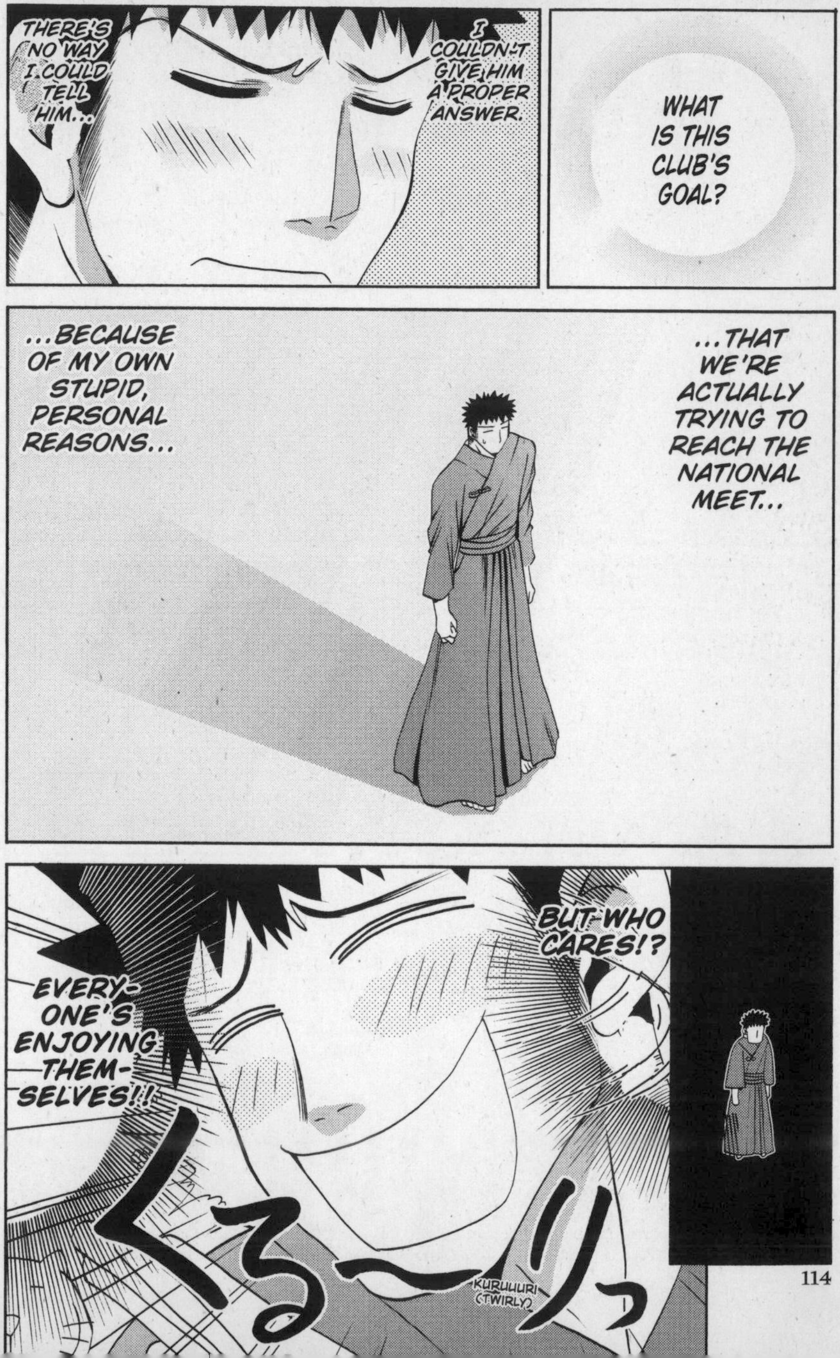
WHAT IS THIS CLUB'S GOAL?
I COULDN'T GIVE HIM A PROPER ANSWER.
THERE'S NO WAY I COULD TELL HIM...
...THAT WE'RE ACTUALLY TRYING TO REACH THE NATIONAL MEET...
...BECAUSE OF MY OWN STUPID, PERSONAL REASONS...
BUT WHO CARES!?
EVERY-ONE'S ENJOYING THEM-SELVES!!
くる～りっ
KURUUURI (TWIRLY)

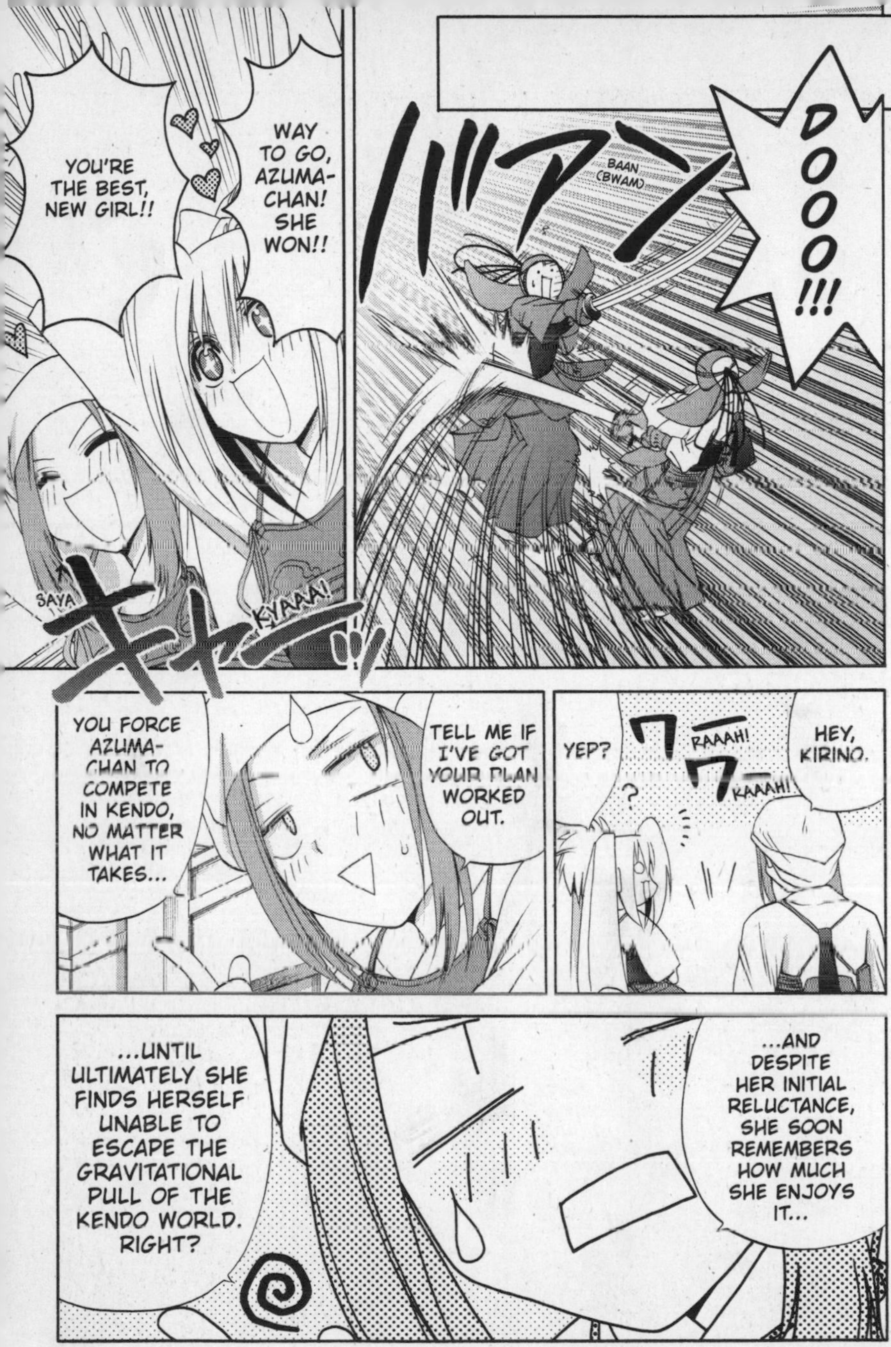
DOOOO!!!
BAAN (BWAM)
WAY TO GO, AZUMA-CHAN! SHE WON!!
YOU'RE THE BEST, NEW GIRL!!
KYAAA!
SAYA
HEY, KIRINO.
RAAAH!
KAAAH!
YEP?
TELL ME IF I'VE GOT YOUR PLAN WORKED OUT.
YOU FORCE AZUMA-CHAN TO COMPETE IN KENDO, NO MATTER WHAT IT TAKES...
...AND DESPITE HER INITIAL RELUCTANCE, SHE SOON REMEMBERS HOW MUCH SHE ENJOYS IT...
...UNTIL ULTIMATELY SHE FINDS HERSELF UNABLE TO ESCAPE THE GRAVITATIONAL PULL OF THE KENDO WORLD. RIGHT?

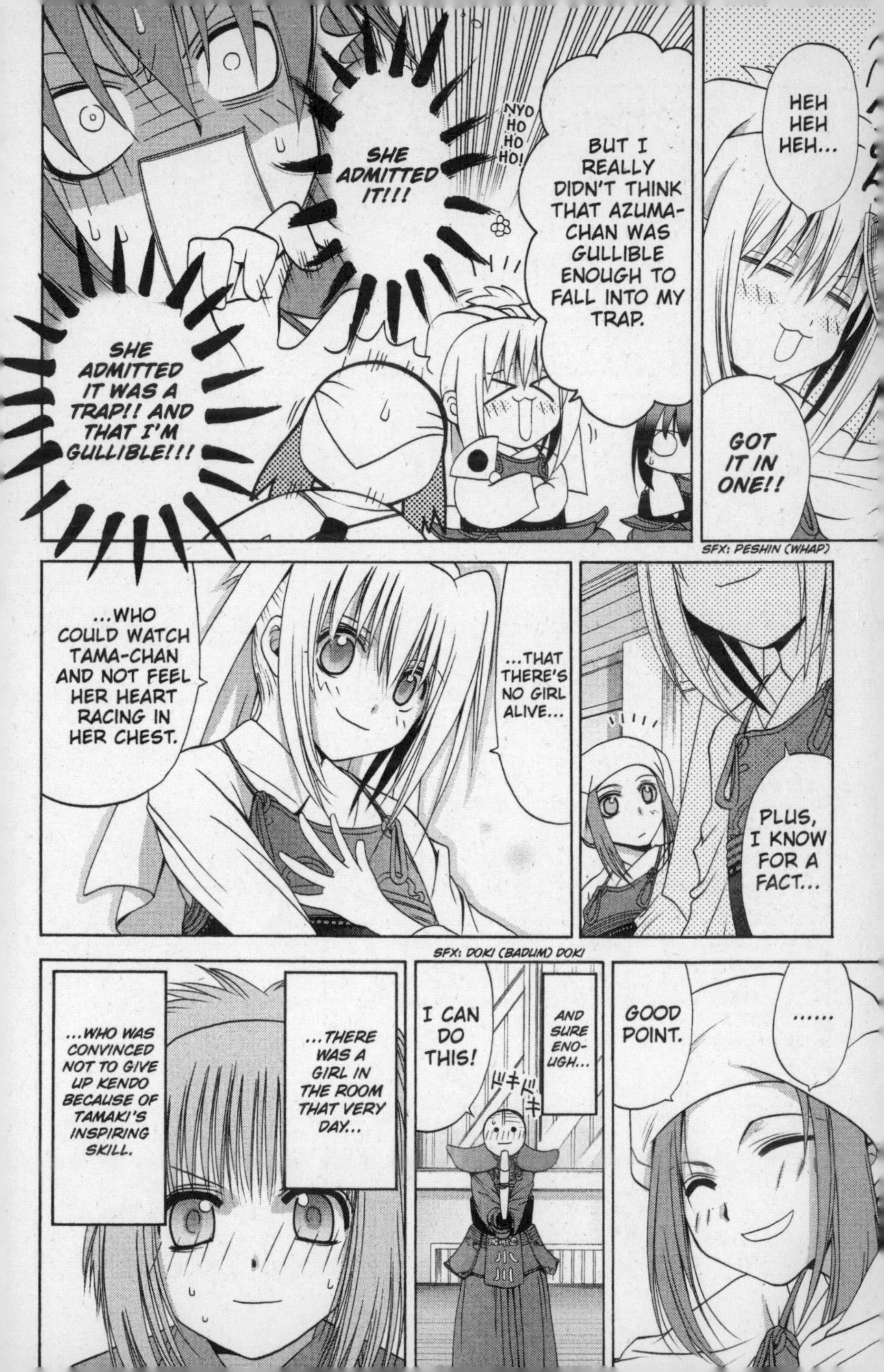
HEH HEH HEH...
GOT IT IN ONE!!
SFX: PESHIN (WHAP)
BUT I REALLY DIDN'T THINK THAT AZUMA-CHAN WAS GULLIBLE ENOUGH TO FALL INTO MY TRAP.
NYO HO HO HO!
SHE ADMITTED IT!!!
SHE ADMITTED IT WAS A TRAP!! AND THAT I'M GULLIBLE!!!
PLUS, I KNOW FOR A FACT...
...THAT THERE'S NO GIRL ALIVE...
...WHO COULD WATCH TAMA-CHAN AND NOT FEEL HER HEART RACING IN HER CHEST.
SFX: DOKI (BADUM) DOKI
......
GOOD POINT.
AND SURE ENOUGH...
I CAN DO THIS!
ドキドキ
...THERE WAS A GIRL IN THE ROOM THAT VERY DAY...
...WHO WAS CONVINCED NOT TO GIVE UP KENDO BECAUSE OF TAMAKI'S INSPIRING SKILL.

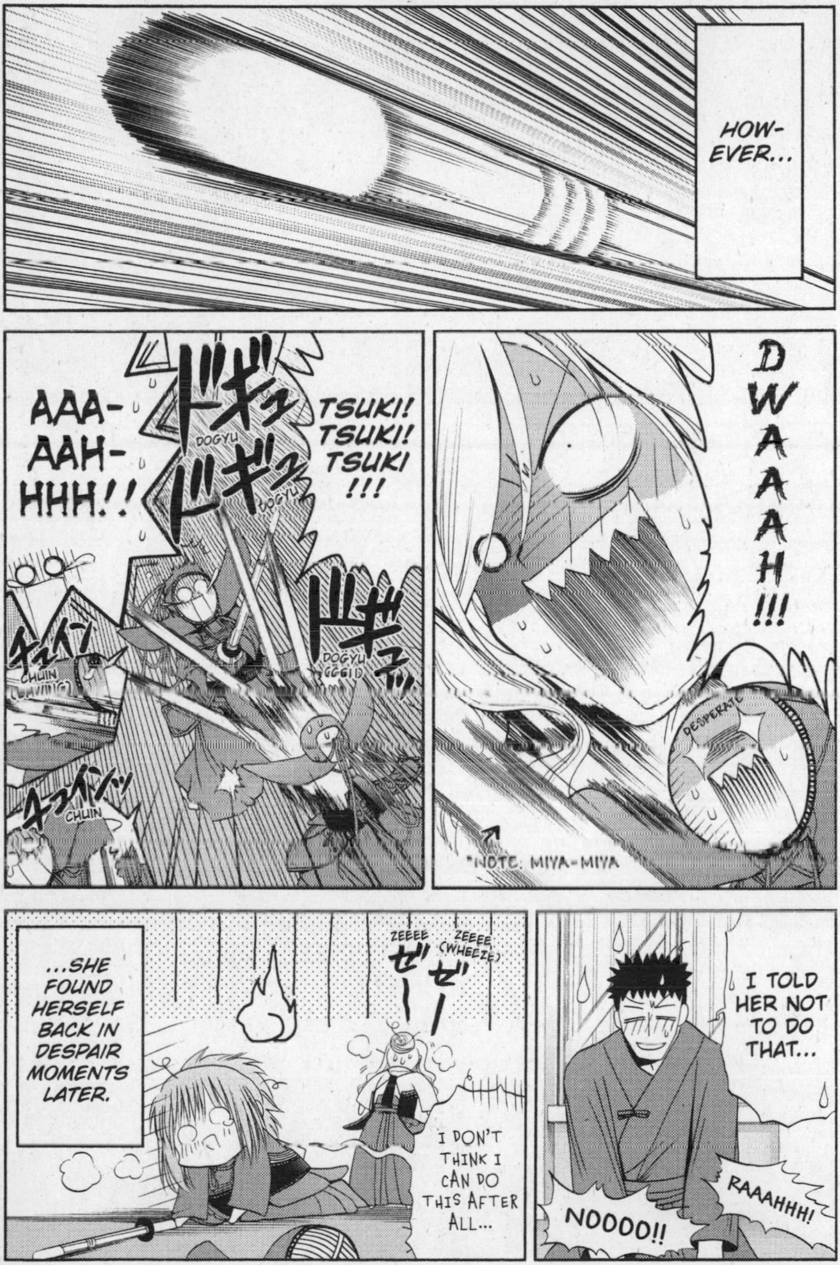
HOW-EVER...
DWAAAAH!!!
DESPERAT
*NOTE: MIYA-MIYA
TSUKI! TSUKI! TSUKI!!!
AAA-AAH-HHH!!
DOGYU
DOGYU
DOGYU
CHUIN
CHUIN
I TOLD HER NOT TO DO THAT...
RAAAHHH!
NOOOO!!
ZEEEE
ZEEEE (WHEEZE)
...SHE FOUND HERSELF BACK IN DESPAIR MOMENTS LATER.
I DON'T THINK I CAN DO THIS AFTER ALL...

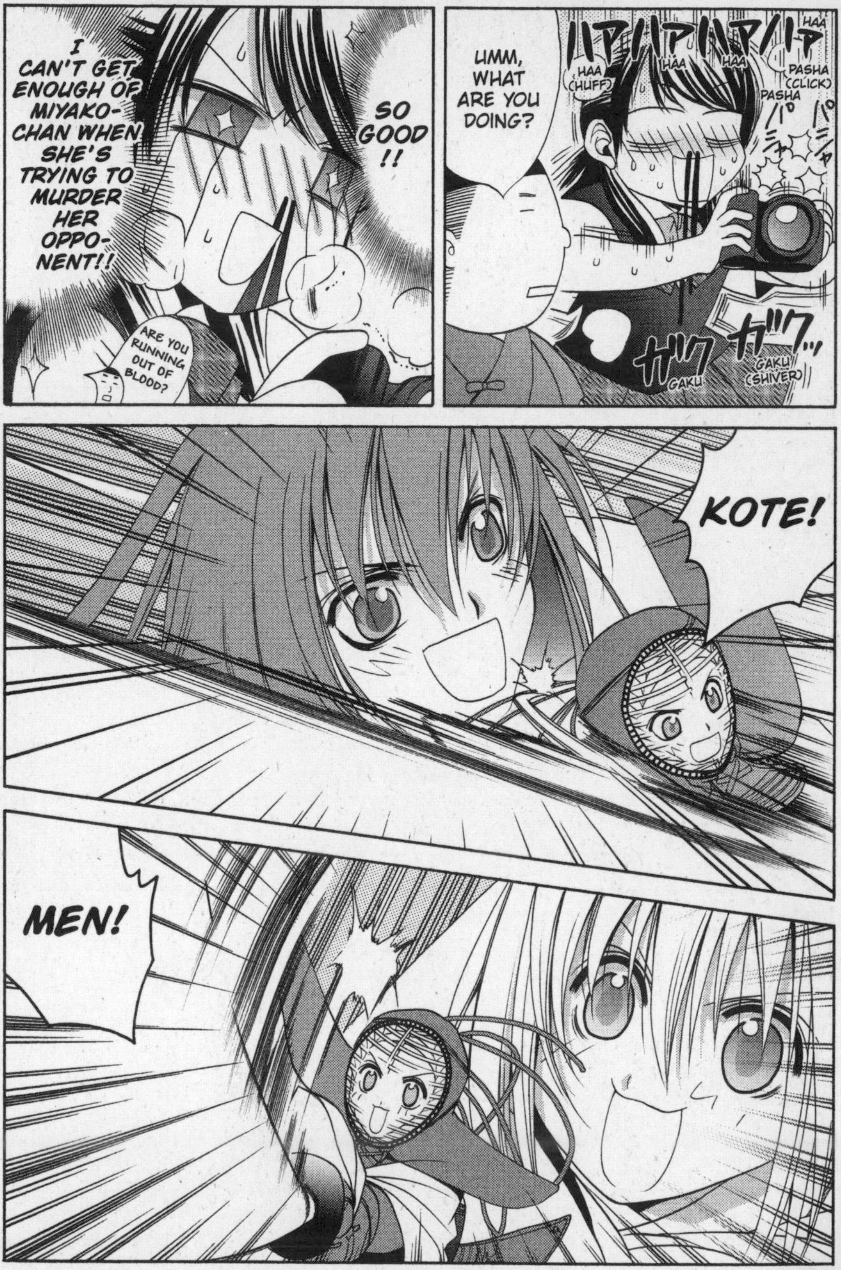
UMM, WHAT ARE YOU DOING?
ハァハァハァハァ
HAA HAA HAA HAA (HUFF)
パシャ パシャ
PASHA (CLICK) PASHA
ガクガク
GAKU GAKU (SHIVER)
I CAN'T GET ENOUGH OF MIYAKO-CHAN WHEN SHE'S TRYING TO MURDER HER OPPO-NENT!!
SO GOOD!!
ARE YOU RUNNING OUT OF BLOOD?
KOTE!
MEN!

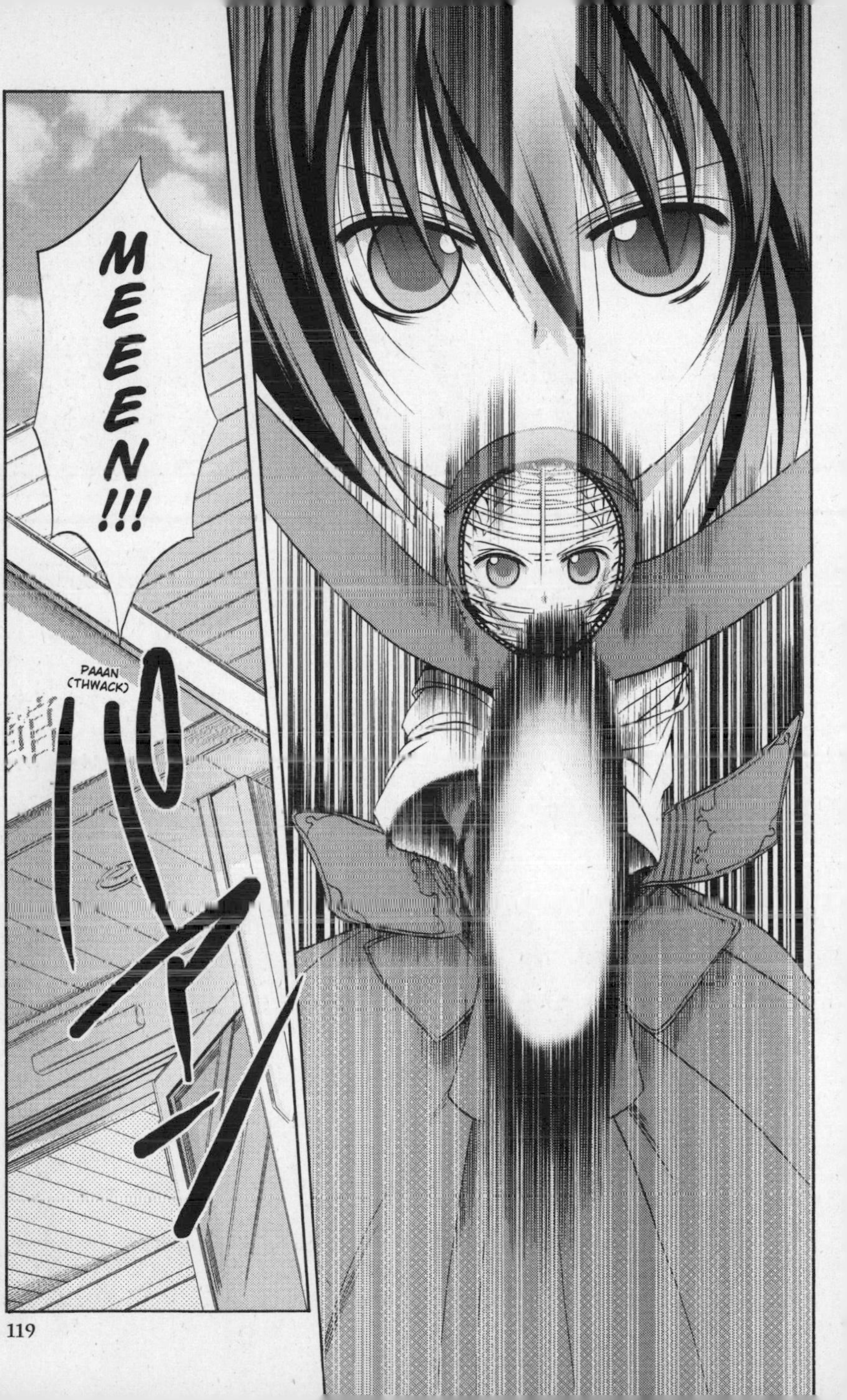
MEEEEN!!!
PAAAN (THWACK)

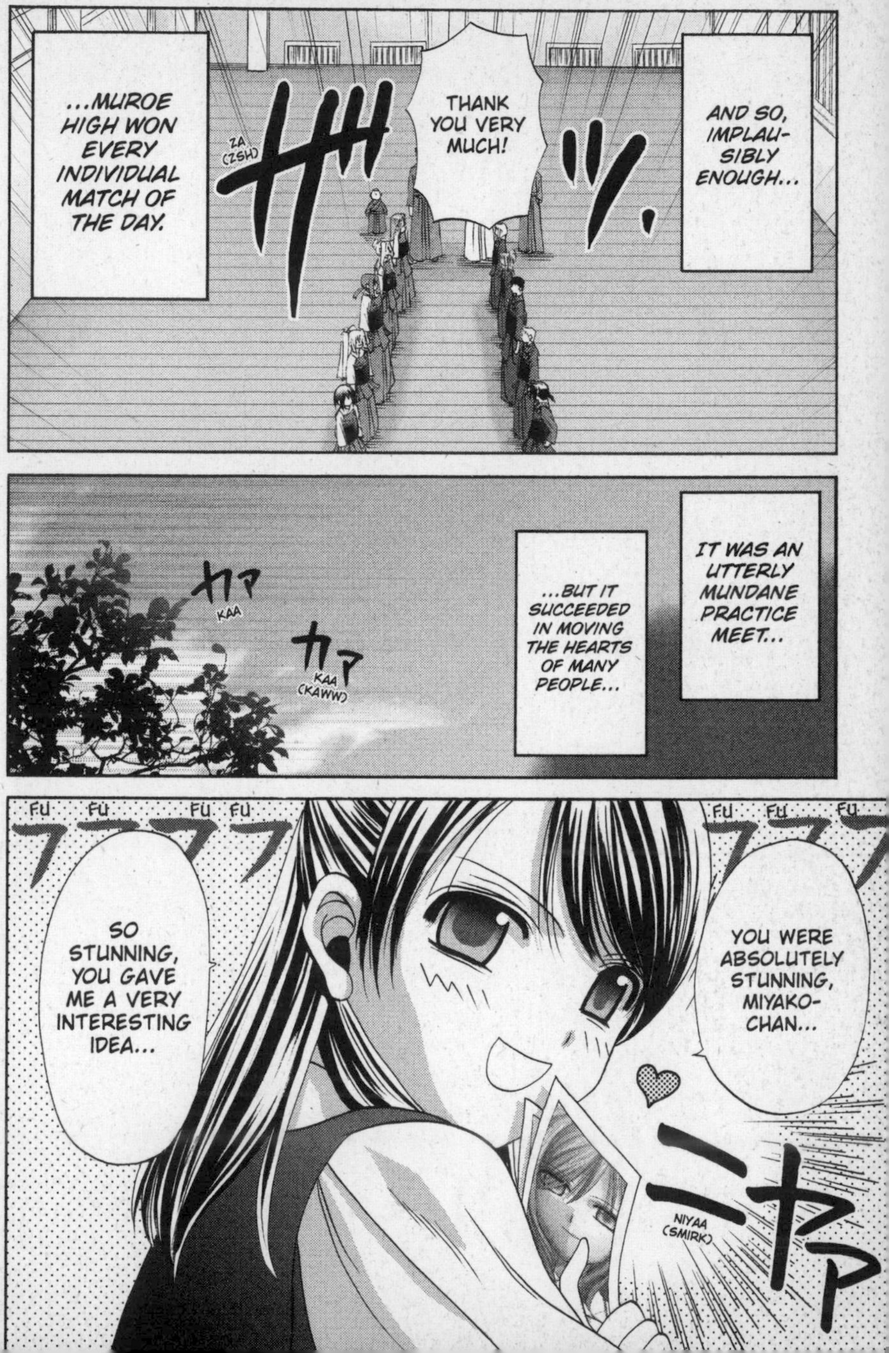

AND SO, IMPLAUSIBLY ENOUGH...
THANK YOU VERY MUCH!
ZA (ZSH)
...MUROE HIGH WON EVERY INDIVIDUAL MATCH OF THE DAY.
IT WAS AN UTTERLY MUNDANE PRACTICE MEET...
...BUT IT SUCCEEDED IN MOVING THE HEARTS OF MANY PEOPLE...
KAA (KAWW)
KAA
FU FU FU
YOU WERE ABSOLUTELY STUNNING, MIYAKO-CHAN...
NIYAA (SMIRK)
SO STUNNING, YOU GAVE ME A VERY INTERESTING IDEA...
FU FU FU FU

BAMBOO BLADE

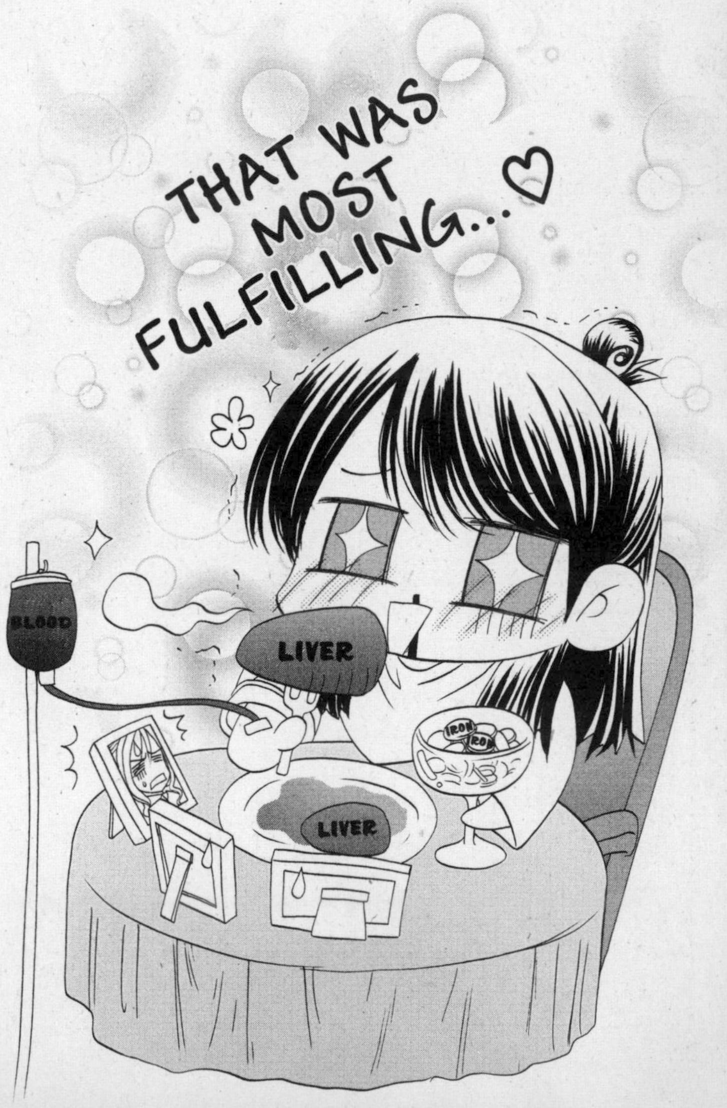
THAT WAS MOST FULFILLING...♡
BLOOD
LIVER
LIVER
IRON
IRON

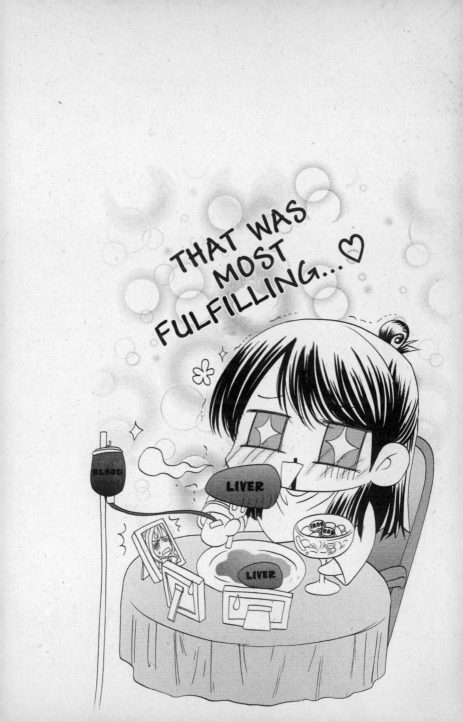

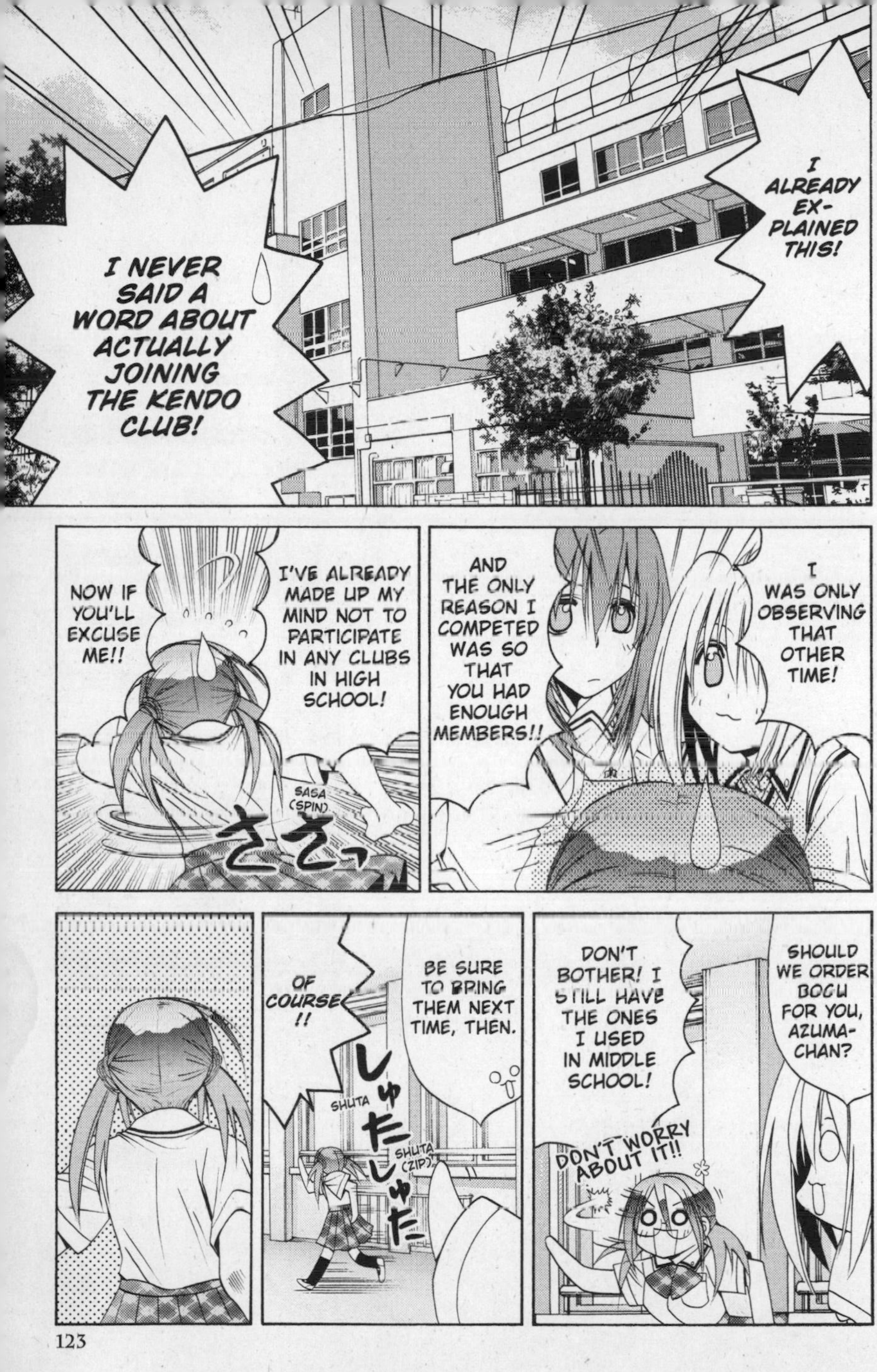
I ALREADY EX-PLAINED THIS!
I NEVER SAID A WORD ABOUT ACTUALLY JOINING THE KENDO CLUB!
I WAS ONLY OBSERVING THAT OTHER TIME!
AND THE ONLY REASON I COMPETED WAS SO THAT YOU HAD ENOUGH MEMBERS!!
I'VE ALREADY MADE UP MY MIND NOT TO PARTICIPATE IN ANY CLUBS IN HIGH SCHOOL!
NOW IF YOU'LL EXCUSE ME!!
SASA (SPIN)
さそっ
SHOULD WE ORDER BOGU FOR YOU, AZUMA-CHAN?
DON'T BOTHER! I STILL HAVE THE ONES I USED IN MIDDLE SCHOOL!
DON'T WORRY ABOUT IT!!
BE SURE TO BRING THEM NEXT TIME, THEN.
OF COURSE!!
SHUTA
しゅたしゅた
SHUTA (ZIP)

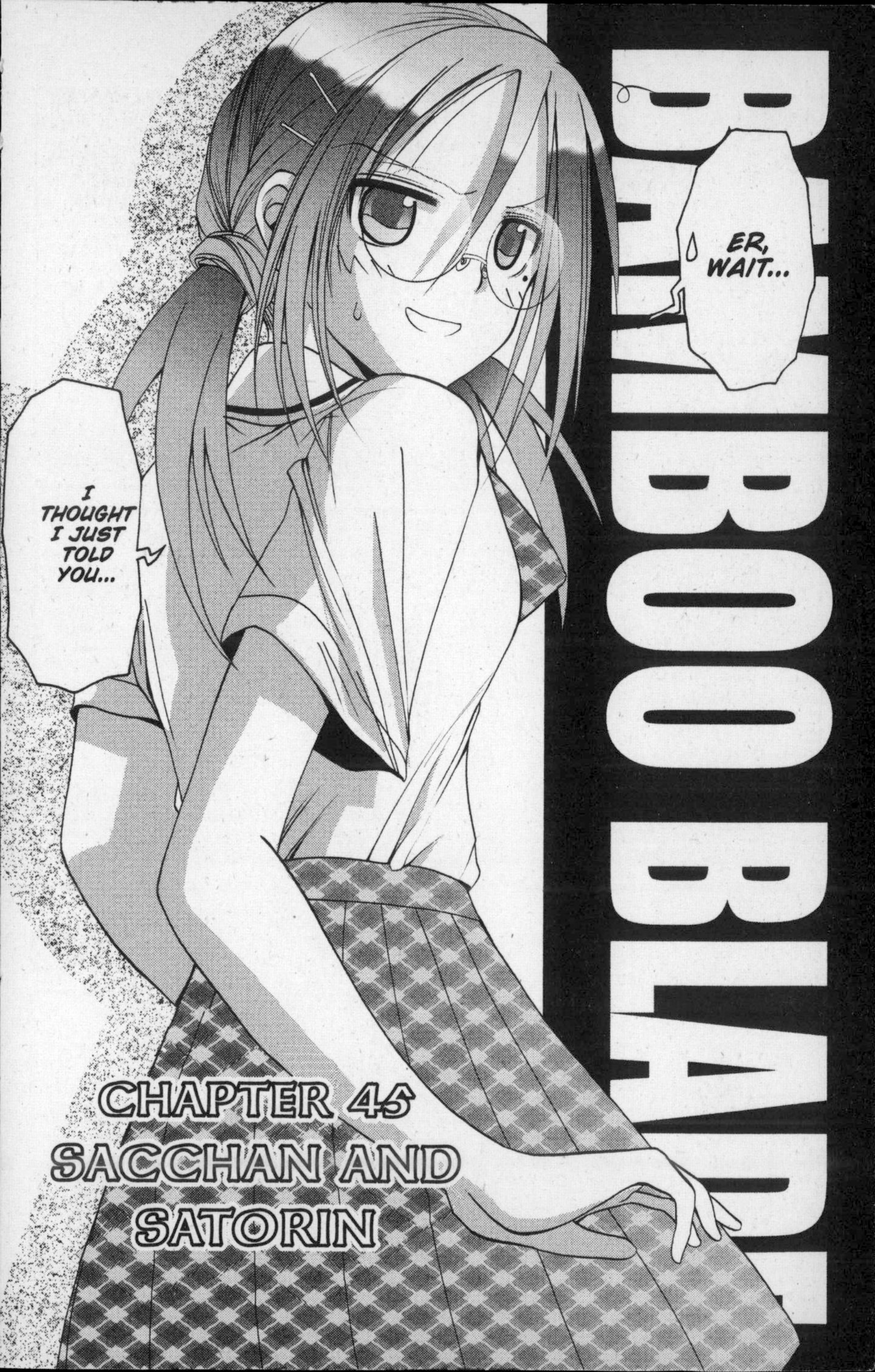
ER, WAIT...
I THOUGHT I JUST TOLD YOU...
CHAPTER 45
SACCHAN AND SATORIN

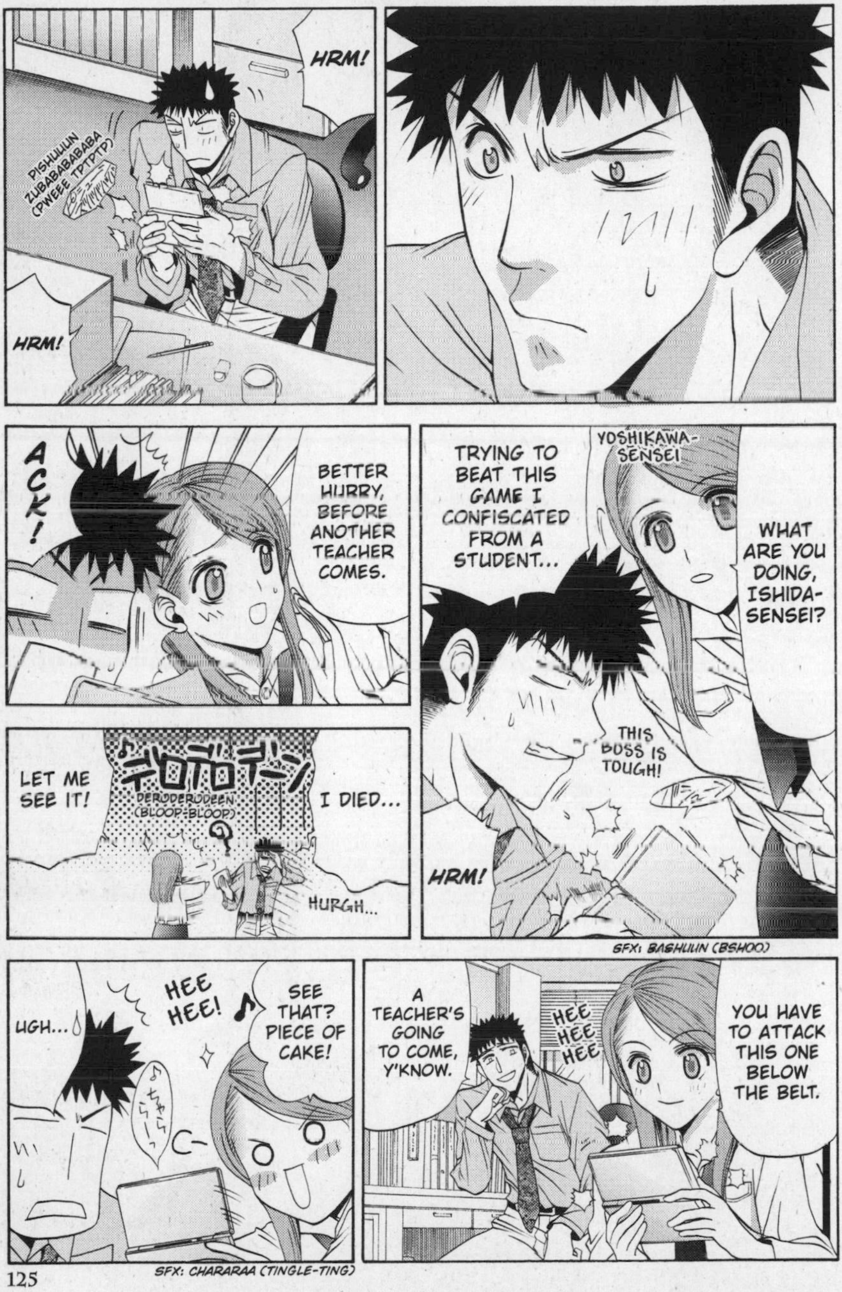
HRM!
PISHUUUN ZUBABABABABA (PWEEE TPTPTP)
HRM!
YOSHIKAWA-SENSEI
WHAT ARE YOU DOING, ISHIDA-SENSEI?
TRYING TO BEAT THIS GAME I CONFISCATED FROM A STUDENT...
THIS BOSS IS TOUGH!
HRM!
SFX: BASHUUN (BSHOO)
BETTER HURRY, BEFORE ANOTHER TEACHER COMES.
ACK!
I DIED...
DERODERODEEN (BLOOP-BLOOP)
LET ME SEE IT!
HURGH...
YOU HAVE TO ATTACK THIS ONE BELOW THE BELT.
HEE HEE HEE
A TEACHER'S GOING TO COME, Y'KNOW.
SEE THAT? PIECE OF CAKE!
HEE HEE!
UGH...
SFX: CHARARAA (TINGLE-TING)

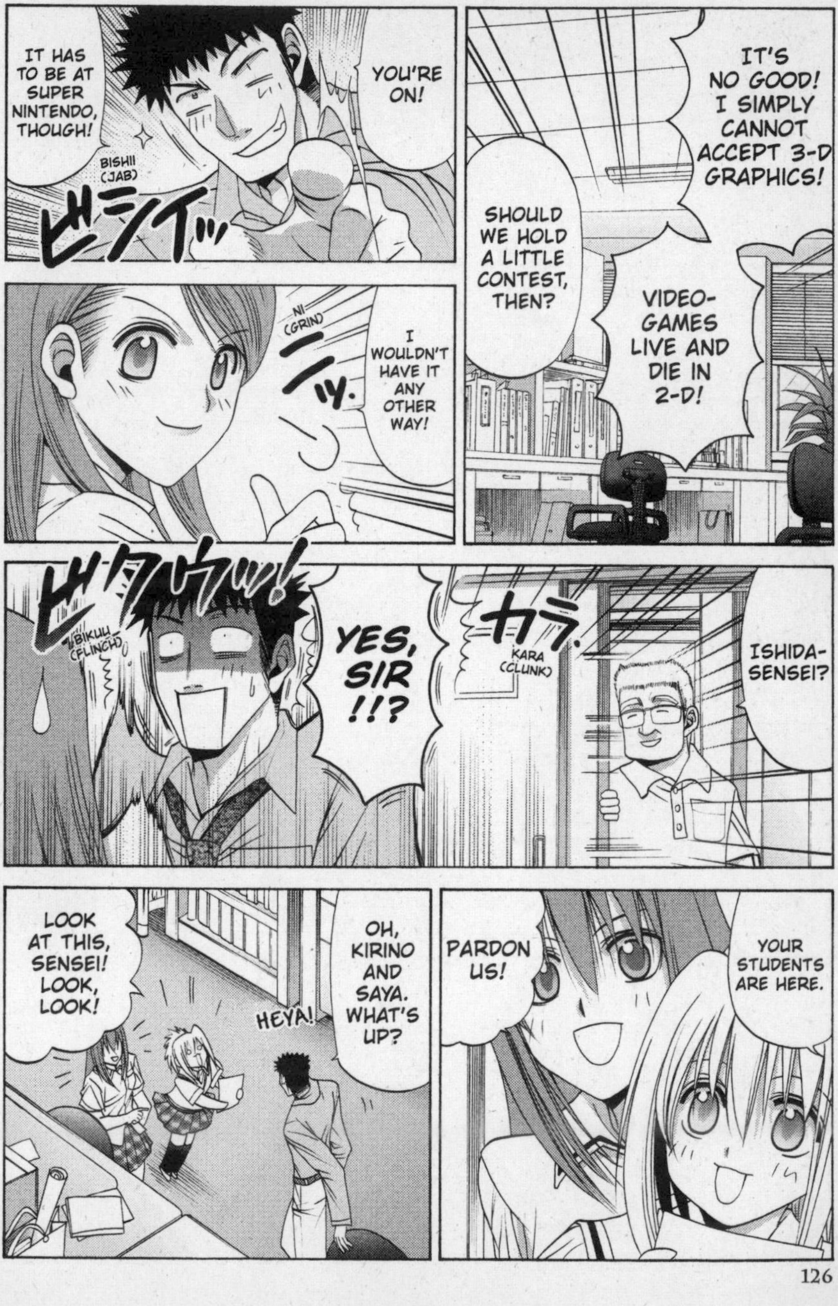
IT'S NO GOOD! I SIMPLY CANNOT ACCEPT 3-D GRAPHICS!
SHOULD WE HOLD A LITTLE CONTEST, THEN?
VIDEO-GAMES LIVE AND DIE IN 2-D!
YOU'RE ON!
IT HAS TO BE AT SUPER NINTENDO, THOUGH!
BISHII (JAB)
NI (GRIN)
I WOULDN'T HAVE IT ANY OTHER WAY!
ISHIDA-SENSEI?
KARA (CLUNK)
YES, SIR!!?
BIKUU (FLINCH)
YOUR STUDENTS ARE HERE.
PARDON US!
OH, KIRINO AND SAYA. WHAT'S UP?
HEYA!
LOOK AT THIS, SENSEI! LOOK, LOOK!

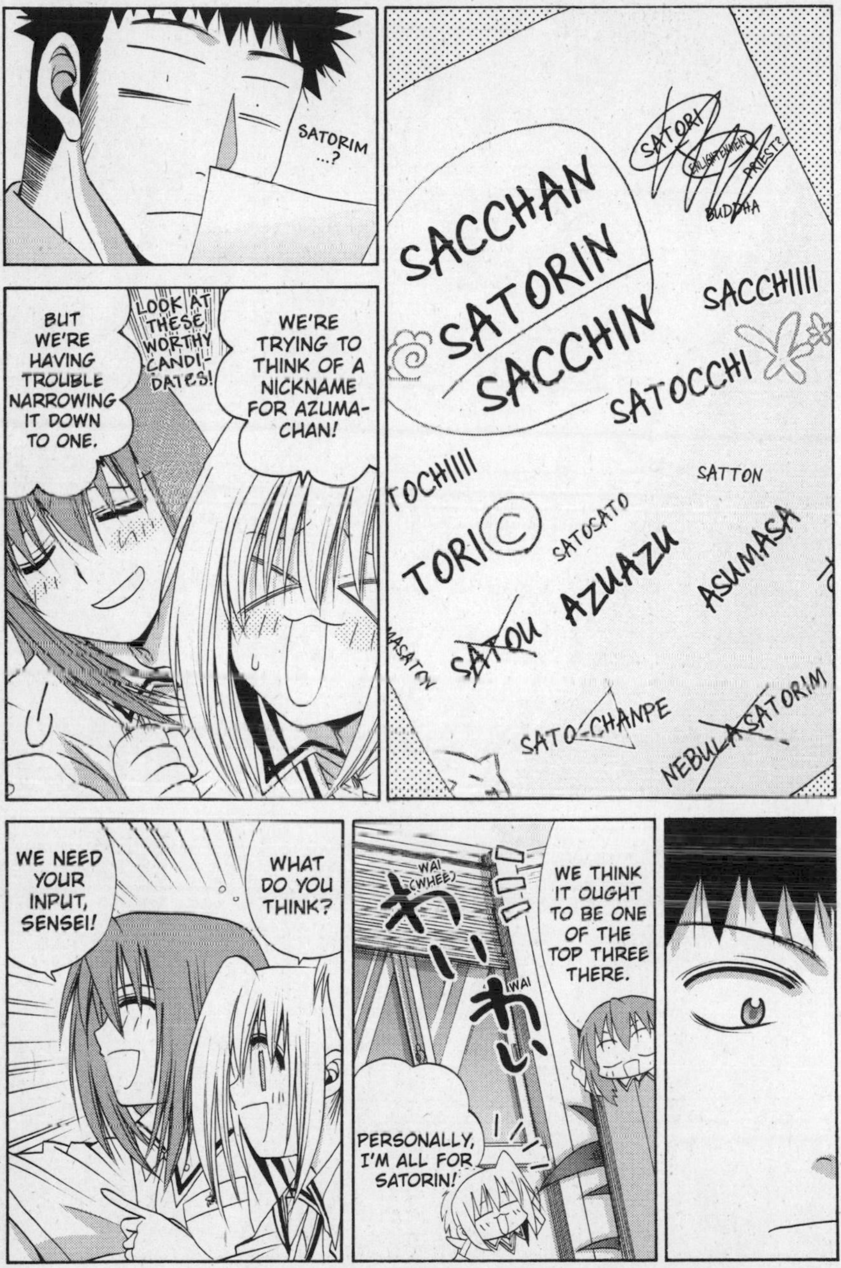
SATORI
ENLIGHTENMENT
PRIEST?
BUDDHA
SACCHAN
SATORIN
SACCHIN
SACCHIIII
SATOCCHI
TOCHIIII
SATTON
TORI
SATOCATO
AZUAZU
ASUMASA
SATOU
MASATON
SATO-CHANPE
NEBULA SATORIM
SATORIM ...?
WE'RE TRYING TO THINK OF A NICKNAME FOR AZUMA-CHAN!
LOOK AT THESE WORTHY CANDIDATES!
BUT WE'RE HAVING TROUBLE NARROWING IT DOWN TO ONE.
WE THINK IT OUGHT TO BE ONE OF THE TOP THREE THERE.
WAI (WHEE)
WAI
PERSONALLY, I'M ALL FOR SATORIN!
WHAT DO YOU THINK?
WE NEED YOUR INPUT, SENSEI!

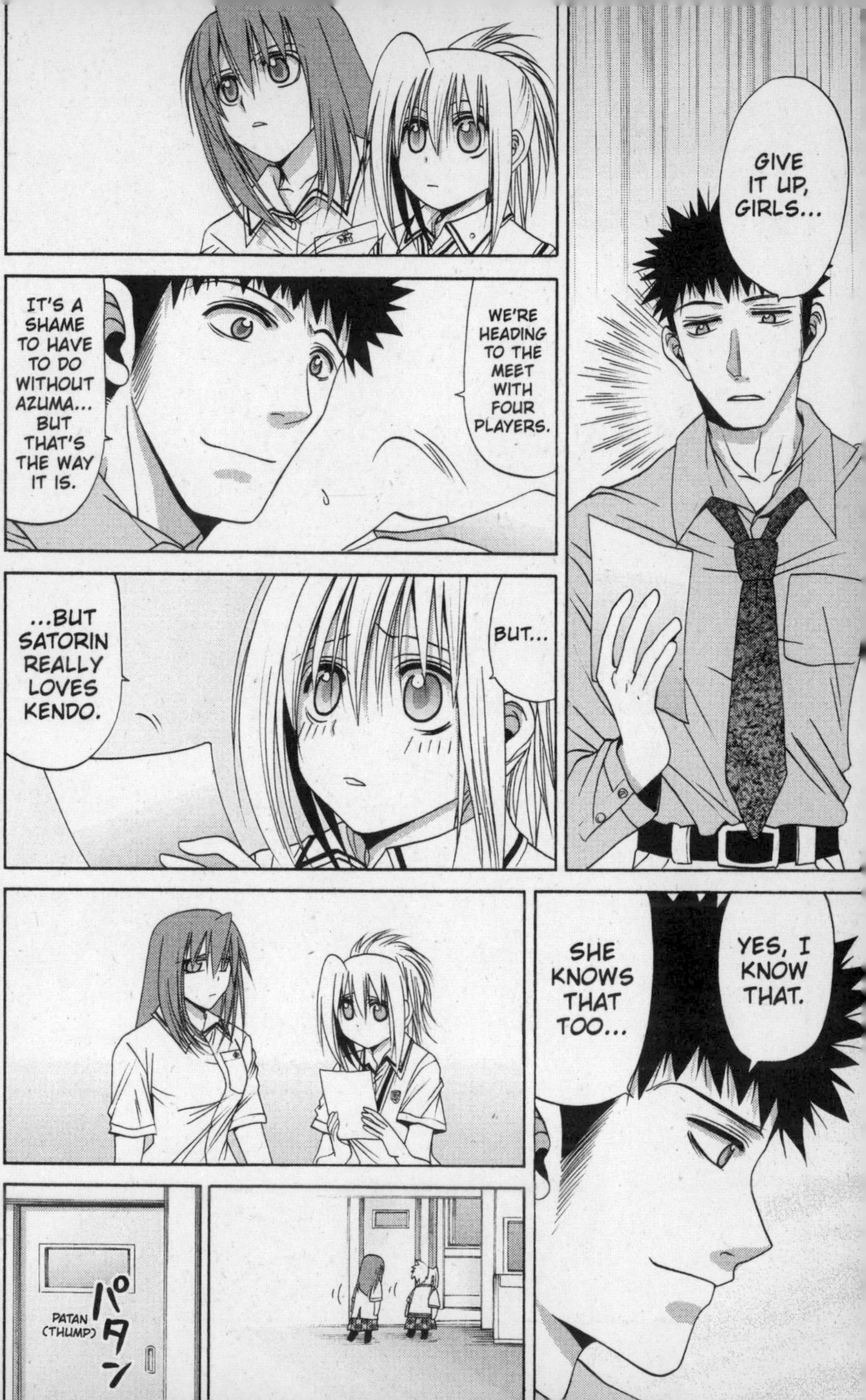
GIVE IT UP, GIRLS...
WE'RE HEADING TO THE MEET WITH FOUR PLAYERS.
IT'S A SHAME TO HAVE TO DO WITHOUT AZUMA... BUT THAT'S THE WAY IT IS.
BUT...
...BUT SATORIN REALLY LOVES KENDO.
YES, I KNOW THAT.
SHE KNOWS THAT TOO...
パタン
PATAN (THUMP)

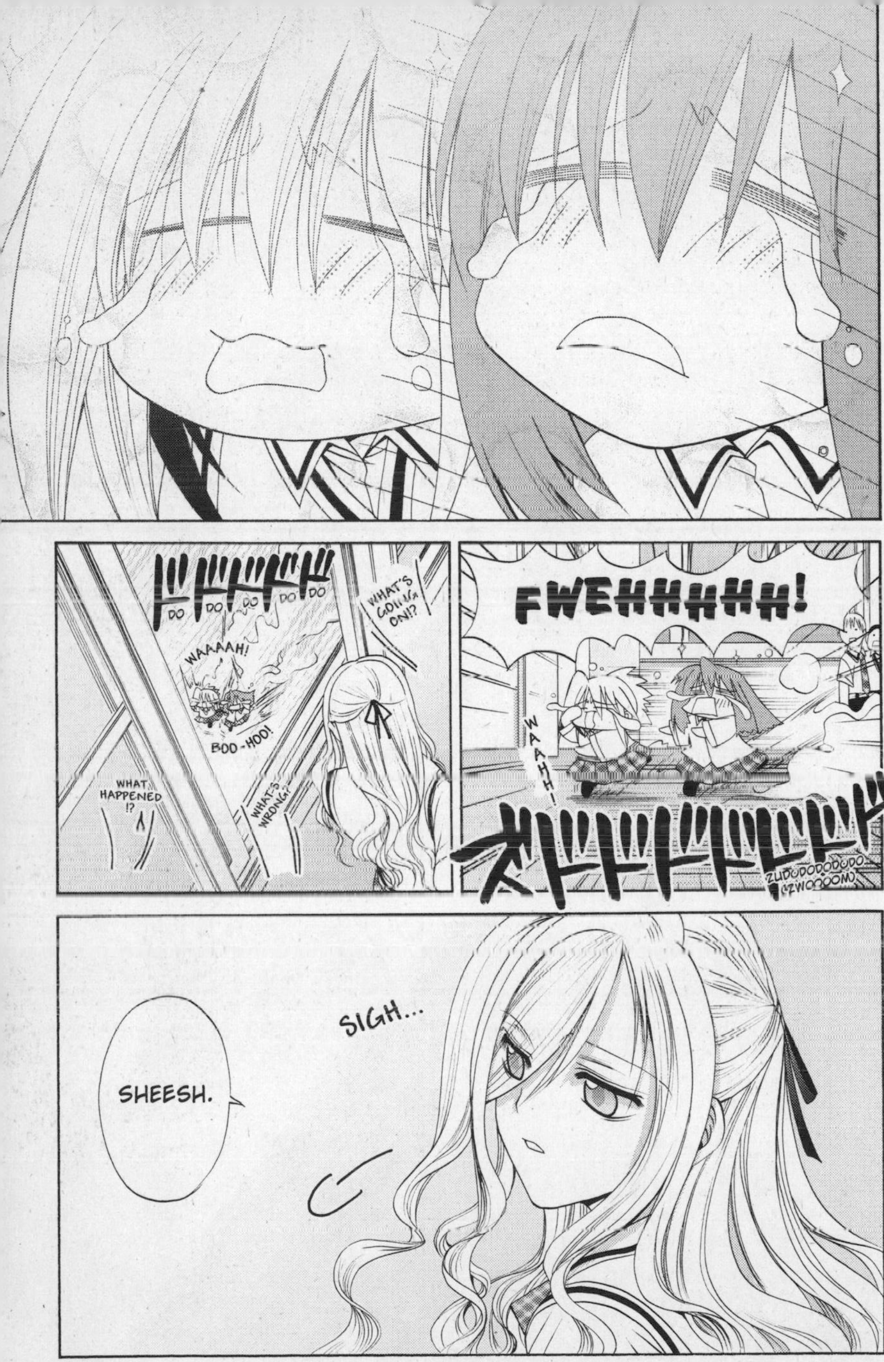
FWEHHHHHH!
WAAHH!
ZUDODODODODO (ZWOOOOM)
DO DO DO DO DO
WHAT'S GOING ON!?
WAAAAH!
BOO-HOO!
WHAT'S WRONG!?
WHAT HAPPENED!?
SIGH...
SHEESH.

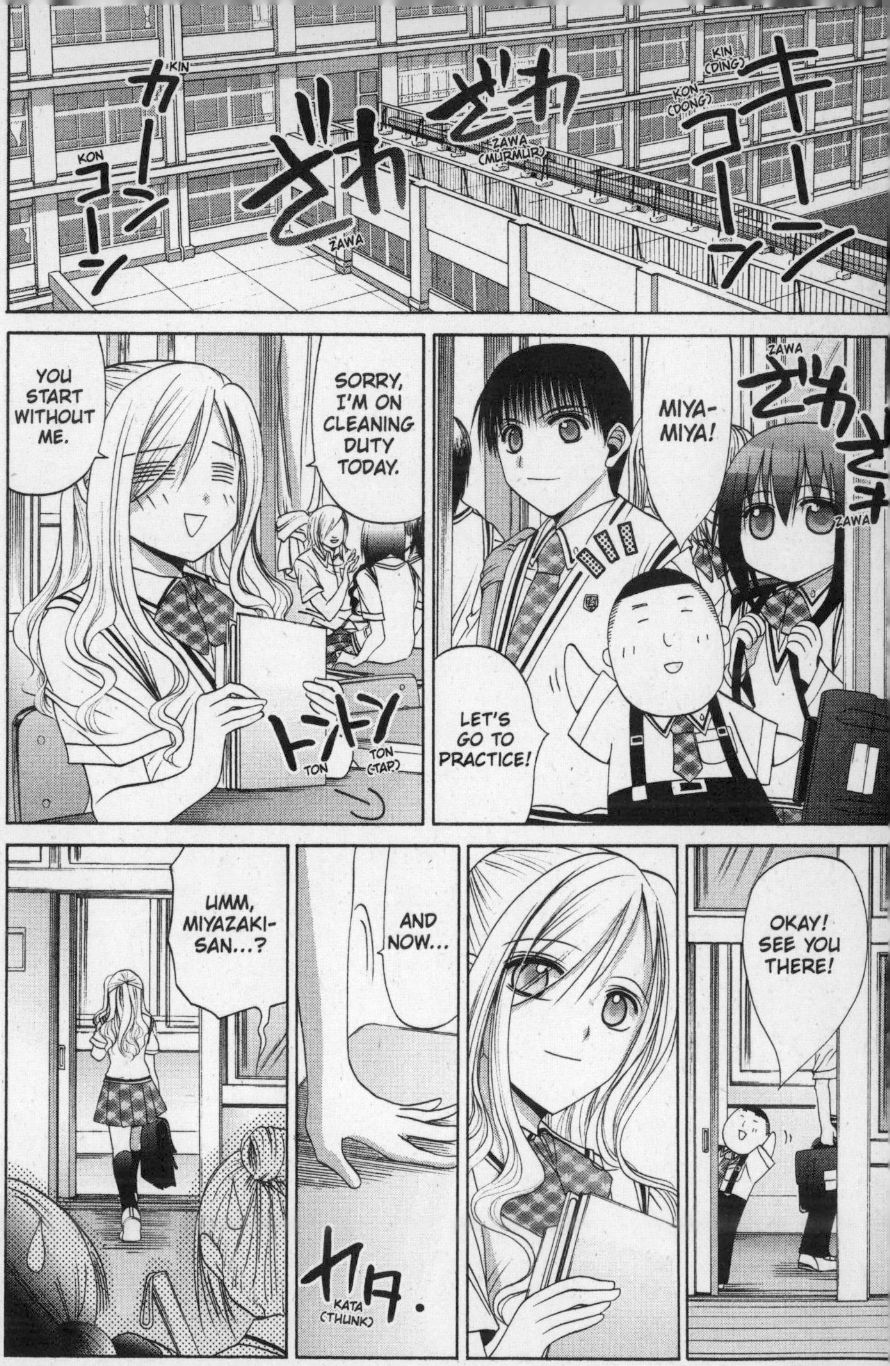
KIN (DING)
KON (DONG)
ZAWA (MURMUR)
ZAWA
KIN
KON
ZAWA
ZAWA
MIYA-MIYA!
LET'S GO TO PRACTICE!
SORRY, I'M ON CLEANING DUTY TODAY.
YOU START WITHOUT ME.
TON
TON (TAP)
OKAY! SEE YOU THERE!
AND NOW...
KATA (THUNK)
UMM, MIYAZAKI-SAN...?

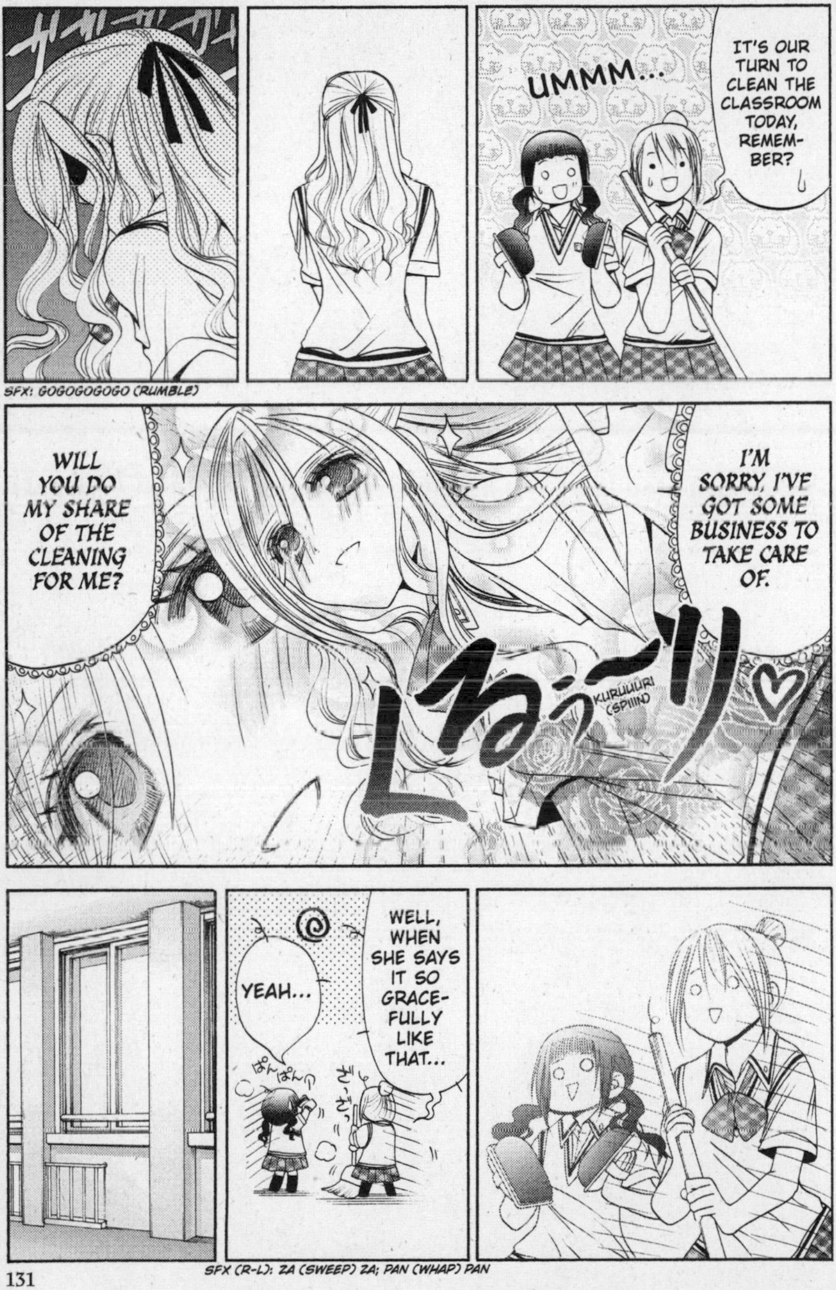
UMMM...
IT'S OUR TURN TO CLEAN THE CLASSROOM TODAY, REMEMBER?
SFX: GOGOGOGOGO (RUMBLE)
I'M SORRY, I'VE GOT SOME BUSINESS TO TAKE CARE OF.
WILL YOU DO MY SHARE OF THE CLEANING FOR ME?
KURUUURI (SPIIIN)
WELL, WHEN SHE SAYS IT SO GRACEFULLY LIKE THAT...
YEAH...
SFX (R-L): ZA (SWEEP) ZA; PAN (WHAP) PAN

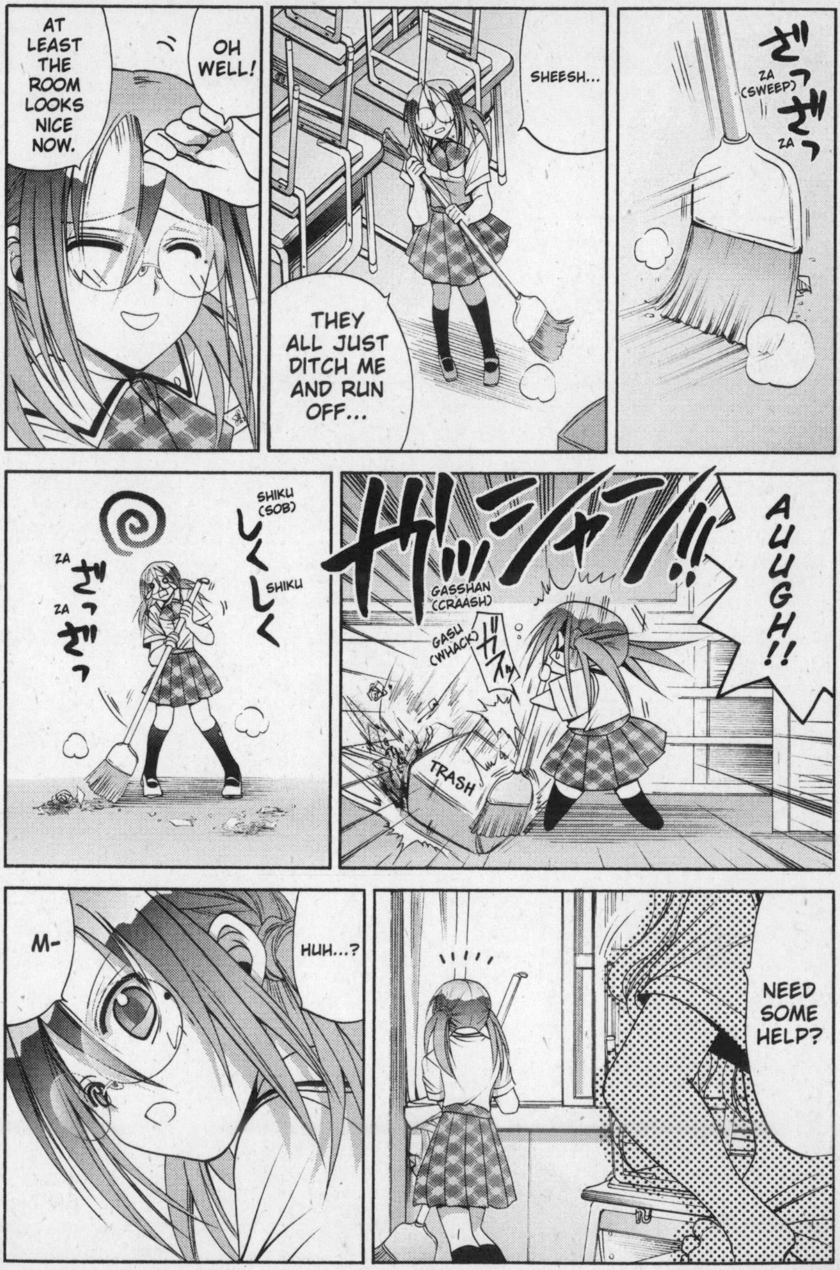
ざっ
ZA (SWEEP)
ざっ
ZA
SHEESH...
THEY ALL JUST DITCH ME AND RUN OFF...
OH WELL!
AT LEAST THE ROOM LOOKS NICE NOW.
AUUGH!!
ガッシャン!!
GASSHAN (CRAASH)
ガスッ
GASU (WHACK)
TRASH
SHIKU (SOB)
しくしく
SHIKU
ZA
ざっざっ
ZA
NEED SOME HELP?
HUH...?
M-

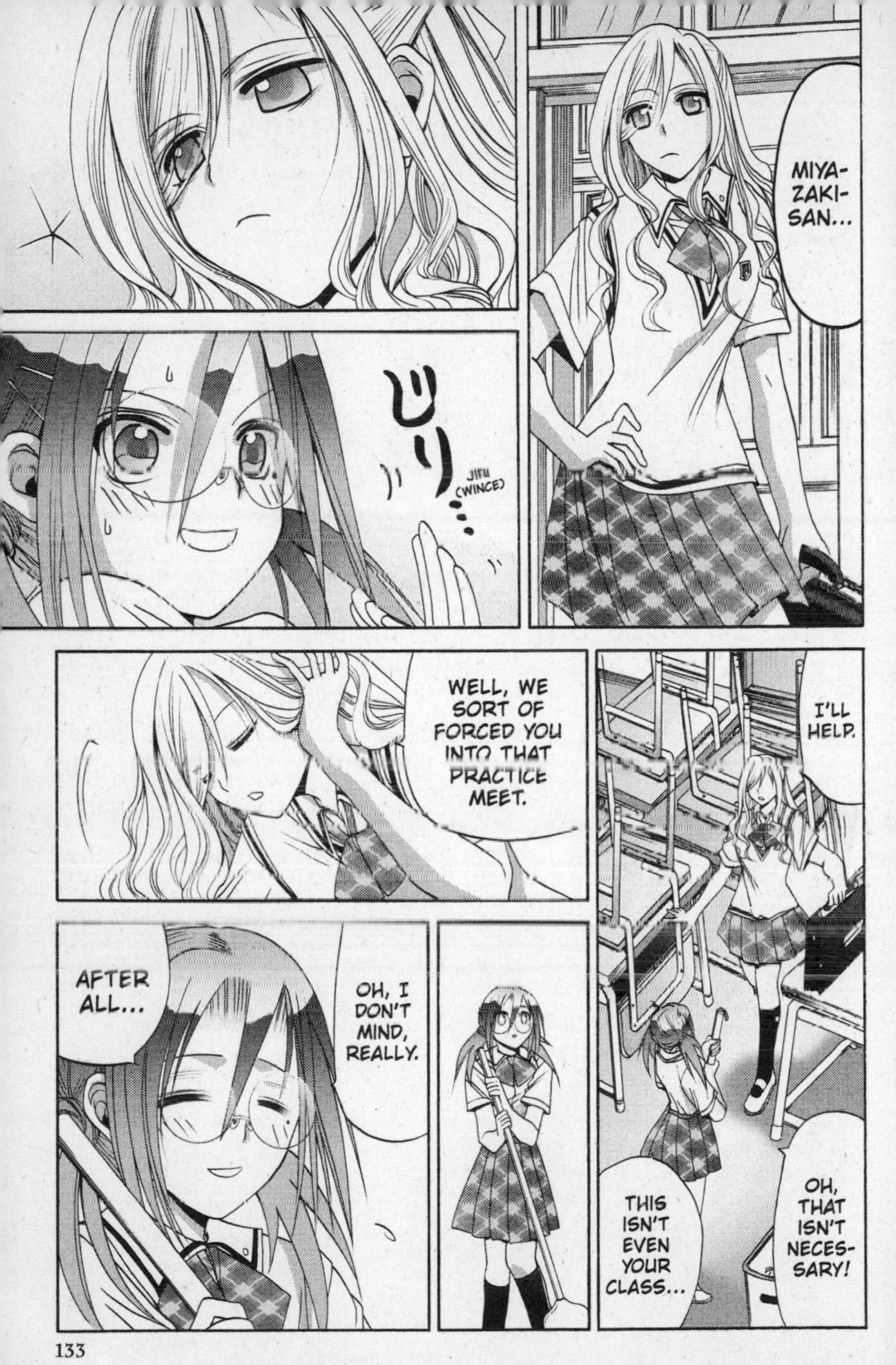
MIYA-ZAKI-SAN...
ジリ
JIRI (WINCE)
I'LL HELP.
OH, THAT ISN'T NECES-SARY!
THIS ISN'T EVEN YOUR CLASS...
WELL, WE SORT OF FORCED YOU INTO THAT PRACTICE MEET.
OH, I DON'T MIND, REALLY.
AFTER ALL...

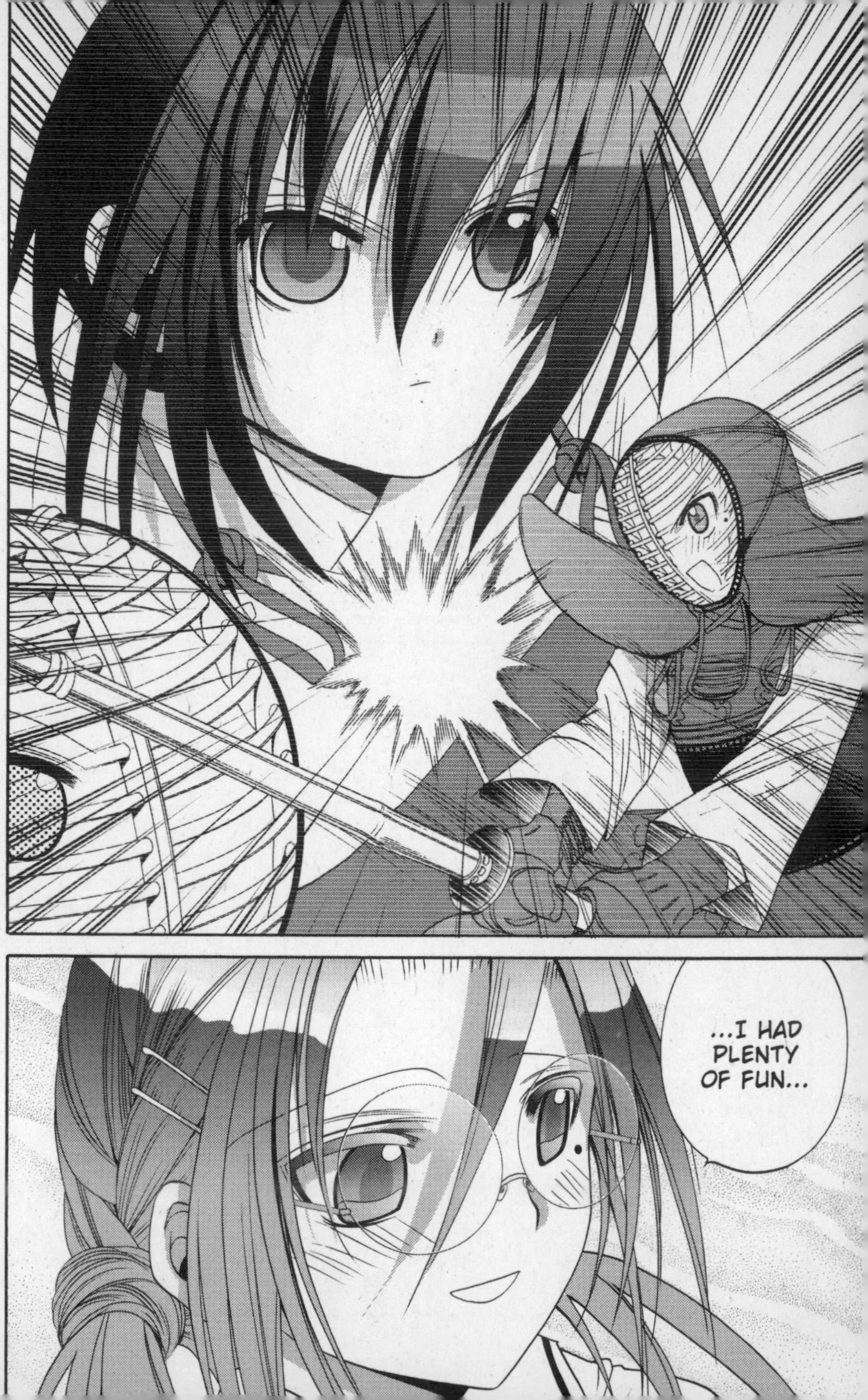
...I HAD PLENTY OF FUN...

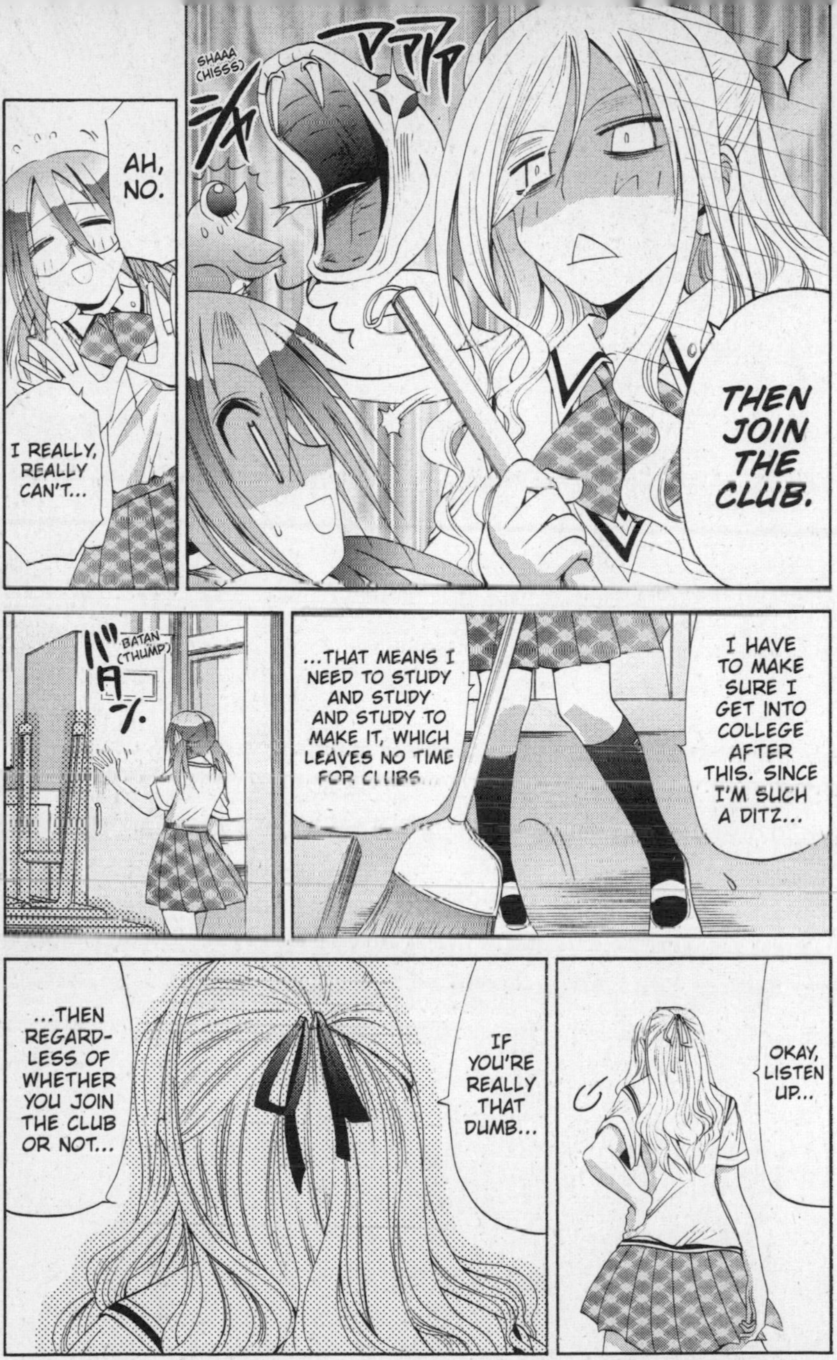
SHAAA (HISSS)
THEN JOIN THE CLUB.
AH, NO.
I REALLY, REALLY CAN'T...
I HAVE TO MAKE SURE I GET INTO COLLEGE AFTER THIS. SINCE I'M SUCH A DITZ...
...THAT MEANS I NEED TO STUDY AND STUDY AND STUDY TO MAKE IT, WHICH LEAVES NO TIME FOR CLUBS...
BATAN (THUMP)
OKAY, LISTEN UP...
IF YOU'RE REALLY THAT DUMB...
...THEN REGARDLESS OF WHETHER YOU JOIN THE CLUB OR NOT...

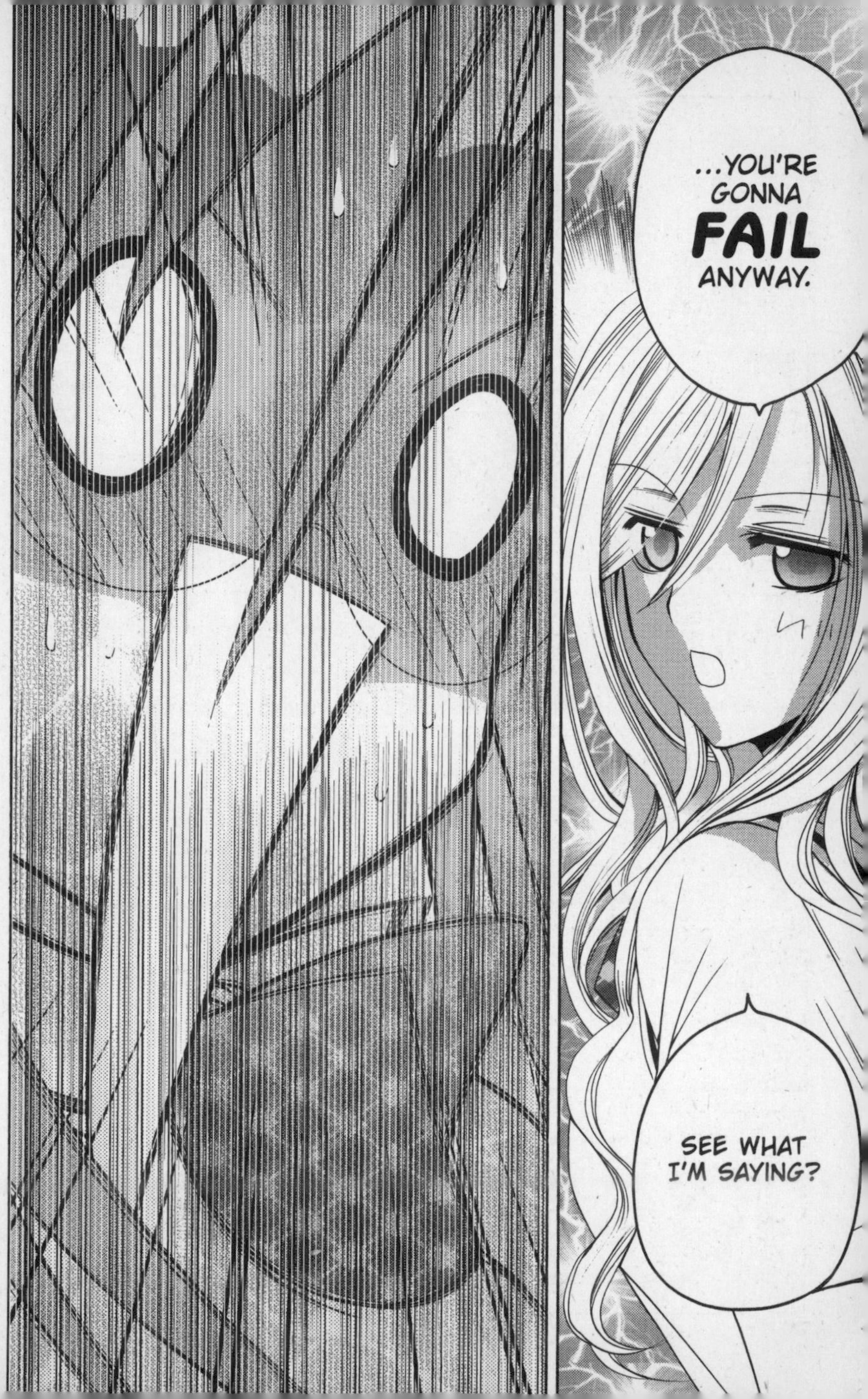
...YOU'RE GONNA **FAIL** ANYWAY.
SEE WHAT I'M SAYING?

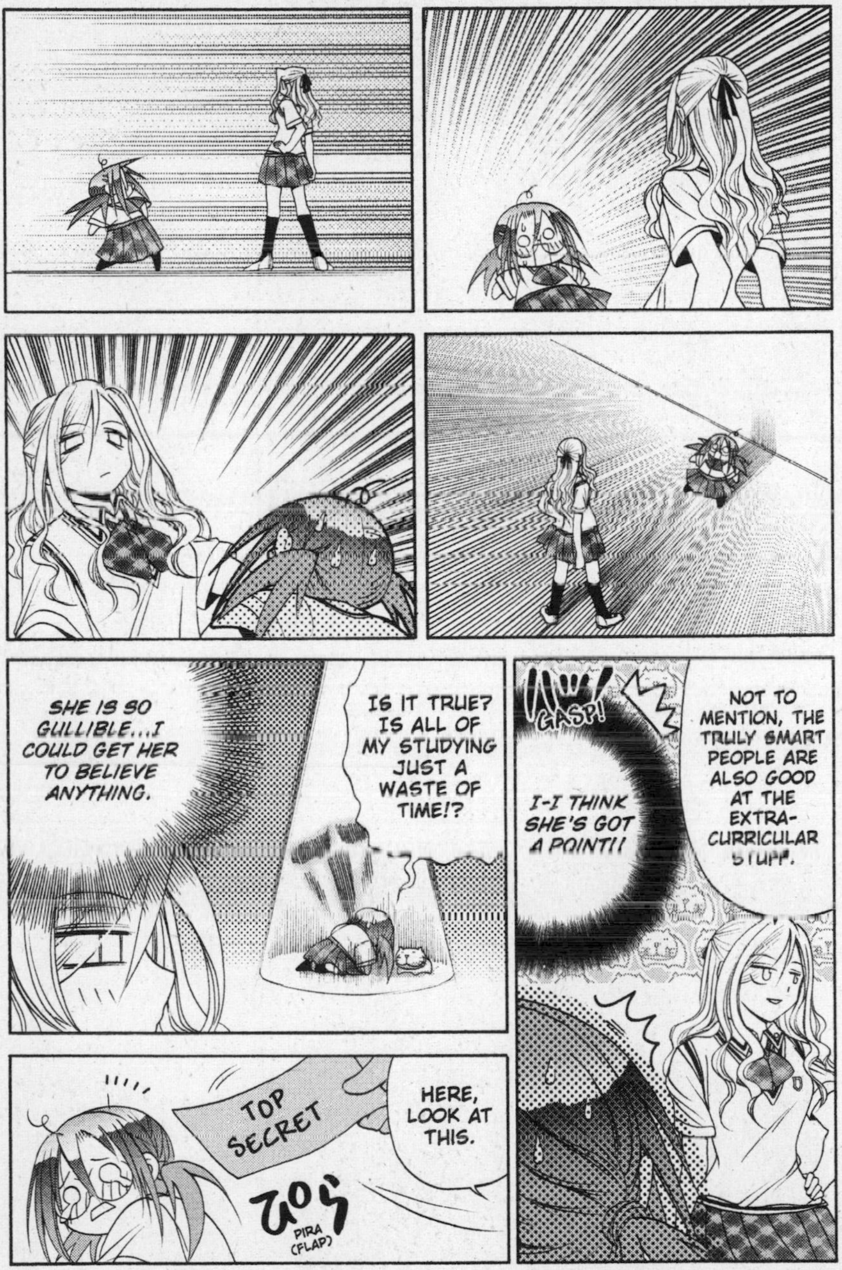

NOT TO MENTION, THE TRULY SMART PEOPLE ARE ALSO GOOD AT THE EXTRA-CURRICULAR STUFF.
ハッ!
GASP!
I-I THINK SHE'S GOT A POINT!!
IS IT TRUE? IS ALL OF MY STUDYING JUST A WASTE OF TIME!?
SHE IS SO GULLIBLE...I COULD GET HER TO BELIEVE ANYTHING.
HERE, LOOK AT THIS.
TOP SECRET
ぴら
PIRA (FLAP)

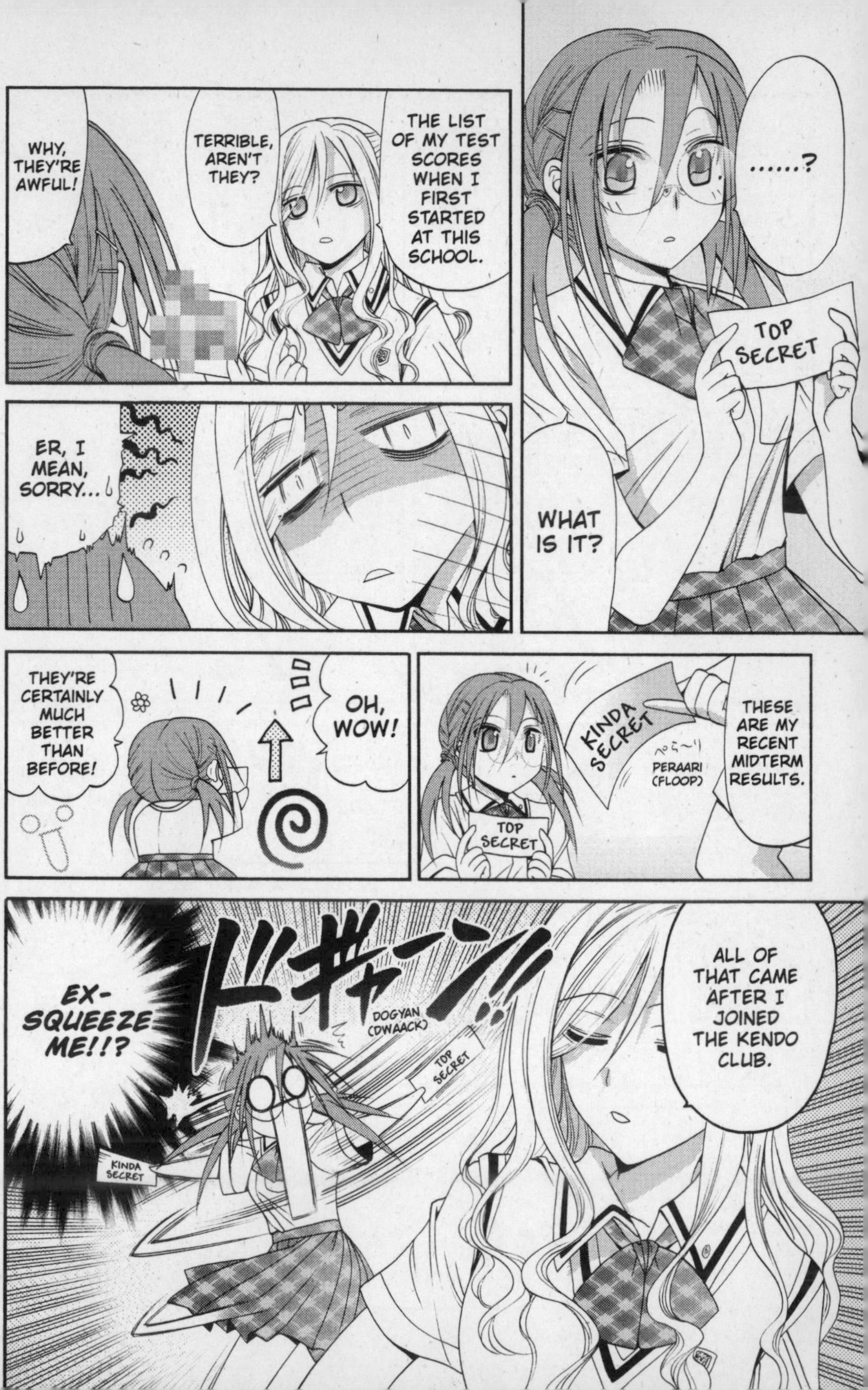
......?
TOP SECRET
WHAT IS IT?
THE LIST OF MY TEST SCORES WHEN I FIRST STARTED AT THIS SCHOOL.
TERRIBLE, AREN'T THEY?
WHY, THEY'RE AWFUL!
ER, I MEAN, SORRY...
THESE ARE MY RECENT MIDTERM RESULTS.
KINDA SECRET
ぺら～り
PERAARI (FLOOP)
TOP SECRET
OH, WOW!
THEY'RE CERTAINLY MUCH BETTER THAN BEFORE!
ALL OF THAT CAME AFTER I JOINED THE KENDO CLUB.
ドギャーン!!
DOGYAN (DWAACK)
TOP SECRET
EX-SQUEEZE ME!!?
KINDA SECRET

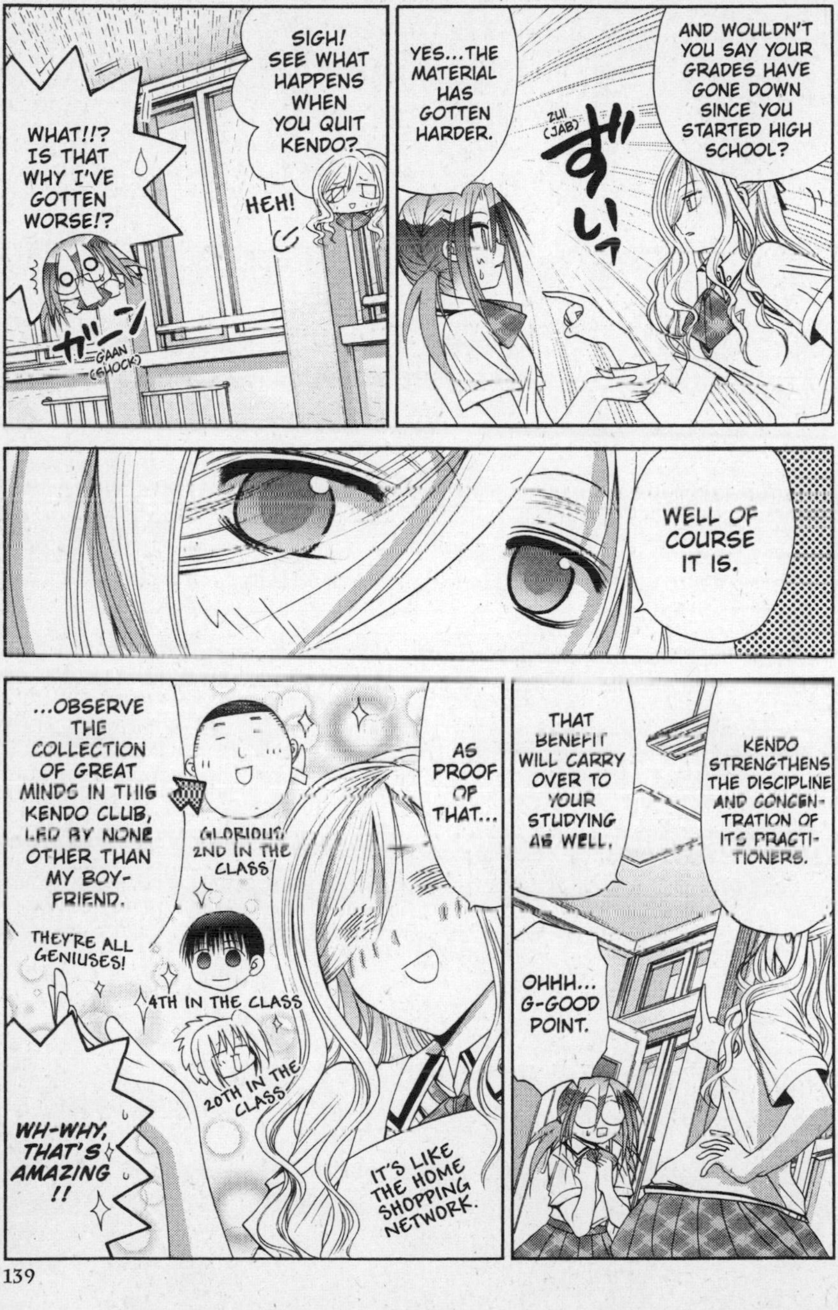
AND WOULDN'T YOU SAY YOUR GRADES HAVE GONE DOWN SINCE YOU STARTED HIGH SCHOOL?
ずい
ZUI (JAB)
YES...THE MATERIAL HAS GOTTEN HARDER.
SIGH! SEE WHAT HAPPENS WHEN YOU QUIT KENDO?
HEH!
WHAT!!? IS THAT WHY I'VE GOTTEN WORSE!?
ガーン
GAAN (SHOCK)
WELL OF COURSE IT IS.
KENDO STRENGTHENS THE DISCIPLINE AND CONCENTRATION OF ITS PRACTITIONERS.
THAT BENEFIT WILL CARRY OVER TO YOUR STUDYING AS WELL.
OHHH... G-GOOD POINT.
AS PROOF OF THAT...
...OBSERVE THE COLLECTION OF GREAT MINDS IN THIS KENDO CLUB, LED BY NONE OTHER THAN MY BOYFRIEND.
GLORIOUS 2ND IN THE CLASS
THEY'RE ALL GENIUSES!
4TH IN THE CLASS
20TH IN THE CLASS
IT'S LIKE THE HOME SHOPPING NETWORK.
WH-WHY, THAT'S AMAZING!!

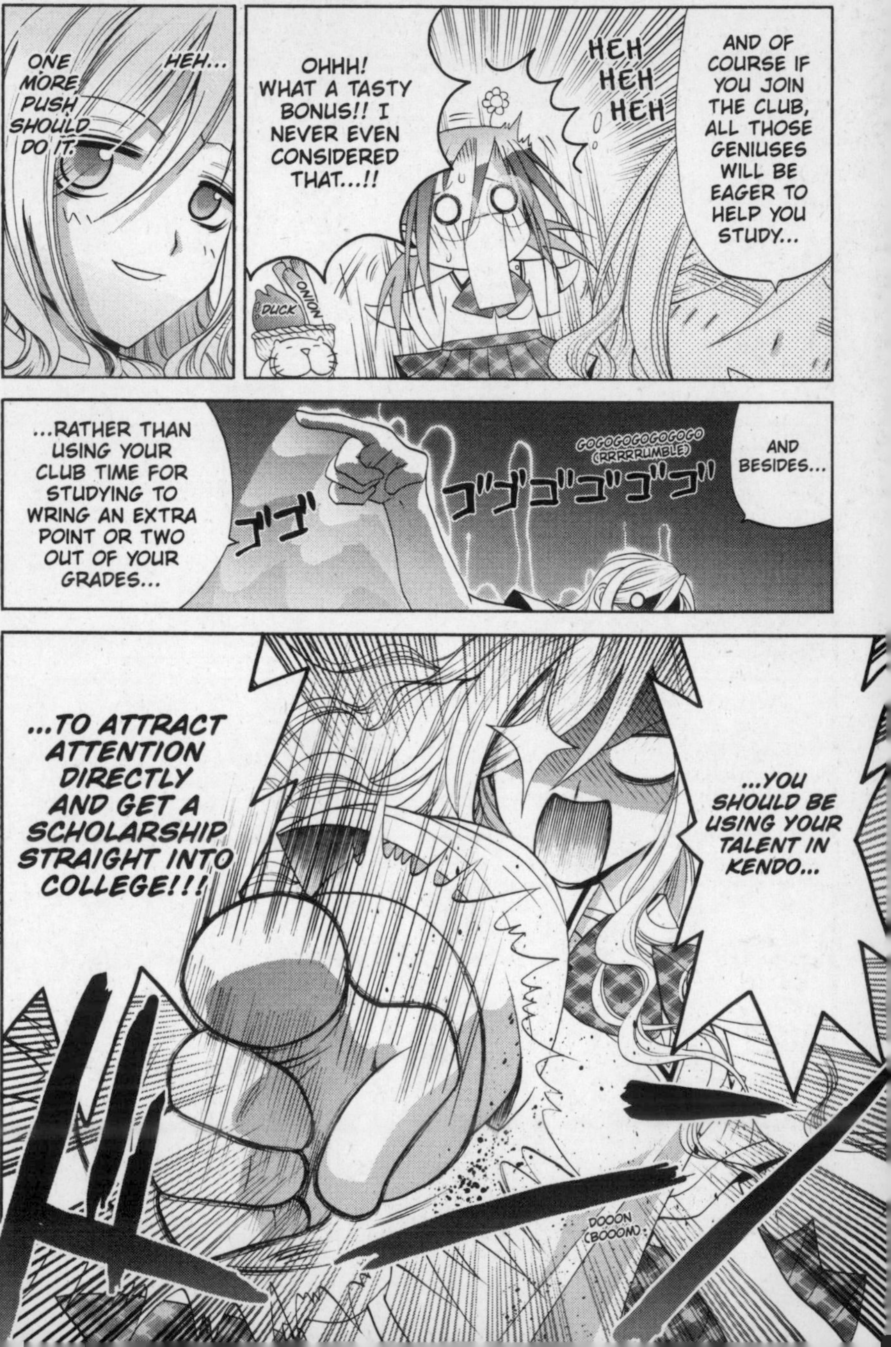
AND OF COURSE IF YOU JOIN THE CLUB, ALL THOSE GENIUSES WILL BE EAGER TO HELP YOU STUDY...
HEH HEH HEH
OHHH! WHAT A TASTY BONUS!! I NEVER EVEN CONSIDERED THAT...!!
ONION
DUCK
HEH...
ONE MORE PUSH SHOULD DO IT.
AND BESIDES...
GOGOGOGOGOGOGO (RRRRRUMBLE)
ゴゴゴゴゴゴ
ゴゴ
...RATHER THAN USING YOUR CLUB TIME FOR STUDYING TO WRING AN EXTRA POINT OR TWO OUT OF YOUR GRADES...
...YOU SHOULD BE USING YOUR TALENT IN KENDO...
...TO ATTRACT ATTENTION DIRECTLY AND GET A SCHOLARSHIP STRAIGHT INTO COLLEGE!!!
DOOON (BOOOM)

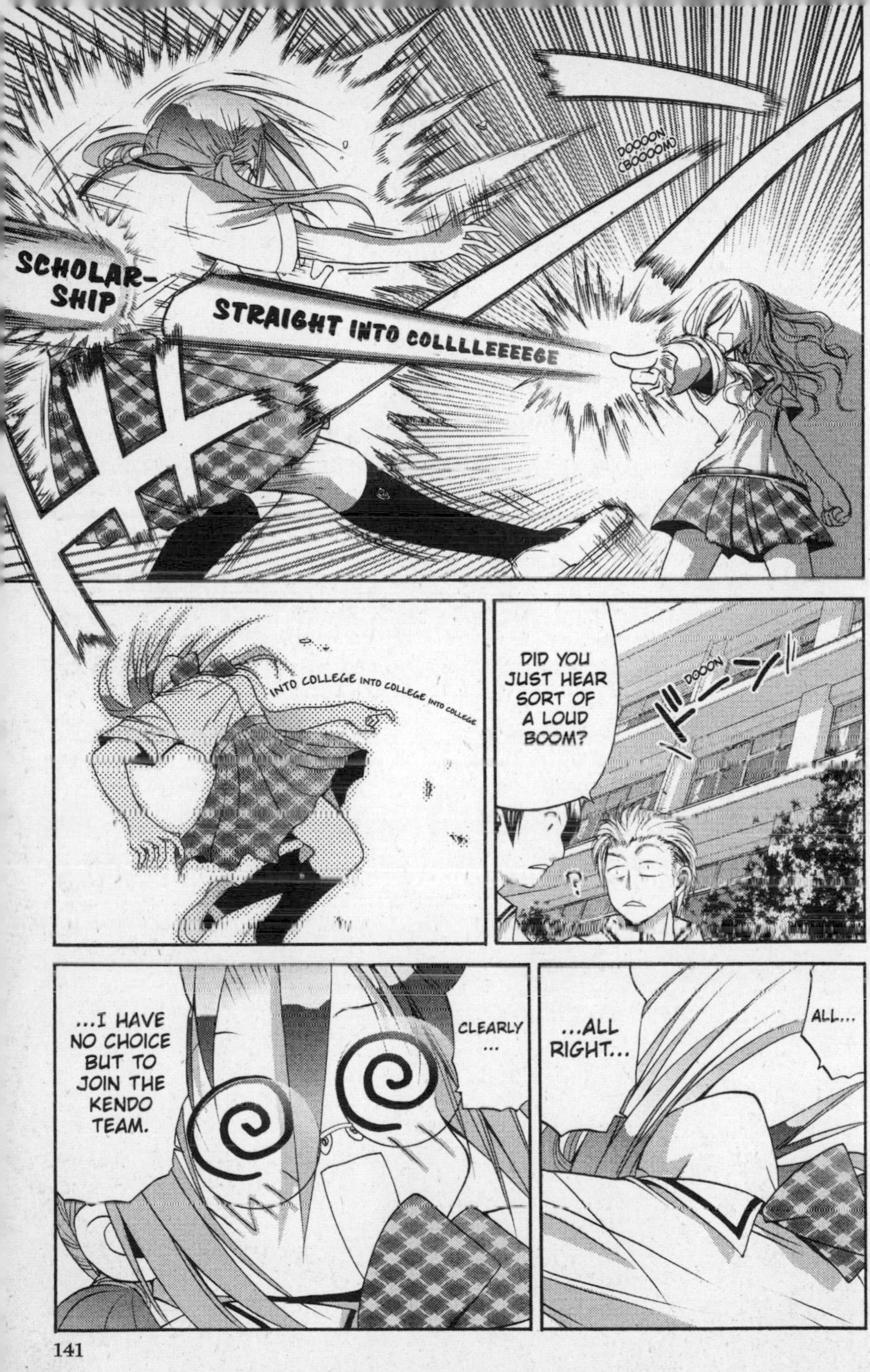
DOOOON (BOOOOM)
SCHOLAR-SHIP
STRAIGHT INTO COLLLLEEEEGE
DID YOU JUST HEAR SORT OF A LOUD BOOM?
DOOON
INTO COLLEGE INTO COLLEGE INTO COLLEGE
ALL...
...ALL RIGHT...
CLEARLY ...
...I HAVE NO CHOICE BUT TO JOIN THE KENDO TEAM.

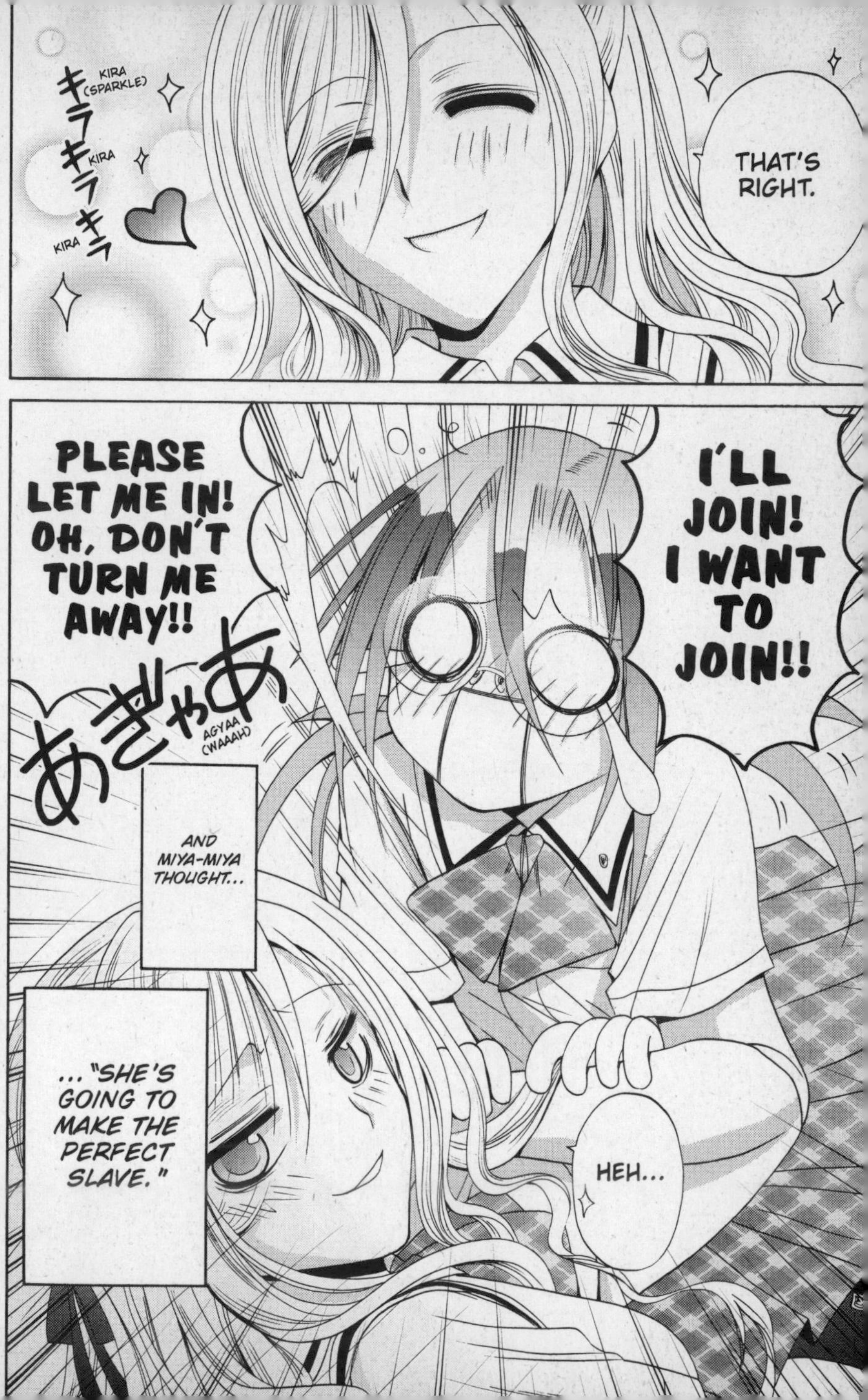
THAT'S RIGHT.
キラキラキラ KIRA (SPARKLE) KIRA KIRA
I'LL JOIN! I WANT TO JOIN!!
PLEASE LET ME IN! OH, DON'T TURN ME AWAY!!
あぎゃあ AGYAA (WAAAH)
AND MIYA-MIYA THOUGHT...
HEH...
..."SHE'S GOING TO MAKE THE PERFECT SLAVE."

BAMBOO BLADE

SAYAKO KUWAHARA

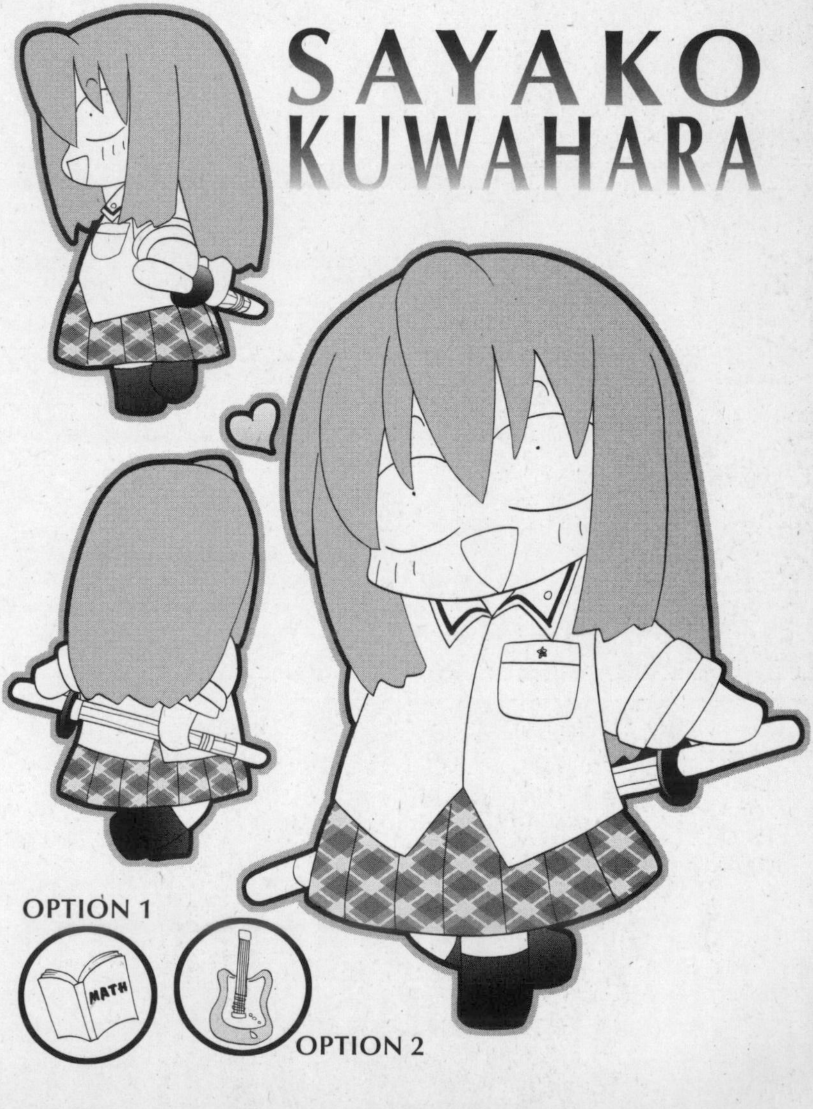
OPTION 1
MATH
OPTION 2

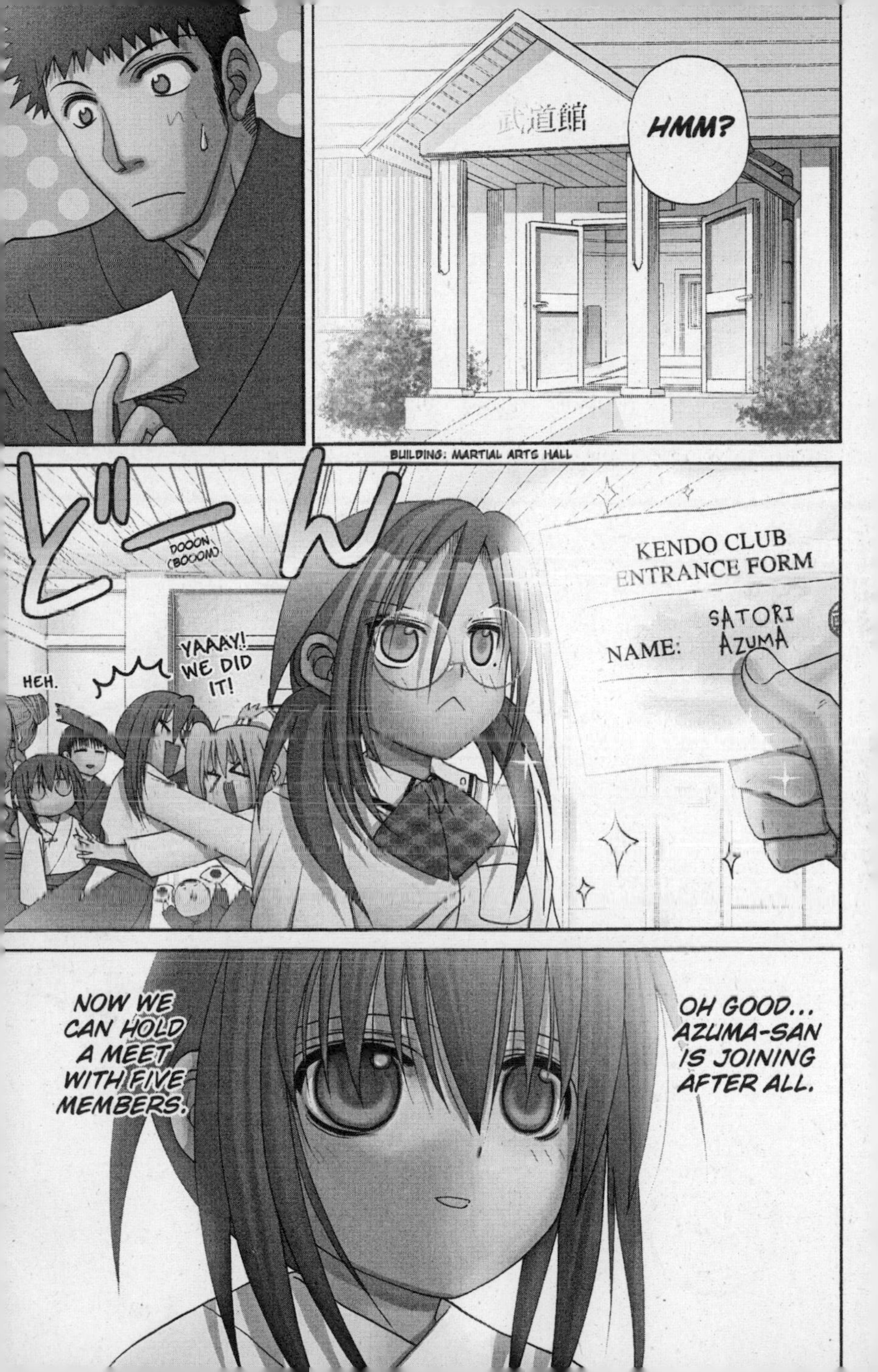
HMM?
武道館
BUILDING: MARTIAL ARTS HALL
KENDO CLUB ENTRANCE FORM
NAME: SATORI AZUMA
どーん
DOOON (BOOOM)
YAAAY! WE DID IT!
HEH.
OH GOOD... AZUMA-SAN IS JOINING AFTER ALL.
NOW WE CAN HOLD A MEET WITH FIVE MEMBERS.

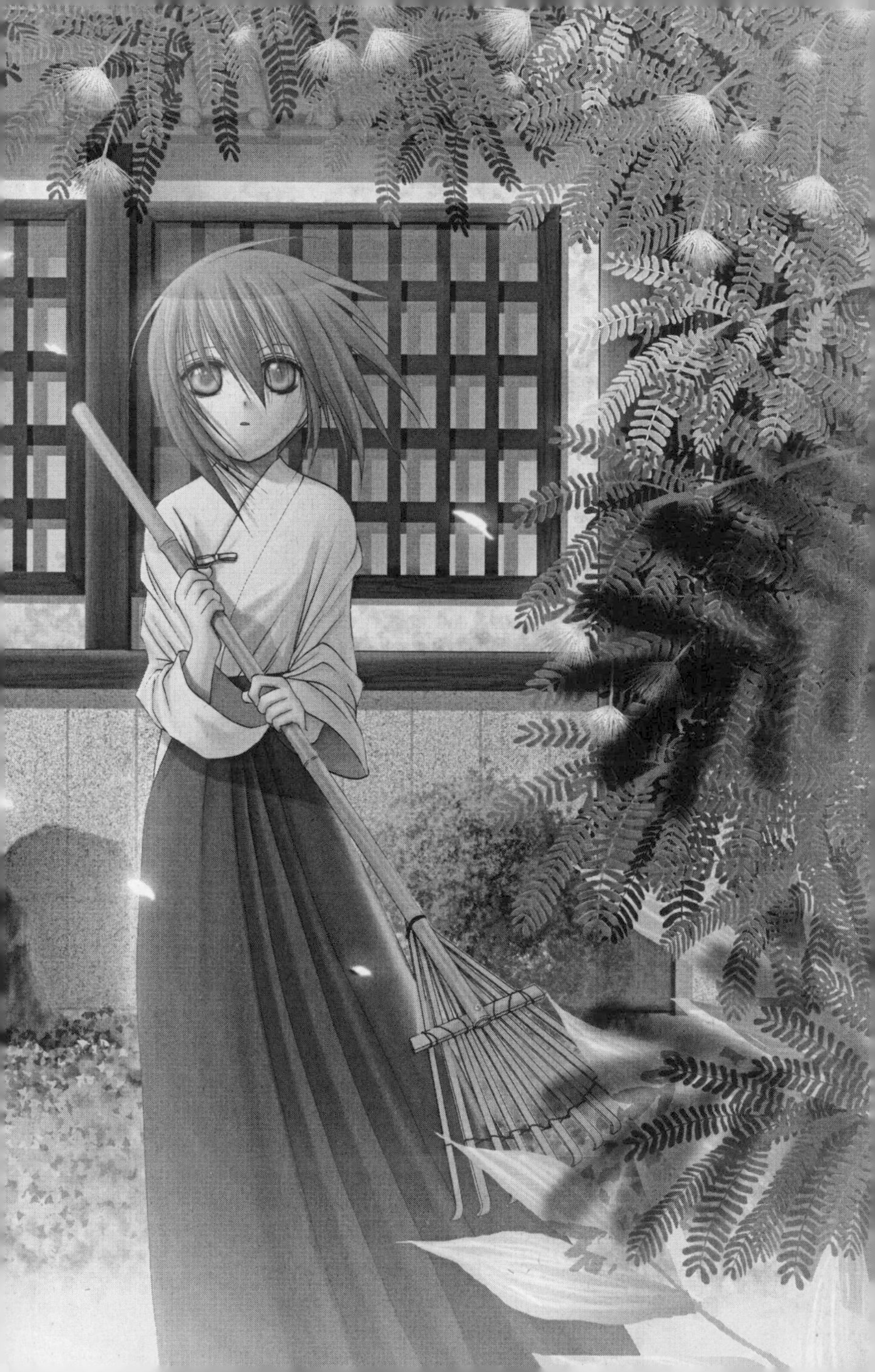

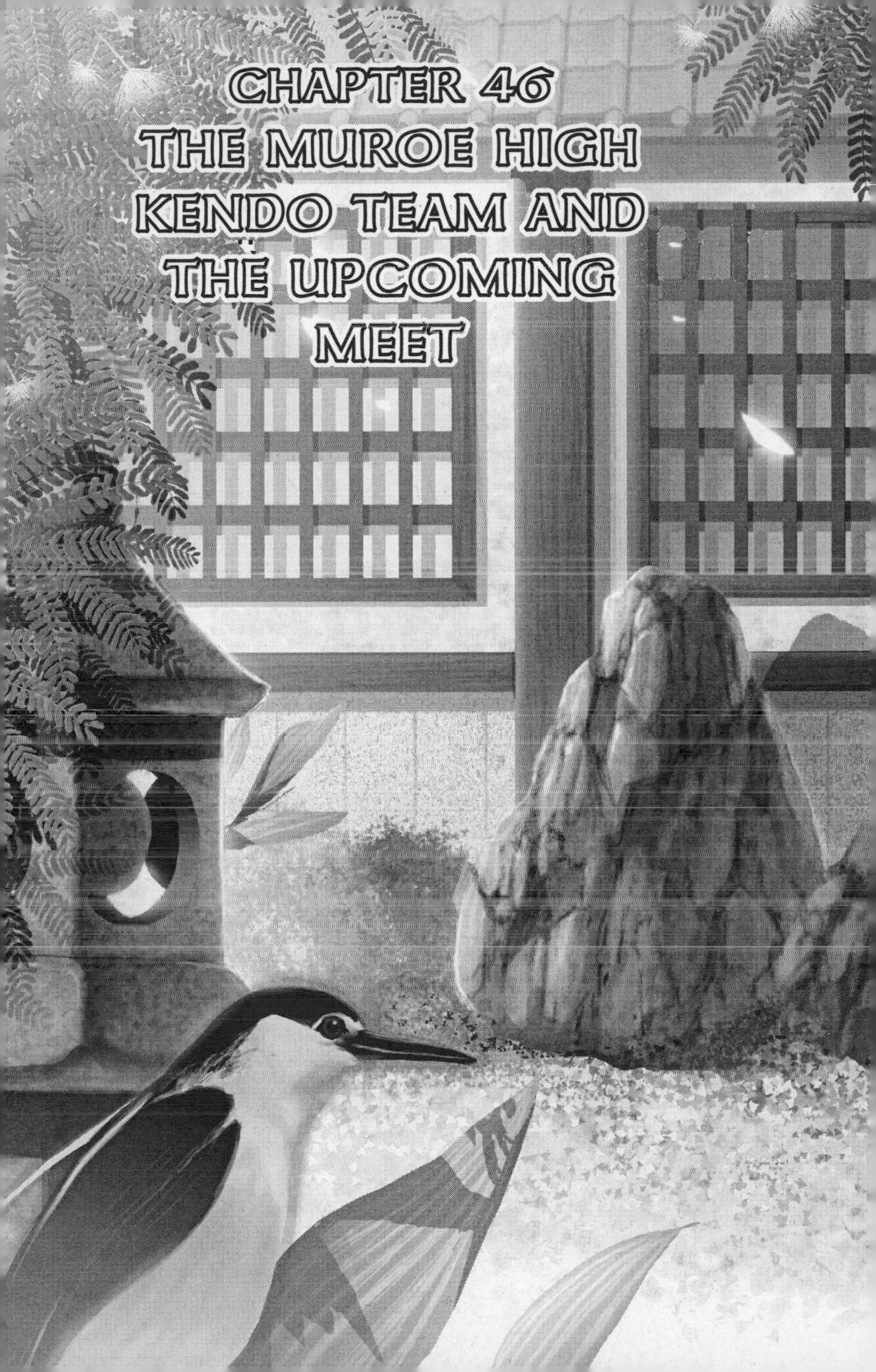
CHAPTER 46
THE MUROE HIGH KENDO TEAM AND THE UPCOMING MEET

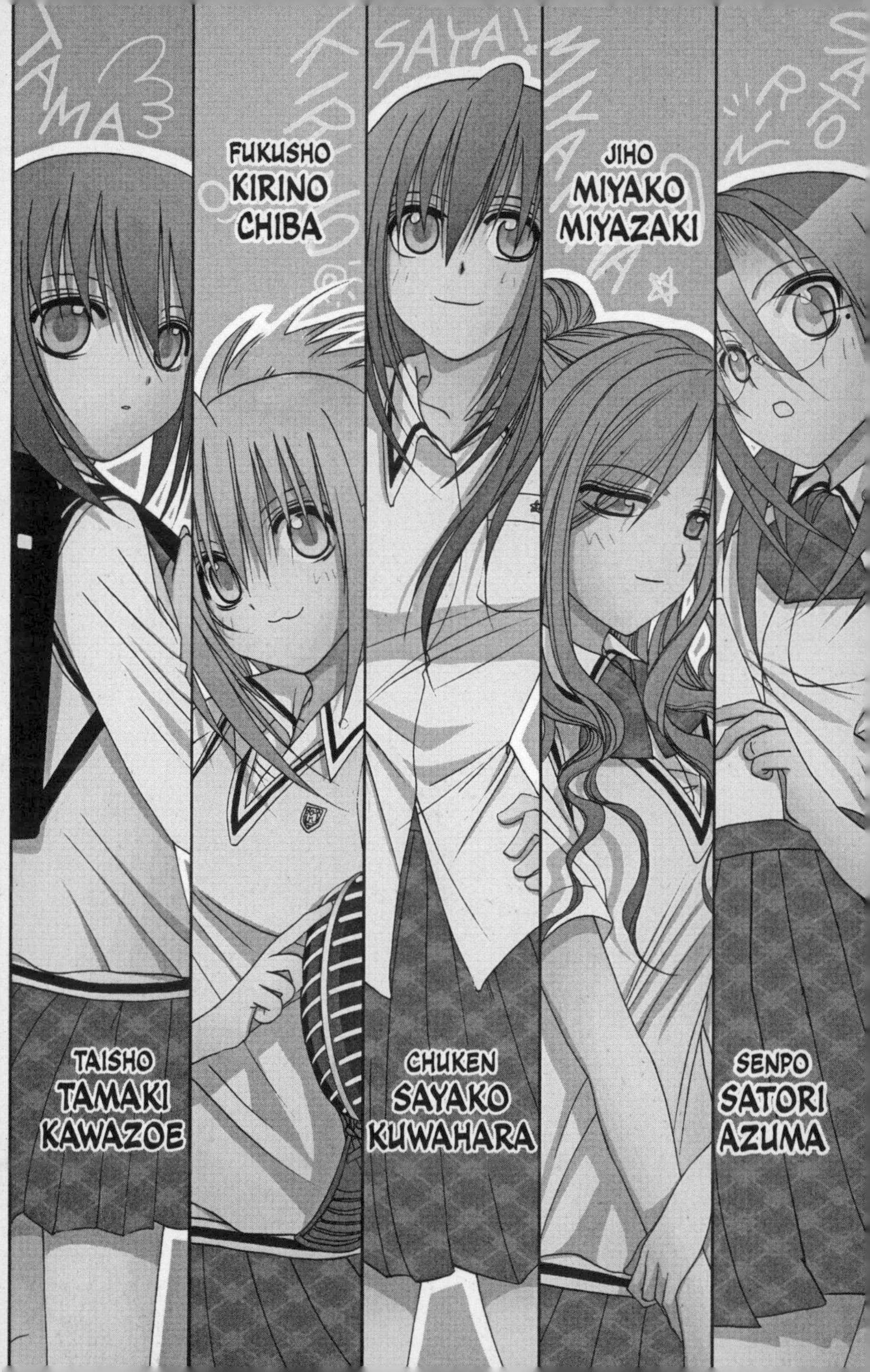
SENPO
SATORI
AZUMA
JIHO
MIYAKO
MIYAZAKI
SAYA!
CHUKEN
SAYAKO
KUWAHARA
FUKUSHO
KIRINO
CHIBA
TAMA
TAISHO
TAMAKI
KAWAZOE

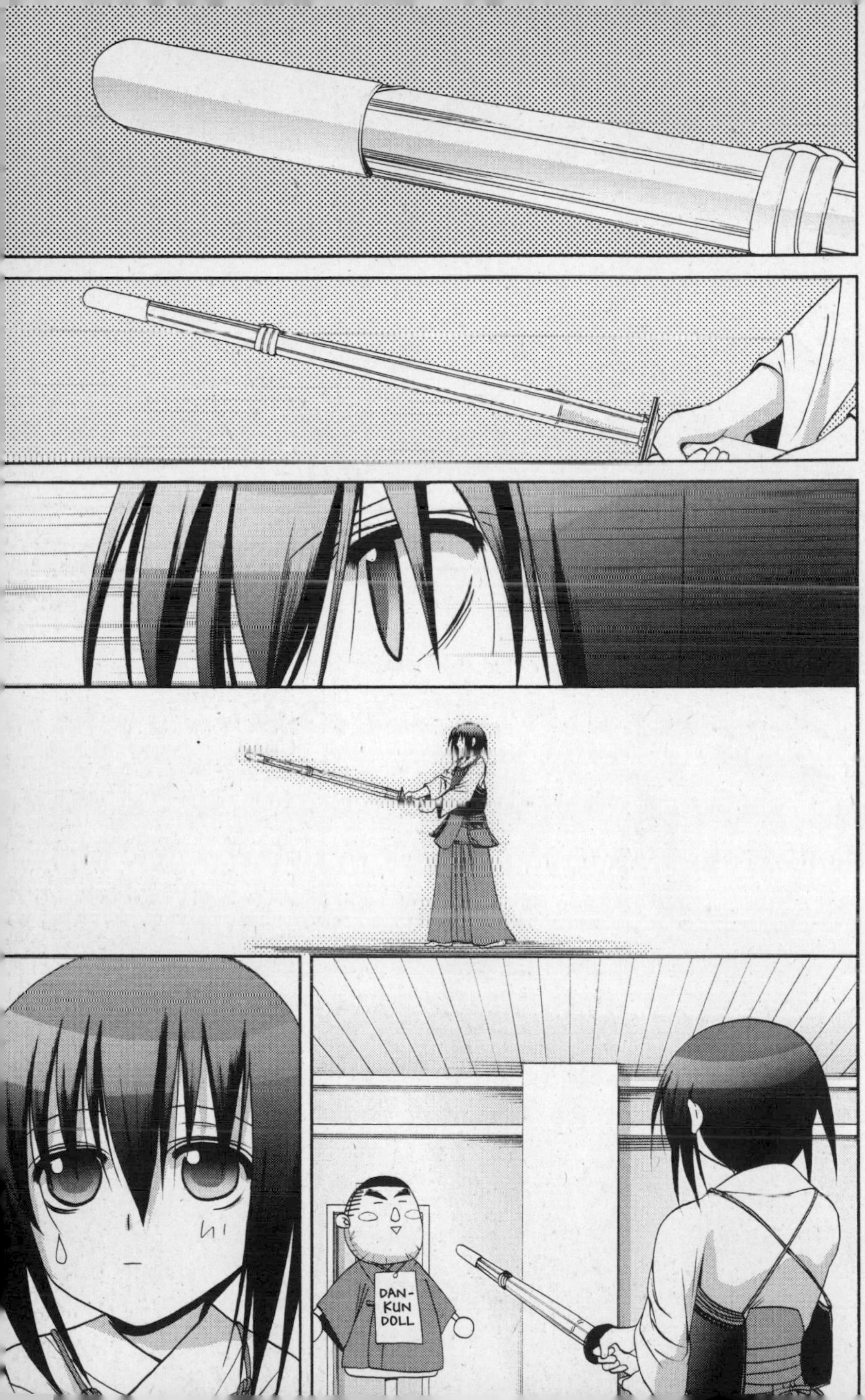
DAN-
KUN
DOLL

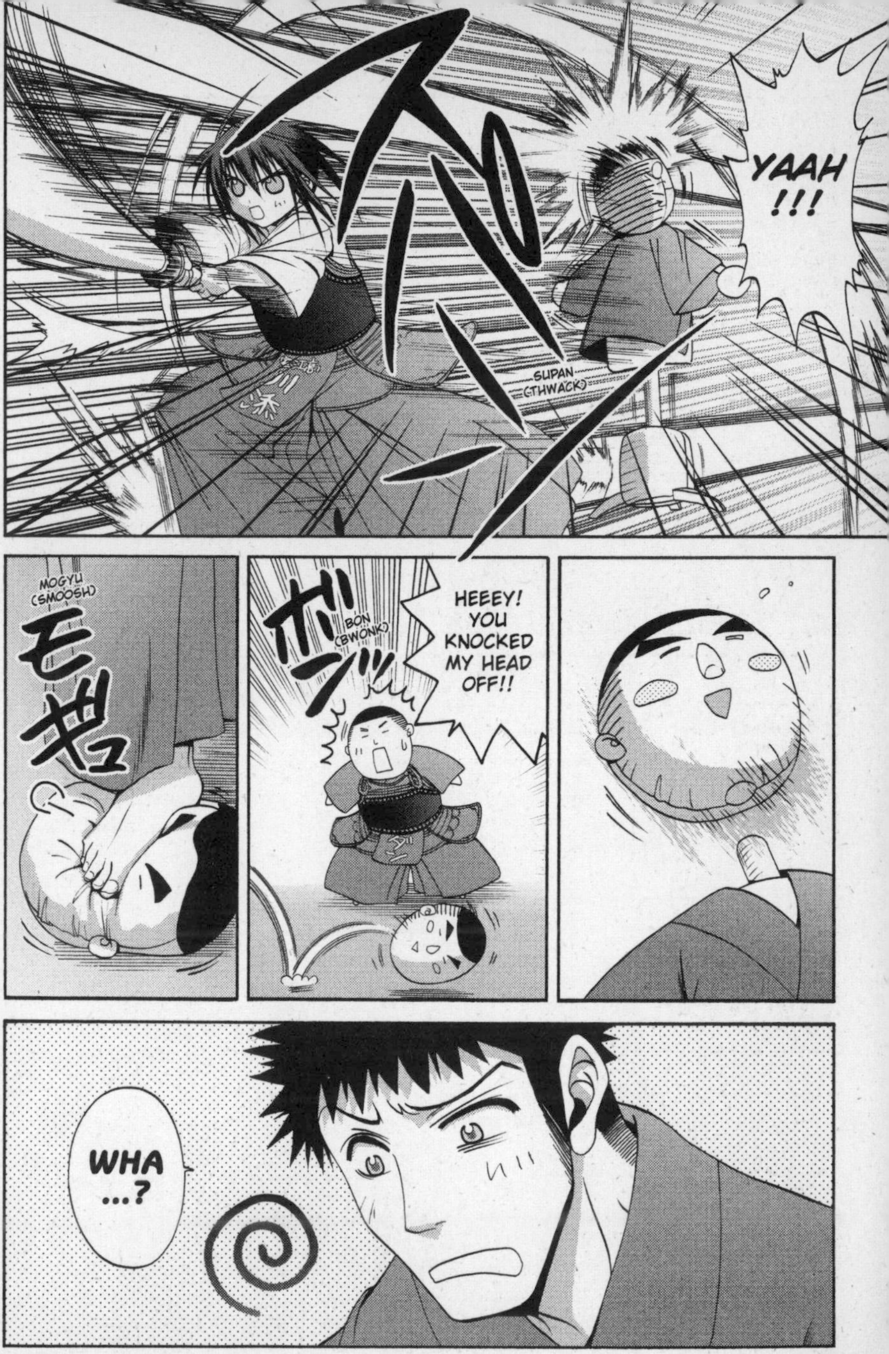
YAAH !!!
SUPAN (THWACK)
HEEEY! YOU KNOCKED MY HEAD OFF!!
BON (BWONK)
MOGYU (SMOOSH)
WHA ...?

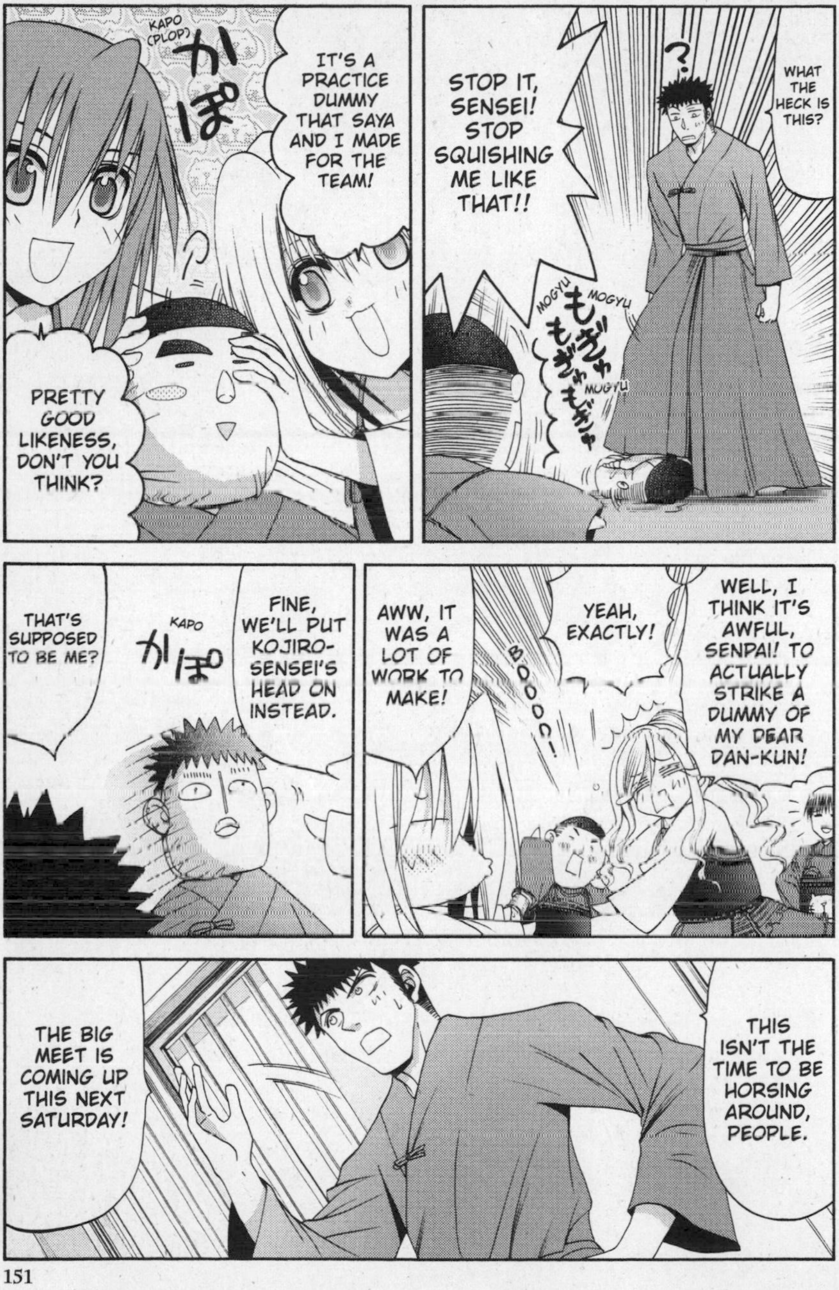
WHAT THE HECK IS THIS?
?
STOP IT, SENSEI! STOP SQUISHING ME LIKE THAT!!
MOGYU MOGYU MOGYU
もぎゅもぎゅもぎゅもぎゅ
IT'S A PRACTICE DUMMY THAT SAYA AND I MADE FOR THE TEAM!
KAPO (PLOP)
かぽ
PRETTY GOOD LIKENESS, DON'T YOU THINK?
WELL, I THINK IT'S AWFUL, SENPAI! TO ACTUALLY STRIKE A DUMMY OF MY DEAR DAN-KUN!
YEAH, EXACTLY!
BOOOON!
AWW, IT WAS A LOT OF WORK TO MAKE!
FINE, WE'LL PUT KOJIRO-SENSEI'S HEAD ON INSTEAD.
KAPO
かぽ
THAT'S SUPPOSED TO BE ME?
THIS ISN'T THE TIME TO BE HORSING AROUND, PEOPLE.
THE BIG MEET IS COMING UP THIS NEXT SATURDAY!

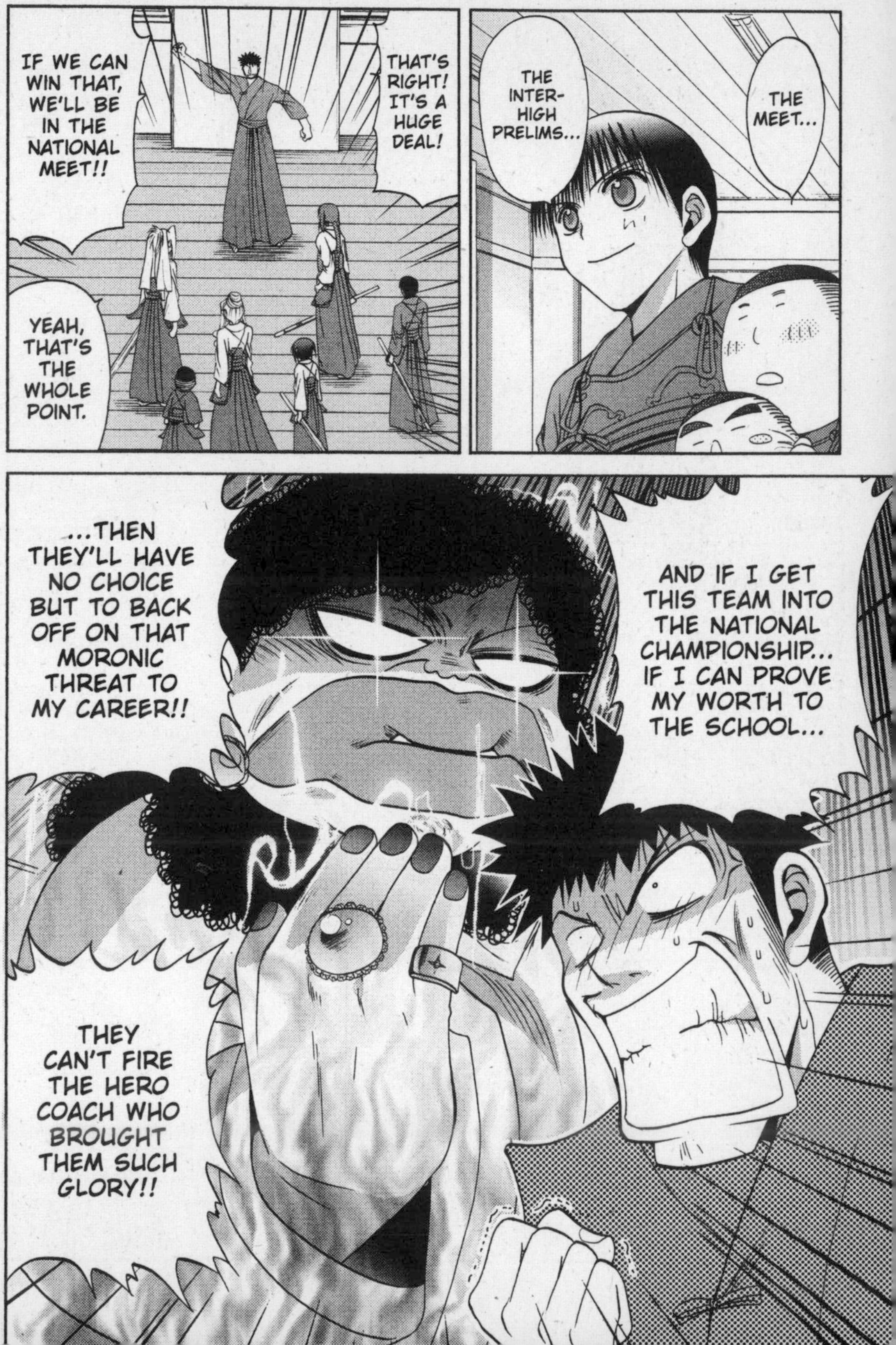
THE MEET...
THE INTER-HIGH PRELIMS...
THAT'S RIGHT! IT'S A HUGE DEAL!
IF WE CAN WIN THAT, WE'LL BE IN THE NATIONAL MEET!!
YEAH, THAT'S THE WHOLE POINT.
AND IF I GET THIS TEAM INTO THE NATIONAL CHAMPIONSHIP... IF I CAN PROVE MY WORTH TO THE SCHOOL...
...THEN THEY'LL HAVE NO CHOICE BUT TO BACK OFF ON THAT MORONIC THREAT TO MY CAREER!!
THEY CAN'T FIRE THE HERO COACH WHO BROUGHT THEM SUCH GLORY!!

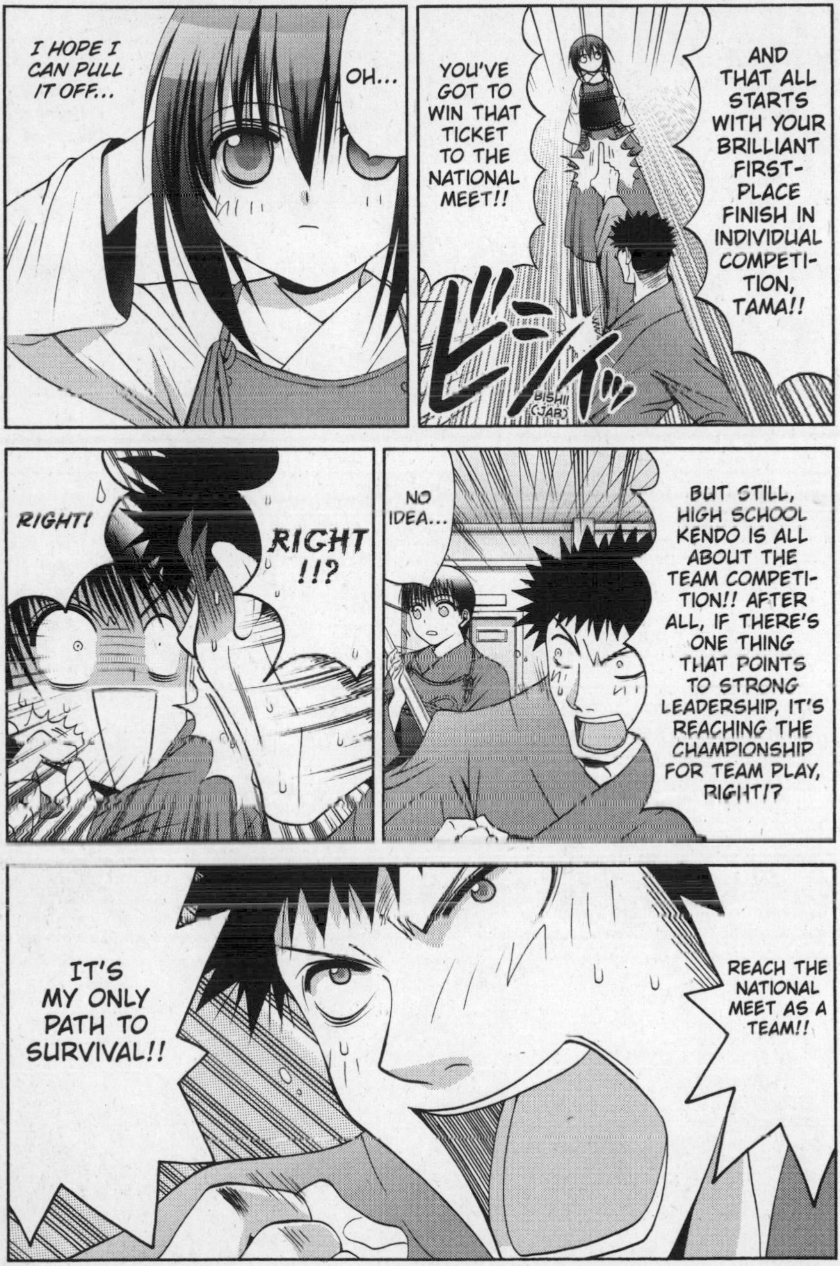
YOU'VE GOT TO WIN THAT TICKET TO THE NATIONAL MEET!!
AND THAT ALL STARTS WITH YOUR BRILLIANT FIRST-PLACE FINISH IN INDIVIDUAL COMPETITION, TAMA!!
BISHI! (JAB)
OH...
I HOPE I CAN PULL IT OFF...
BUT STILL, HIGH SCHOOL KENDO IS ALL ABOUT THE TEAM COMPETITION!! AFTER ALL, IF THERE'S ONE THING THAT POINTS TO STRONG LEADERSHIP, IT'S REACHING THE CHAMPIONSHIP FOR TEAM PLAY, RIGHT!?
NO IDEA...
RIGHT !!?
RIGHT!
REACH THE NATIONAL MEET AS A TEAM!!
IT'S MY ONLY PATH TO SURVIVAL!!

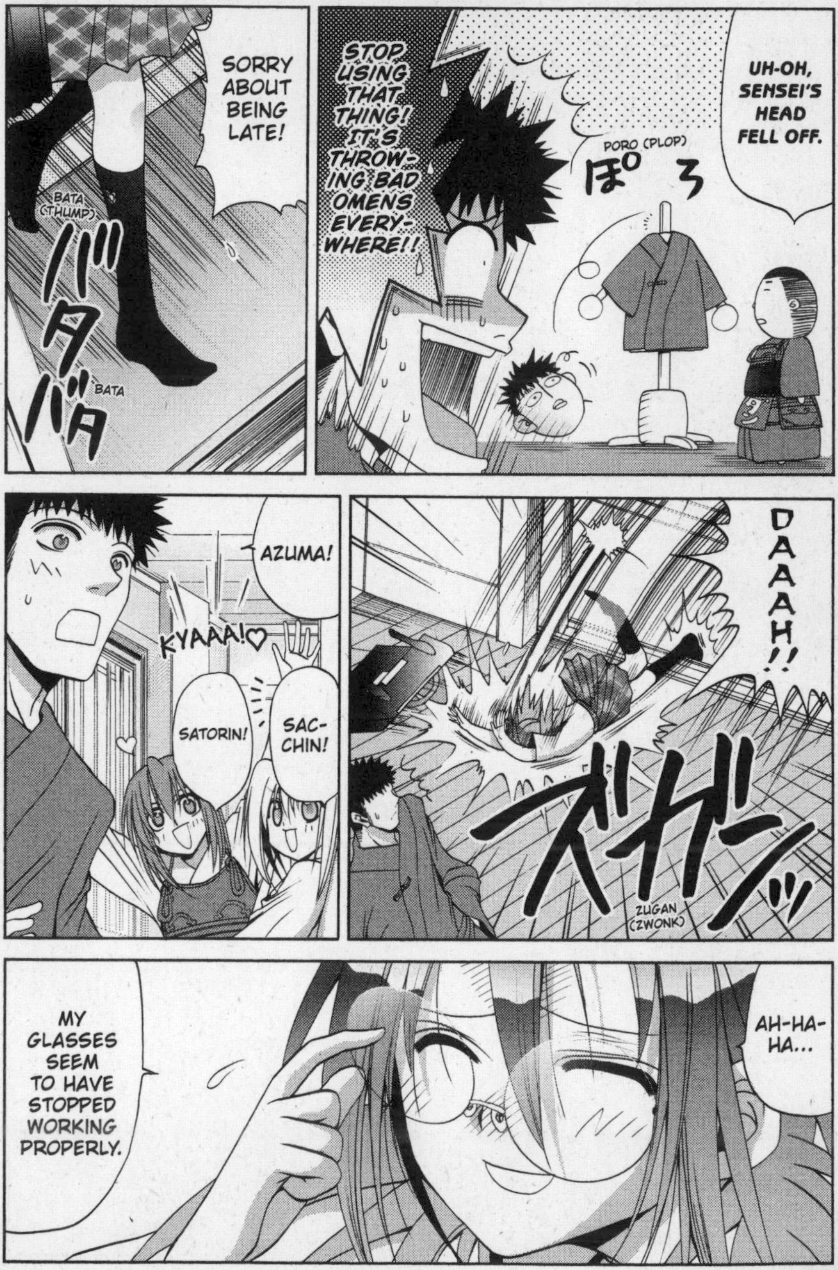
UH-OH, SENSEI'S HEAD FELL OFF.
ぽろ
PORO (PLOP)
STOP USING THAT THING! IT'S THROWING BAD OMENS EVERYWHERE!!
SORRY ABOUT BEING LATE!
バタバタ
BATA (THUMP)
BATA
DAAAH!!
ズガンッ
ZUGAN (ZWONK)
AZUMA!
KYAAA!♡
SAC-CHIN!
SATORIN!
AH-HA-HA...
MY GLASSES SEEM TO HAVE STOPPED WORKING PROPERLY.

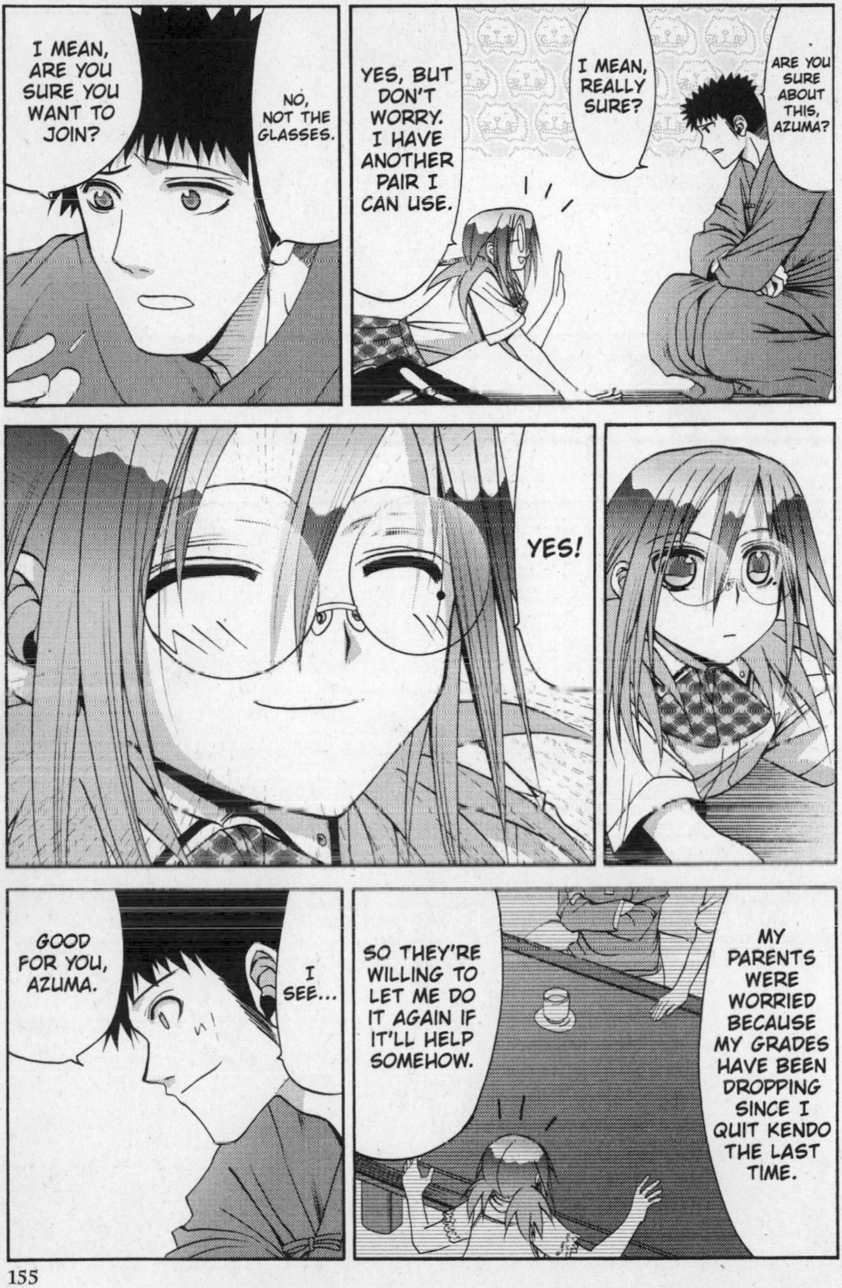
ARE YOU SURE ABOUT THIS, AZUMA?
I MEAN, REALLY SURE?
YES, BUT DON'T WORRY. I HAVE ANOTHER PAIR I CAN USE.
NO, NOT THE GLASSES.
I MEAN, ARE YOU SURE YOU WANT TO JOIN?
YES!
MY PARENTS WERE WORRIED BECAUSE MY GRADES HAVE BEEN DROPPING SINCE I QUIT KENDO THE LAST TIME.
SO THEY'RE WILLING TO LET ME DO IT AGAIN IF IT'LL HELP SOMEHOW.
I SEE...
GOOD FOR YOU, AZUMA.

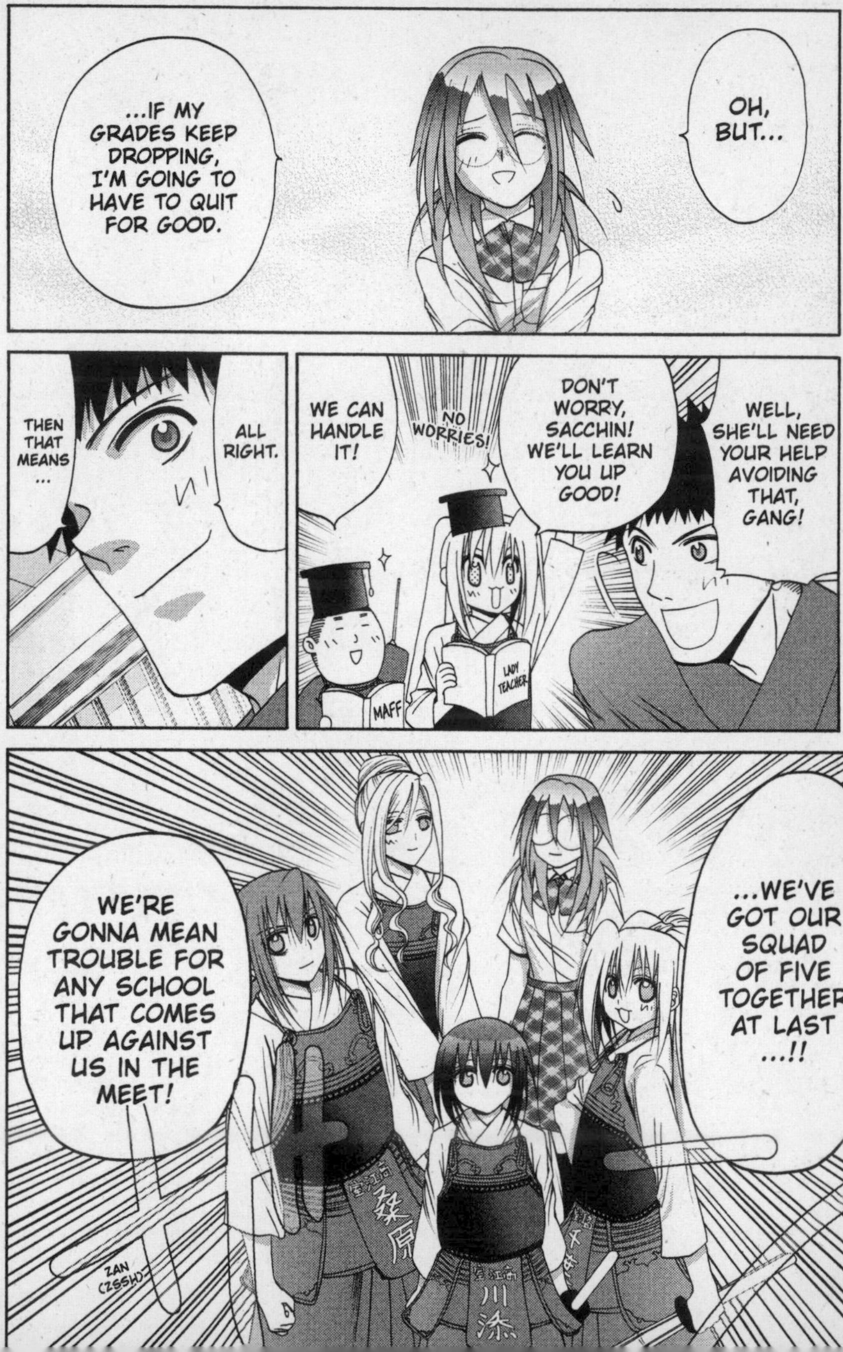
OH, BUT...
...IF MY GRADES KEEP DROPPING, I'M GOING TO HAVE TO QUIT FOR GOOD.
WELL, SHE'LL NEED YOUR HELP AVOIDING THAT, GANG!
DON'T WORRY, SACCHIN! WE'LL LEARN YOU UP GOOD!
NO WORRIES!
WE CAN HANDLE IT!
LADY TEACHER
MAFF
ALL RIGHT.
THEN THAT MEANS ...
...WE'VE GOT OUR SQUAD OF FIVE TOGETHER AT LAST ...!!
WE'RE GONNA MEAN TROUBLE FOR ANY SCHOOL THAT COMES UP AGAINST US IN THE MEET!
ZAN (ZSSH)

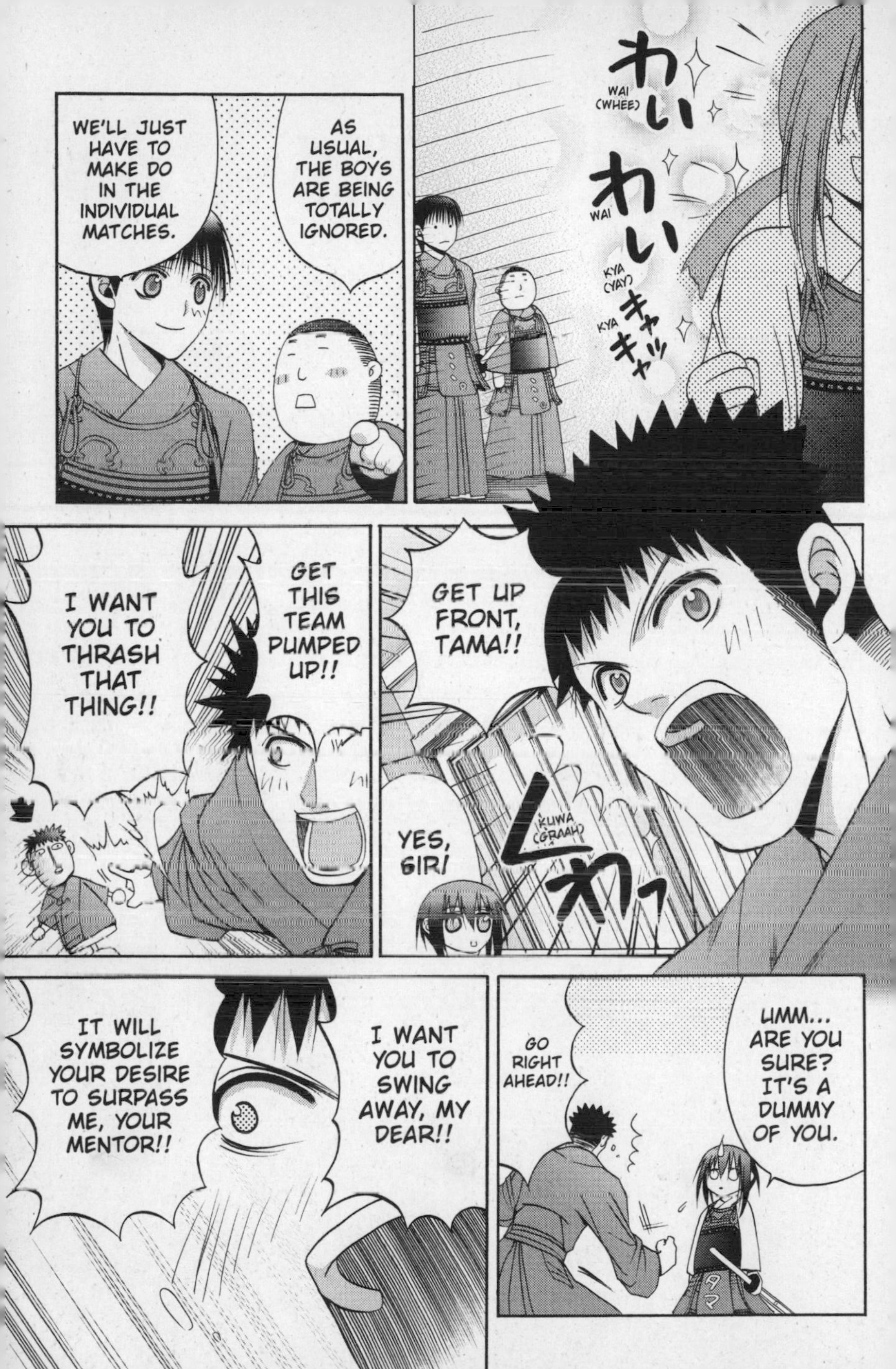
わい
WAI (WHEE)
わい
WAI
キャッ
KYA (YAY)
キャ
KYA
AS USUAL, THE BOYS ARE BEING TOTALLY IGNORED.
WE'LL JUST HAVE TO MAKE DO IN THE INDIVIDUAL MATCHES.
GET UP FRONT, TAMA!!
くわっ
KUWA (GRAAH)
YES, SIR!
GET THIS TEAM PUMPED UP!!
I WANT YOU TO THRASH THAT THING!!
UMM... ARE YOU SURE? IT'S A DUMMY OF YOU.
GO RIGHT AHEAD!!
タマ
I WANT YOU TO SWING AWAY, MY DEAR!!
IT WILL SYMBOLIZE YOUR DESIRE TO SURPASS ME, YOUR MENTOR!!

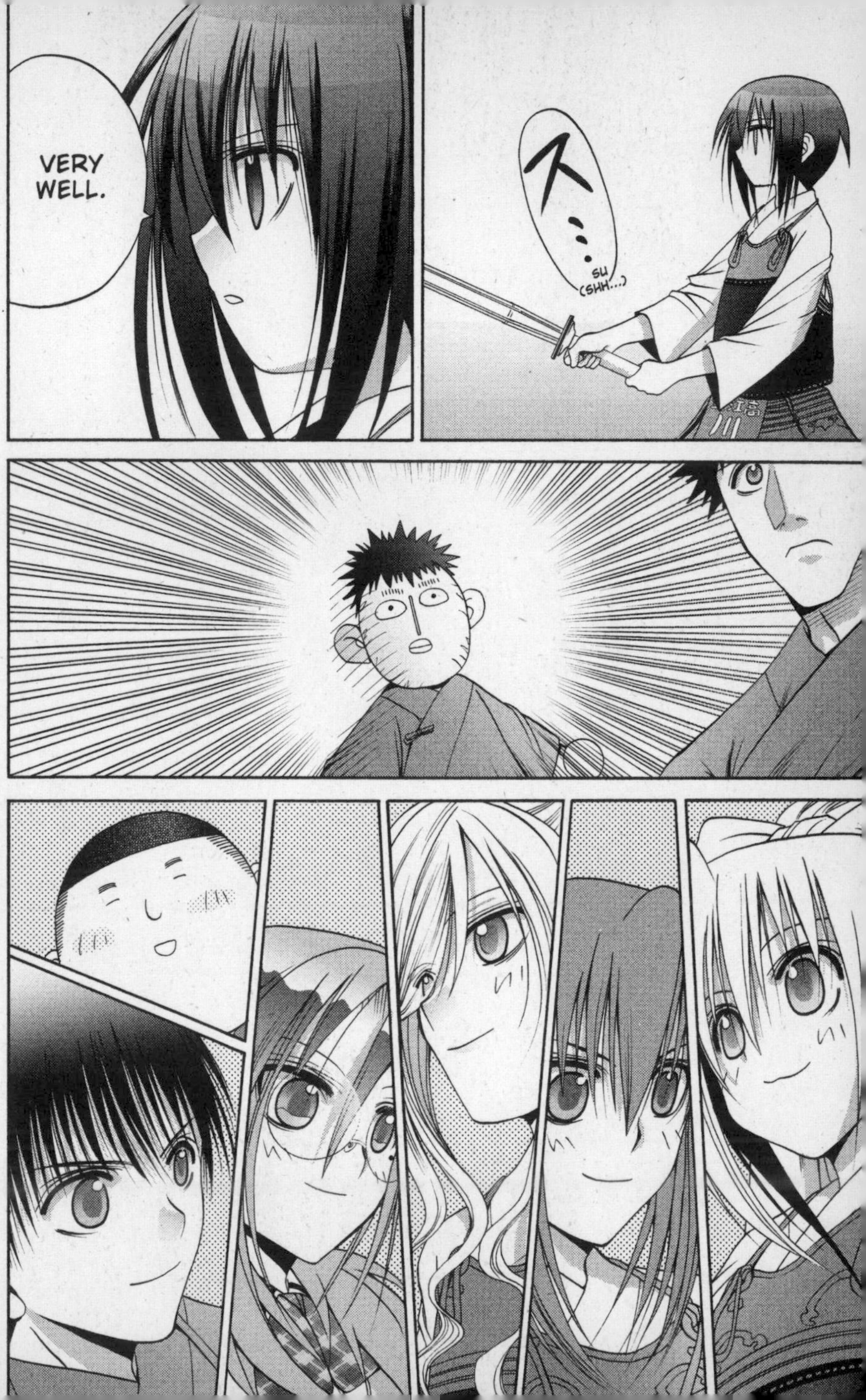
ス…
SU (SHH...)
VERY WELL.

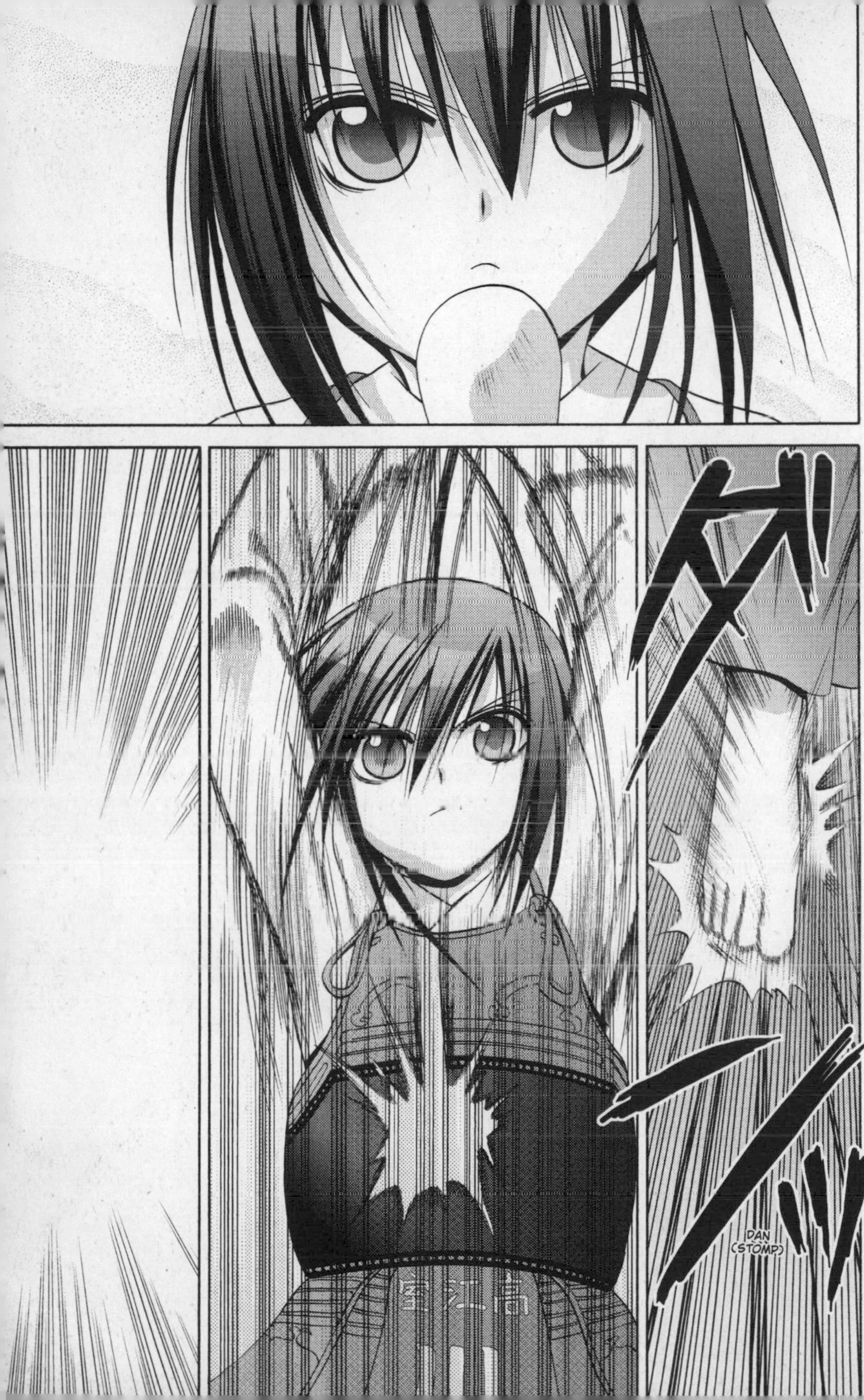
DAN
(STOMP)

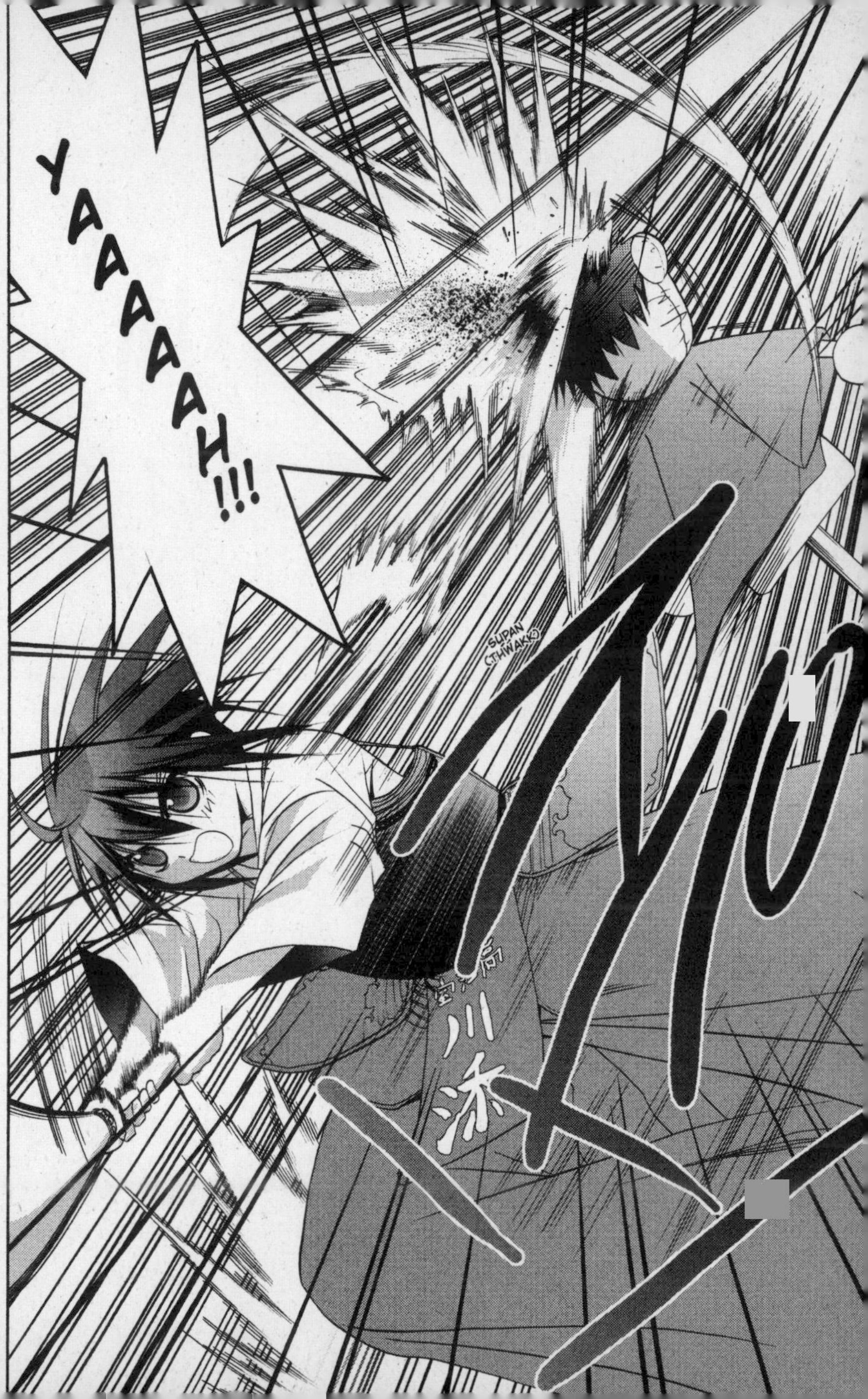
YAAAAAH!!!
SUPAN (THWAKK)

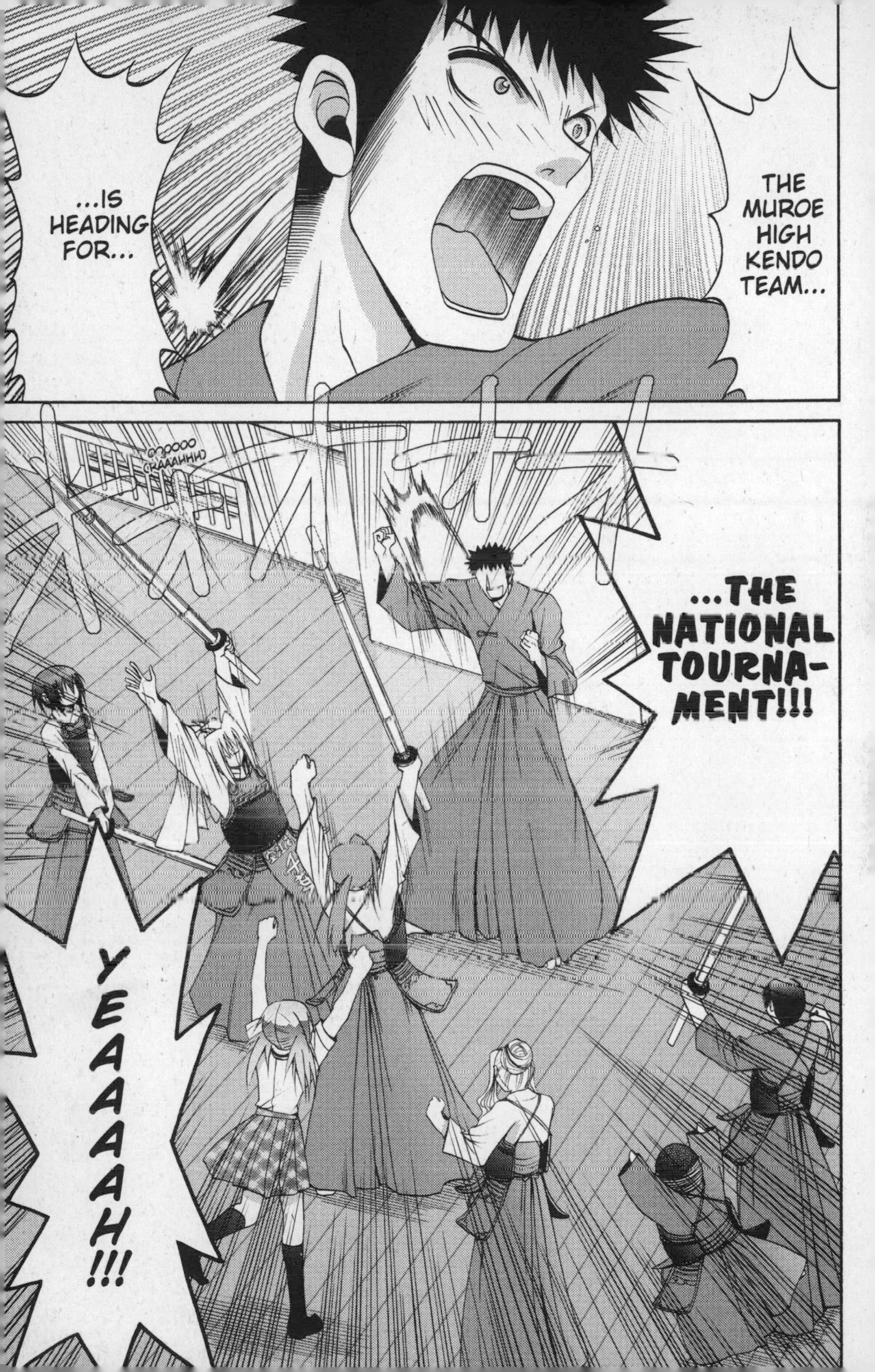
THE MUROE HIGH KENDO TEAM...
...IS HEADING FOR...
...THE NATIONAL TOURNAMENT!!!
YEAAAAAH!!!

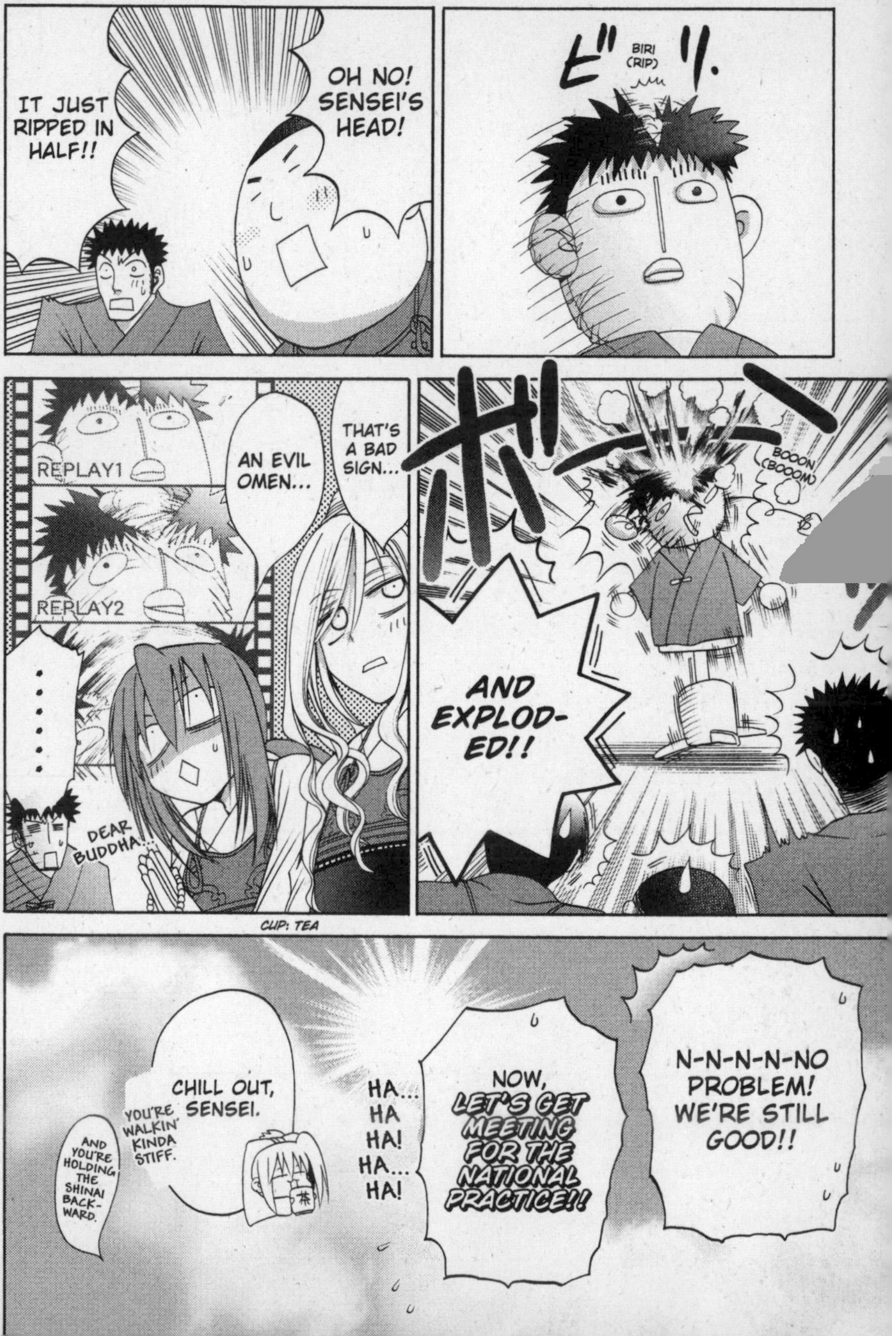
BIRI (RIP)
OH NO! SENSEI'S HEAD!
IT JUST RIPPED IN HALF!!
BOOON (BOOOM)
AND EXPLODED!!
THAT'S A BAD SIGN...
AN EVIL OMEN...
REPLAY1
REPLAY2
......
DEAR BUDDHA...
CUP: TEA
N-N-N-N-NO PROBLEM! WE'RE STILL GOOD!!
NOW, LET'S GET MEETING FOR THE NATIONAL PRACTICE!!
HA... HA HA! HA... HA!
CHILL OUT, SENSEI.
YOU'RE WALKIN' KINDA STIFF.
AND YOU'RE HOLDING THE SHINAI BACKWARD.

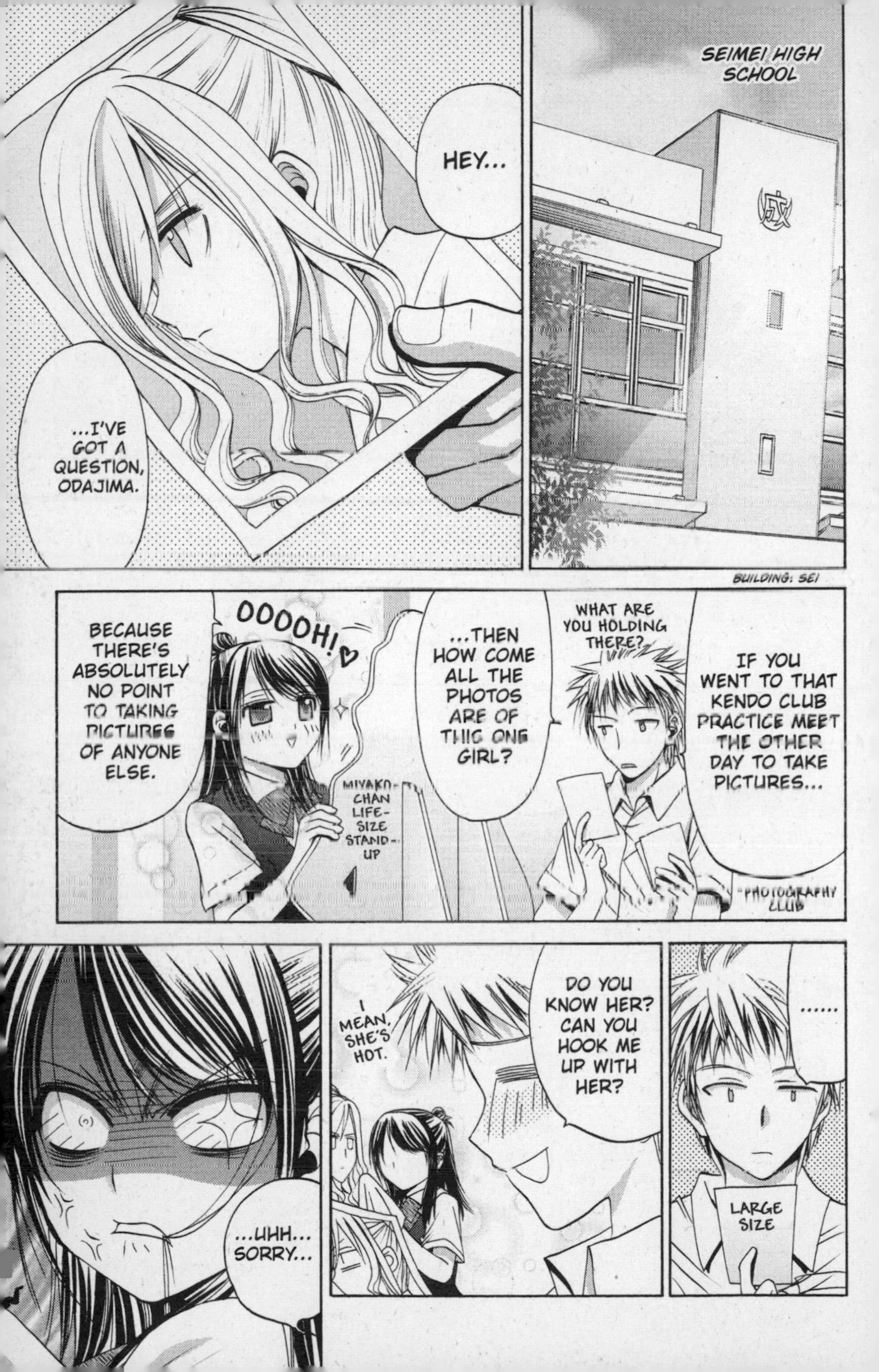
SEIMEI HIGH SCHOOL
BUILDING: SEI
HEY...
...I'VE GOT A QUESTION, ODAJIMA.
IF YOU WENT TO THAT KENDO CLUB PRACTICE MEET THE OTHER DAY TO TAKE PICTURES...
PHOTOGRAPHY CLUB
WHAT ARE YOU HOLDING THERE?
...THEN HOW COME ALL THE PHOTOS ARE OF THIS ONE GIRL?
OOOOH! ♥
MIYAKO-CHAN LIFE-SIZE STAND-UP
BECAUSE THERE'S ABSOLUTELY NO POINT TO TAKING PICTURES OF ANYONE ELSE.
......
LARGE SIZE
DO YOU KNOW HER? CAN YOU HOOK ME UP WITH HER?
I MEAN, SHE'S HOT.
...UHH... SORRY...

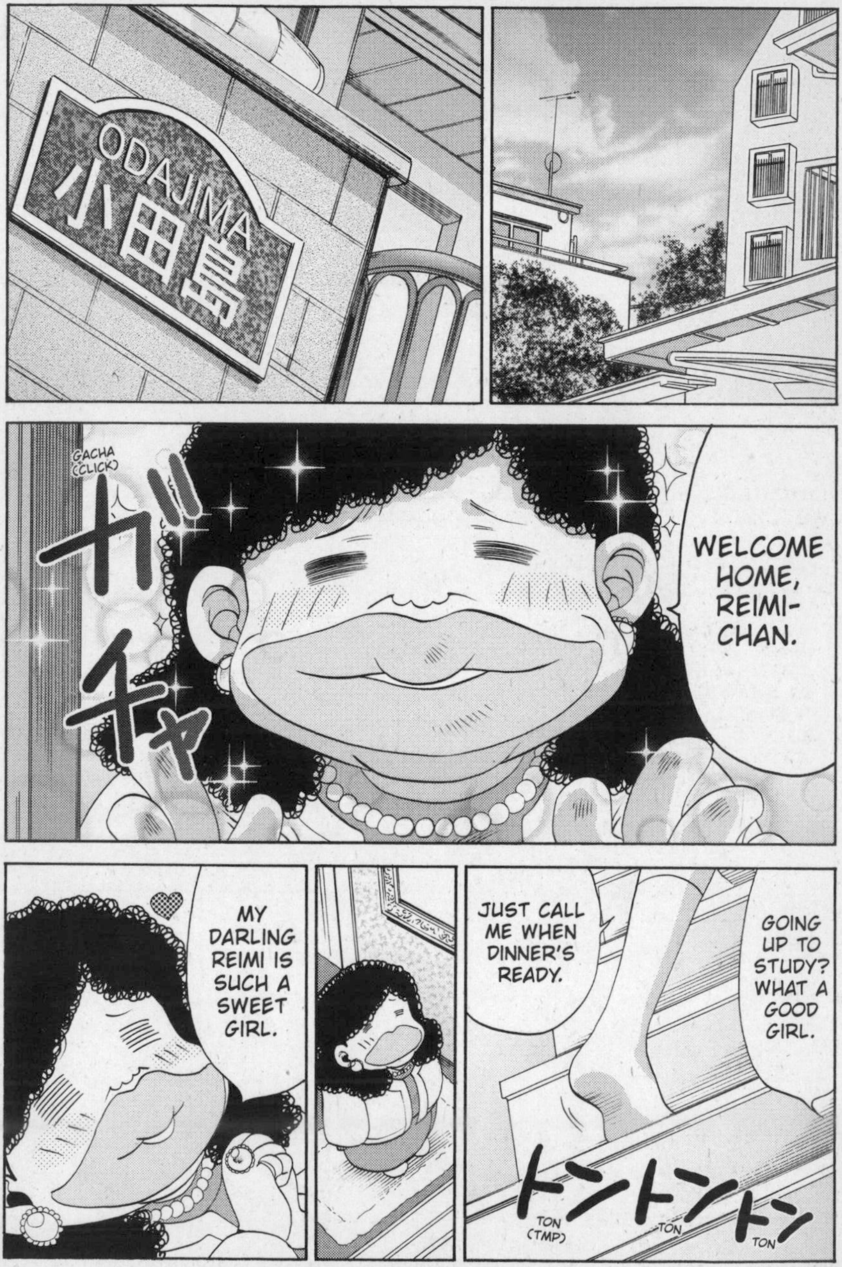
ODAJIMA
小田島
WELCOME HOME, REIMI-CHAN.
ガチャ
GACHA (CLICK)
GOING UP TO STUDY? WHAT A GOOD GIRL.
JUST CALL ME WHEN DINNER'S READY.
トントントン
TON (TMP)
TON
TON
MY DARLING REIMI IS SUCH A SWEET GIRL.

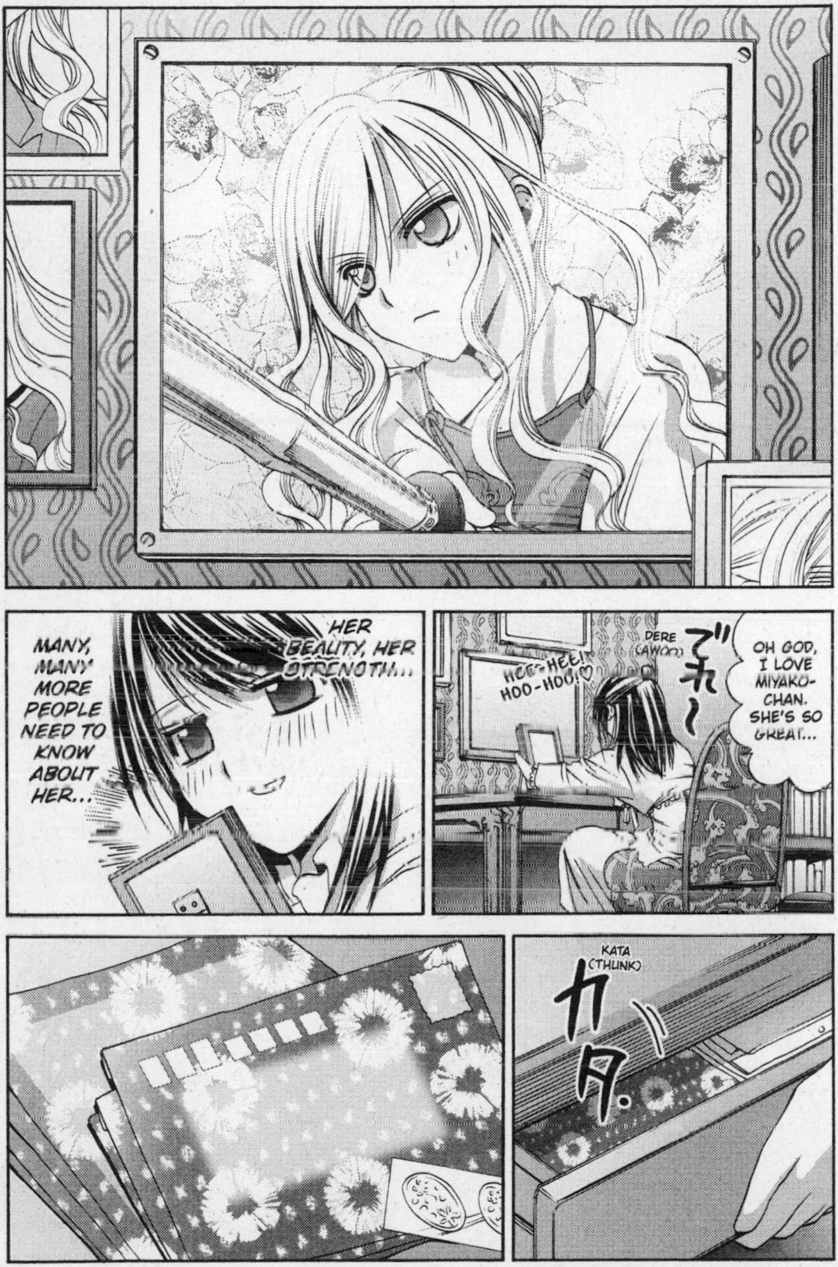
OH GOD, I LOVE MIYAKO-CHAN. SHE'S SO GREAT...
デレ~
DERE (AWOO)
HOO-HEE! HOO-HOO!♡
HER BEAUTY, HER STRENGTH...
MANY, MANY MORE PEOPLE NEED TO KNOW ABOUT HER...
KATA (THUNK)
カタ.

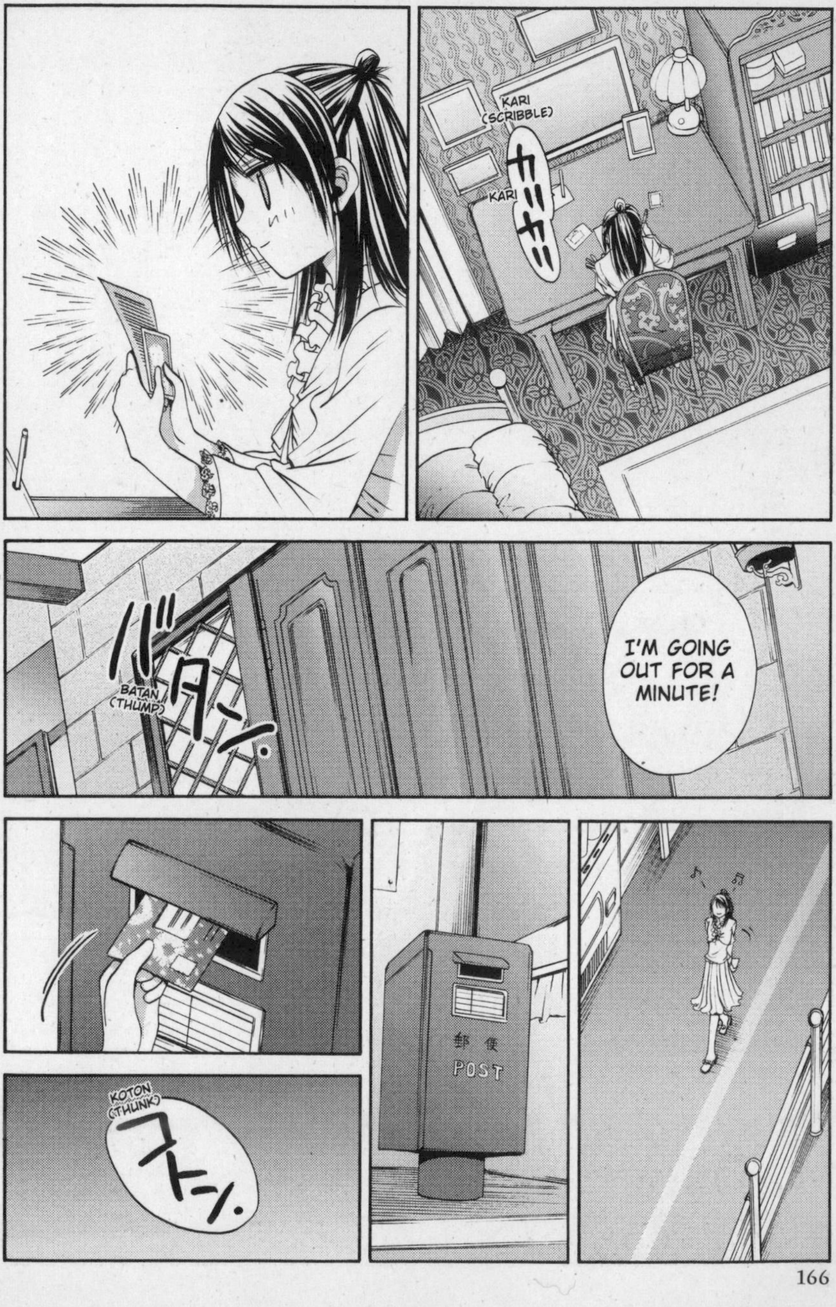
KARI (SCRIBBLE)
カリカリ
KARI
I'M GOING OUT FOR A MINUTE!
BATAN (THUMP)
バターン。
郵便
POST
KOTON (THUNK)
コトーン。

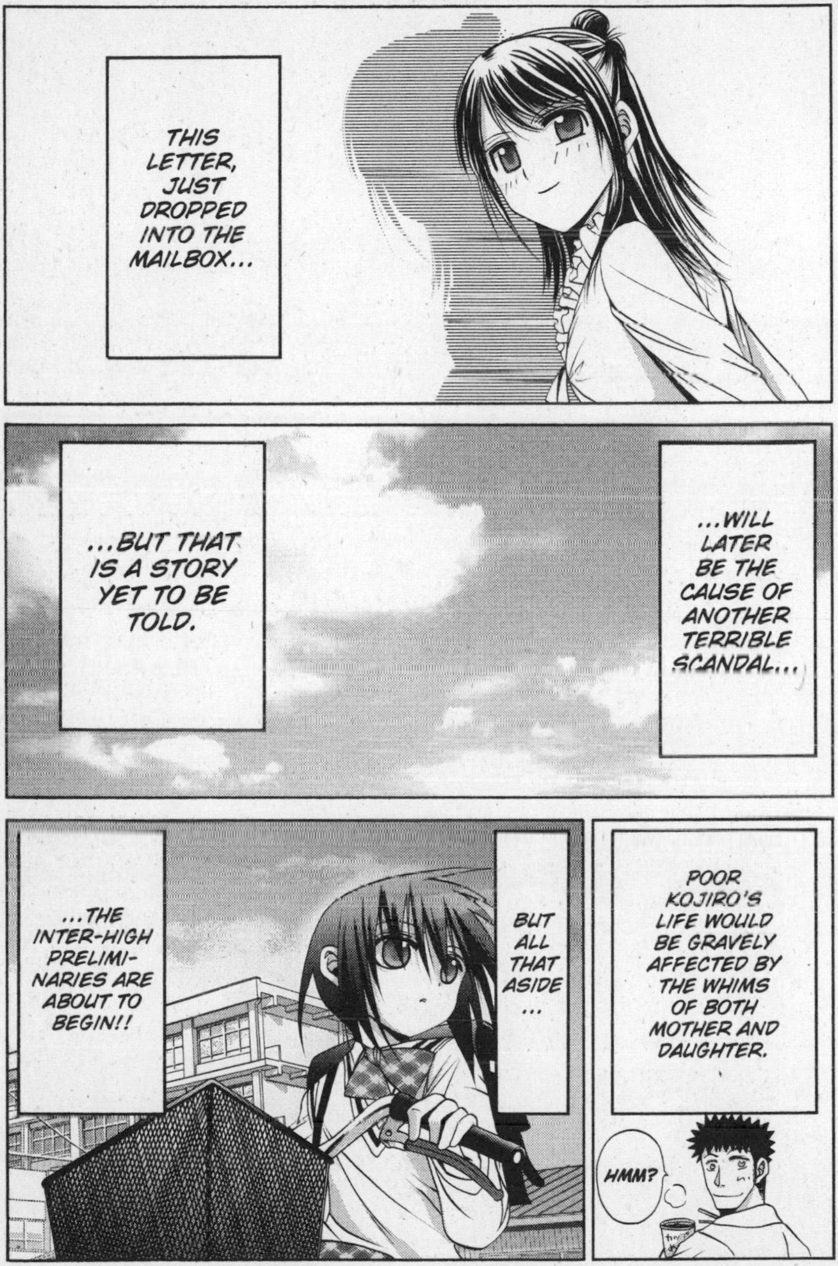
THIS LETTER, JUST DROPPED INTO THE MAILBOX...
...WILL LATER BE THE CAUSE OF ANOTHER TERRIBLE SCANDAL...
...BUT THAT IS A STORY YET TO BE TOLD.
POOR KOJIRO'S LIFE WOULD BE GRAVELY AFFECTED BY THE WHIMS OF BOTH MOTHER AND DAUGHTER.
HMM?
BUT ALL THAT ASIDE...
...THE INTER-HIGH PRELIMI-NARIES ARE ABOUT TO BEGIN!!

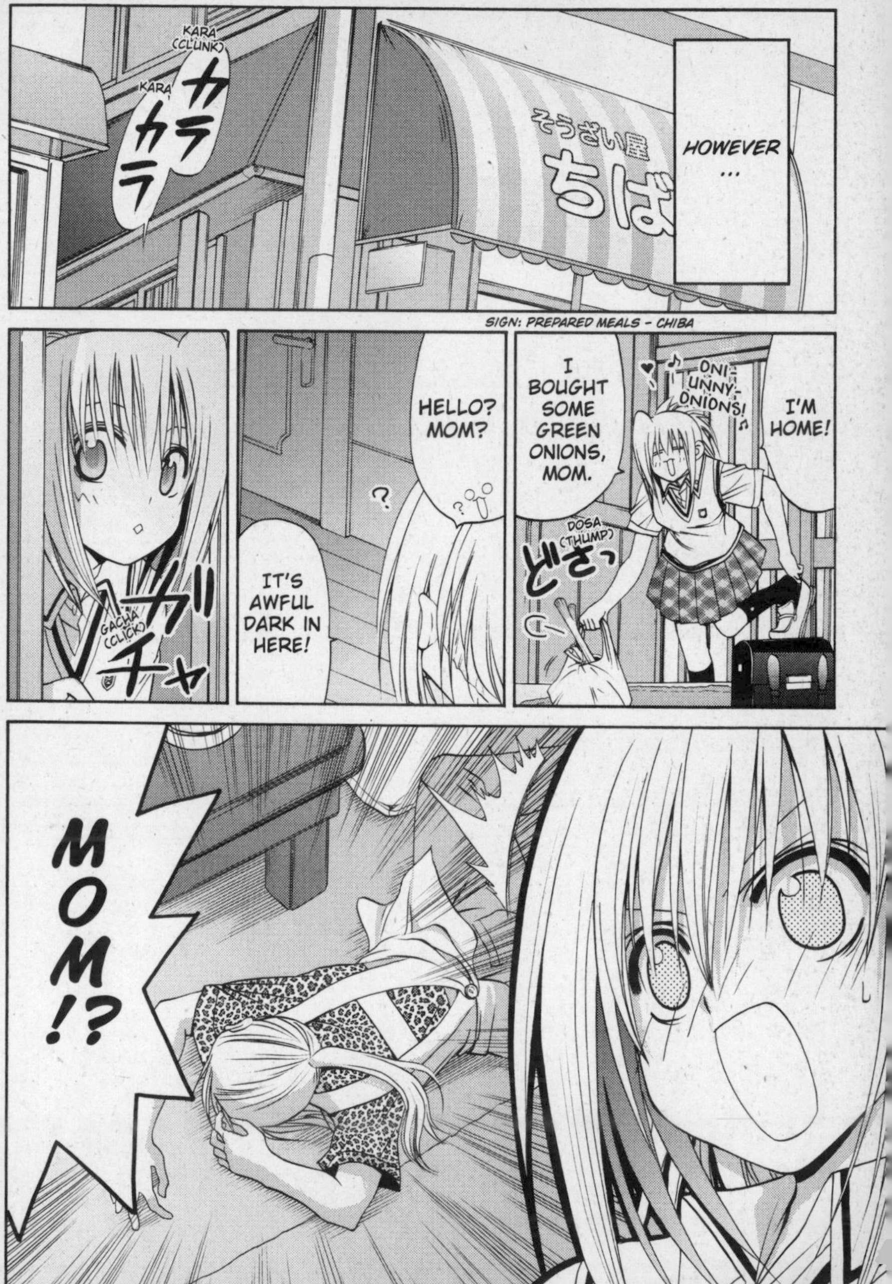
HOWEVER ...
KARA (CLUNK)
カラ
KARA
カラ
そうざい屋
ちば
SIGN: PREPARED MEALS - CHIBA
I'M HOME!
ONI-UNNY ONIONS!
I BOUGHT SOME GREEN ONIONS, MOM.
DOSA (THUMP)
どさっ
HELLO? MOM?
IT'S AWFUL DARK IN HERE!
GACHA (CLICK)
ガチャ
MOM!?

BAMBOO BLADE

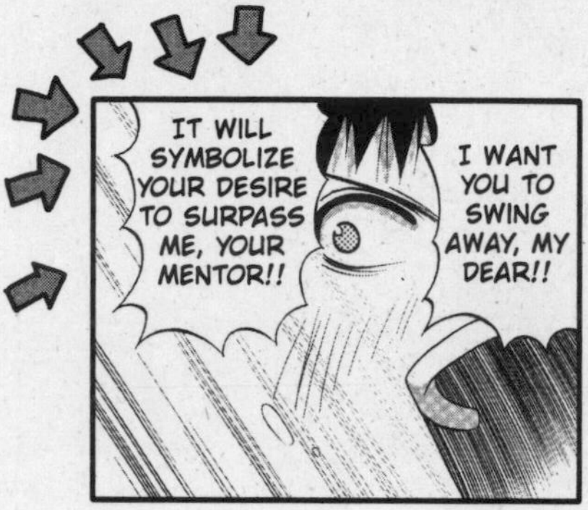
I WANT YOU TO SWING AWAY, MY DEAR!!
IT WILL SYMBOLIZE YOUR DESIRE TO SURPASS ME, YOUR MENTOR!!

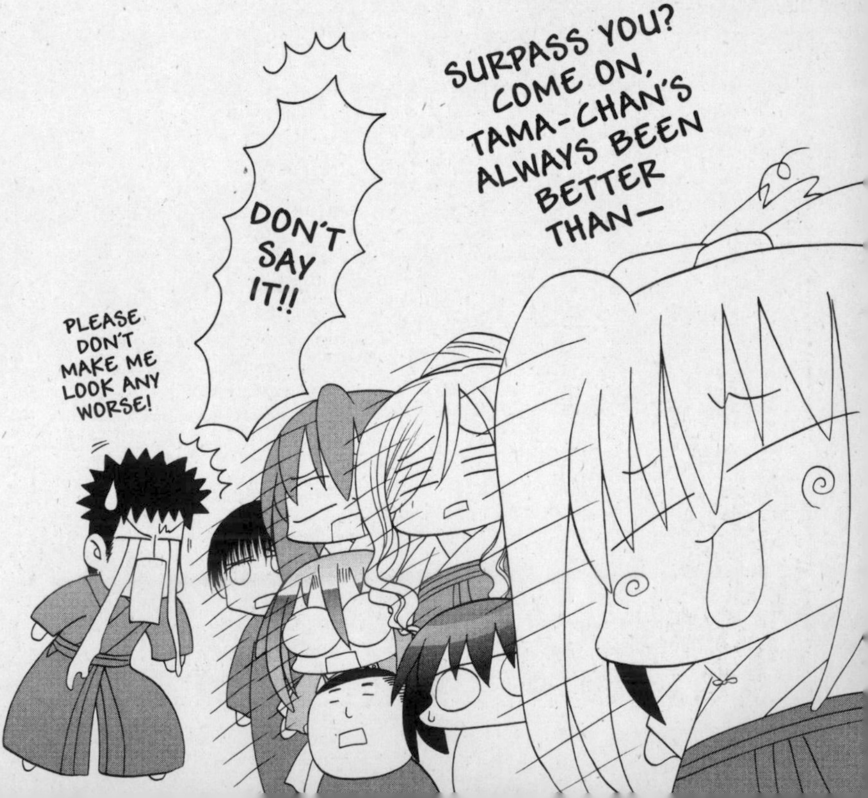
SURPASS YOU? COME ON, TAMA-CHAN'S ALWAYS BEEN BETTER THAN—
DON'T SAY IT!!
PLEASE DON'T MAKE ME LOOK ANY WORSE!

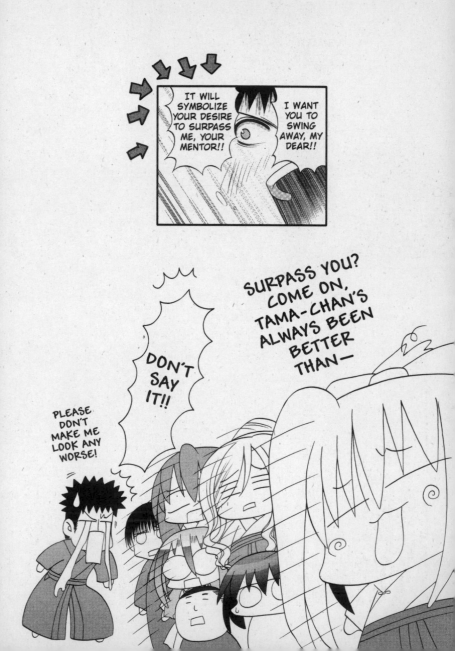

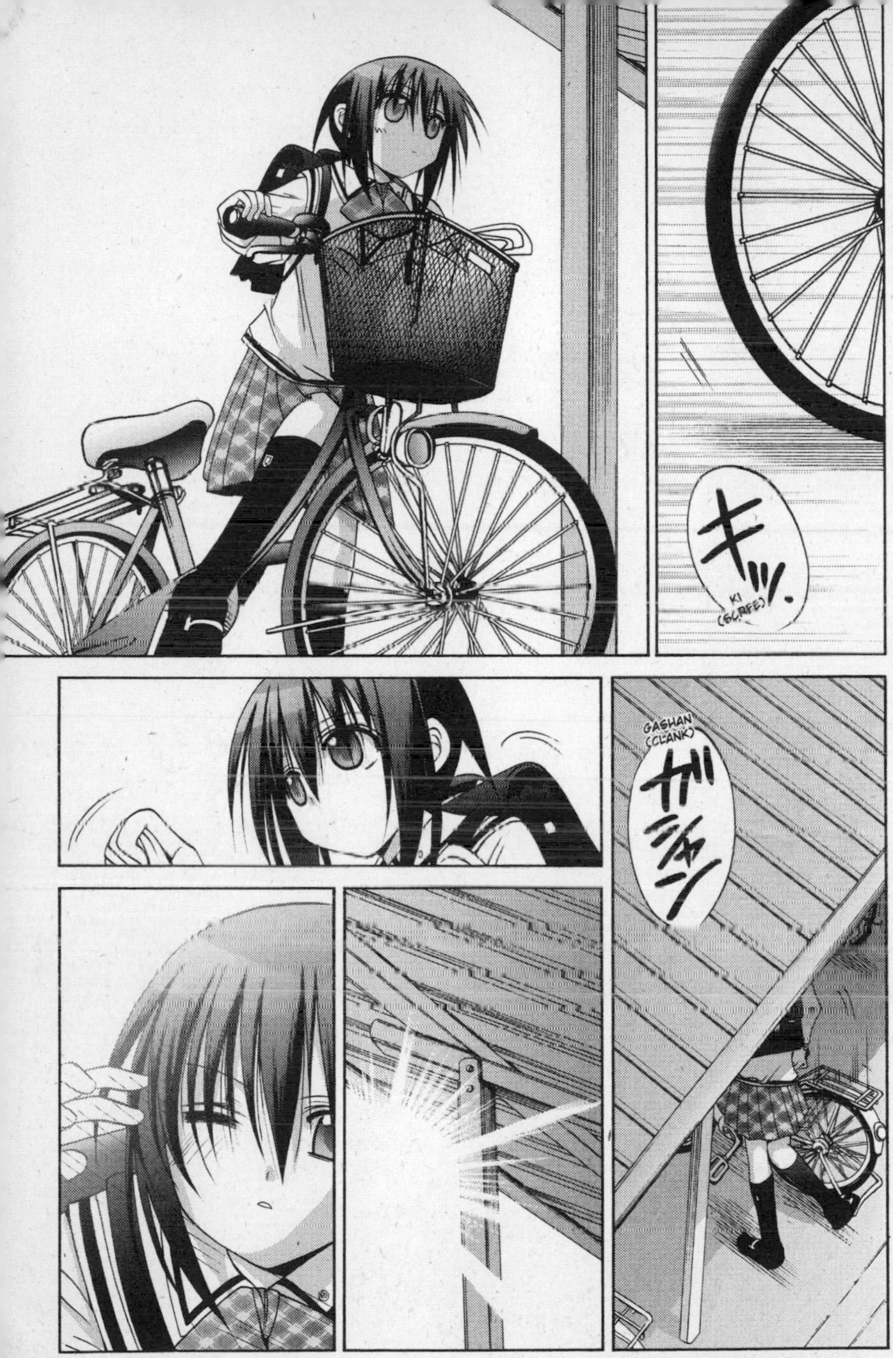
キッ。
KI (SCRAPE)
GASHAN (CLANK)
ガシャン

CHAPTER 47 KIRINO AND HER MOTHER

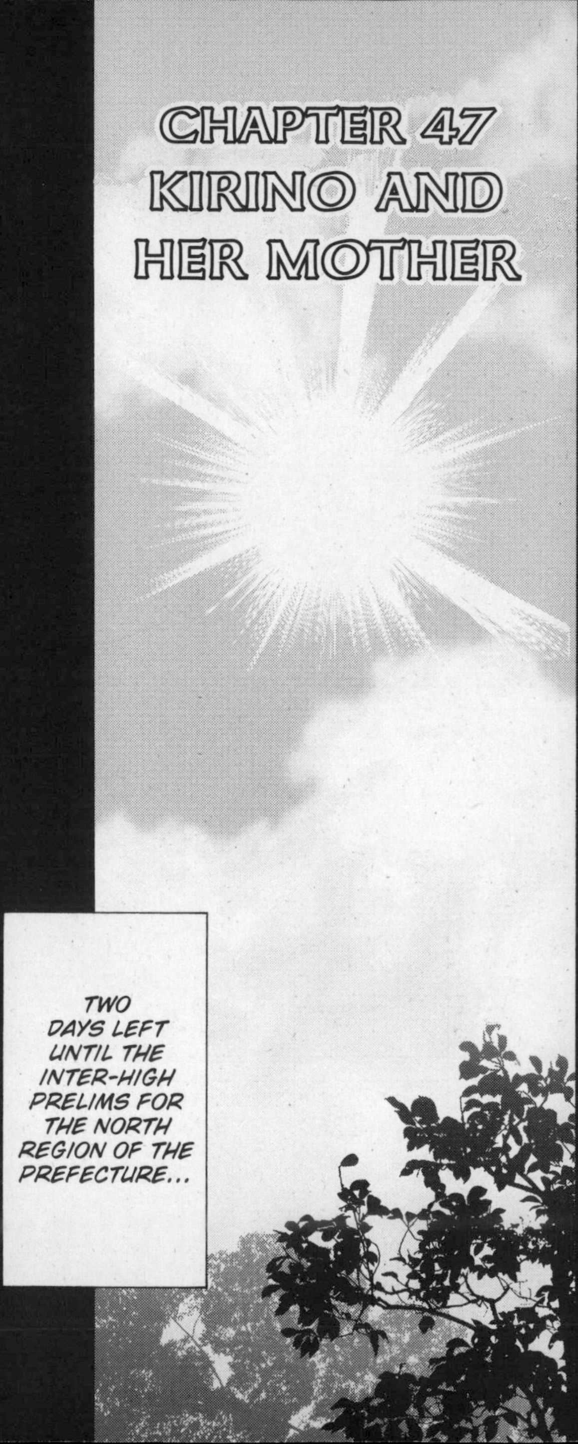
TWO DAYS LEFT UNTIL THE INTER-HIGH PRELIMS FOR THE NORTH REGION OF THE PREFECTURE...

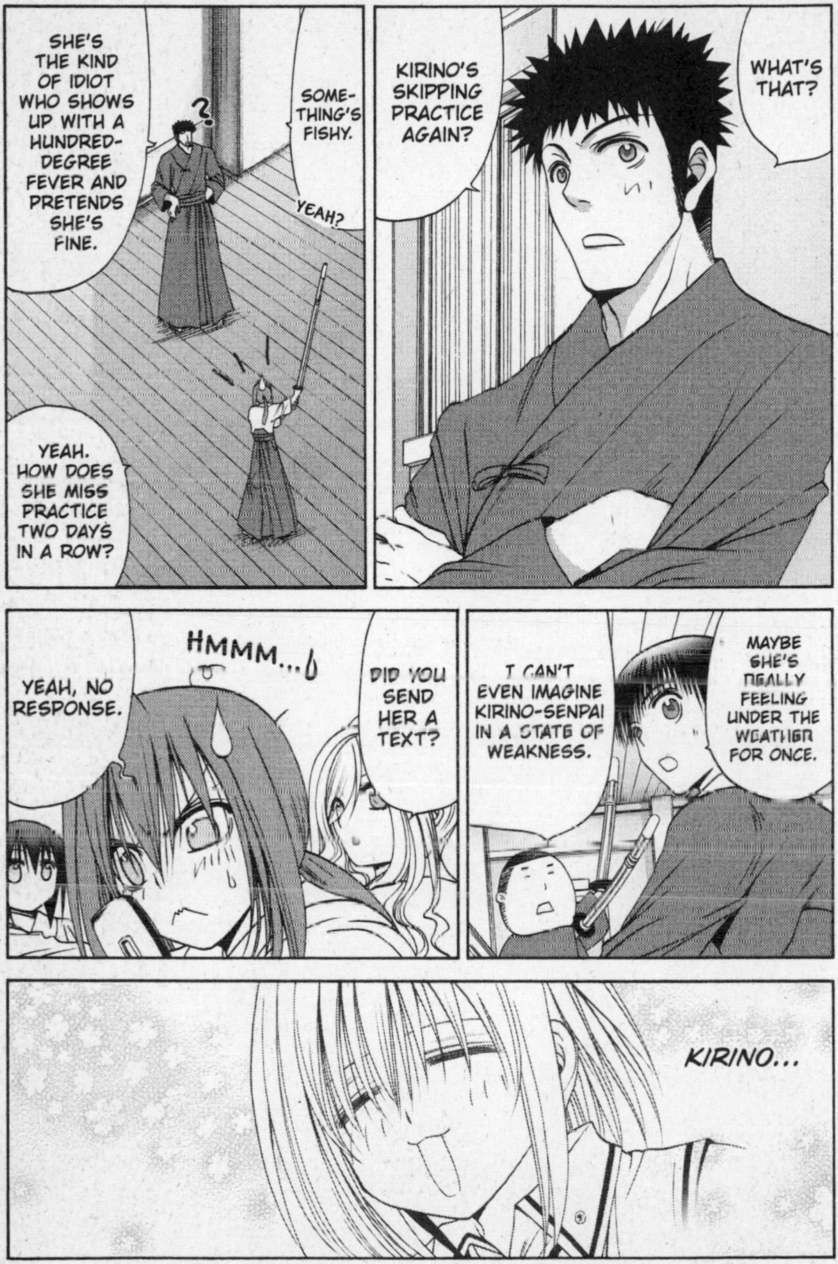
WHAT'S THAT?
KIRINO'S SKIPPING PRACTICE AGAIN?
SOME-THING'S FISHY.
YEAH?
SHE'S THE KIND OF IDIOT WHO SHOWS UP WITH A HUNDRED-DEGREE FEVER AND PRETENDS SHE'S FINE.
YEAH. HOW DOES SHE MISS PRACTICE TWO DAYS IN A ROW?
MAYBE SHE'S REALLY FEELING UNDER THE WEATHER FOR ONCE.
I CAN'T EVEN IMAGINE KIRINO-SENPAI IN A STATE OF WEAKNESS.
DID YOU SEND HER A TEXT?
HMMM...
YEAH, NO RESPONSE.
KIRINO...

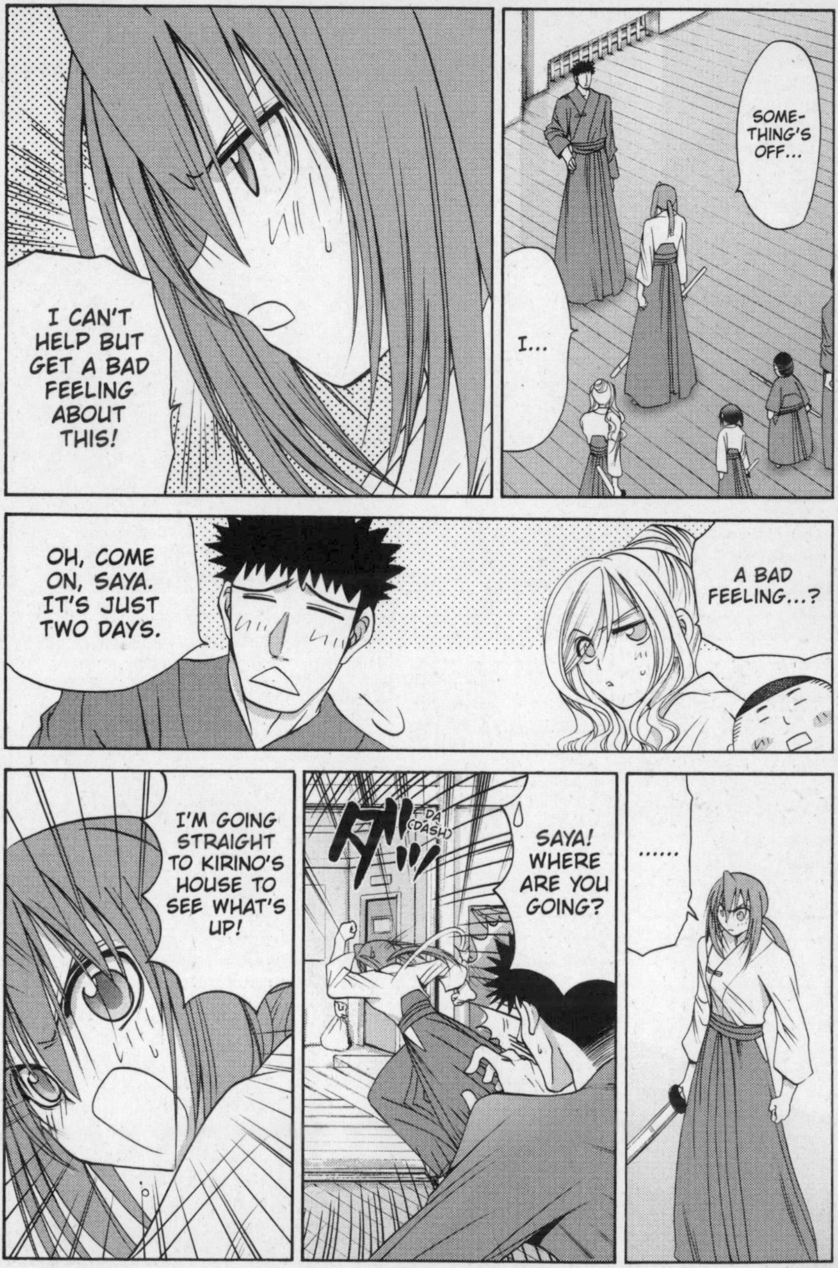
SOME-THING'S OFF...
I...
I CAN'T HELP BUT GET A BAD FEELING ABOUT THIS!
A BAD FEELING...?
OH, COME ON, SAYA. IT'S JUST TWO DAYS.
......
SAYA! WHERE ARE YOU GOING?
DA (DASH)
I'M GOING STRAIGHT TO KIRINO'S HOUSE TO SEE WHAT'S UP!

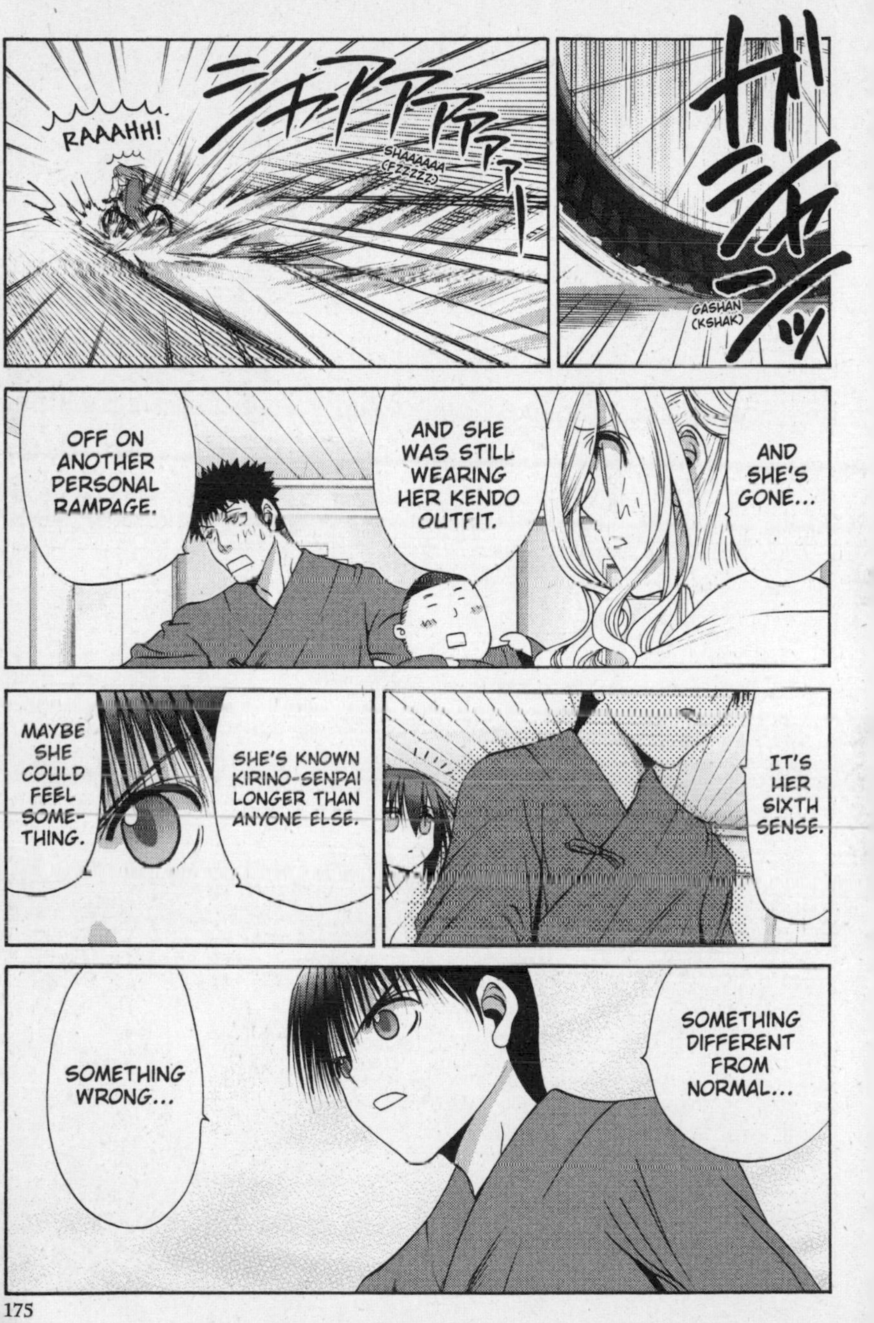
GASHAN (KSHAK)
RAAAHH!
SHAAAAAA (FZZZZZ)
AND SHE'S GONE...
AND SHE WAS STILL WEARING HER KENDO OUTFIT.
OFF ON ANOTHER PERSONAL RAMPAGE.
IT'S HER SIXTH SENSE.
SHE'S KNOWN KIRINO-SENPAI LONGER THAN ANYONE ELSE.
MAYBE SHE COULD FEEL SOME-THING.
SOMETHING DIFFERENT FROM NORMAL...
SOMETHING WRONG...

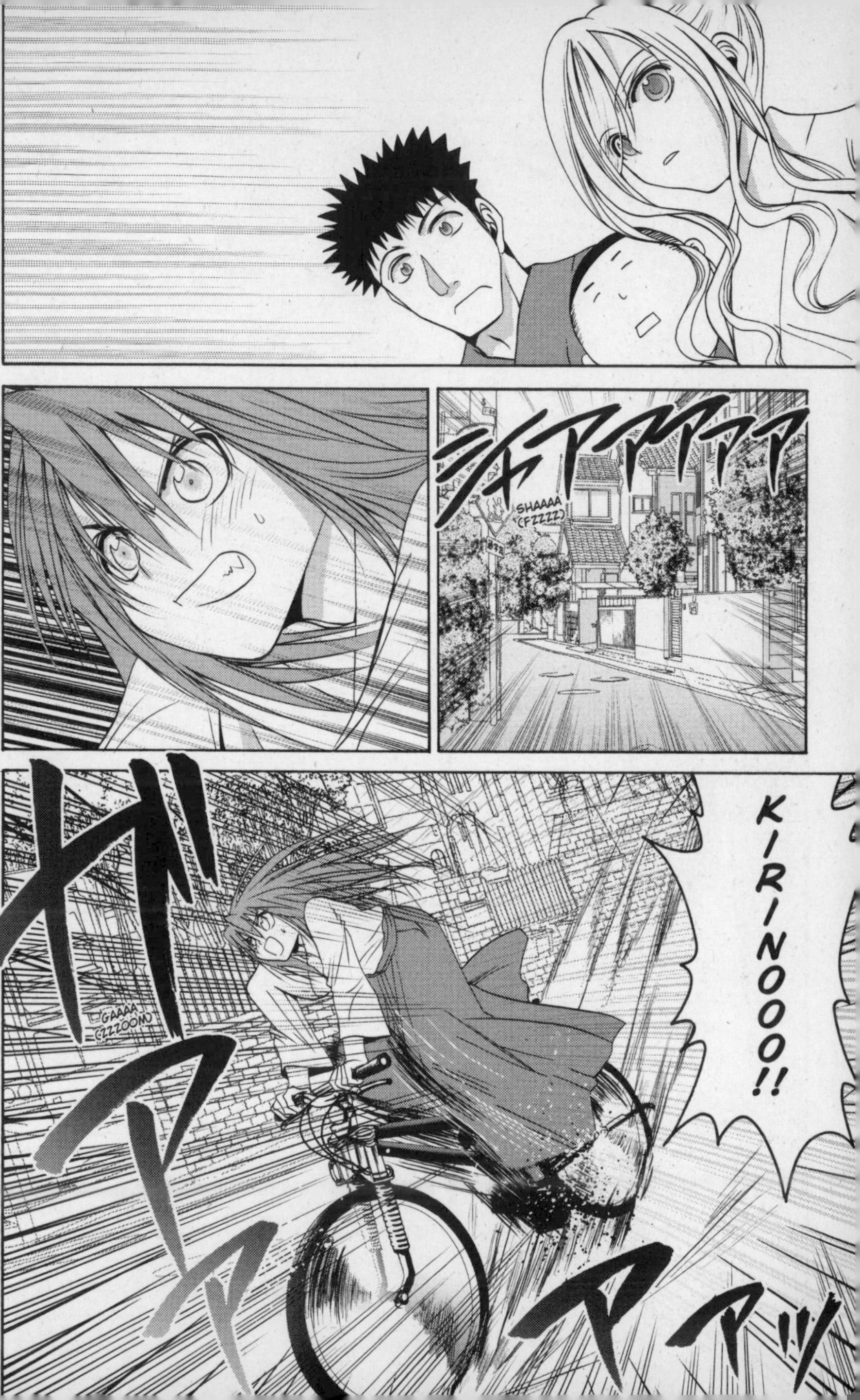
シャアアアア
SHAAAA (FZZZZ)
KIRINOOOO!!
GAAAA (ZZZOOM)

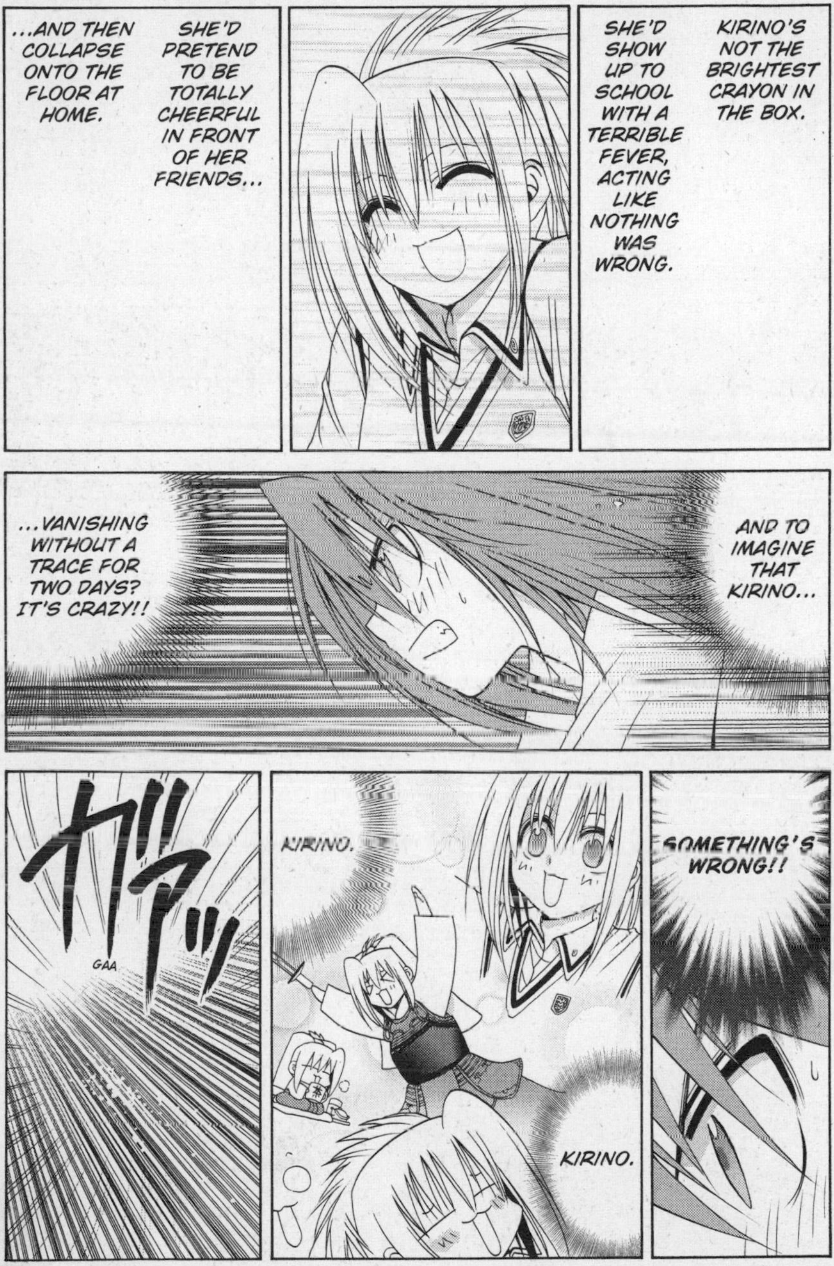
KIRINO'S NOT THE BRIGHTEST CRAYON IN THE BOX.
SHE'D SHOW UP TO SCHOOL WITH A TERRIBLE FEVER, ACTING LIKE NOTHING WAS WRONG.
SHE'D PRETEND TO BE TOTALLY CHEERFUL IN FRONT OF HER FRIENDS...
...AND THEN COLLAPSE ONTO THE FLOOR AT HOME.
AND TO IMAGINE THAT KIRINO...
...VANISHING WITHOUT A TRACE FOR TWO DAYS? IT'S CRAZY!!
SOMETHING'S WRONG!!
KIRINO.
KIRINO.
ガァッ
GAA

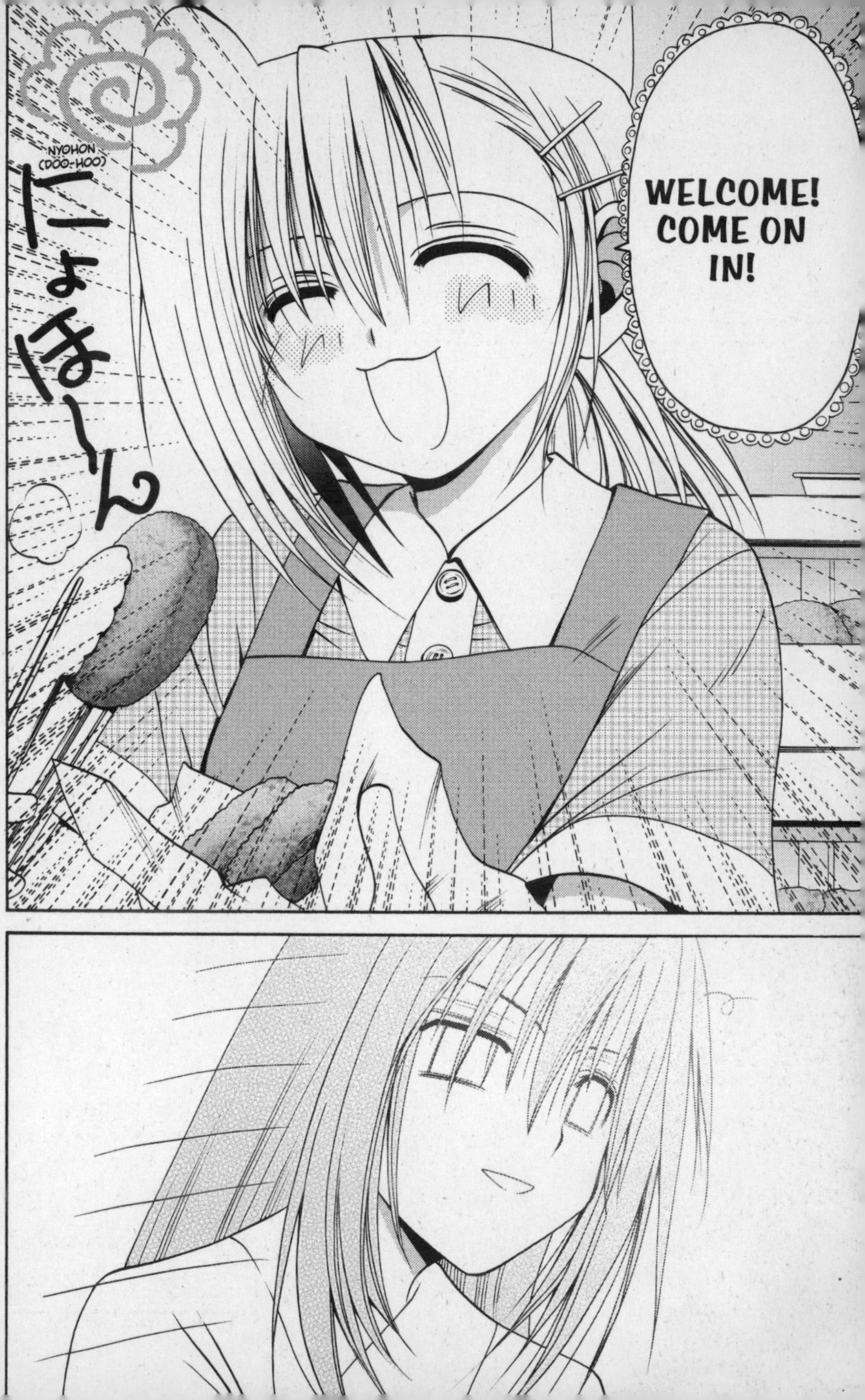
WELCOME! COME ON IN!
にょほ～ん
NYOHON (DOO-HOO)

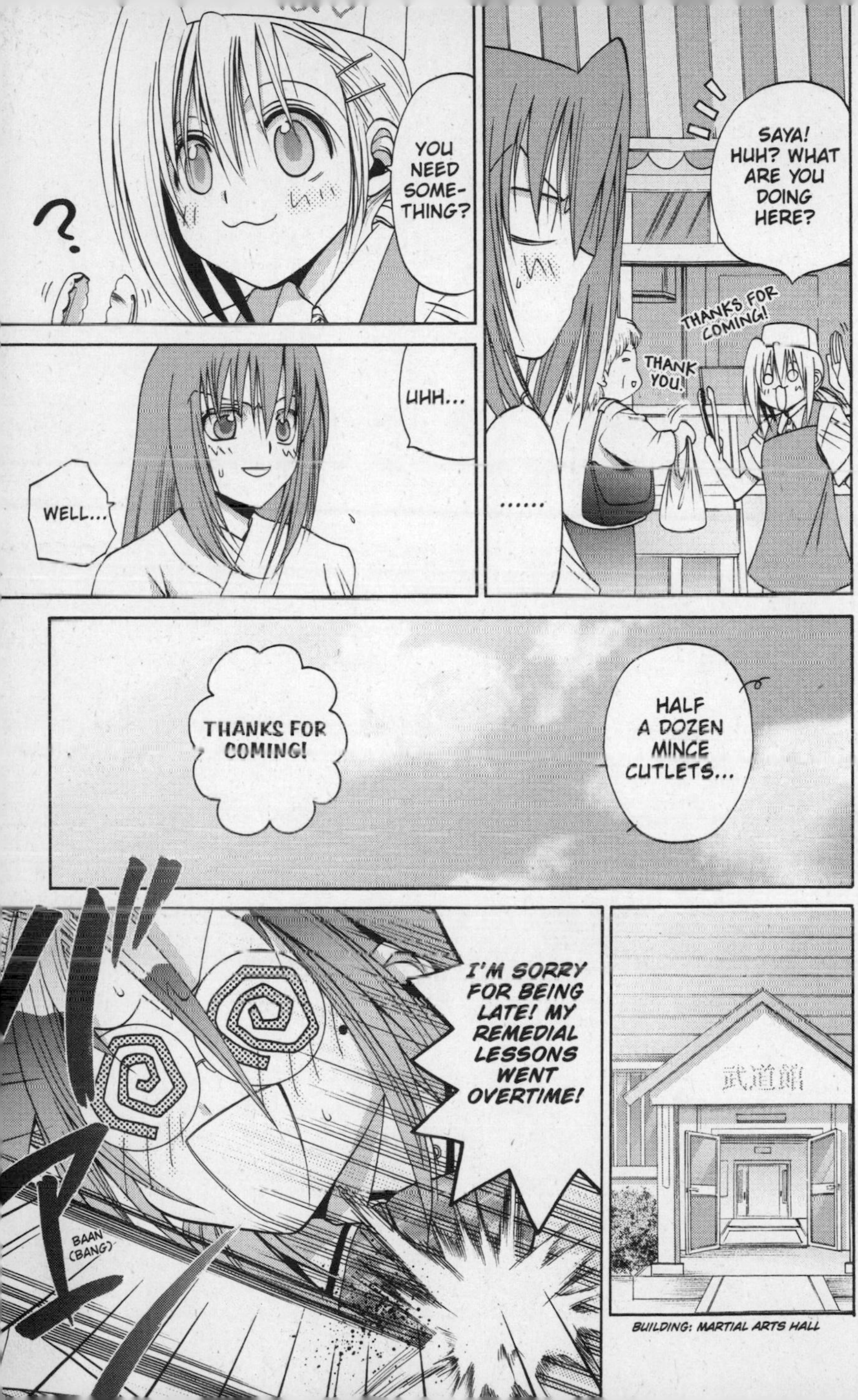
SAYA! HUH? WHAT ARE YOU DOING HERE?
THANKS FOR COMING!
THANK YOU!
......
YOU NEED SOME-THING?
UHH...
WELL...
HALF A DOZEN MINCE CUTLETS...
THANKS FOR COMING!
武道館
BUILDING: MARTIAL ARTS HALL
I'M SORRY FOR BEING LATE! MY REMEDIAL LESSONS WENT OVERTIME!
BAAN (BANG)

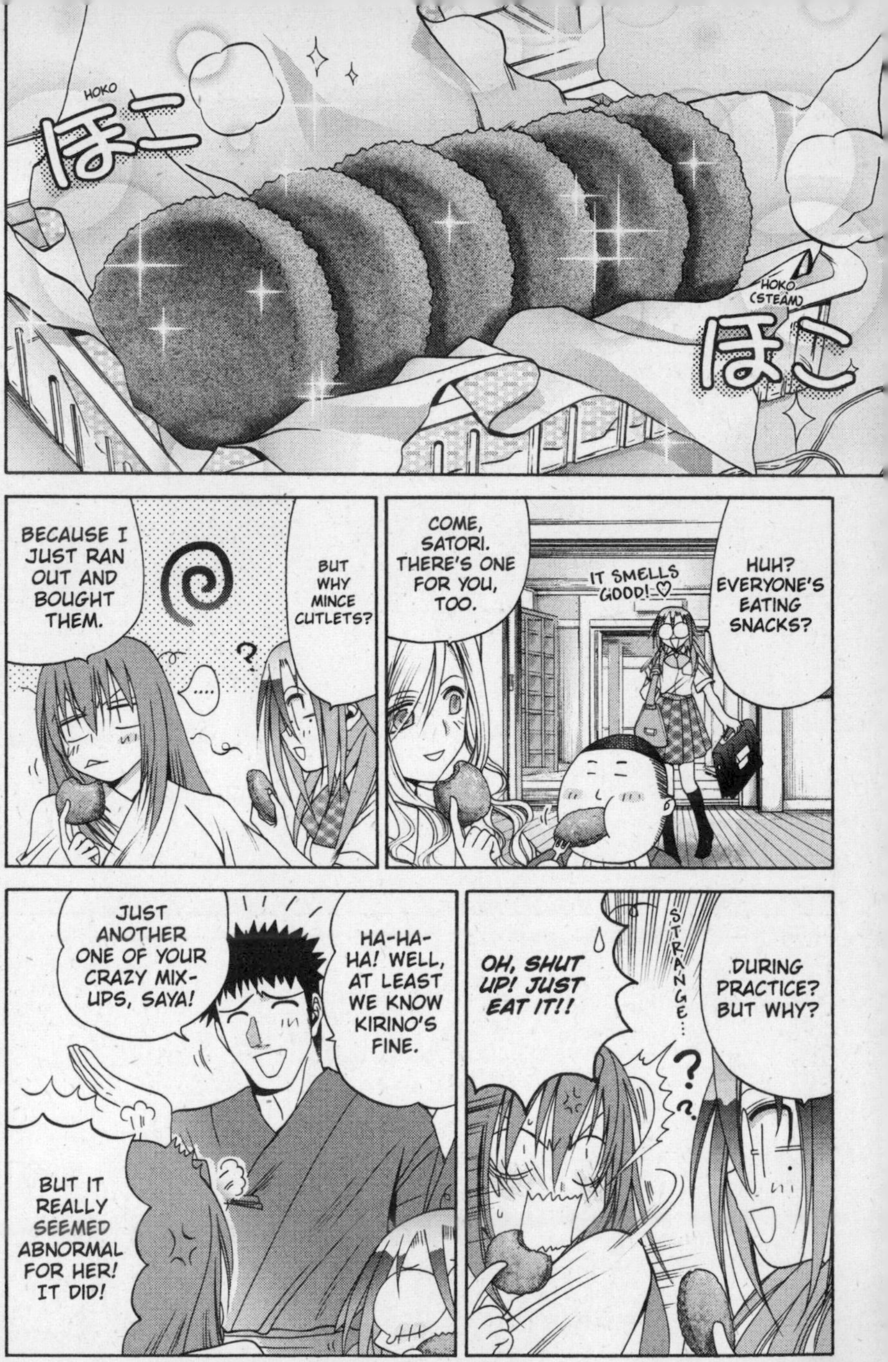

HOKO (STEAM)
ほこ
HOKO
ほこ
HUH? EVERYONE'S EATING SNACKS?
IT SMELLS GOOD! ♡
COME, SATORI. THERE'S ONE FOR YOU, TOO.
BUT WHY MINCE CUTLETS?
BECAUSE I JUST RAN OUT AND BOUGHT THEM.
....
DURING PRACTICE? BUT WHY?
STRANGE...
OH, SHUT UP! JUST EAT IT!!
HA-HA-HA! WELL, AT LEAST WE KNOW KIRINO'S FINE.
JUST ANOTHER ONE OF YOUR CRAZY MIX-UPS, SAYA!
BUT IT REALLY SEEMED ABNORMAL FOR HER! IT DID!

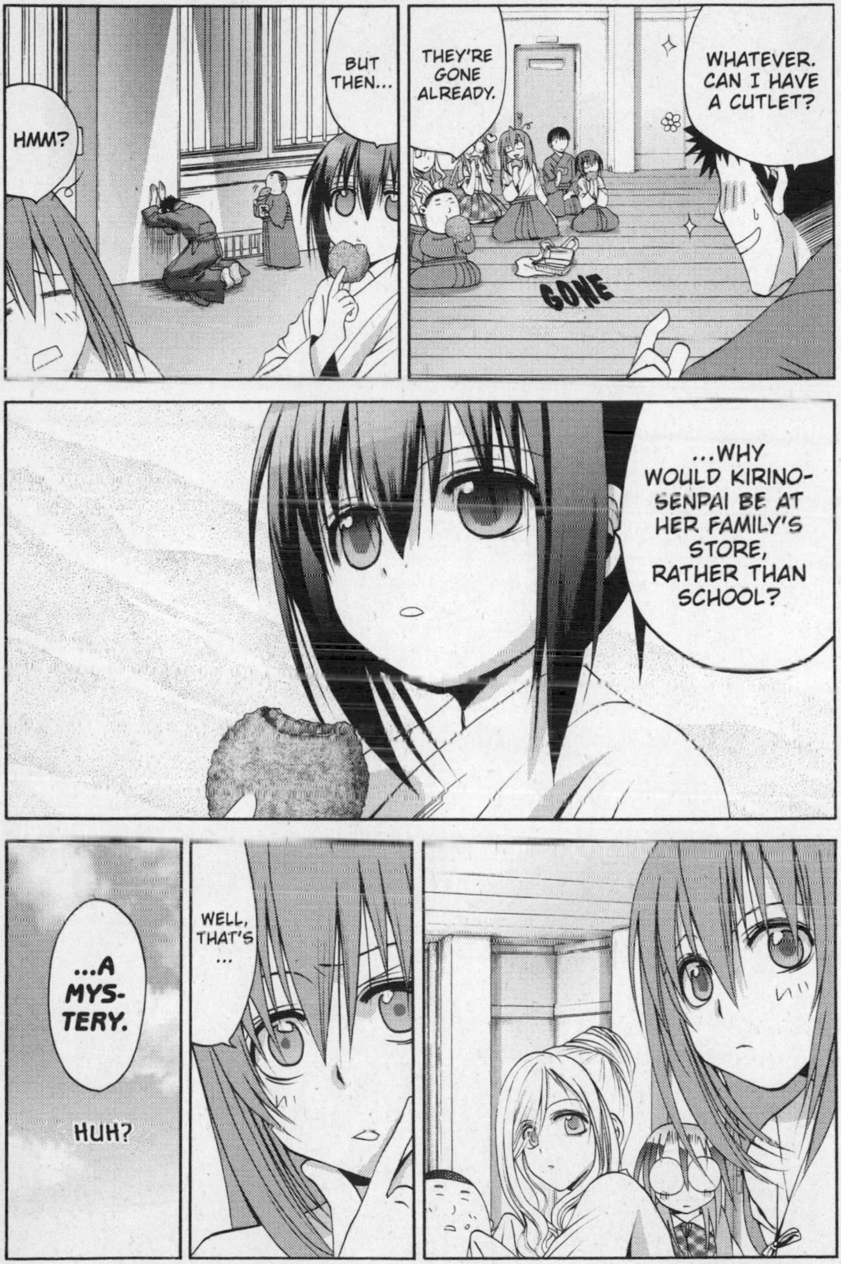
WHATEVER. CAN I HAVE A CUTLET?
THEY'RE GONE ALREADY.
GONE
BUT THEN...
HMM?
...WHY WOULD KIRINO-SENPAI BE AT HER FAMILY'S STORE, RATHER THAN SCHOOL?
WELL, THAT'S ...
...A MYS-TERY.
HUH?

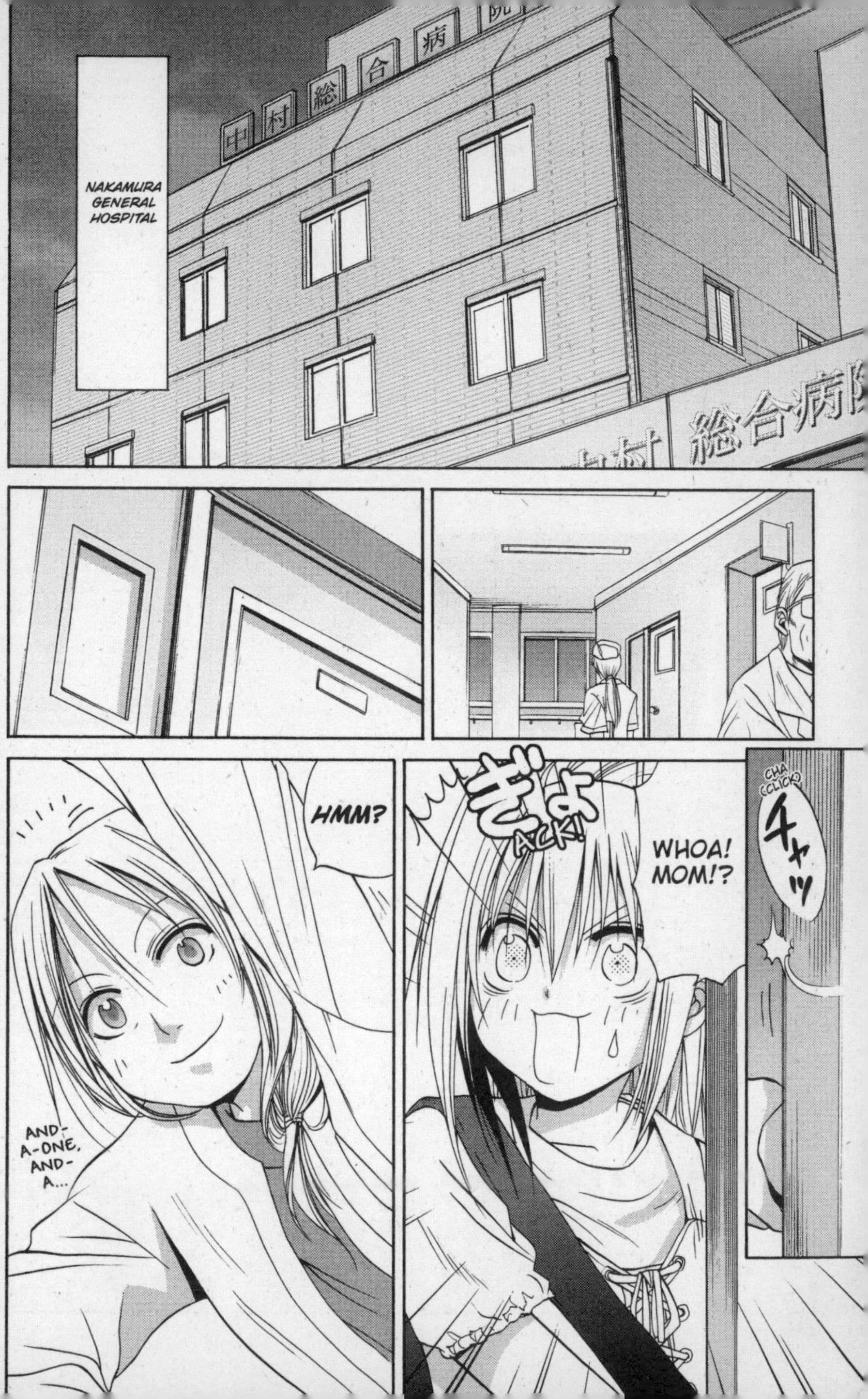

中村総合病院
NAKAMURA GENERAL HOSPITAL
CHA (CLICK)
チャッ
ぎょ
ACK!
WHOA! MOM!?
HMM?
AND-A-ONE, AND-A...

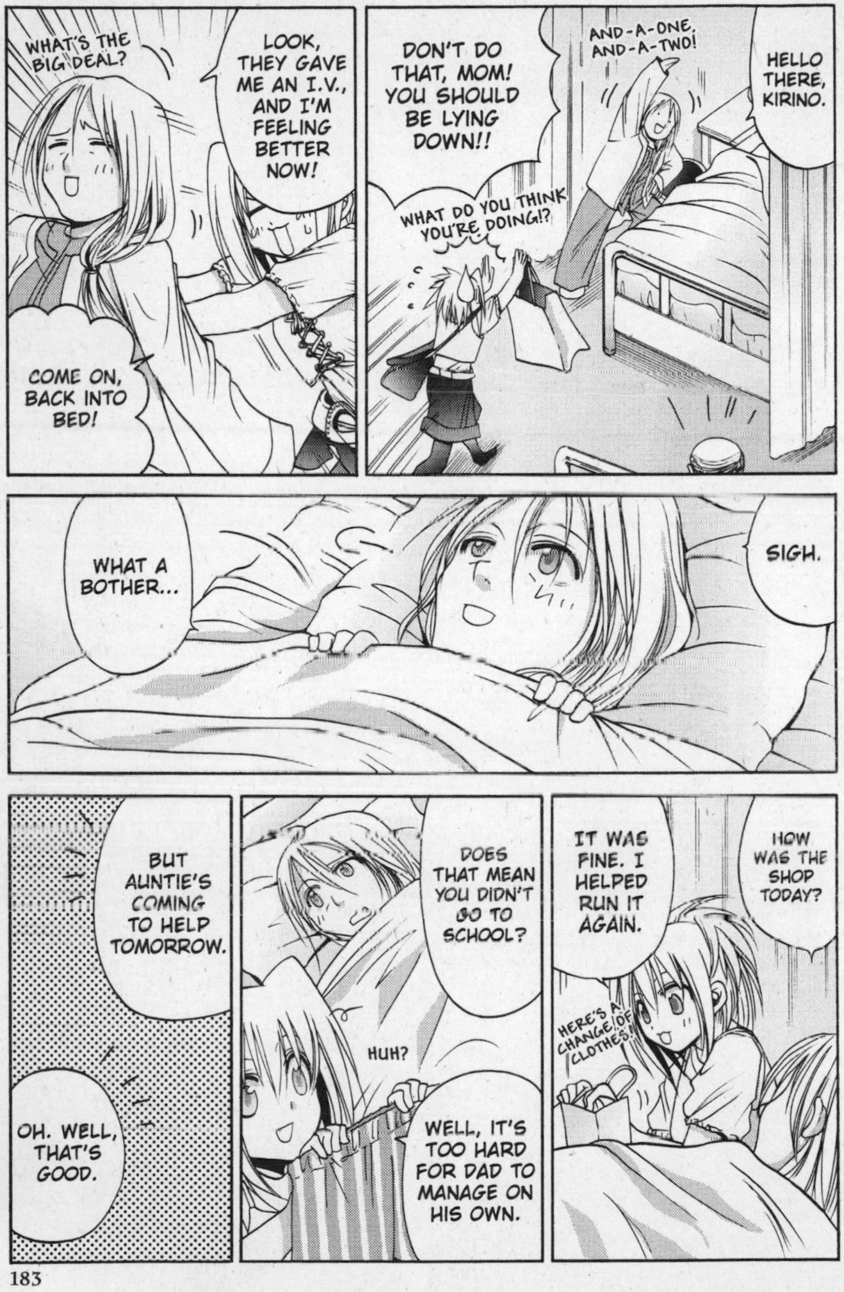
HELLO THERE, KIRINO.
AND-A-ONE, AND-A-TWO!
DON'T DO THAT, MOM! YOU SHOULD BE LYING DOWN!!
WHAT DO YOU THINK YOU'RE DOING!?
LOOK, THEY GAVE ME AN I.V., AND I'M FEELING BETTER NOW!
WHAT'S THE BIG DEAL?
COME ON, BACK INTO BED!
SIGH.
WHAT A BOTHER...
HOW WAS THE SHOP TODAY?
IT WAS FINE. I HELPED RUN IT AGAIN.
HERE'S A CHANGE OF CLOTHES!
DOES THAT MEAN YOU DIDN'T GO TO SCHOOL?
HUH?
WELL, IT'S TOO HARD FOR DAD TO MANAGE ON HIS OWN.
BUT AUNTIE'S COMING TO HELP TOMORROW.
OH. WELL, THAT'S GOOD.

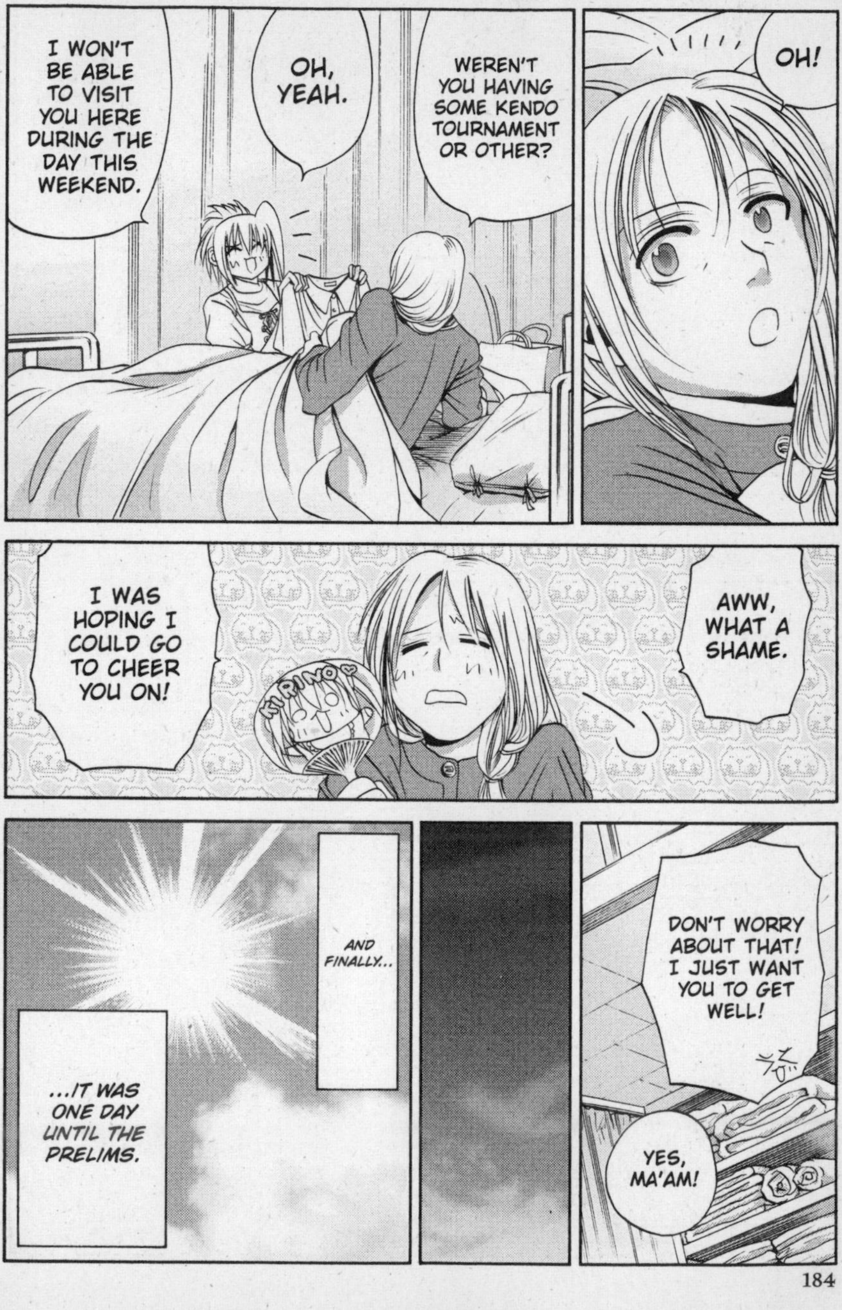
OH!
WEREN'T YOU HAVING SOME KENDO TOURNAMENT OR OTHER?
OH, YEAH.
I WON'T BE ABLE TO VISIT YOU HERE DURING THE DAY THIS WEEKEND.
AWW, WHAT A SHAME.
I WAS HOPING I COULD GO TO CHEER YOU ON!
DON'T WORRY ABOUT THAT! I JUST WANT YOU TO GET WELL!
YES, MA'AM!
AND FINALLY...
...IT WAS ONE DAY UNTIL THE PRELIMS.

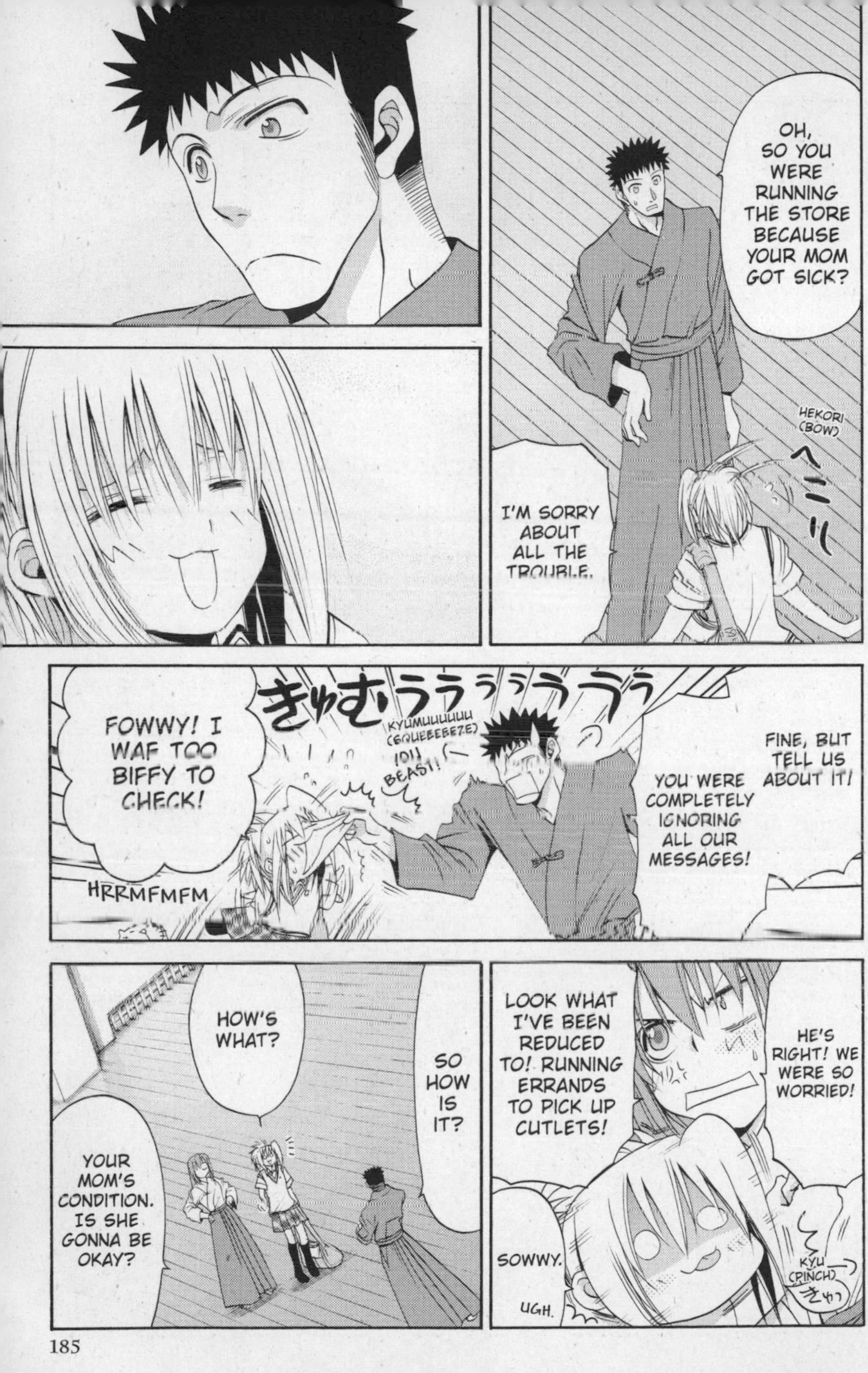

OH, SO YOU WERE RUNNING THE STORE BECAUSE YOUR MOM GOT SICK?
HEKORI (BOW)
I'M SORRY ABOUT ALL THE TROUBLE.
FINE, BUT TELL US ABOUT IT!
YOU WERE COMPLETELY IGNORING ALL OUR MESSAGES!
KYUMUUUUUU (SQUEEEEEZE)
!?!! BEAST!
FOWWY! I WAF TOO BIFFY TO CHECK!
HRRMFMFM
HE'S RIGHT! WE WERE SO WORRIED!
LOOK WHAT I'VE BEEN REDUCED TO! RUNNING ERRANDS TO PICK UP CUTLETS!
KYU (PINCH)
SOWWY.
UGH.
SO HOW IS IT?
HOW'S WHAT?
YOUR MOM'S CONDITION. IS SHE GONNA BE OKAY?

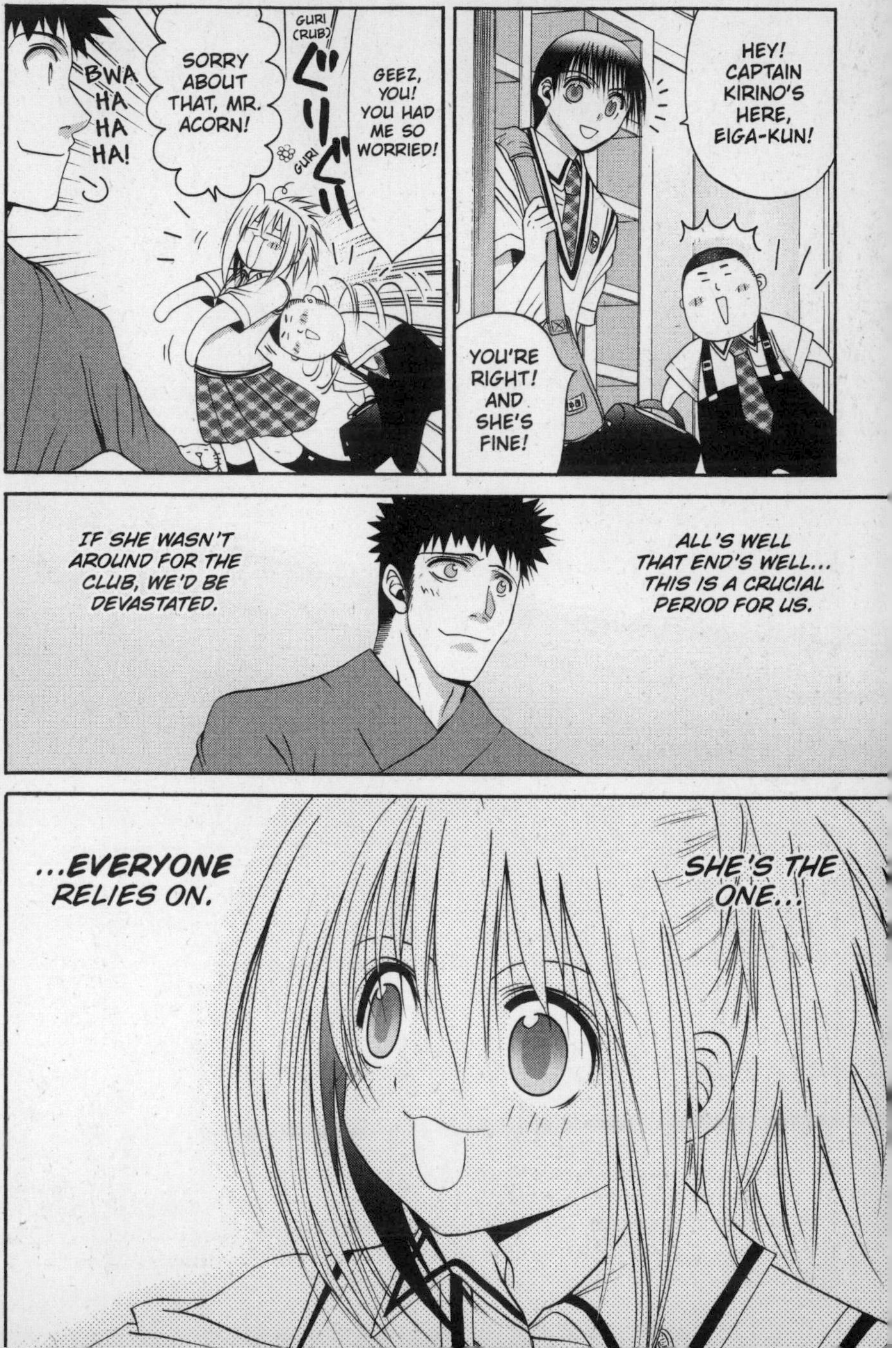
HEY! CAPTAIN KIRINO'S HERE, EIGA-KUN!
YOU'RE RIGHT! AND SHE'S FINE!
GEEZ, YOU! YOU HAD ME SO WORRIED!
GURI (RUB)
GURI
SORRY ABOUT THAT, MR. ACORN!
BWA HA HA HA!
ALL'S WELL THAT END'S WELL... THIS IS A CRUCIAL PERIOD FOR US.
IF SHE WASN'T AROUND FOR THE CLUB, WE'D BE DEVASTATED.
SHE'S THE ONE...
...EVERYONE RELIES ON.

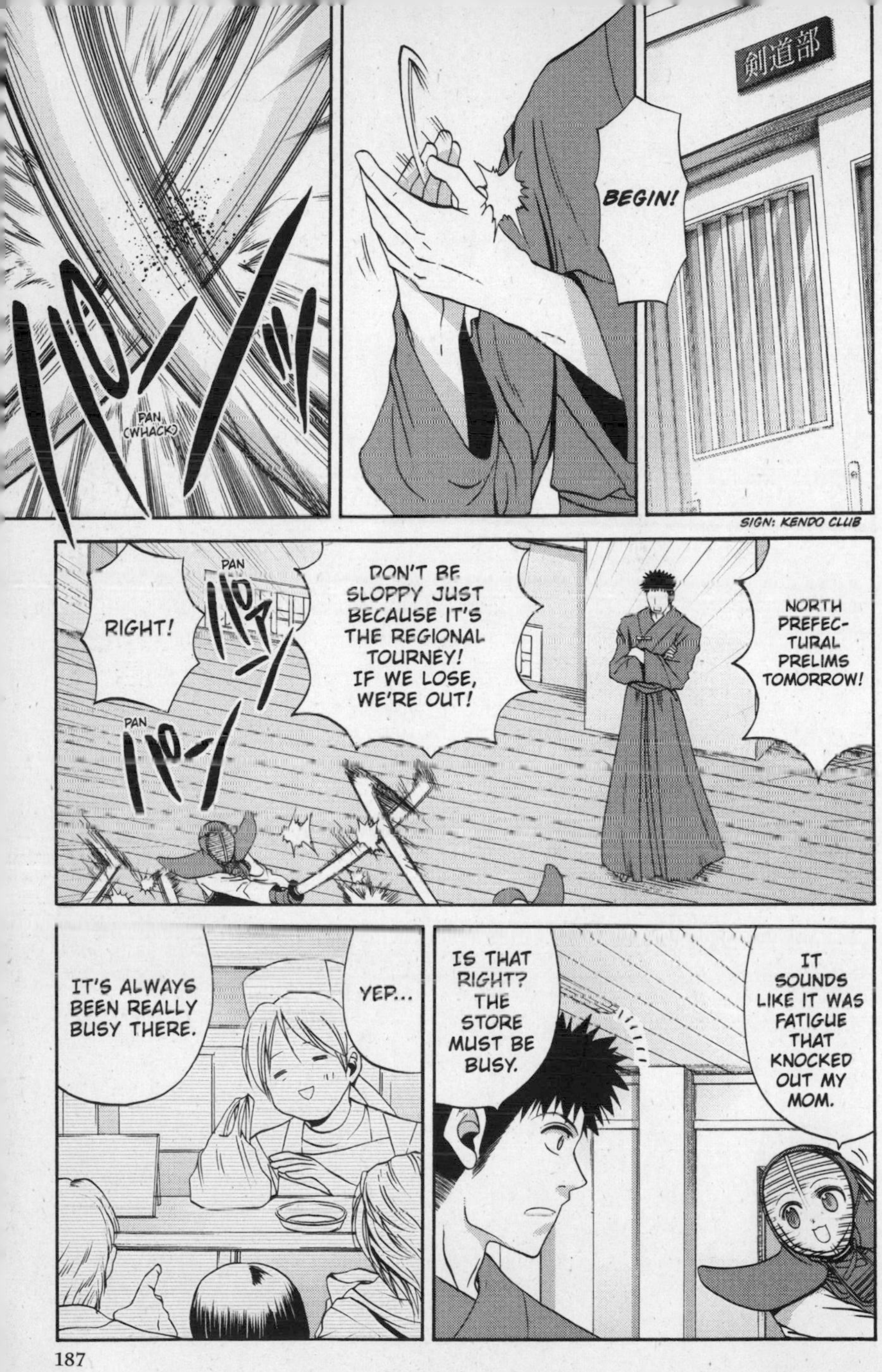
剣道部
SIGN: KENDO CLUB
BEGIN!
PAN (WHACK)
NORTH PREFECTURAL PRELIMS TOMORROW!
DON'T BE SLOPPY JUST BECAUSE IT'S THE REGIONAL TOURNEY! IF WE LOSE, WE'RE OUT!
PAN
RIGHT!
PAN
IT SOUNDS LIKE IT WAS FATIGUE THAT KNOCKED OUT MY MOM.
IS THAT RIGHT? THE STORE MUST BE BUSY.
YEP...
IT'S ALWAYS BEEN REALLY BUSY THERE.

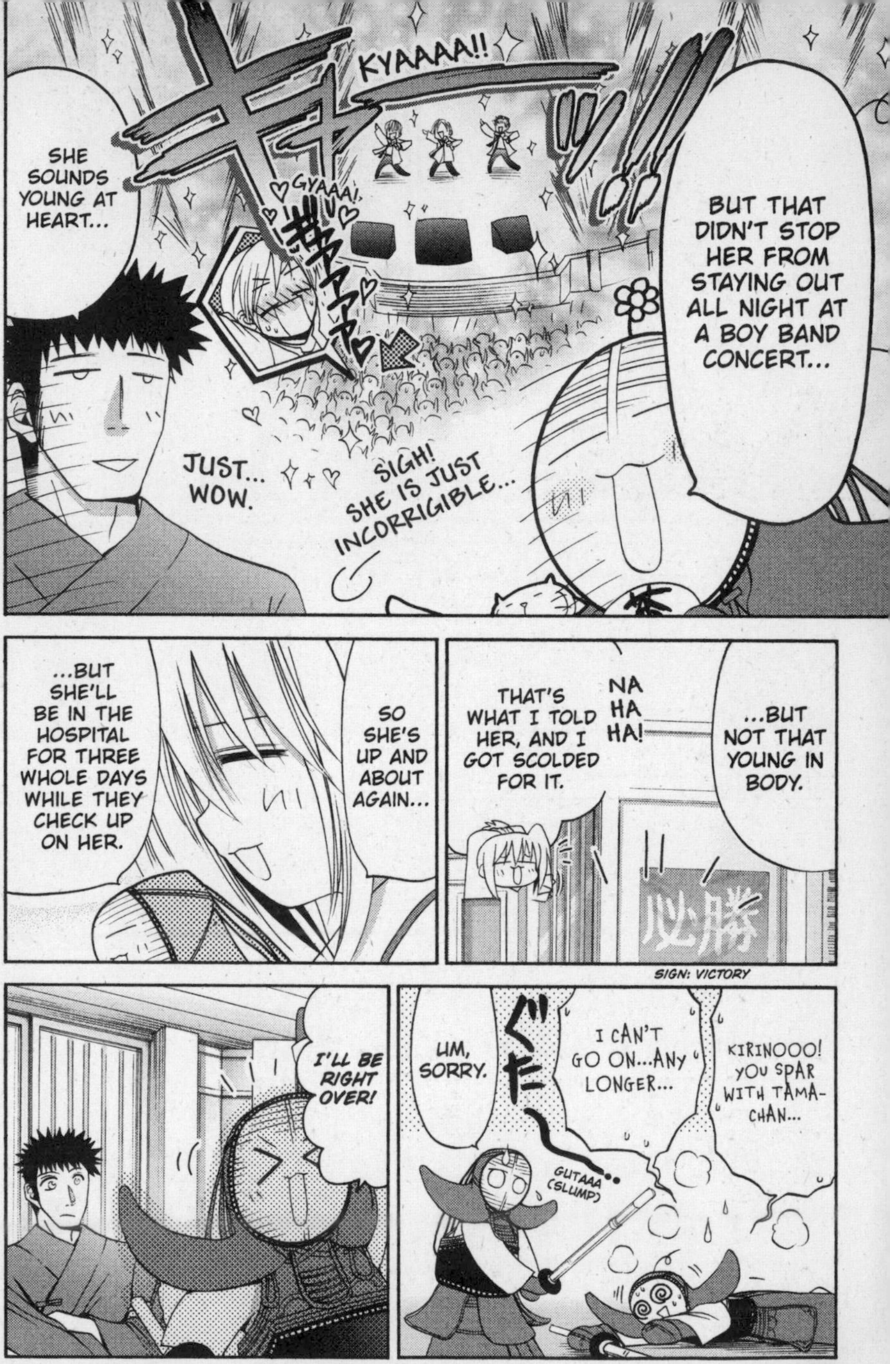
KYAAAA!!
BUT THAT DIDN'T STOP HER FROM STAYING OUT ALL NIGHT AT A BOY BAND CONCERT...
GYAAA!
SHE SOUNDS YOUNG AT HEART...
SIGH! SHE IS JUST INCORRIGIBLE...
JUST... WOW.
...BUT NOT THAT YOUNG IN BODY.
NA HA HA!
THAT'S WHAT I TOLD HER, AND I GOT SCOLDED FOR IT.
SIGN: VICTORY
SO SHE'S UP AND ABOUT AGAIN...
...BUT SHE'LL BE IN THE HOSPITAL FOR THREE WHOLE DAYS WHILE THEY CHECK UP ON HER.
KIRINOOO! YOU SPAR WITH TAMA-CHAN...
I CAN'T GO ON...ANY LONGER...
UM, SORRY.
GUTAAA (SLUMP)
I'LL BE RIGHT OVER!

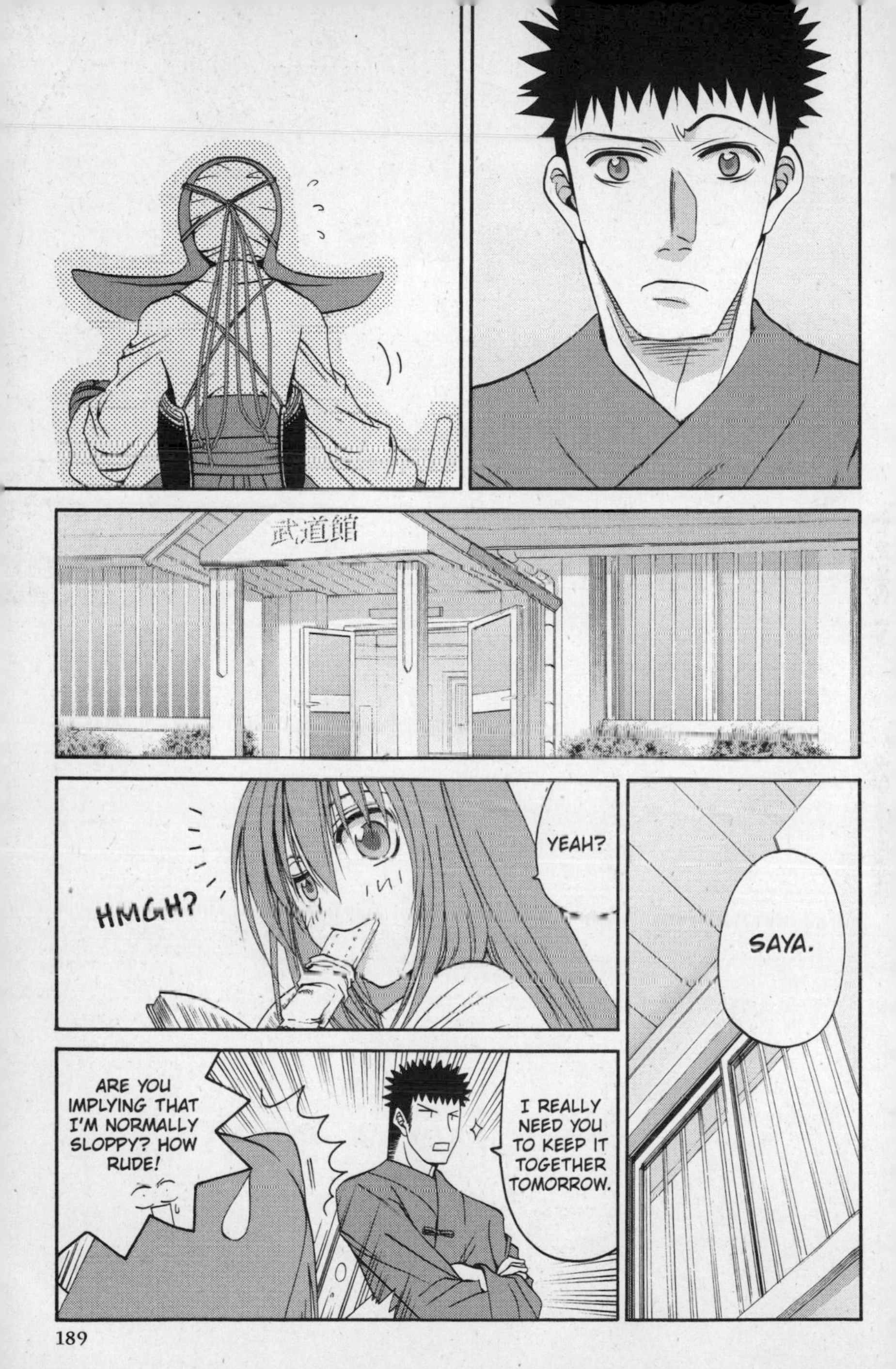
武道館
SAYA.
YEAH?
HMGH?
I REALLY NEED YOU TO KEEP IT TOGETHER TOMORROW.
ARE YOU IMPLYING THAT I'M NORMALLY SLOPPY? HOW RUDE!

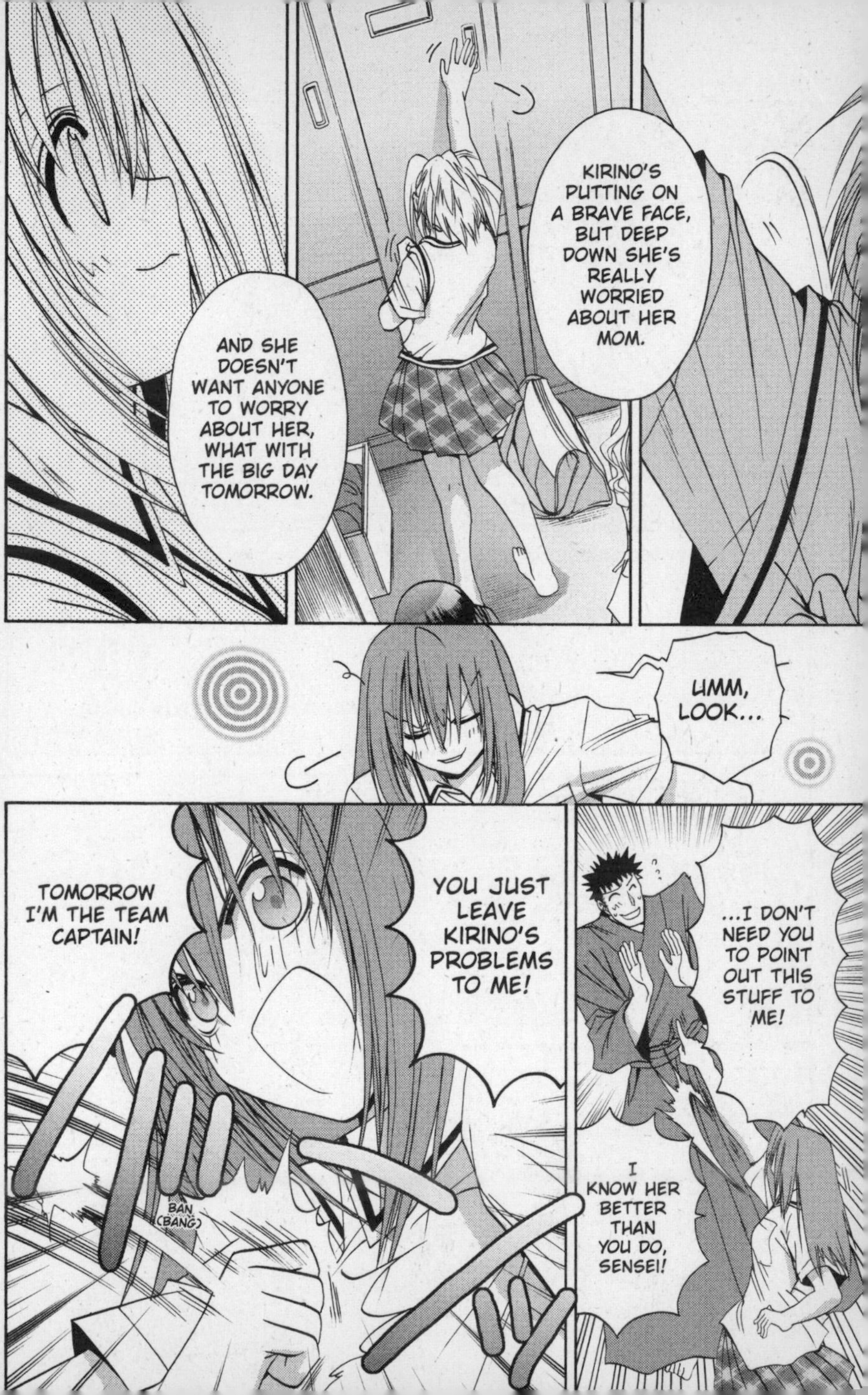
KIRINO'S PUTTING ON A BRAVE FACE, BUT DEEP DOWN SHE'S REALLY WORRIED ABOUT HER MOM.
AND SHE DOESN'T WANT ANYONE TO WORRY ABOUT HER, WHAT WITH THE BIG DAY TOMORROW.
UMM, LOOK...
...I DON'T NEED YOU TO POINT OUT THIS STUFF TO ME!
I KNOW HER BETTER THAN YOU DO, SENSEI!
YOU JUST LEAVE KIRINO'S PROBLEMS TO ME!
TOMORROW I'M THE TEAM CAPTAIN!
BAN (BANG)

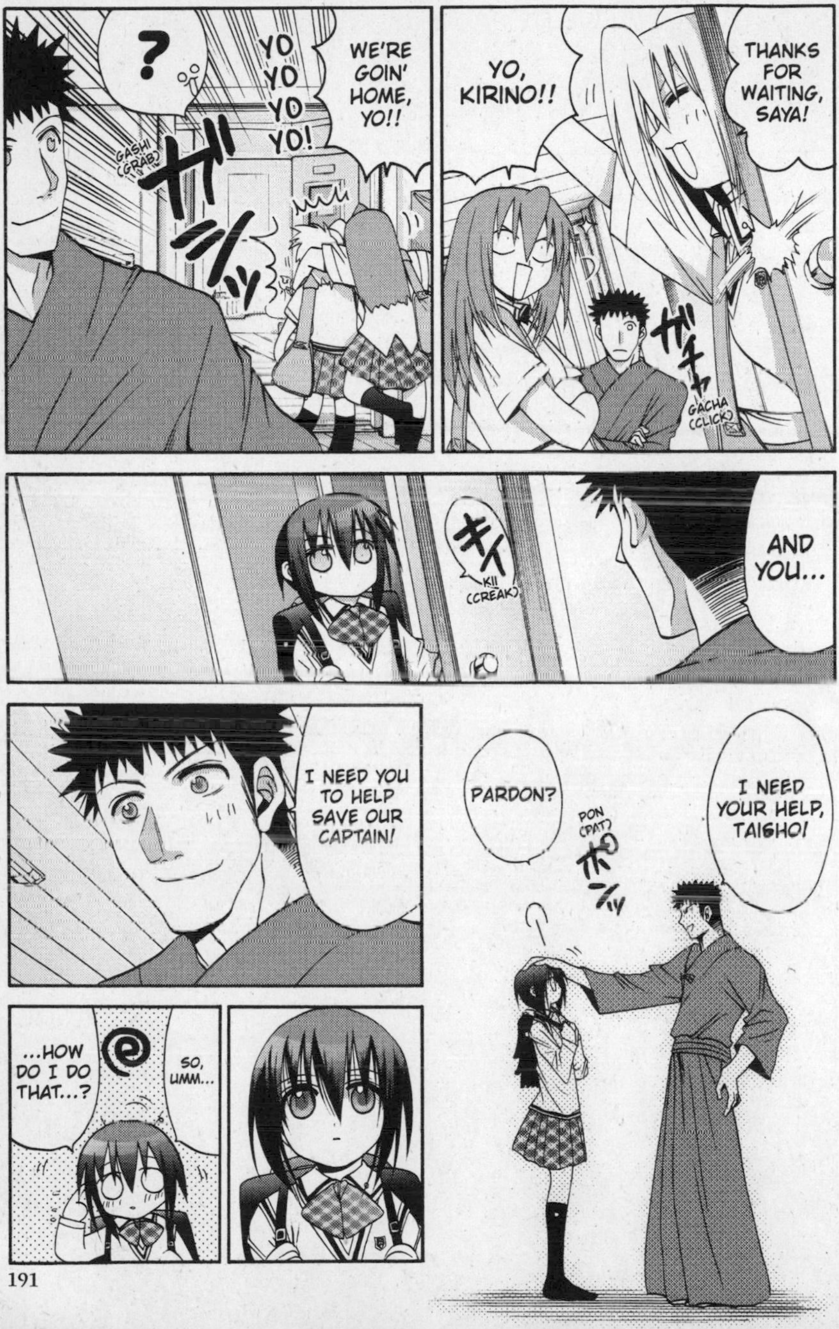
THANKS FOR WAITING, SAYA!
YO, KIRINO!!
GACHA (CLICK)
WE'RE GOIN' HOME, YO!!
YO YO YO YO!
?
GASHI (GRAB)
AND YOU...
KII (CREAK)
I NEED YOUR HELP, TAISHO!
PON (PAT)
PARDON?
I NEED YOU TO HELP SAVE OUR CAPTAIN!
SO, UMM...
...HOW DO I DO THAT...?

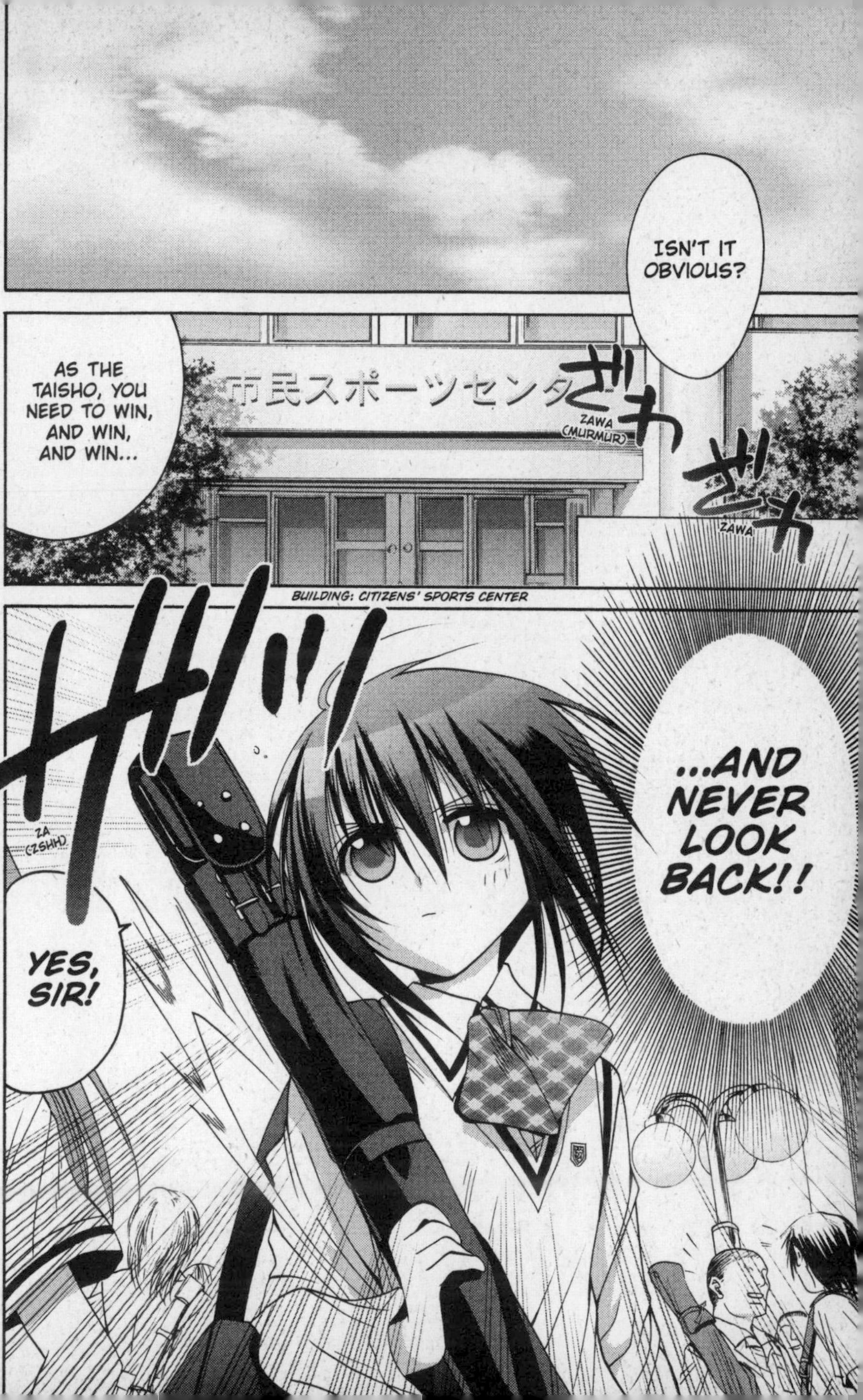
ISN'T IT OBVIOUS?
ZAWA (MURMUR)
ZAWA
市民スポーツセンタ
AS THE TAISHO, YOU NEED TO WIN, AND WIN, AND WIN...
BUILDING: CITIZENS' SPORTS CENTER
...AND NEVER LOOK BACK!!
ZA (ZSHH)
YES, SIR!

BAMBOO BLADE

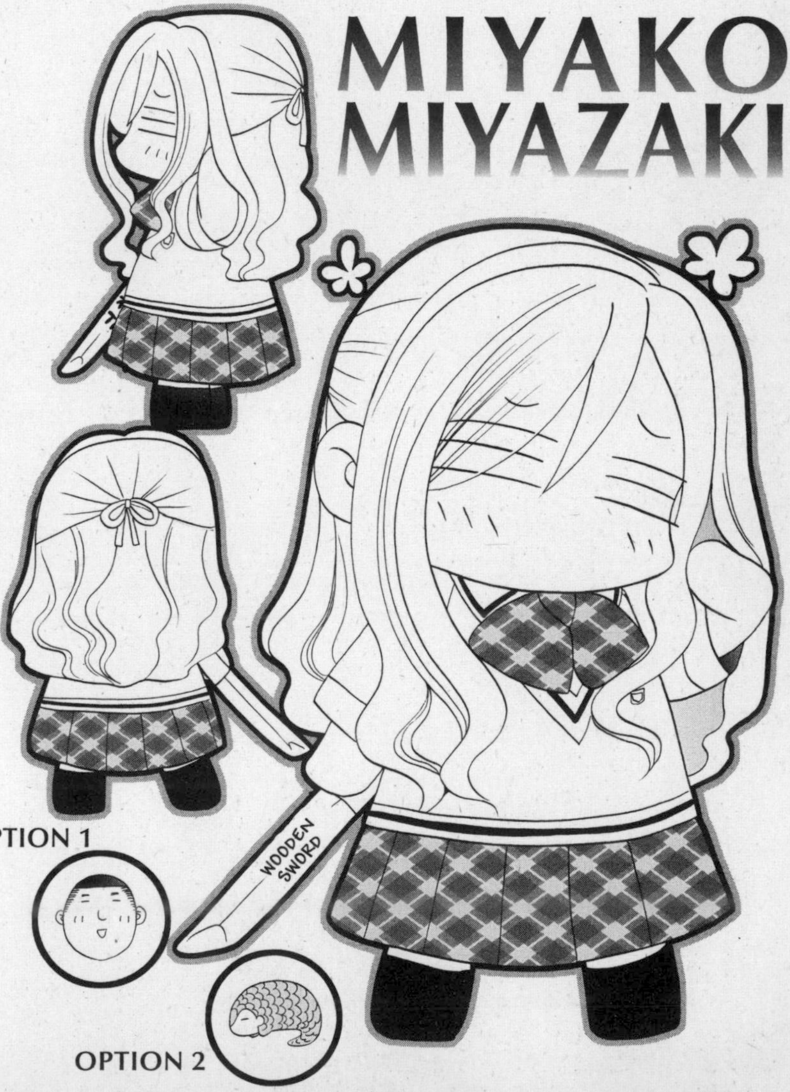
MIYAKO
MIYAZAKI
WOODEN
SWORD
OPTION 1
OPTION 2

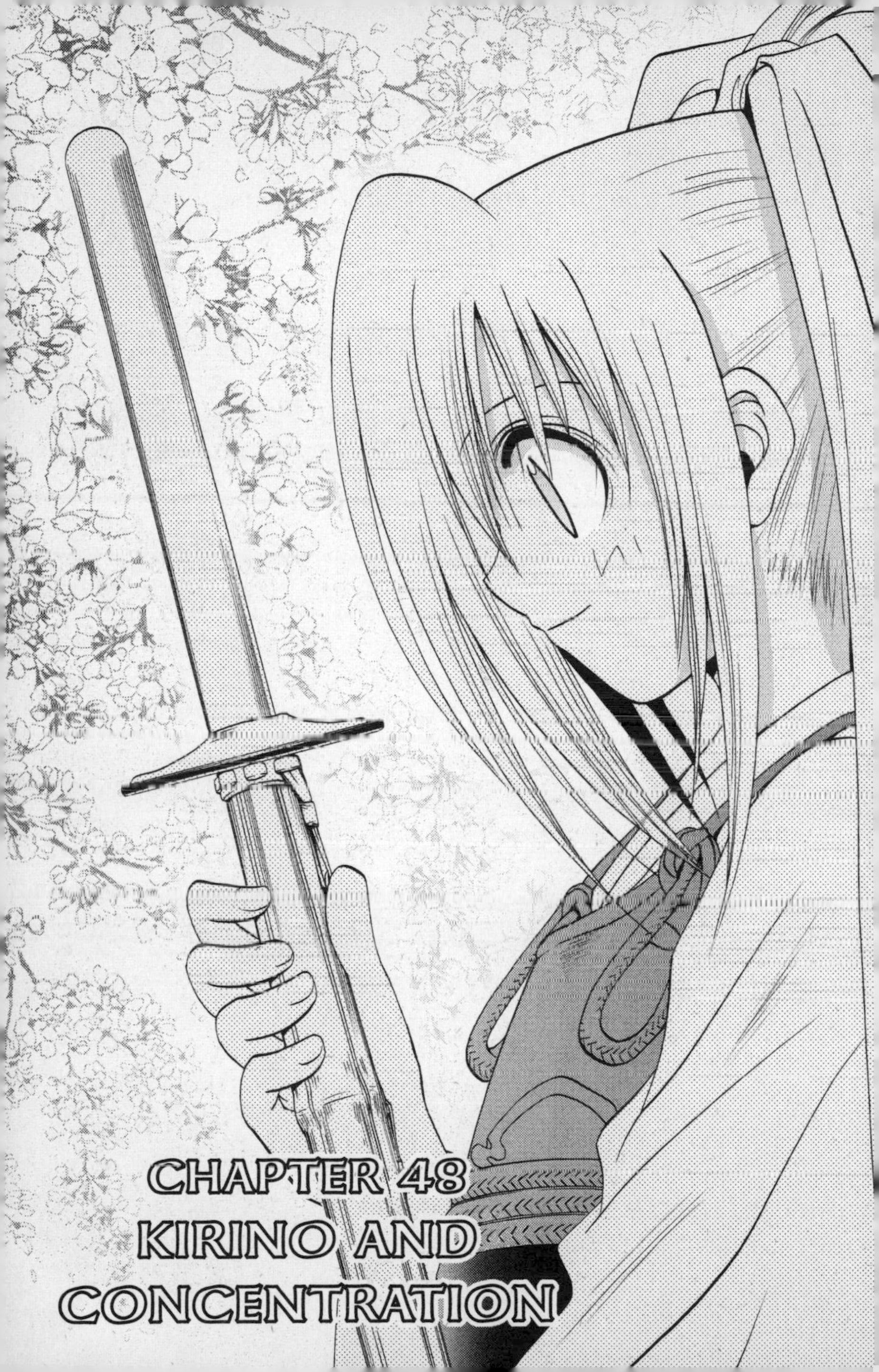
CHAPTER 48
KIRINO AND
CONCENTRATION

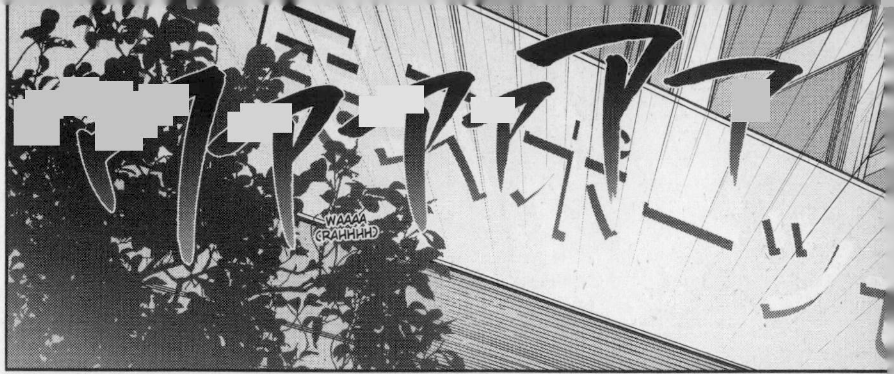
WAAAA
(RAHHHH)
SIGN: CITIZEN'S SPORTS CENTER

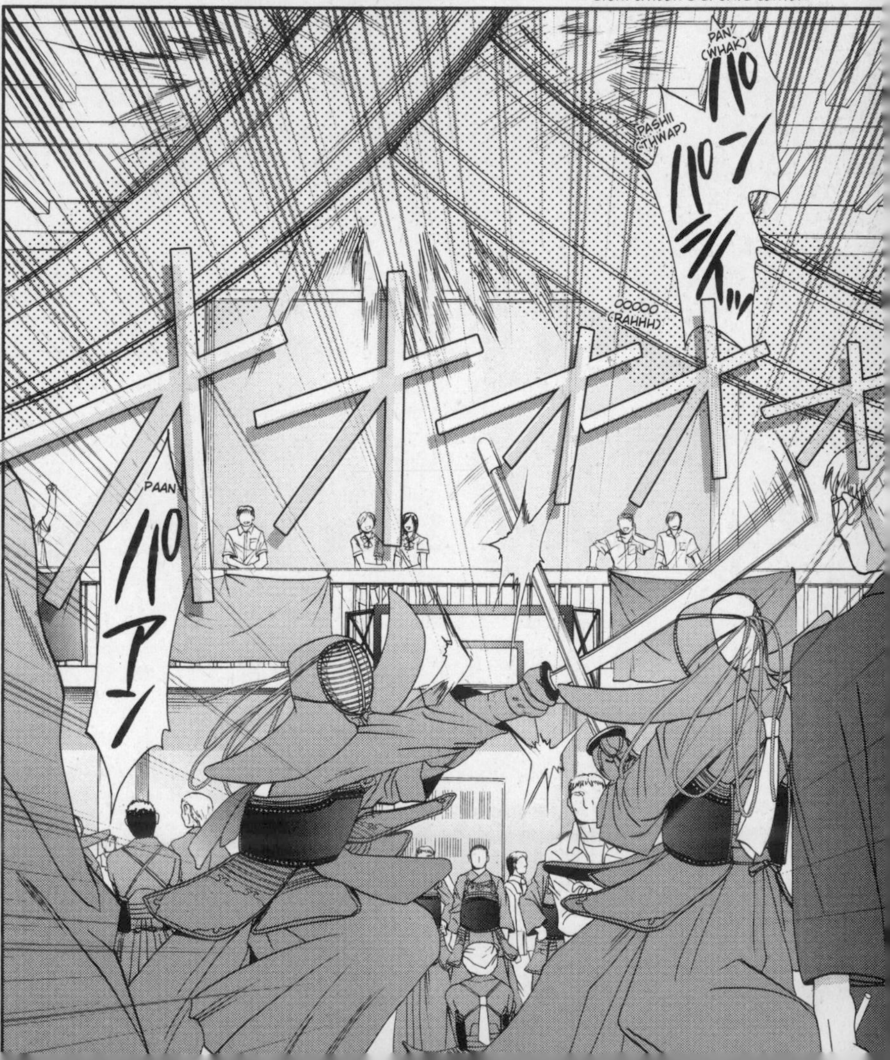
PAN
(WHAK)
PASHII
(THWAP)
OOOOO
(RAHHH)
PAAN

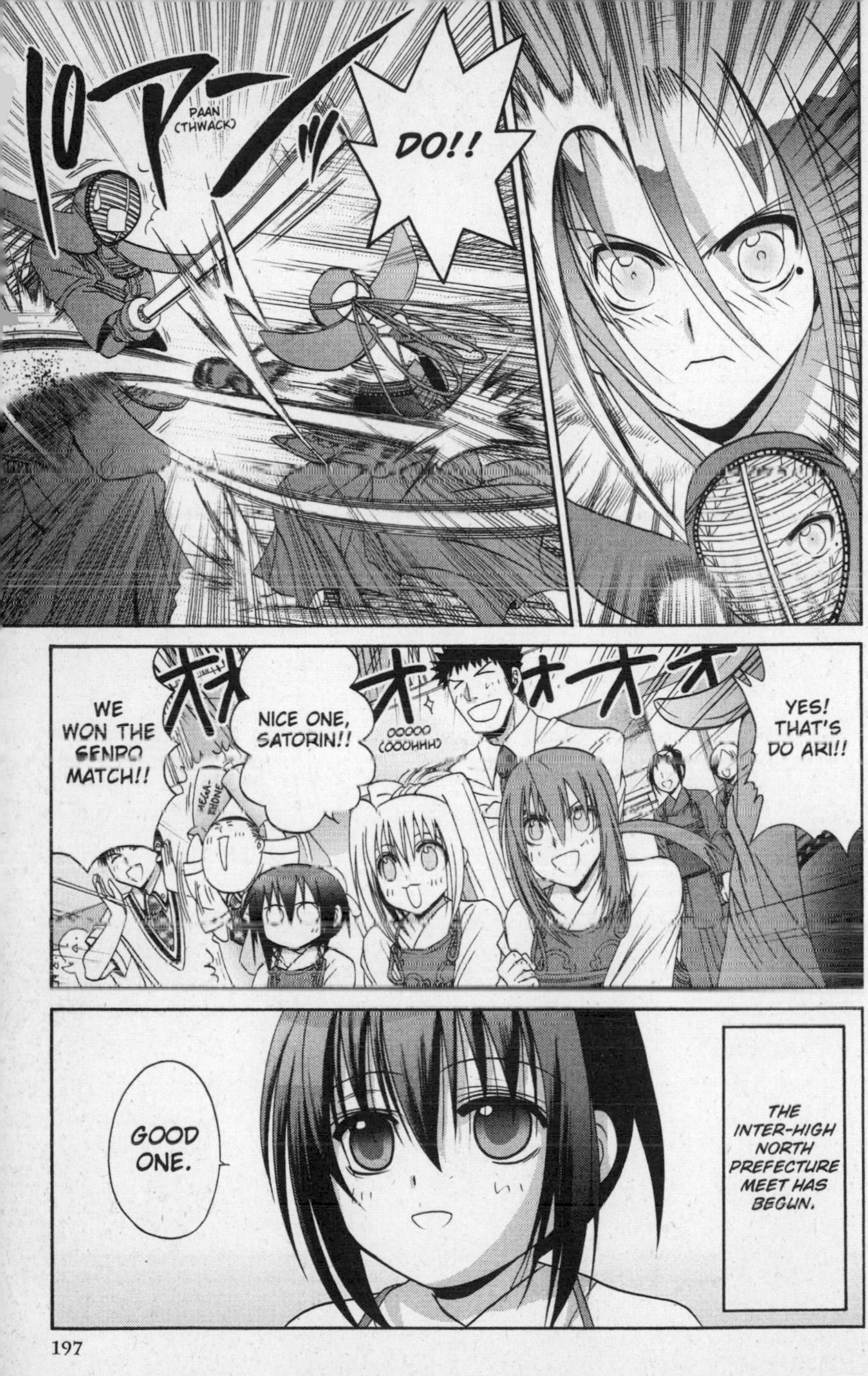
PAAN (THWACK)
DO!!
YES! THAT'S DO ARI!!
OOOOO (OOOHHH)
NICE ONE, SATORIN!!
WE WON THE SENPO MATCH!!
THE INTER-HIGH NORTH PREFECTURE MEET HAS BEGUN.
GOOD ONE.

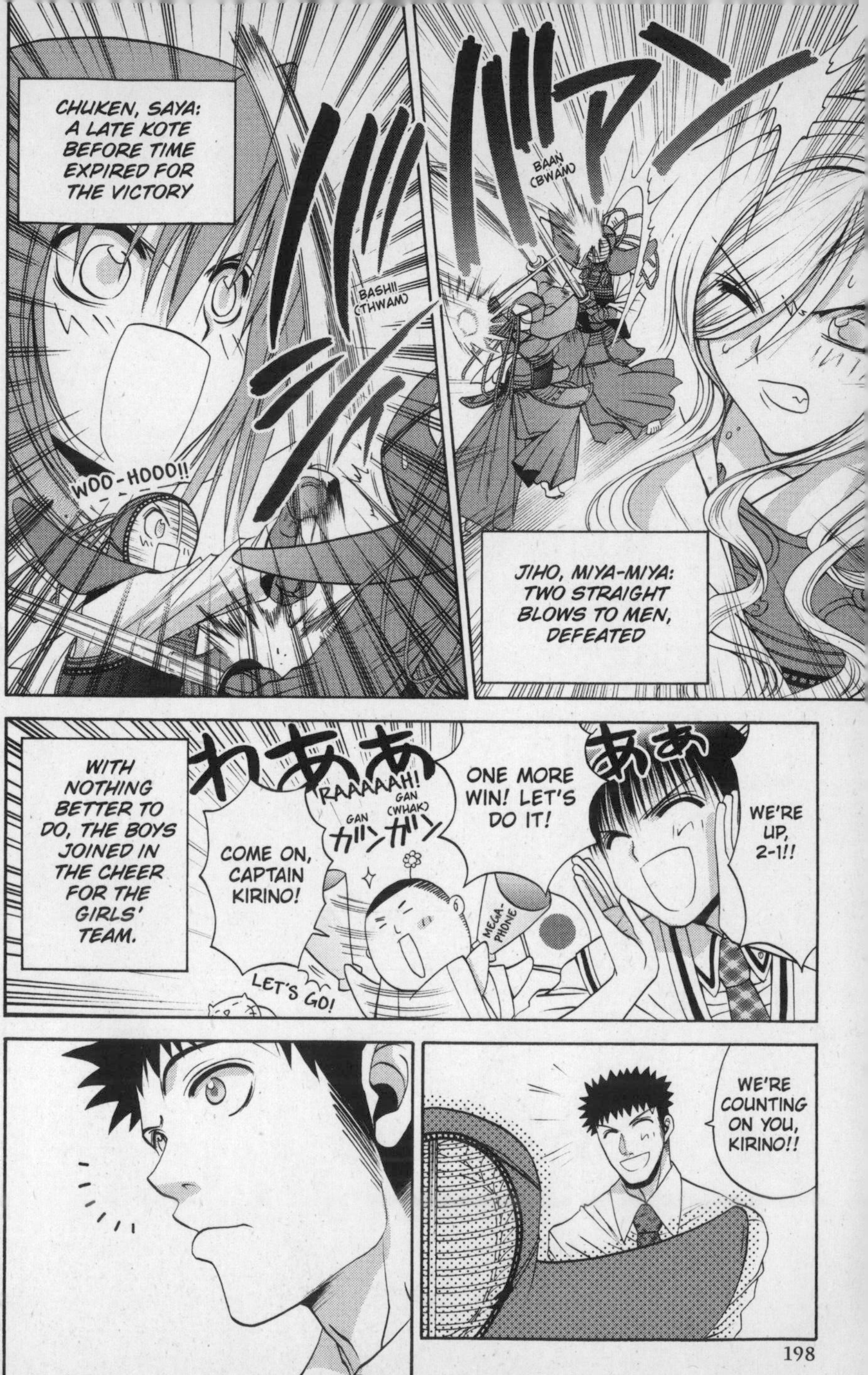
バァン
BAAN (BWAM)
JIHO, MIYA-MIYA: TWO STRAIGHT BLOWS TO MEN, DEFEATED
CHUKEN, SAYA: A LATE KOTE BEFORE TIME EXPIRED FOR THE VICTORY
BASHII (THWAM)
WOO-HOOO!!
WE'RE UP, 2-1!!
ああ
ONE MORE WIN! LET'S DO IT!
MEGA-PHONE
RAAAAAH!
GAN GAN (WHAK)
ガンガン
わあぁ
COME ON, CAPTAIN KIRINO!
LET'S GO!
WITH NOTHING BETTER TO DO, THE BOYS JOINED IN THE CHEER FOR THE GIRLS' TEAM.
WE'RE COUNTING ON YOU, KIRINO!!

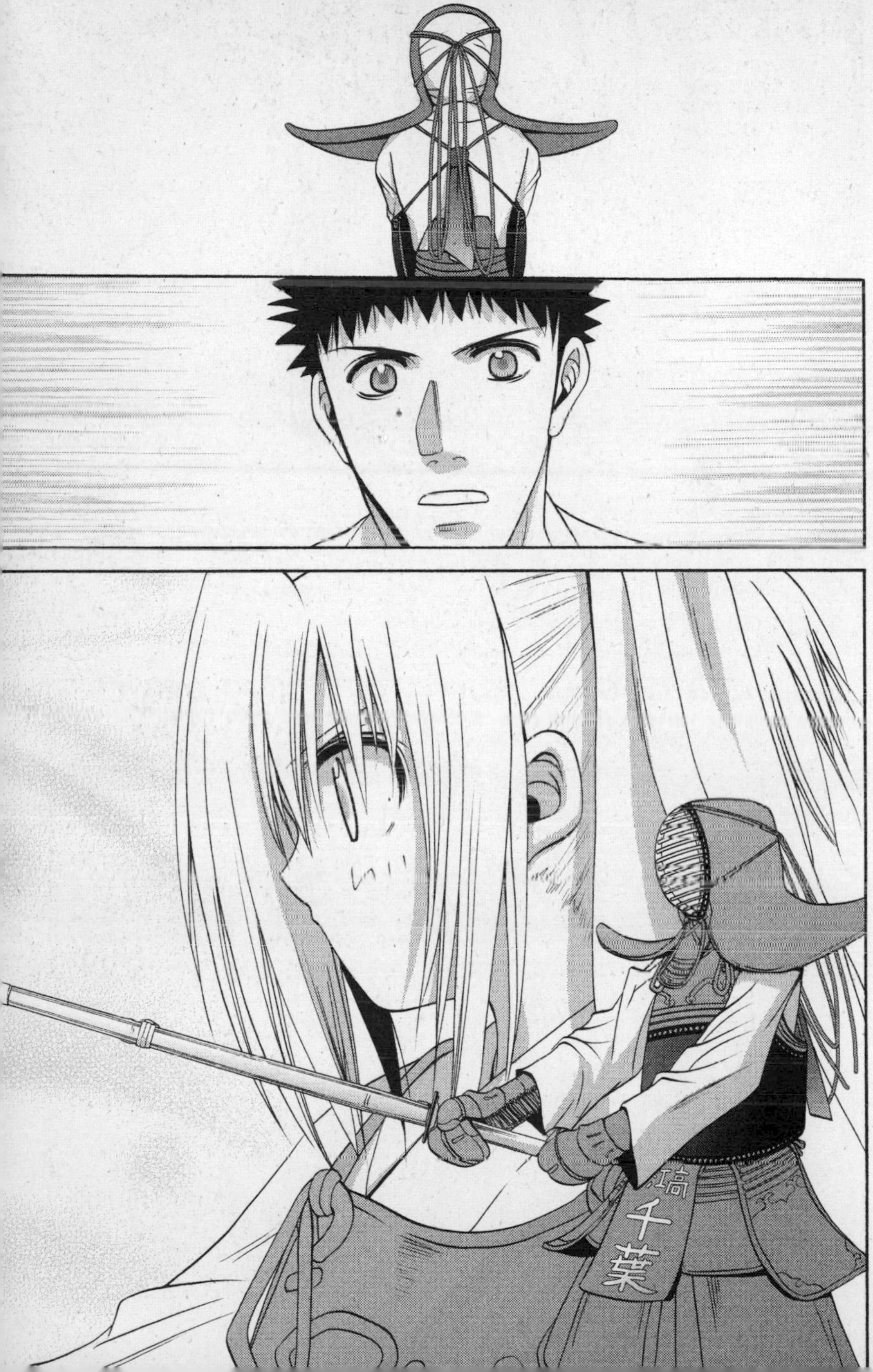
千葉

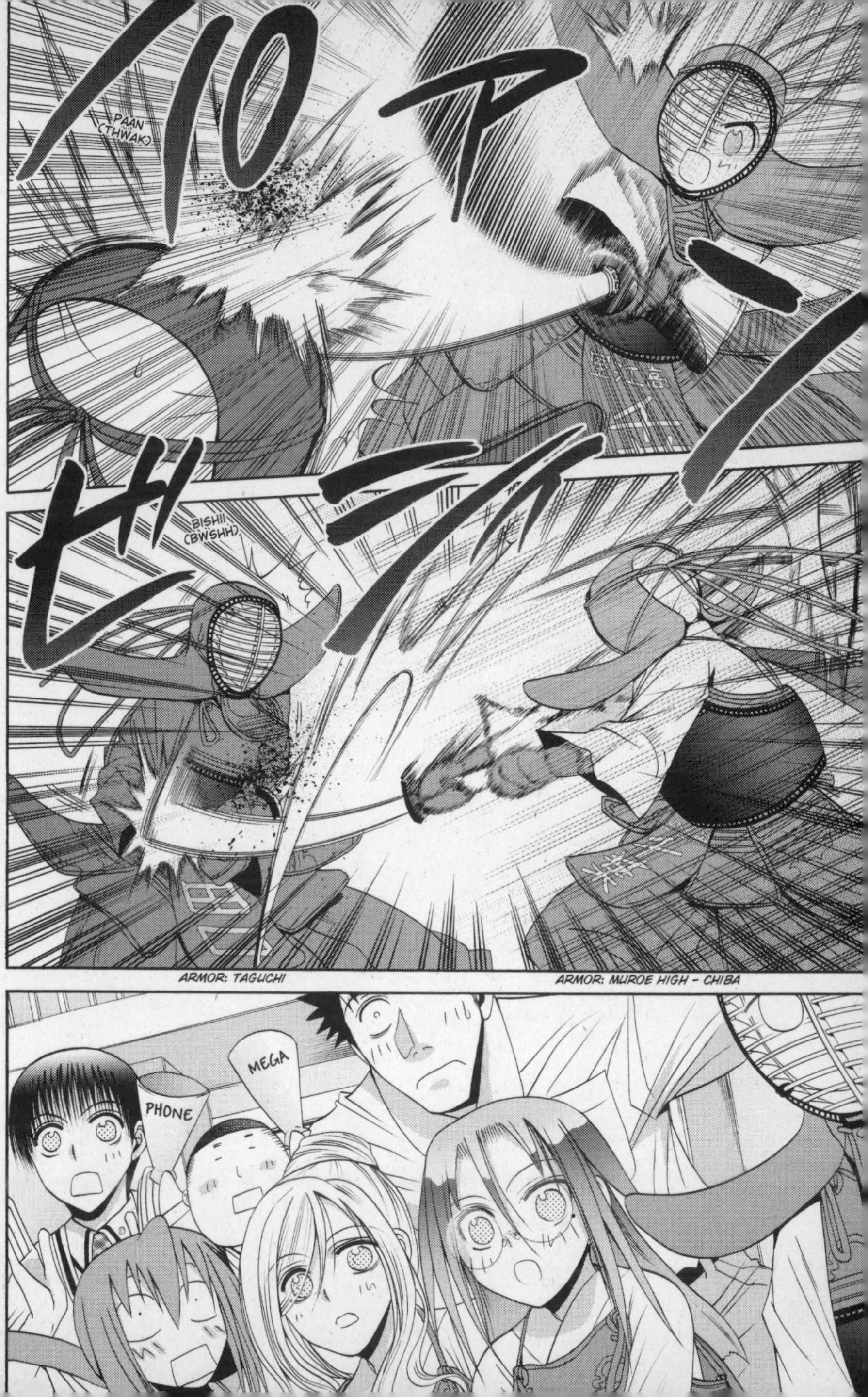
PAAN (THWAK)
BISHI (BWSHH)
ARMOR: MUROE HIGH - CHIBA
ARMOR: TAGUCHI
MEGA
PHONE

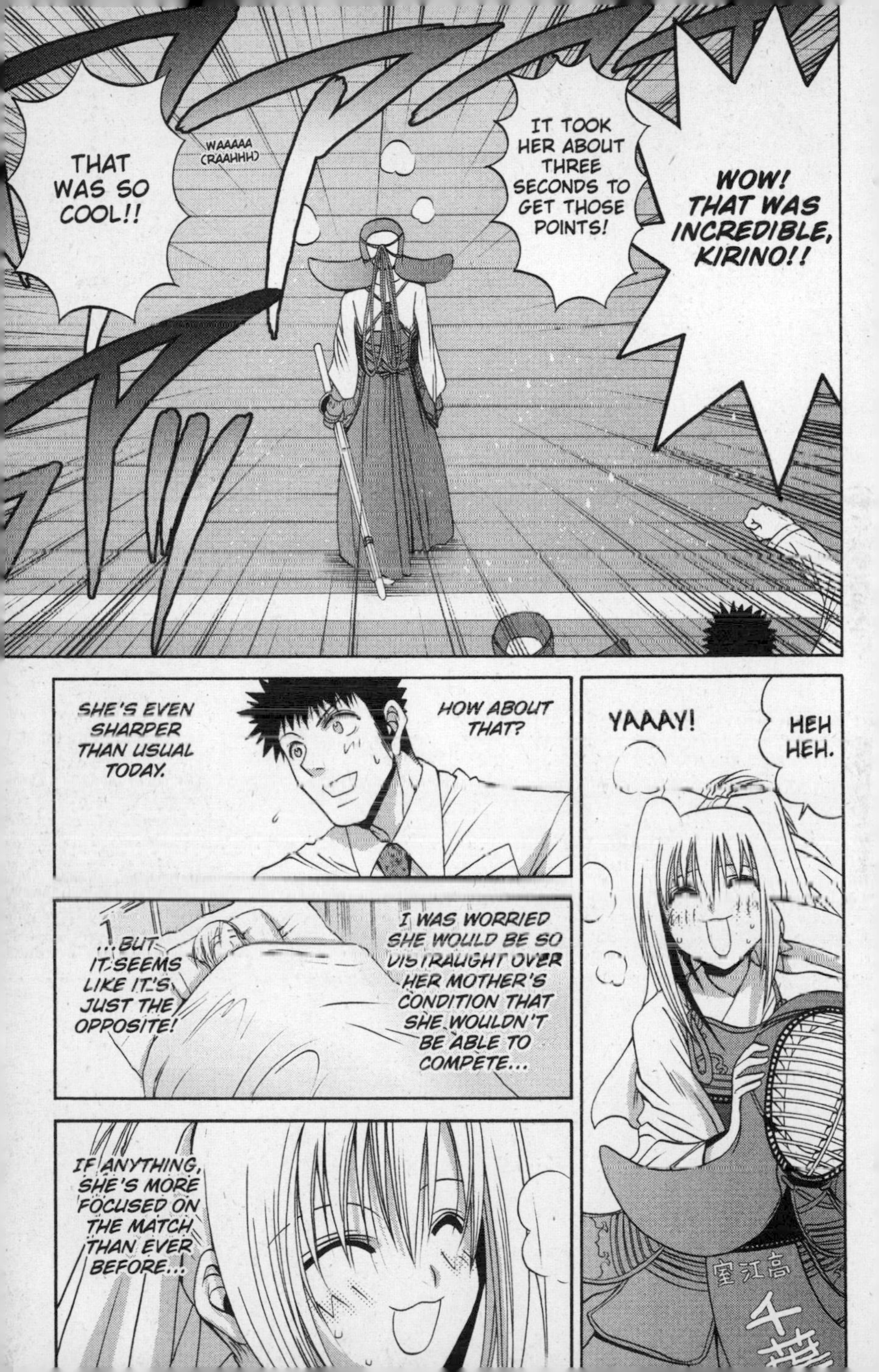

WOW! THAT WAS INCREDIBLE, KIRINO!!
IT TOOK HER ABOUT THREE SECONDS TO GET THOSE POINTS!
WAAAAA (RAAHHH)
THAT WAS SO COOL!!
HEH HEH.
YAAAY!
室江高
HOW ABOUT THAT?
SHE'S EVEN SHARPER THAN USUAL TODAY.
I WAS WORRIED SHE WOULD BE SO DISTRAUGHT OVER HER MOTHER'S CONDITION THAT SHE WOULDN'T BE ABLE TO COMPETE...
...BUT IT SEEMS LIKE IT'S JUST THE OPPOSITE!
IF ANYTHING, SHE'S MORE FOCUSED ON THE MATCH THAN EVER BEFORE...

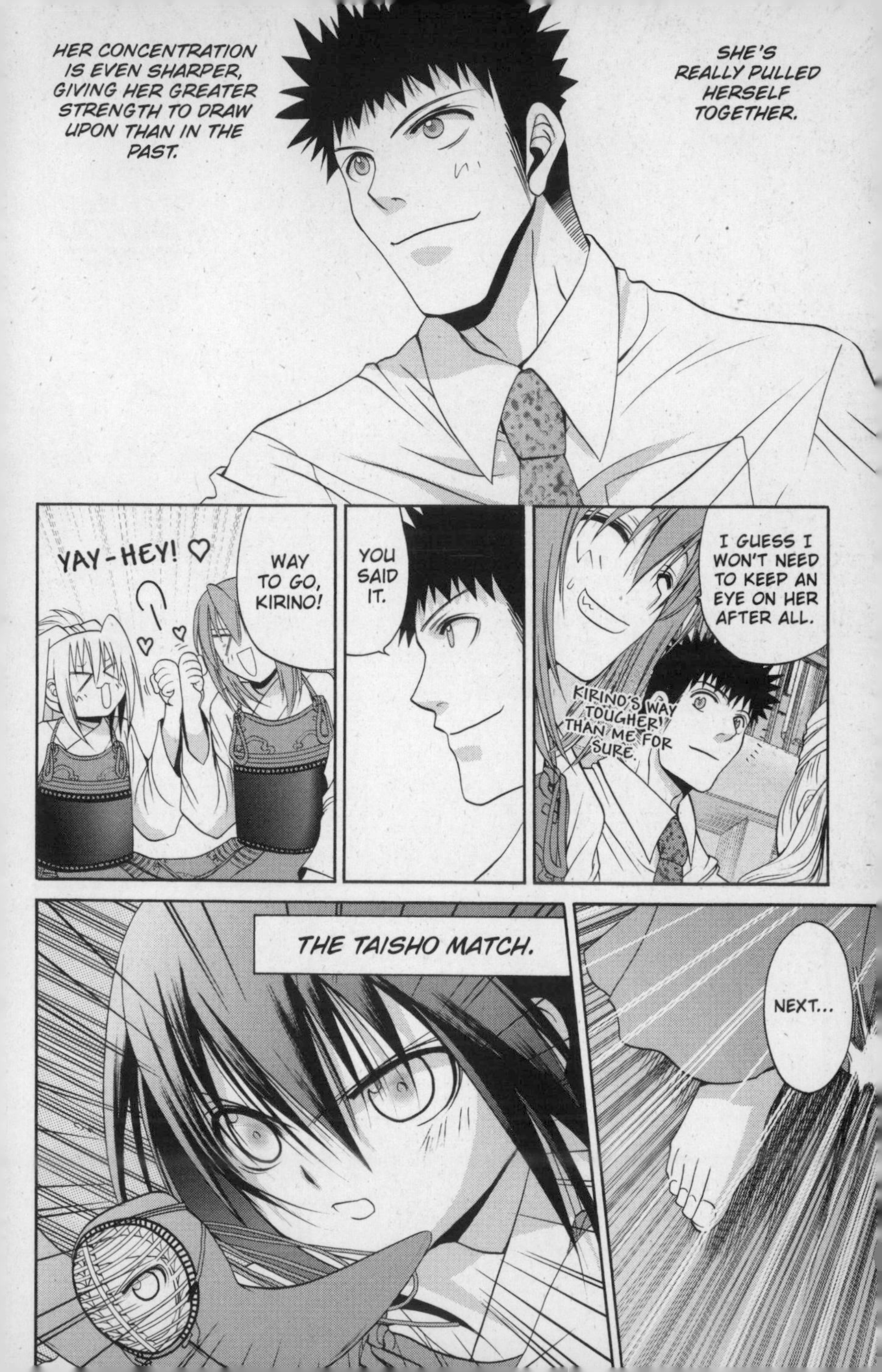
SHE'S REALLY PULLED HERSELF TOGETHER.
HER CONCENTRATION IS EVEN SHARPER, GIVING HER GREATER STRENGTH TO DRAW UPON THAN IN THE PAST.
I GUESS I WON'T NEED TO KEEP AN EYE ON HER AFTER ALL.
KIRINO'S WAY TOUGHER THAN ME FOR SURE.
YOU SAID IT.
WAY TO GO, KIRINO!
YAY-HEY! ♡
NEXT...
THE TAISHO MATCH.

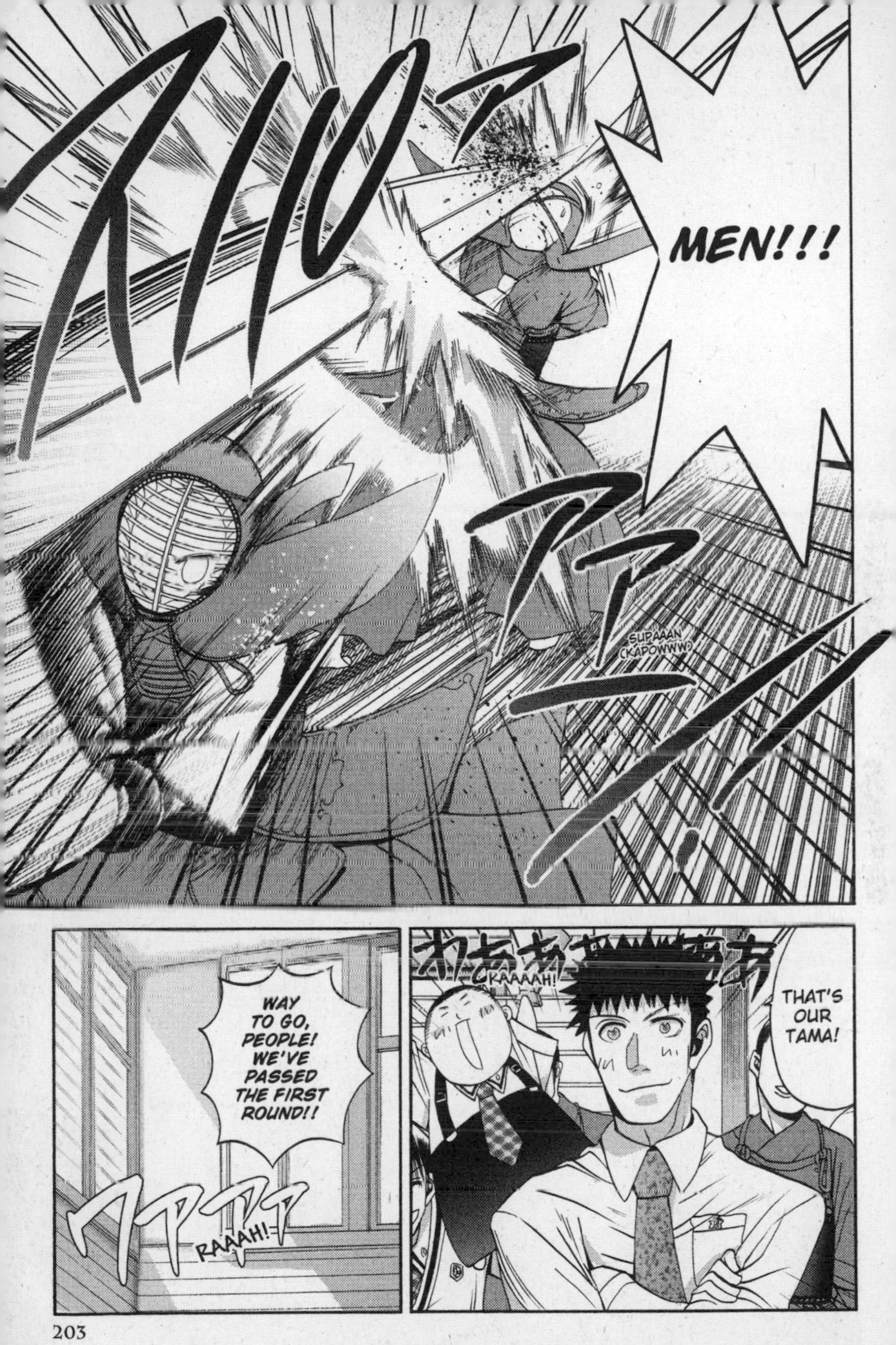
MEN!!!
SUPAAAN (KAPOWWW)
KAAAAH!
THAT'S OUR TAMA!
WAY TO GO, PEOPLE! WE'VE PASSED THE FIRST ROUND!!
RAAAH!

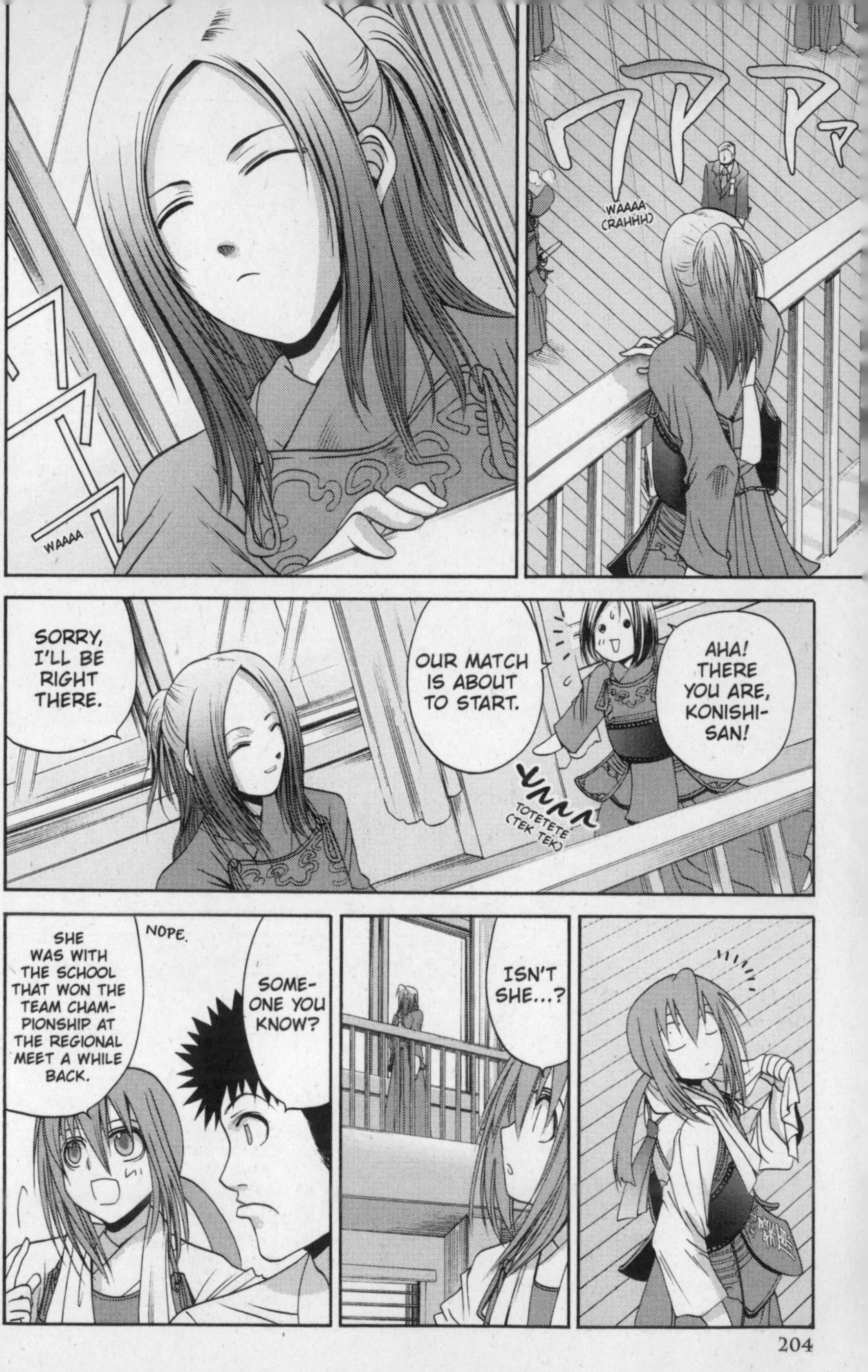
WAAAA (RAHHH)
WAAAA
AHA! THERE YOU ARE, KONISHI-SAN!
TOTETETE (TEK TEK)
OUR MATCH IS ABOUT TO START.
SORRY, I'LL BE RIGHT THERE.
ISN'T SHE...?
SOME-ONE YOU KNOW?
NOPE.
SHE WAS WITH THE SCHOOL THAT WON THE TEAM CHAM-PIONSHIP AT THE REGIONAL MEET A WHILE BACK.

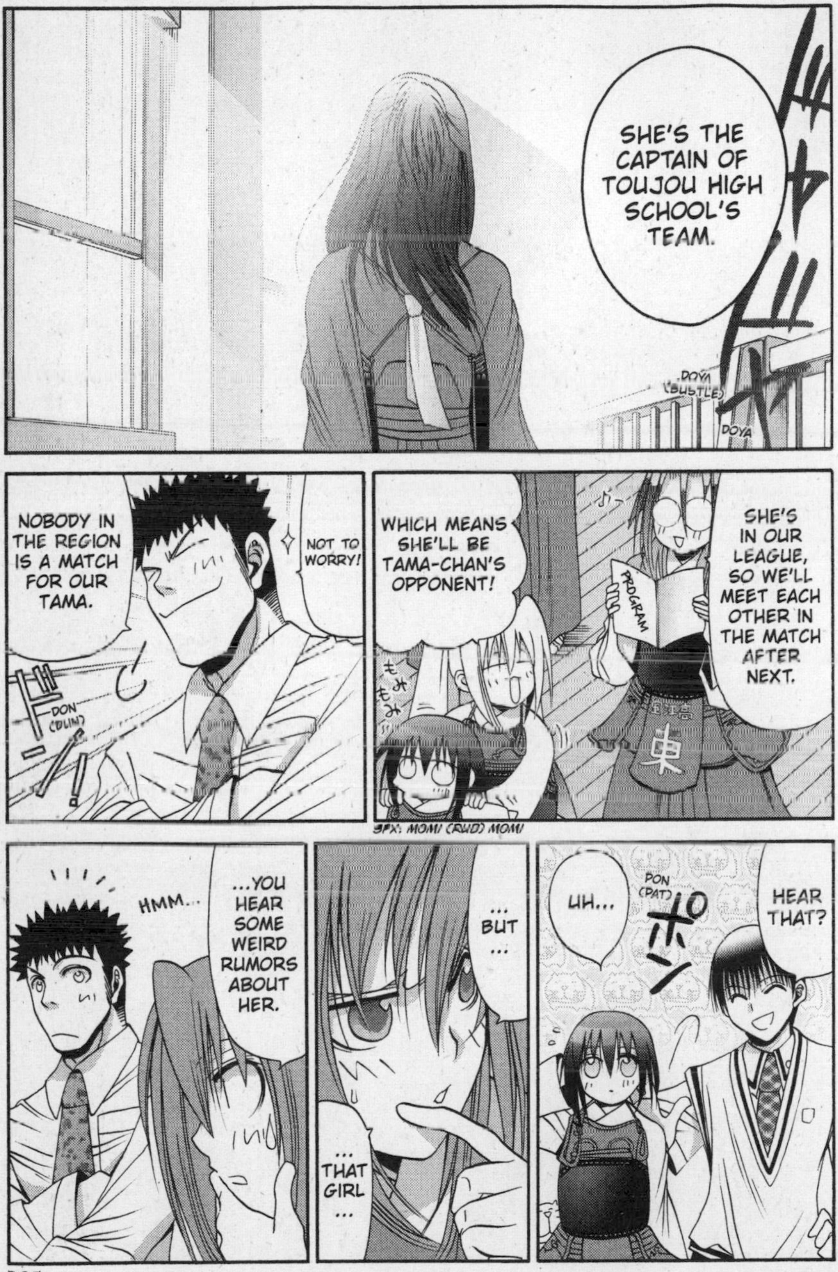

SHE'S THE CAPTAIN OF TOUJOU HIGH SCHOOL'S TEAM.
DOYA (BUSTLE)
DOYA
SHE'S IN OUR LEAGUE, SO WE'LL MEET EACH OTHER IN THE MATCH AFTER NEXT.
PROGRAM
WHICH MEANS SHE'LL BE TAMA-CHAN'S OPPONENT!
SFX: MOMI (RUB) MOMI
NOT TO WORRY!
NOBODY IN THE REGION IS A MATCH FOR OUR TAMA.
DON (DUN)
HEAR THAT?
PON (PAT)
UH...
... BUT ...
... THAT GIRL ...
...YOU HEAR SOME WEIRD RUMORS ABOUT HER.
HMM...

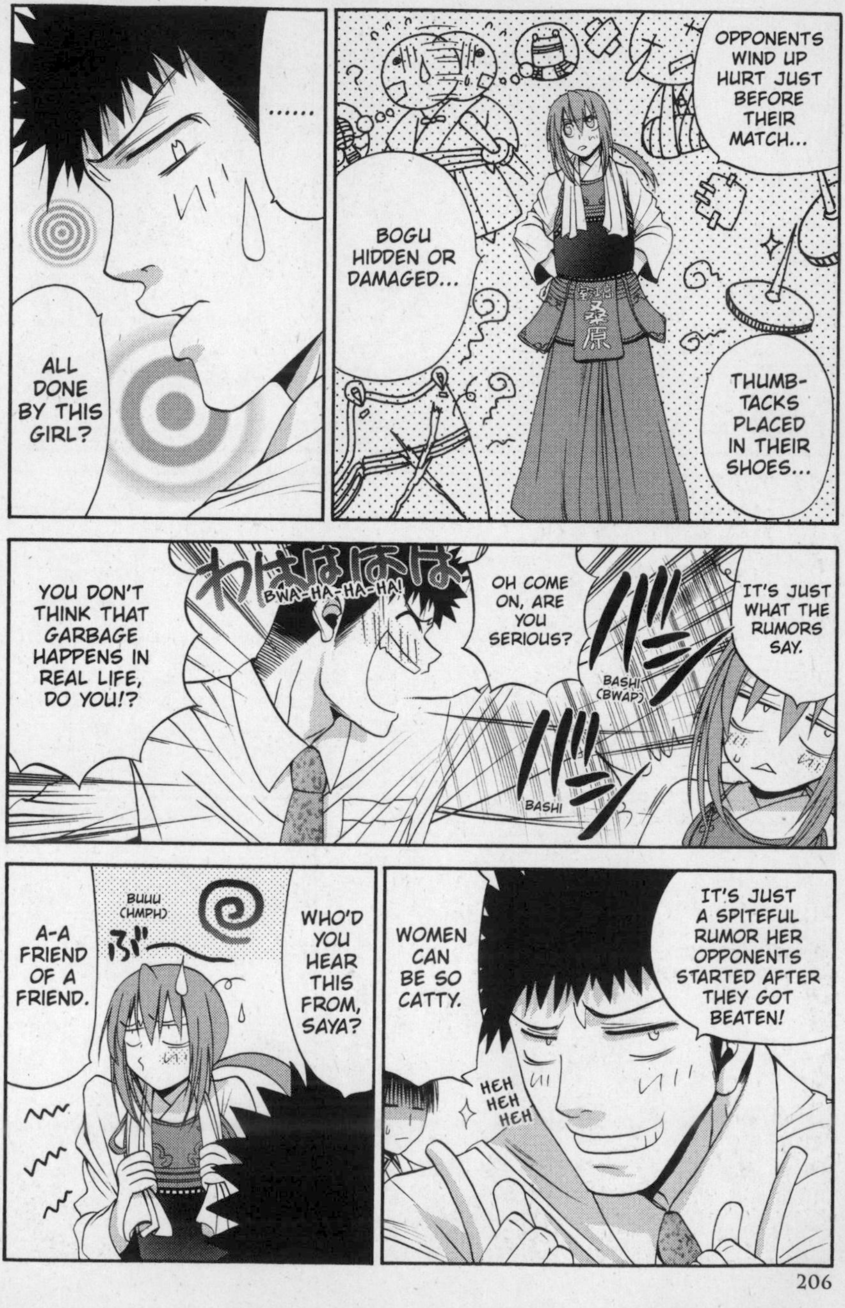
OPPONENTS WIND UP HURT JUST BEFORE THEIR MATCH...
THUMB-TACKS PLACED IN THEIR SHOES...
BOGU HIDDEN OR DAMAGED...
......
ALL DONE BY THIS GIRL?
IT'S JUST WHAT THE RUMORS SAY.
バシ
BASHI (BWAP)
バシ
BASHI
OH COME ON, ARE YOU SERIOUS?
わははははは
BWA-HA-HA-HA!
YOU DON'T THINK THAT GARBAGE HAPPENS IN REAL LIFE, DO YOU!?
IT'S JUST A SPITEFUL RUMOR HER OPPONENTS STARTED AFTER THEY GOT BEATEN!
HEH HEH HEH
WOMEN CAN BE SO CATTY.
WHO'D YOU HEAR THIS FROM, SAYA?
ぶー
BUUU (HMPH)
A-A FRIEND OF A FRIEND.

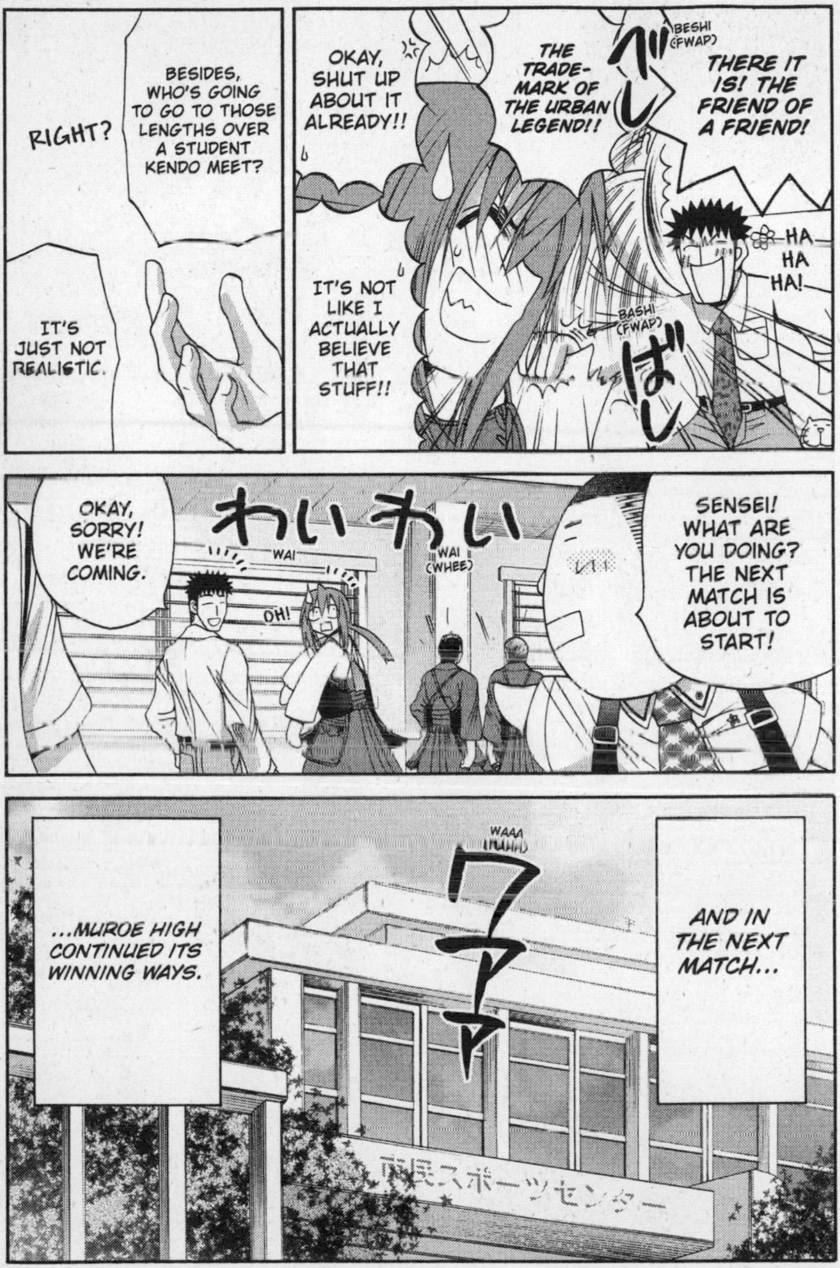
べし
BESHI (FWAP)
THERE IT IS! THE FRIEND OF A FRIEND!
THE TRADE-MARK OF THE URBAN LEGEND!!
OKAY, SHUT UP ABOUT IT ALREADY!!
HA HA HA!
ばし
BASHI (FWAP)
IT'S NOT LIKE I ACTUALLY BELIEVE THAT STUFF!!
BESIDES, WHO'S GOING TO GO TO THOSE LENGTHS OVER A STUDENT KENDO MEET?
RIGHT?
IT'S JUST NOT REALISTIC.
SENSEI! WHAT ARE YOU DOING? THE NEXT MATCH IS ABOUT TO START!
わいわい
WAI WAI (WHEE)
OH!
OKAY, SORRY! WE'RE COMING.
AND IN THE NEXT MATCH...
ワァ
WAAA
...MUROE HIGH CONTINUED ITS WINNING WAYS.

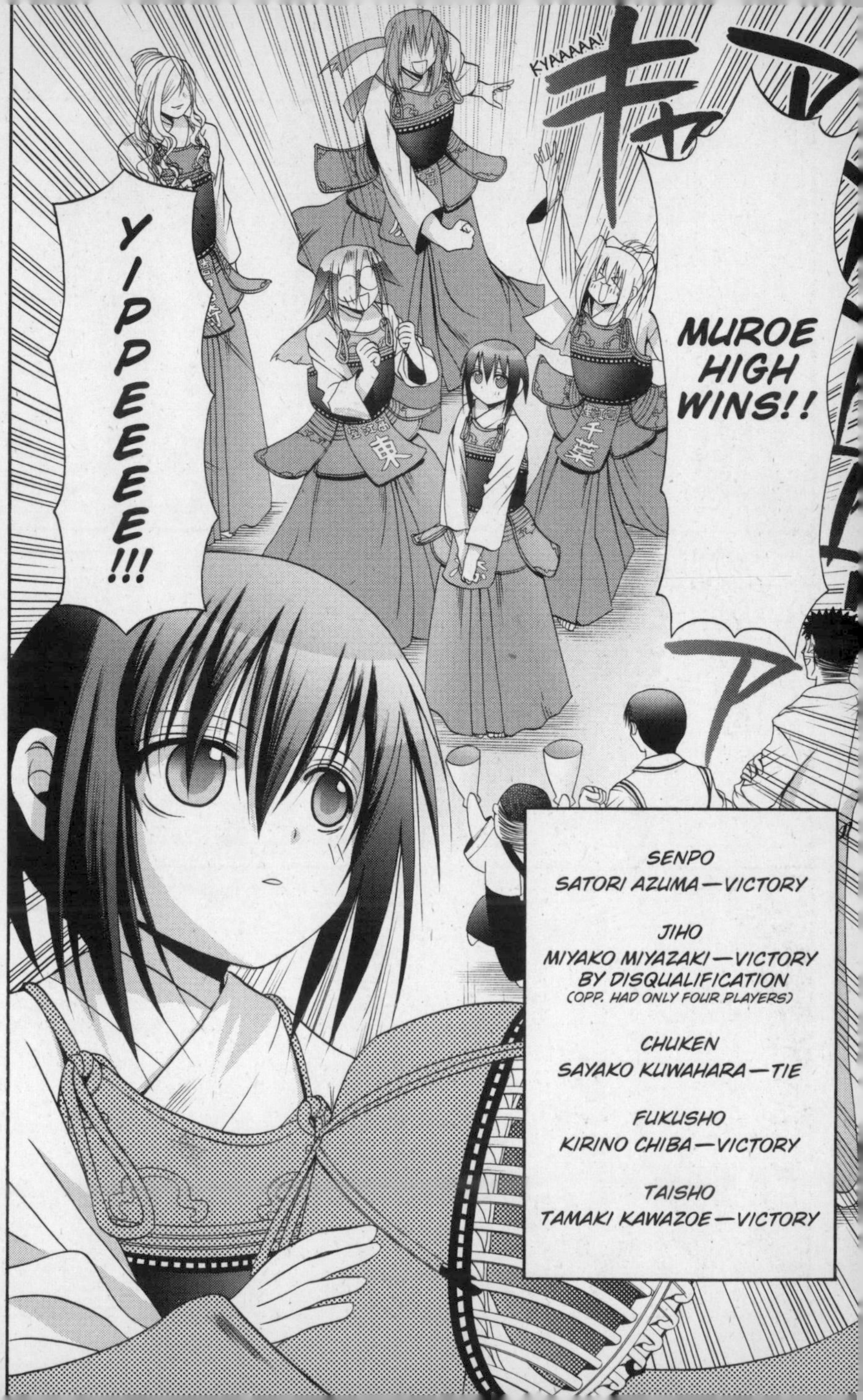
KYAAAAA!
MUROE HIGH WINS!!
YIPPEEEEE!!!
SENPO
SATORI AZUMA—VICTORY
JIHO
MIYAKO MIYAZAKI—VICTORY BY DISQUALIFICATION
(OPP. HAD ONLY FOUR PLAYERS)
CHUKEN
SAYAKO KUWAHARA—TIE
FUKUSHO
KIRINO CHIBA—VICTORY
TAISHO
TAMAKI KAWAZOE—VICTORY

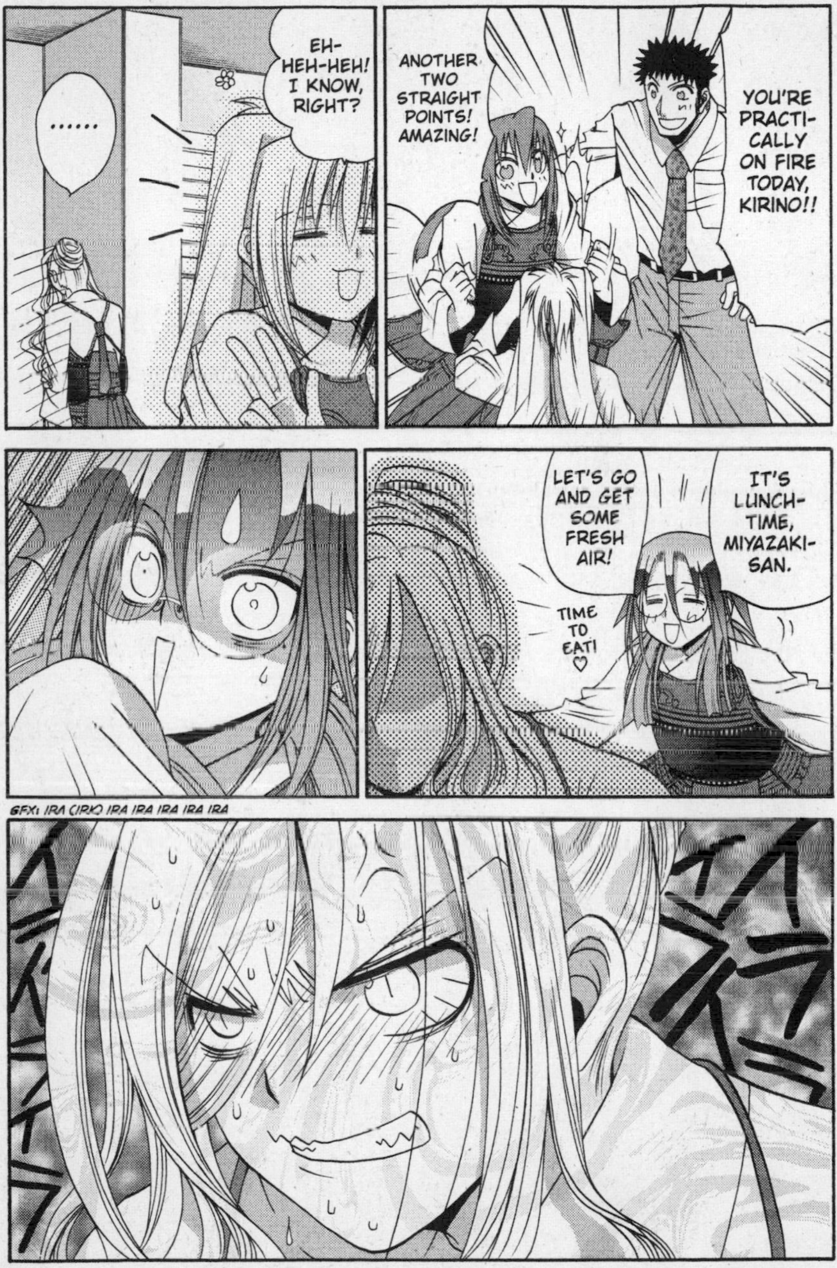
YOU'RE PRACTI-CALLY ON FIRE TODAY, KIRINO!!
ANOTHER TWO STRAIGHT POINTS! AMAZING!
EH-HEH-HEH! I KNOW, RIGHT?
......
IT'S LUNCH-TIME, MIYAZAKI-SAN.
LET'S GO AND GET SOME FRESH AIR!
TIME TO EAT! ♡
SFX: IRA (IRK) IRA IRA IRA IRA IRA

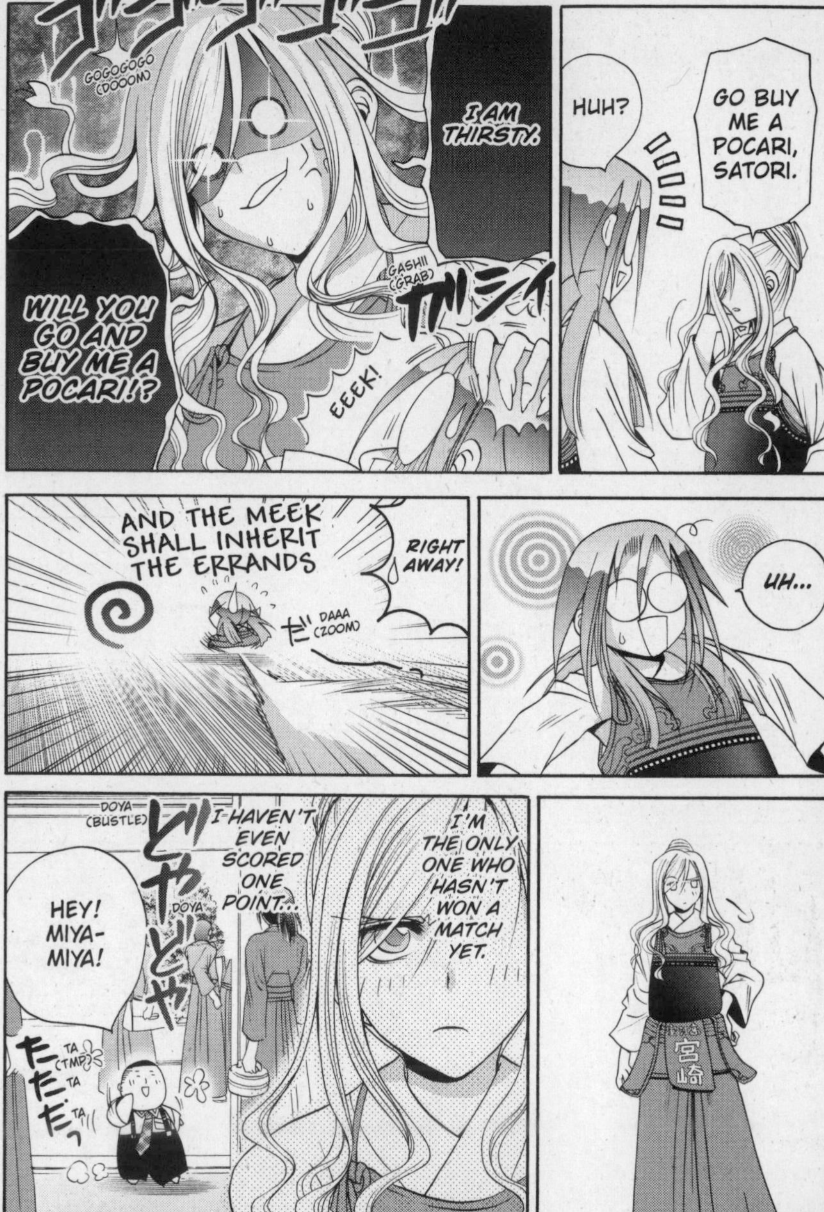
GO BUY ME A POCARI, SATORI.
HUH?
I AM THIRSTY.
GOGOGOGO (DOOOM)
GASHII (GRAB)
WILL YOU GO AND BUY ME A POCARI!?
EEEK!
UH...
RIGHT AWAY!
AND THE MEEK SHALL INHERIT THE ERRANDS
DAAA (ZOOM)
宮崎
I'M THE ONLY ONE WHO HASN'T WON A MATCH YET.
I HAVEN'T EVEN SCORED ONE POINT...
DOYA (BUSTLE)
DOYA
HEY! MIYA-MIYA!
TA (TMP) TA TA

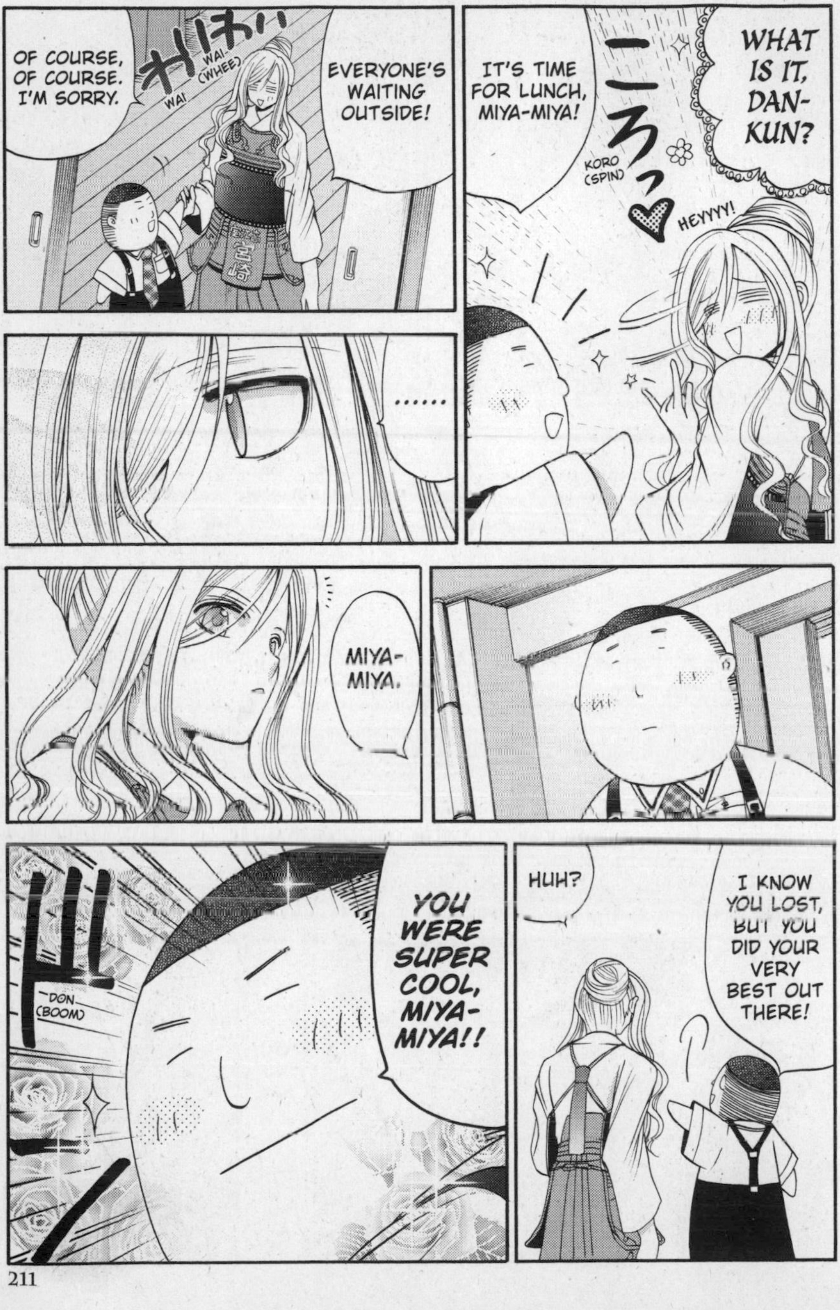

WHAT IS IT, DAN-KUN?
IT'S TIME FOR LUNCH, MIYA-MIYA!
KORO (SPIN)
HEYYYY!
EVERYONE'S WAITING OUTSIDE!
WAI-WAI (WHEE)
OF COURSE, OF COURSE. I'M SORRY.
......
MIYA-MIYA.
I KNOW YOU LOST, BUT YOU DID YOUR VERY BEST OUT THERE!
HUH?
YOU WERE SUPER COOL, MIYA-MIYA!!
DON (BOOM)

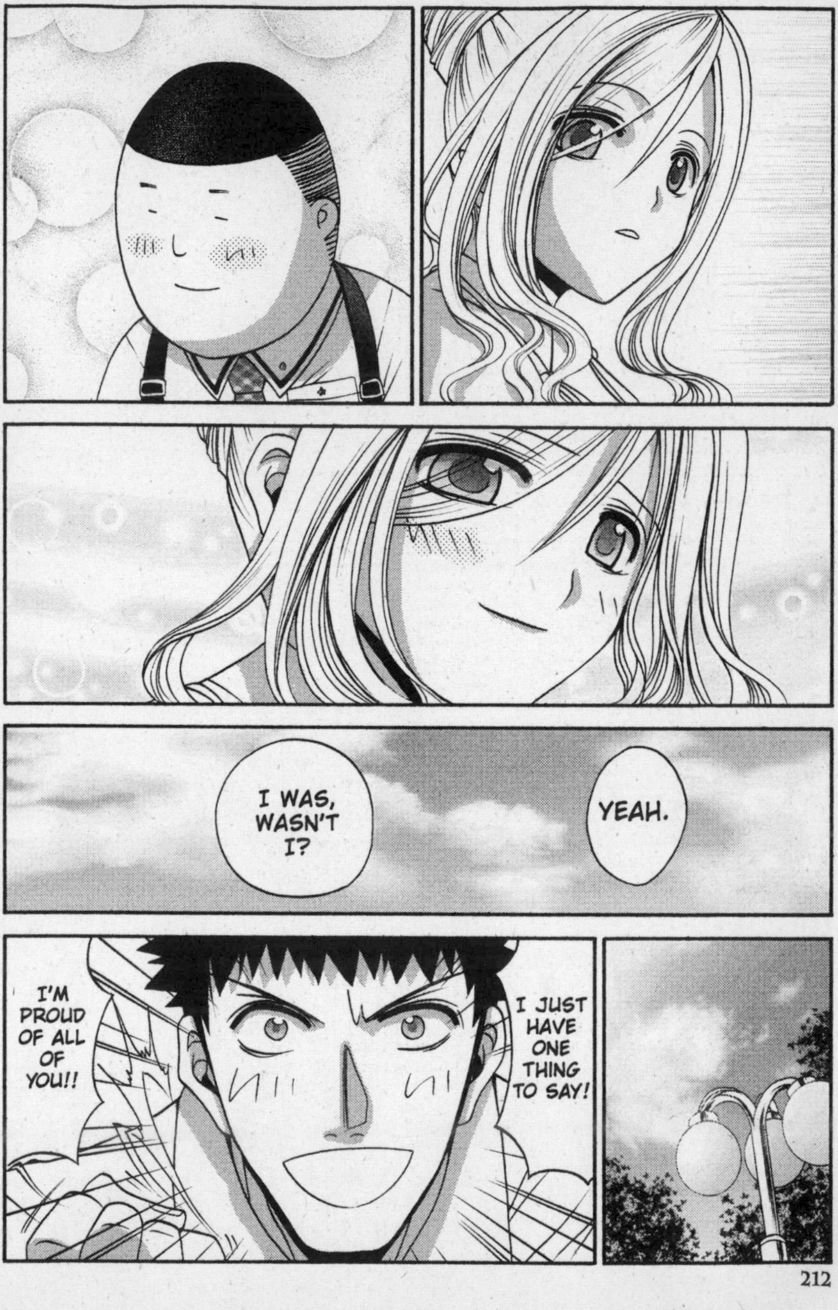
YEAH.
I WAS, WASN'T I?
I JUST HAVE ONE THING TO SAY!
I'M PROUD OF ALL OF YOU!!

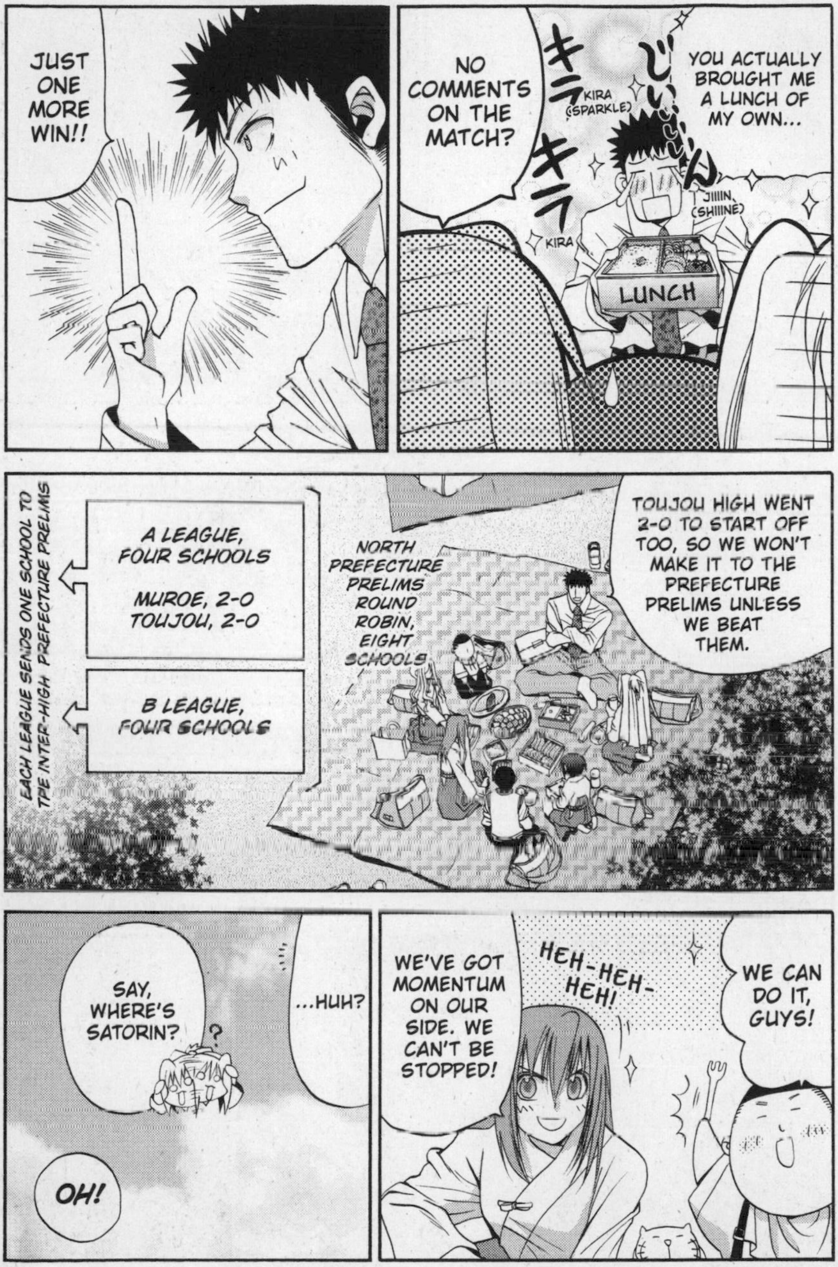
YOU ACTUALLY BROUGHT ME A LUNCH OF MY OWN...
じぃいいいん
JIIIIN (SHIIINE)
キラ
KIRA (SPARKLE)
NO COMMENTS ON THE MATCH?
LUNCH
キラ
KIRA
JUST ONE MORE WIN!!
TOUJOU HIGH WENT 2-0 TO START OFF TOO, SO WE WON'T MAKE IT TO THE PREFECTURE PRELIMS UNLESS WE BEAT THEM.
NORTH PREFECTURE PRELIMS ROUND ROBIN, EIGHT SCHOOLS
A LEAGUE, FOUR SCHOOLS
MUROE, 2-0
TOUJOU, 2-0
B LEAGUE, FOUR SCHOOLS
EACH LEAGUE SENDS ONE SCHOOL TO THE INTER-HIGH PREFECTURE PRELIMS
WE CAN DO IT, GUYS!
HEH-HEH-HEH!
WE'VE GOT MOMENTUM ON OUR SIDE. WE CAN'T BE STOPPED!
...HUH?
SAY, WHERE'S SATORIN?
?
OH!

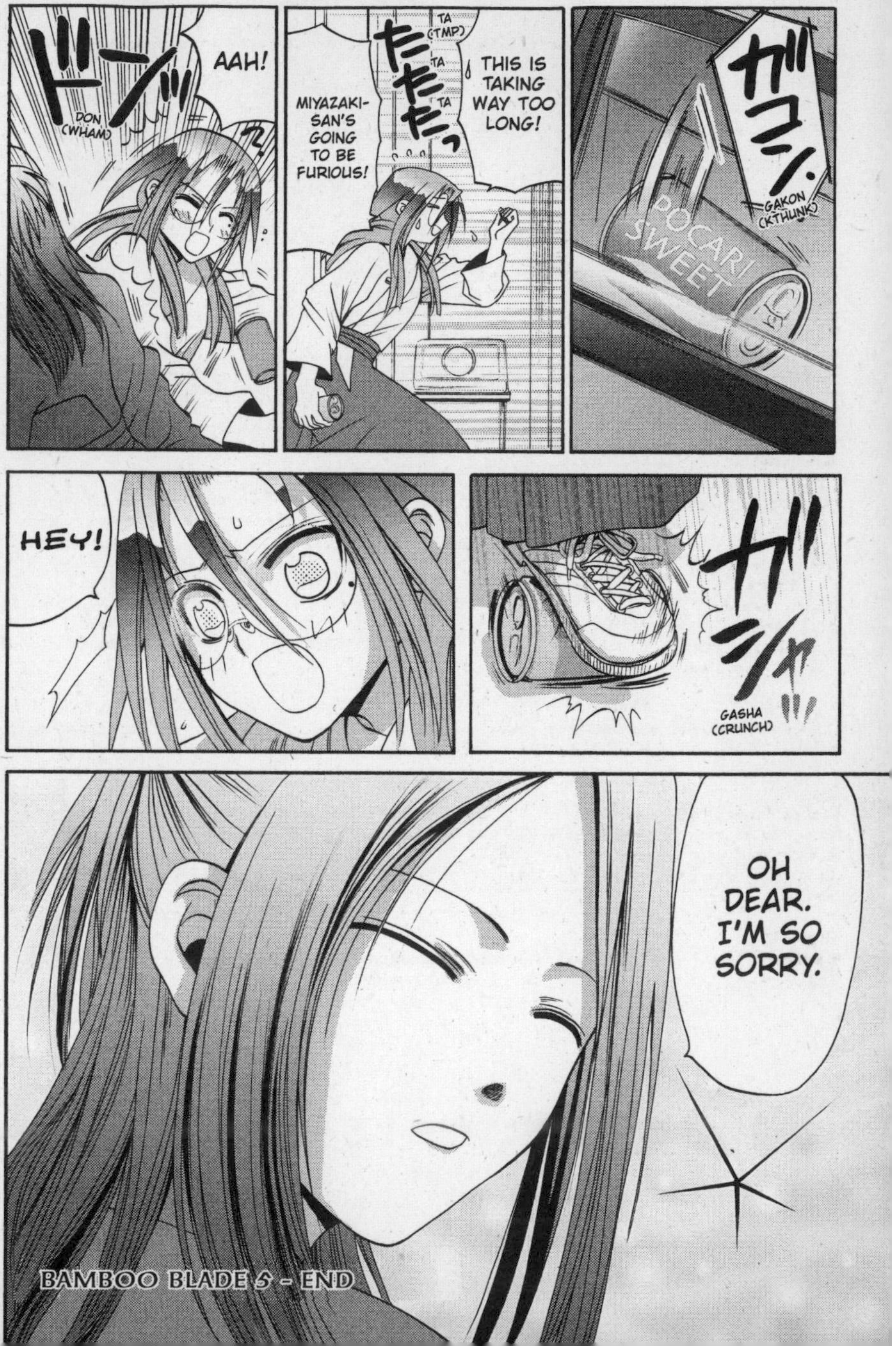
ガコン
GAKON (KTHUNK)
POCARI SWEET
たたたっ
TA (TMP)
TA
TA
THIS IS TAKING WAY TOO LONG!
MIYAZAKI-SAN'S GOING TO BE FURIOUS!
ドーン
DON (WHAM)
AAH!
ガシャ
GASHA (CRUNCH)
HEY!
OH DEAR. I'M SO SORRY.
BAMBOO BLADE 5 - END

TRANSLATION NOTES

Common Honorifics

No honorific: Indicates familiarity or closeness; if used without permission or reason, addresssing someone in this manner would constitute an insult.

-san: The Japanese equivalent of Mr./Mrs./Miss. If a situation calls for politeness, this is the failsafe honorific.

-sama: Conveys great respect; may also indicate that the social status of the speaker is lower than that of the addressee.

-kun: Used most often when referring to boys, this indicates affection or familiarity. Occasionally used by older men among their peers, but it may also be used by anyone referring to a person of lower standing.

-chan: An affectionate honorific indicating familiarity used mostly in reference to girls; also used in reference to cute persons or animals of either gender.

-senpai: A suffix used in addressing one's upperclassmen.

-sensei: A respectful term for teachers, artists, or high-level professionals.

Page 20

Going-home club: Because extracurricular clubs in Japan meet up after school, those students who don't belong to a club would be going home at the time the rest are engaging in their club activities, thus spawning the nickname "going-home club" for any student not affiliated with any club.

Page 43

Equipment: The "status screen" shown in the background here is a parody of role playing games (RPGs), particularly the *Dragon Quest* series, in which an "E" is placed in front of items that are currently equipped on the character. Most of these pieces of kendo equipment have been defined and covered in previous volumes, but for reference's sake, here they are again:

Shinai – the titular "bamboo blade"
Do – breastplate
Kote – gauntlets
Men – helmet
Tare – hanging waist protectors
Hakama – traditional underclothing tied around the waist

Page 127

Satori: Though Satori's name is spelled with different characters, the word "*satori*" itself can mean "comprehension" or "enlightenment" in the Buddhist sense.

Page 213

North Prefecture Prelims: Rather than states or counties, Japan is divided into prefectures, of which there are forty-seven. The meet being held in these chapters is the "north prefecture" preliminaries; that is, the local meet covering all the schools in the northern region of the prefecture. By passing to the next round, schools advance to the "prefecture preliminaries" which will cover the entire prefecture.

Page 214

Pocari: A brand of uncarbonated soft drink, similar to Gatorade. The real name of the drink is "Pocari Sweat," but if you ask me, "Pocari Sweet" sounds tastier.

SATORI AZUMA

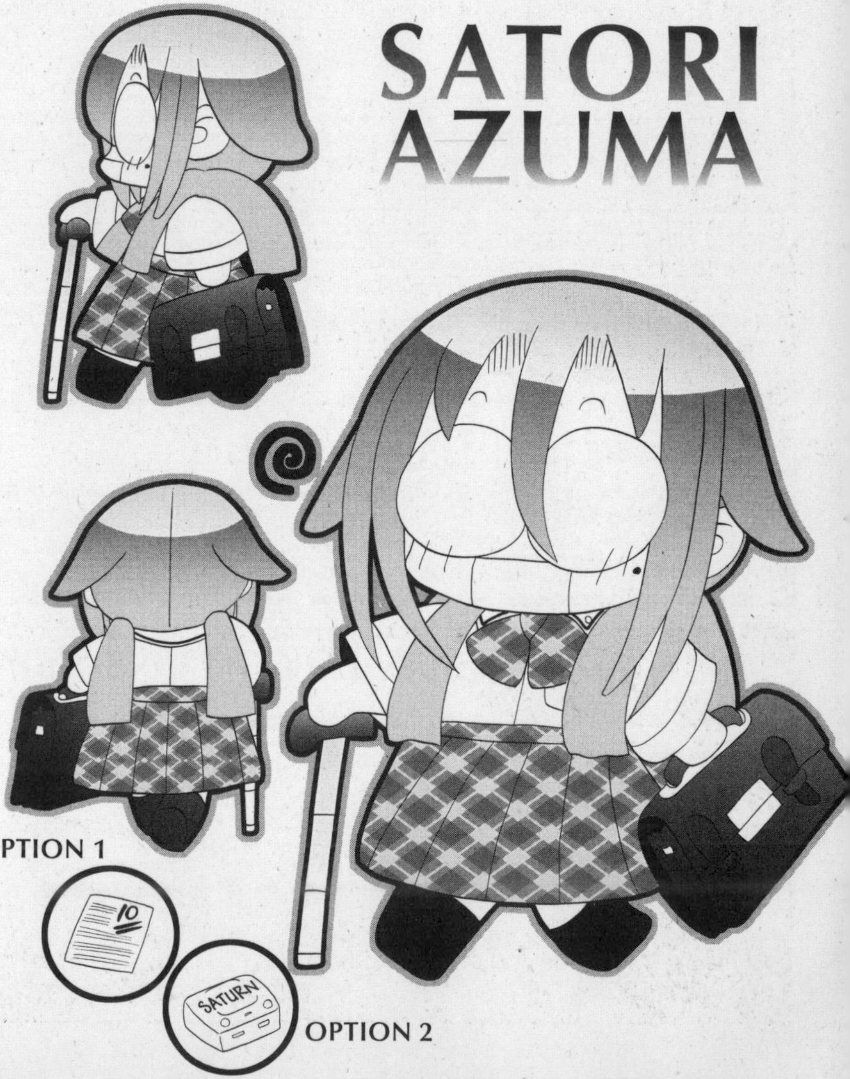
OPTION 1
10
SATURN
OPTION 2

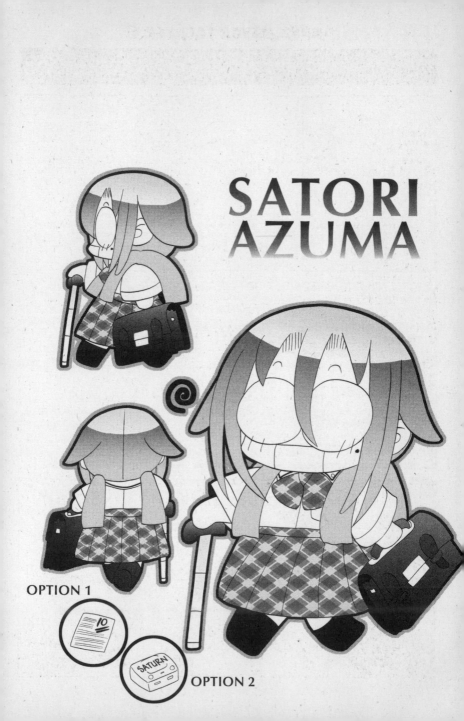

OMAKE MANGA THEATER 1

KIRINO-SAN AND HER THOUGHTS

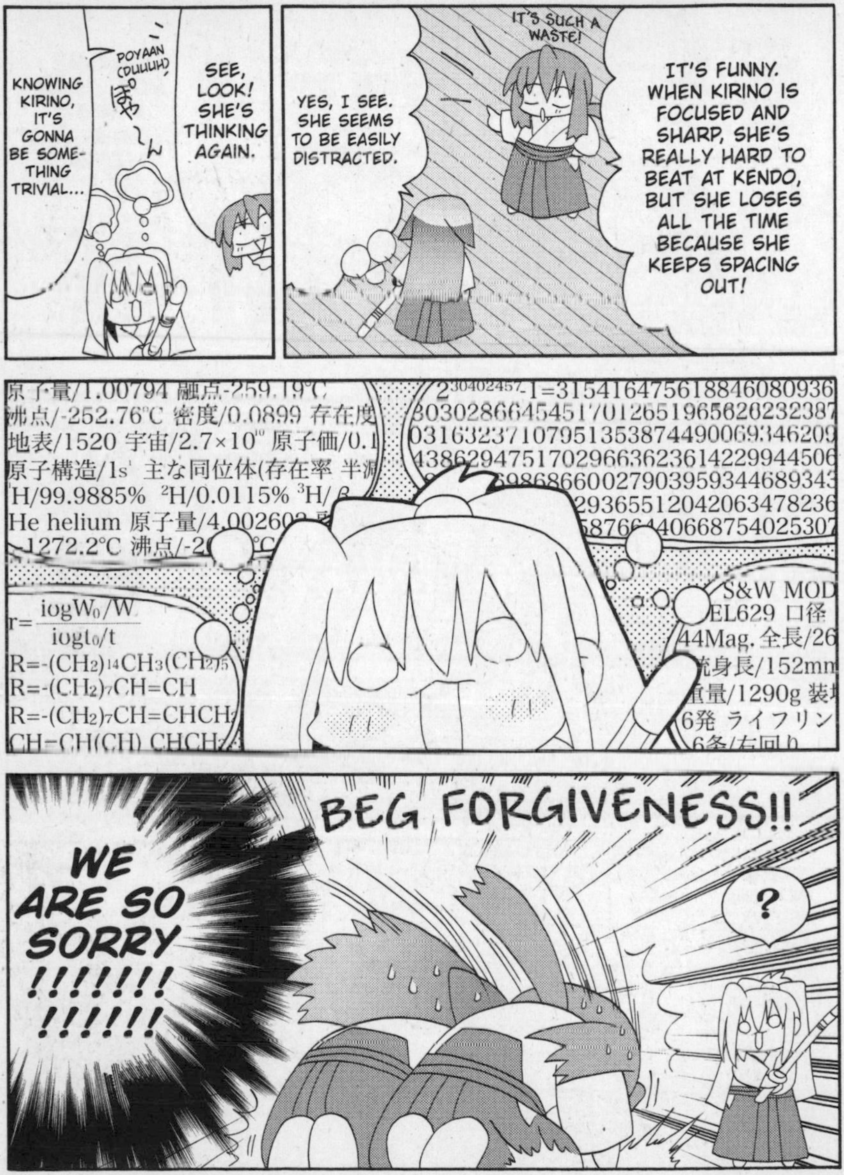

IT'S FUNNY. WHEN KIRINO IS FOCUSED AND SHARP, SHE'S REALLY HARD TO BEAT AT KENDO, BUT SHE LOSES ALL THE TIME BECAUSE SHE KEEPS SPACING OUT!
IT'S SUCH A WASTE!
YES, I SEE. SHE SEEMS TO BE EASILY DISTRACTED.
SEE, LOOK! SHE'S THINKING AGAIN.
POYAAN (DUHHH)
ぽや～ん
KNOWING KIRINO, IT'S GONNA BE SOMETHING TRIVIAL...
原子量/1.00794 融点-259.19℃
沸点/-252.76℃ 密度/0.0899 存在度
地表/1520 宇宙/2.7×10¹⁰ 原子価/0.1
原子構造/1s¹ 主な同位体(存在率 半減
¹H/99.9885% ²H/0.0115% ³H/β
He helium 原子量/4.002602
2³⁰⁴⁰²⁴⁵⁷-1=315416475618846080936
303028664545170126519656202323 87
031632371079513538744900693462 09
438629475170296636236142299445 06
S&W MOD
EL629 口径
44Mag. 全長/26
銃身長/152mm
重量/1290g
6発 ライフリン
R=-(CH2)7CH=CH
BEG FORGIVENESS!!
?
WE ARE SO SORRY !!!!!!! !!!!!!

OMAKE MANGA THEATER ④

THE DAUGHTER AND THE FEELINGS OF A FATHER WHO DOESN'T WANT TO LOSE HER

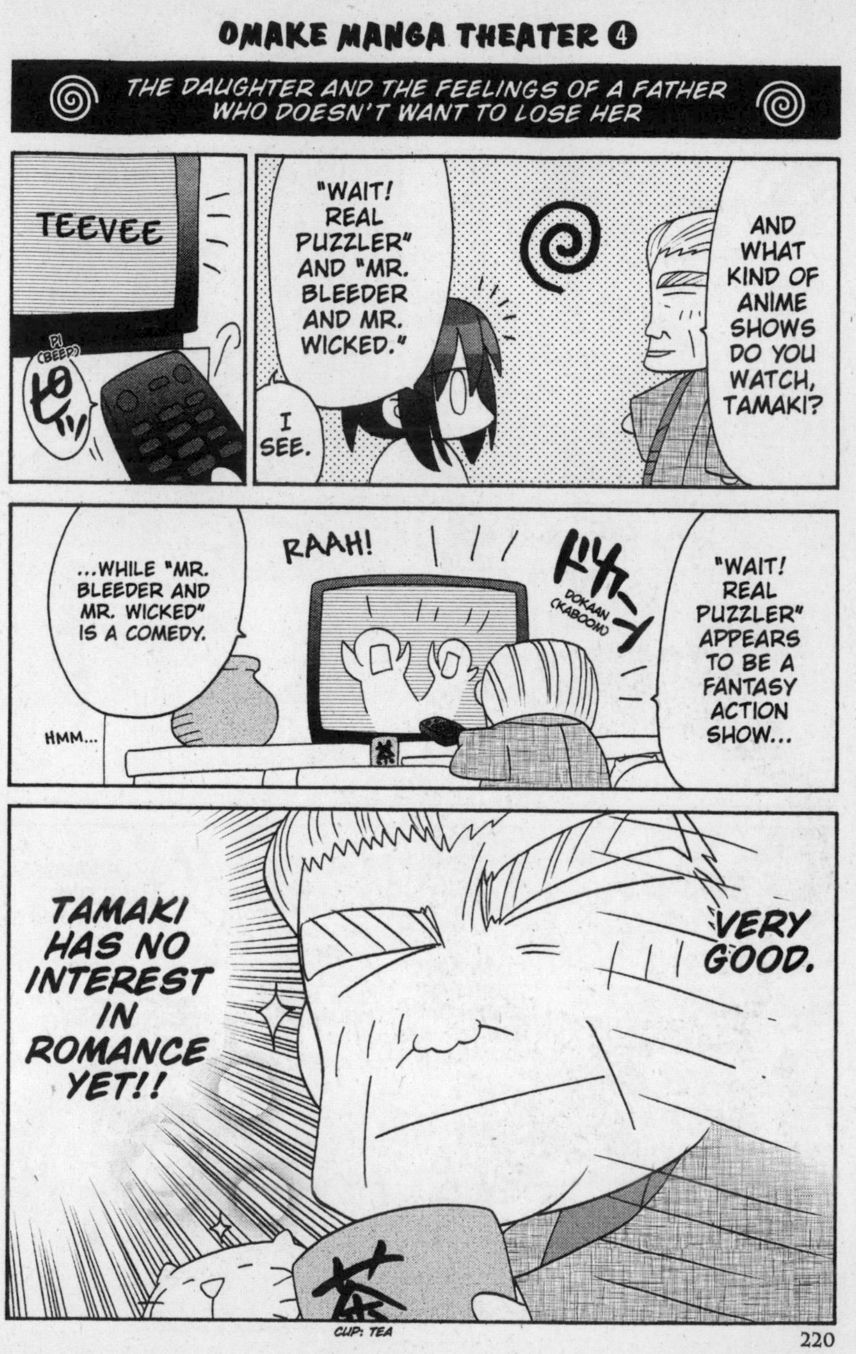
AND WHAT KIND OF ANIME SHOWS DO YOU WATCH, TAMAKI?
"WAIT! REAL PUZZLER" AND "MR. BLEEDER AND MR. WICKED."
I SEE.
TEEVEE
ピッ
PI (BEEP)
"WAIT! REAL PUZZLER" APPEARS TO BE A FANTASY ACTION SHOW...
ドカーン
DOKAAN (KABOOM)
RAAH!
...WHILE "MR. BLEEDER AND MR. WICKED" IS A COMEDY.
HMM...
VERY GOOD.
TAMAKI HAS NO INTEREST IN ROMANCE YET!!

CUP: TEA

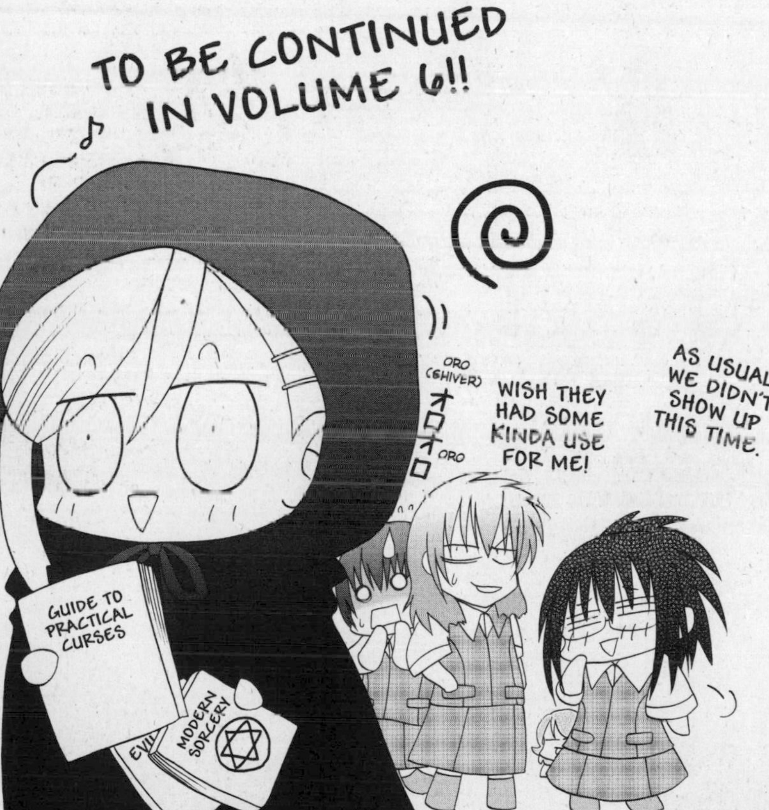
TO BE CONTINUED IN VOLUME 6!!
AS USUAL, WE DIDN'T SHOW UP THIS TIME.
WISH THEY HAD SOME KINDA USE FOR ME!
ORO (SHIVER)
オロオロ
ORO
GUIDE TO PRACTICAL CURSES
MODERN SORCERY
EVIL

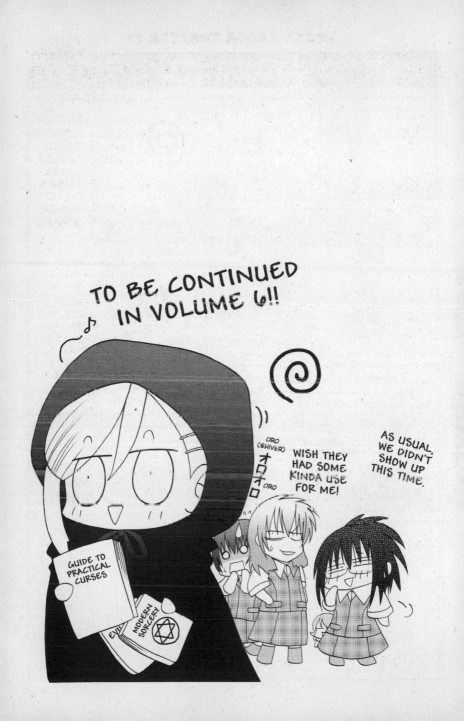

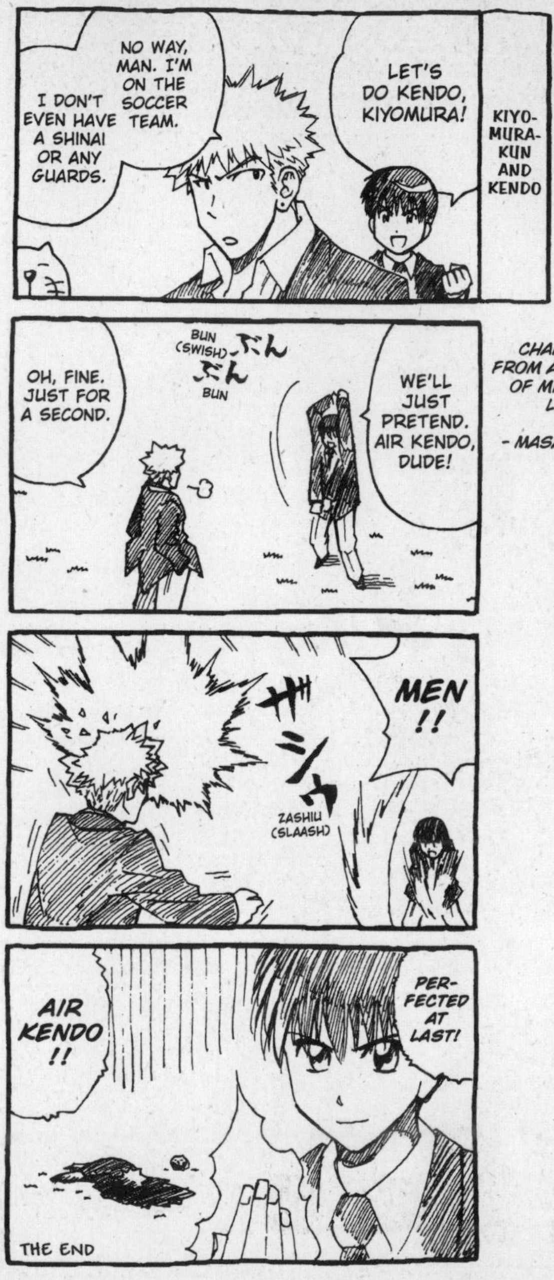
KIYOMURA-KUN AND KENDO
LET'S DO KENDO, KIYOMURA!
NO WAY, MAN. I'M ON THE SOCCER TEAM.
I DON'T EVEN HAVE A SHINAI OR ANY GUARDS.
WE'LL JUST PRETEND. AIR KENDO, DUDE!
BUN (SWISH) ぶん
ぶん BUN
OH, FINE. JUST FOR A SECOND.
MEN !!
ザシュ
ZASHIU (SLAASH)
PERFECTED AT LAST!
AIR KENDO !!
THE END

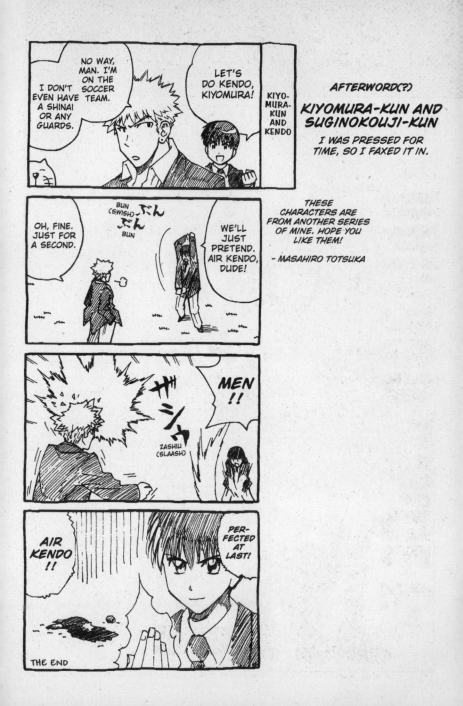

AFTERWORD(?)

KIYOMURA-KUN AND SUGINOKOUJI-KUN

I WAS PRESSED FOR TIME, SO I FAXED IT IN.

THESE CHARACTERS ARE FROM ANOTHER SERIES OF MINE. HOPE YOU LIKE THEM!

- MASAHIRO TOTSUKA

BACKSTAGE AFTERWORD

DRAWN BY IGA

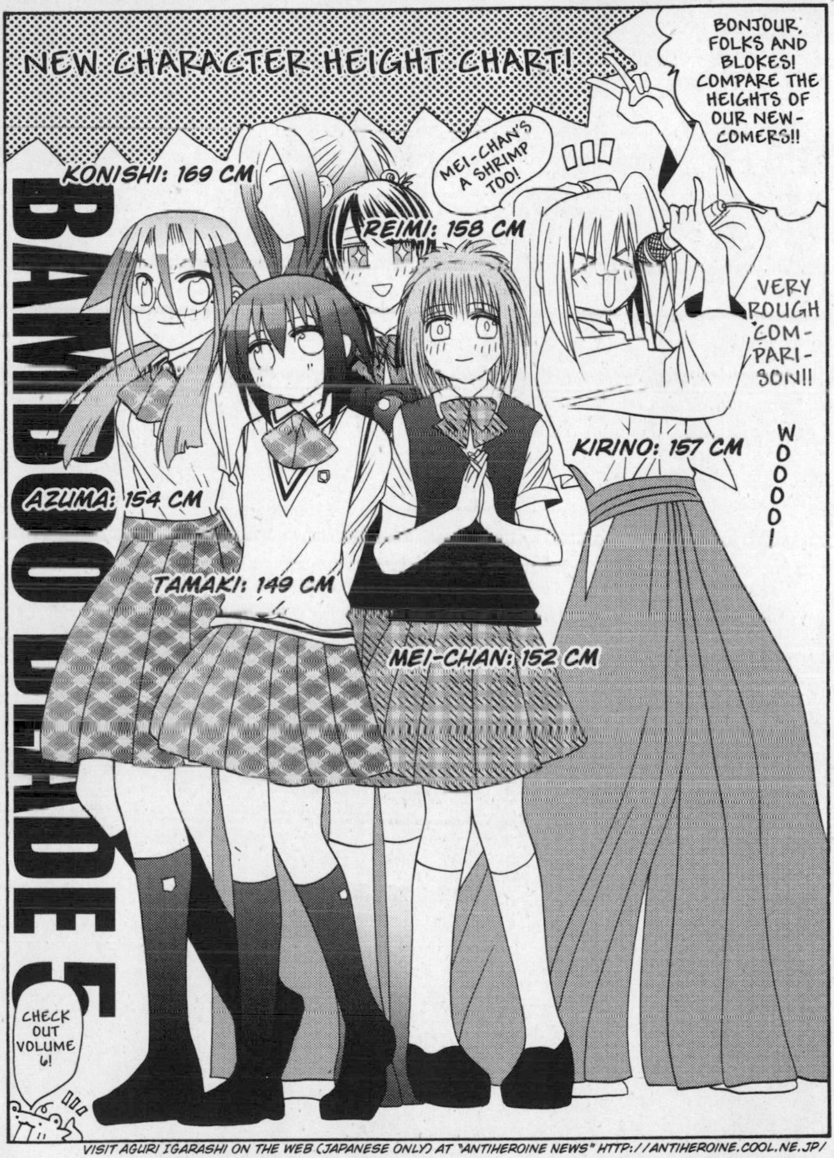

NEW CHARACTER HEIGHT CHART!
BONJOUR, FOLKS AND BLOKES! COMPARE THE HEIGHTS OF OUR NEW-COMERS!!
MEI-CHAN'S A SHRIMP TOO!
KONISHI: 169 CM
REIMI: 158 CM
VERY ROUGH COMPARISON!!
KIRINO: 157 CM
WOOOOO!
AZUMA: 154 CM
TAMAKI: 149 CM
MEI-CHAN: 152 CM
BAMBOO BLADE 5
CHECK OUT VOLUME 6!

VISIT AGURI IGARASHI ON THE WEB (JAPANESE ONLY) AT "ANTIHEROINE NEWS" HTTP://ANTIHEROINE.COOL.NE.JP/

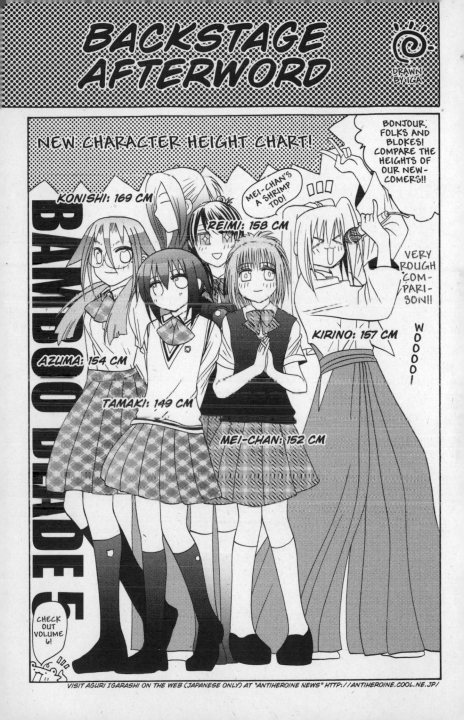

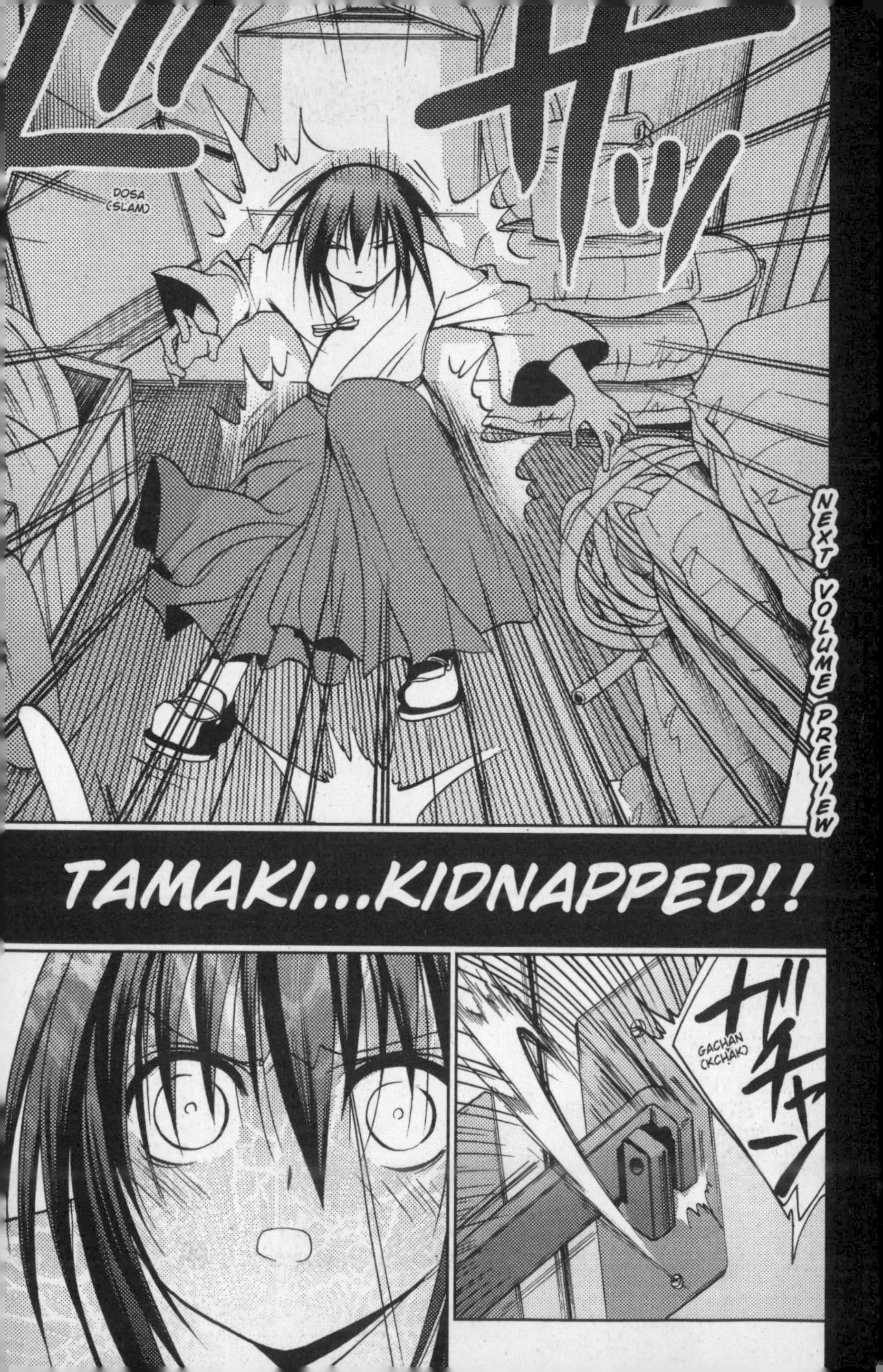
NEXT VOLUME PREVIEW
DOSA (SLAM)
TAMAKI...KIDNAPPED!!
GACHAN (KCHAK)

WHO COULD HAVE DONE THIS!!?

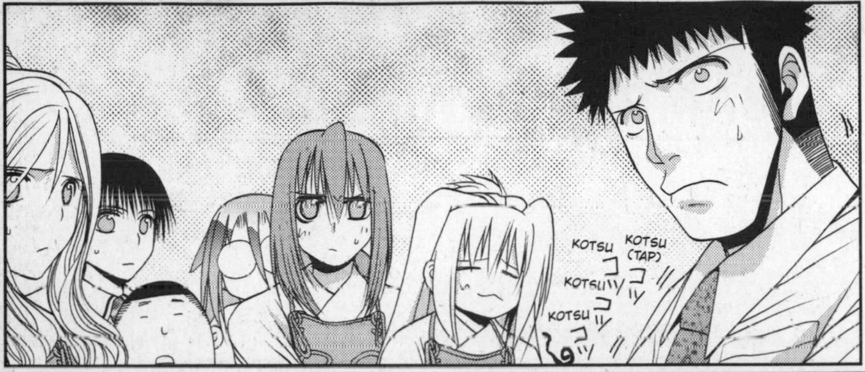
KOTSU
KOTSU (TAP)
KOTSU
KOTSU

THE TEAM GROWS MORE AND MORE ANXIOUS AS MATCH TIME APPROACHES!

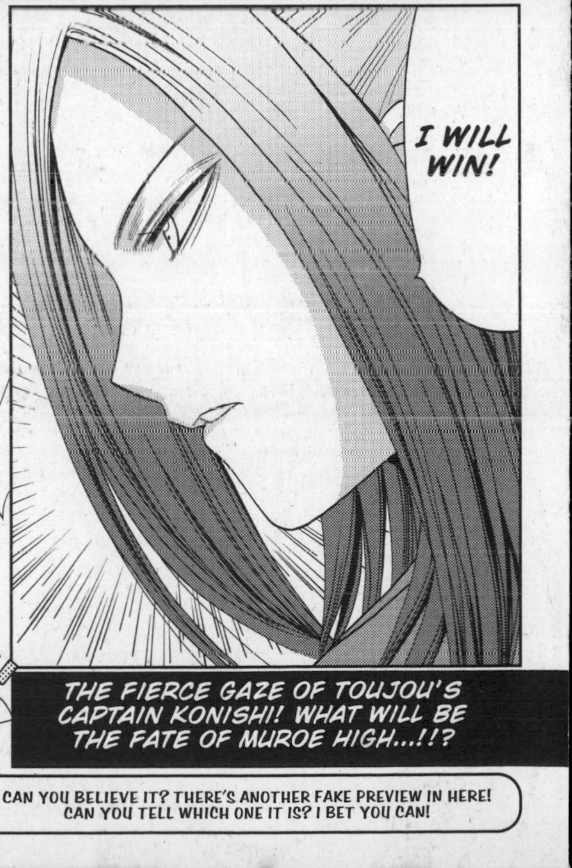
I WILL WIN!

THE FIERCE GAZE OF TOUJOU'S CAPTAIN KONISHI! WHAT WILL BE THE FATE OF MUROE HIGH...!!?

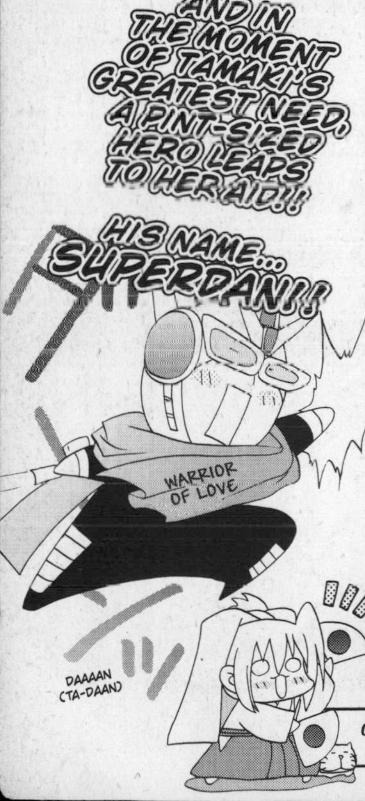
AND IN THE MOMENT OF TAMAKI'S GREATEST NEED, A PINT-SIZED HERO LEAPS TO HER AID!!
HIS NAME... SUPERDAN!!
WARRIOR OF LOVE
DAAAAN (TA-DAAN)

CAN YOU BELIEVE IT? THERE'S ANOTHER FAKE PREVIEW IN HERE! CAN YOU TELL WHICH ONE IT IS? I BET YOU CAN!

BAMBOO BLADE ⑤

MASAHIRO TOTSUKA
AGURI IGARASHI

Translation: Stephen Paul

Lettering: Terri Delgado

BAMBOO BLADE Vol. 5 © 2007 Masahiro Totsuka, Aguri Igarashi /
SQUARE ENIX CO., LTD. All rights reserved. First published in Japan in
2007 by SQUARE ENIX CO., LTD. English translation rights arranged with
SQUARE ENIX CO., LTD. and Hachette Book Group through Tuttle-Mori
Agency, Inc.

Translation © 2010 by SQUARE ENIX CO., LTD.

Yen Press
Hachette Book Group
237 Park Avenue, New York, NY 10017

www.HachetteBookGroup.com
www.YenPress.com

Yen Press is an imprint of Hachette Book Group, Inc. The Yen Press name
and logo are trademarks of Hachette Book Group, Inc.

First Yen Press Edition: June 2010

ISBN: 978-0-316-07298-4

10 9 8 7 6 5 4 3 2 1

BVG

Printed in the United States of America